Mastering Wingz

Mastering
WINGZ

The Official Introduction to
Wingz Presentation Spreadsheet

Fred E. Davis
Elna R. Tymes

BANTAM BOOKS
NEW YORK · TORONTO · LONDON · SYDNEY · AUCKLAND

MASTERING WINGZ
A Bantam Book/April 1989

All rights reserved.
Copyright © 1989 by Fred E. Davis and Elna R. Tymes
Cover art copyright © 1989 by Bantam Books.

This book was produced by Publishing Synthesis, Ltd., New York, NY.

No part of this book may be reproduced or transmitted
in any form or by any means, electronic or mechanical,
including photocopying, recording, or by an information
storage and retrieval system, without permission in writing from
the publisher.
For information address: Bantam Books.

ISBN 0-553-34706-3

Published simultaneously in the United States and Canada

Bantam Books are published by Bantam Book, a division of
Bantam Doubleday Dell Publishing Group, Inc. Its trademark,
consiting of the words "Bantam Books" and the portrayal of
a rooster, is Registered in U.S. Patent and Trademark Office
and in other countries. Marca Registrada, Bantam Books
666 Fifth Avenue, New York, New York 10103

PRINTED IN THE UNITED STATES OF AMERICA

FG   0 9 8 7 6 5 4 3 2 1

Contents

Foreword by Michael J. Brown xv

Chapter 1 Introduction 1
   What is Presentation Software? 1
   What Can Wingz Do? 5
   Charts 13
     Bar Chart 14
     Step Chart 15
     Horizontal Bar Chart 16
     Pie Chart 16
     Line Chart 19
     Layer Chart 21
     Combination Chart 22
     HiLo Chart 24
     Scatter Chart 24
     X-Y Chart 26
     Polar Chart 26
     Wireframe Chart 27
     Surface Chart 27
     Contour Chart 29
   Automating Your Work With Hyperscript 30
   Summary 32
   Case Study 1: Wingz in Environmental Engineering 33

Chapter 2 Getting Started 37
   Loading Wingz 37

Getting Help Fast 38
Tour of the Screen 40

Chapter 3 Entering Data 45

Cells and Ranges 45
Selecting 47
  Entering Data 49
  Text 50
  Numbers 50
  Using Date and Time 51
  Logical Values 52
  Using Fill with Data 53
Formatting 56
  What's Actually Stored 56
  Format Options 58
  Number Formats 58
  Text Formats 59
  Alignment of Data and Text 59
  Changing Column Width or Row Height 61
Formulas and Functions 62
Summary 65
Case Study 2: Wingz in Physics Research 66

Chapter 4 Formulas and Functions 69

Entering Formulas 69
What's a Function? 72
Pasting Functions 75
Explanation of Functions 76
Business Functions 76
  BONDPRICE(yield,value,rate,yearstomaturity,payments) 76
  BONDYTM(price,value,rate,yearstomaturity,payments) 76
  CTERM(rate,futurevalue,presentvalue) 77
  DDB(cost,salvage,life,period) 77
  FV(payment,interest,term) 78
  FVL(payment,interest,term) 78
  INTEREST(principal,payment,term) 79
  IRR(guess,range) 79
  LOANTERM(principal,payment,interest) 80

        NPV(interest,payments)   81
        PRINCIPAL(payment,rate,term)   83
        PV (payment,interest,term)   84
        PVL(payment,interest,term)   84
        RATE (fv,pv,term)   85
        SLN(cost,salvage,life,period)   85
        SYD(cost,salvage,life,period)   85
        TERM(payment,interest,fv)   86
    Date/time Functions   87
        ADATE(datenumber,picture)   87
        ADDDAYS (datenumber,days)   88
        ADDHOURS(datenumber,hours)   88
        ADDMINUTES(datenumber,minutes)   88
        ADDMONTHS(datenumber,months)   89
        ADDSECONDS   89
        ADDYEARS(datenumber,years)   89
        ATIME(datenumber,picture)   89
        CMONTH(month)   89
        CWEEKDAY(weekday)   90
        DATE(year,month,day)   90
        DATEVALUE(datestring)   90
        DAY(datenumber)   91
        DAYNAME(datenumber)   91
        HOUR(datenumber)   91
        MINUTE(datenumber)   92
        MONTH(datenumber)   92
        MONTHNAME(datenumber)   93
        NOW()   93
        SECOND(datenumber)   93
        TIME(hour,minute,second)   94
        TIMEVALUE(timestring)   94
        YEAR(datenumber)   94
    Logical Functions   95
        FALSE()   95
        IF(condition,x,y)   95
        ISBLANK(x)   96
        ISERR(x)   96
        ISNA(x)   96
        ISNUMBER(x)   97

viii   Contents

      ISRANGE(x)   97
      ISSTRING(x)   97
      TRUE()   97
   Statistical Functions   98
      AVG(itemlist)   98
      COUNT(itemlist)   98
      MAX(itemlist)   98
      MIN(itemlist)   99
      STD(itemlist)   99
      STDEV(itemlist)   100
      SUM(itemlist)   100
      SUMSQ(itemlist)   100
      VAR(itemlist)   101
      VARIANCE(itemlist)   101
   Database Functions   102
      DAVG(input,offset,criteria)   103
      DCOUNT(input,offset,criteria)   103
      DMAX(input,offset,criteria)   103
      DMIN(input,offset,criteria)   103
      DSTD(input,offset,criteria)   103
      DSTDEV(input,offset,criteria)   104
      DSUM(input,offset,criteria)   104
      DSUMSQ(input,offset,criteria)   104
      DVAR(input,offset,criteria)   104
      DVARIANCE(input,offset,criteria)   104
   Text Functions   104
      CHAR(x)   104
      CODE(text)   105
      COLLATE(text1,text2)   105
      CONTAINS(textsearch,text)   105
      CURRENCY(x)   106
      EXACT(text1,text2)   106
      FIND(searchtext,text,start)   107
      LEFT(text,n)   107
      LENGTH(text)   107
      LOWER(text)   108
      MATCH(text,searchtext,start)   108
      MID(text,start,n)   108
      N(range)   109

Contents ix

NFORMAT(number,format) 109
PROPER(text) 110
REPEAT(text,n) 110
REPLACE(text,start,n,newtext) 110
RIGHT(text,n) 111
S(range) 111
STR(x,n) 111
STRING(x,n) 111
TRIM(text) 112
UPPER(text) 112
VALUE(text) 112
Spreadsheet Functions 113
  CELL() 113
  CELLTEXT(cell) 113
  CHOOSE(n,itemlist) 114
  COL() 114
  COLOF(range) 115
  COLS(range) 115
  ERR() 115
  HLOOKUP(x,range,row) 115
  INDEX(range,column,row) 116
  INDIRECT(text) 117
  MAKECELL(column,row) 117
  MAKERANGE(colum n1,row1,column2,row2) 118
  NA() 118
  RANGE(text) 118
  ROW() 119
  ROWOF(range) 119
  ROWS(range) 119
  VLOOKUP(x,range,column) 119
Numeric Functions 120
  ABS(x) 120
  ACOS(x) 120
  ACOSH(x) 121
  ASIN(x) 121
  ASINH(x) 121
  ATAN(x) 121
  ATANH(x) 122
  ATAN2(x,y) 122

COS(x)   122
COSH(x)   122
DEGREES(radians)   123
E()   123
EXP(x)   123
EXPONENTIAL(x)   123
FACTORIAL(x)   124
GOAL(initial,result,formula)   124
GUESS()   124
INT(x)   125
LN(x)   125
LOG   125
LOGN(x,logbase)   125
MOD(x,y)   126
NORMAL(x)   126
PI()   126
RADIANS(degrees)   126
RAND()   127
ROUND(x,n)   127
SIGN(number)   127
=SIGN(54–60) = -1SIN(x)   127
SINH(x)   127
SQRT(x)   128
TAN(x)   128
TANH(x)   128
UNIFORM(x)   128
Operators   129
Other Functions   129

Chapter 5   Charts and Graphs   131

Divisions and Series   132
Creating a Chart   132
Tailoring Your Charts   142
  Titles   142
  Legends   142
  Footnotes   142
  Chart, Division, and Series Ranges and Labels   143
  Working with Axes   146
  Repositioning Elements in Your Chart   148

Objects 153
   Adding and Removing Data Elements 154
Copying Or Moving Objects 157
Changing Colors and Patterns 158
Drawing and Working With Graphics 166
Summary 172
Case Study 3: Wingz in Investment Banking 173

Chapter 6   Changing Your Mind   175
Editing 175
A Reminder About Selecting 180
And a Reminder About Undo 180
Removing Data: Clearing and Deleting 180
Inserting 183
Cut and Paste: Moving, Copying, and the Clipboard 187
   What To Do When Things Go Wrong 190
   A Simple Copying Exercise 190
   Using Copy Right or Copy Down 192
   Copying Specific Cell or Data Attributes 193
   Copying Into the Formula Bar 195
   Copying Names or Functions Into a Formula 195
   Copying Objects 196
   Copying and Moving Text Boxes 200
Borders, Patterns, and Color 200
Adding Text to Your Worksheet 205
Using Windows 210
External References 212
Finding Specific Data 212
Protecting Your Work 213
Summary 215
Case Study 4: Wingz in a Law Firm 216

Chapter 7   File Management   217
Opening a New Worksheet 217
Saving Your Work 219
Closing a File 221
Retrieving a Saved File 222
Closing a File When You Quit Wingz 222

Summary 223
Case Study 5: Wingz in a Publishing House 224

Chapter 8 Using Wingz as a Database 229
What's a Database 229
  Creating Your Own Database 231
  Finding Specific Data 238
  Criteria Ranges 241
  Sorting Your Data 247
  Inserting and Deleting Data 250
Summary 254
Case Study 6: Wingz in TV Election Result 255

Chapter 9 Printing 257
Preparing Your Printer 257
Page Size and Orientation 258
Creating a Report 259
Previewing Your Page 261
Printing Your Work 262
Summary 263

Chapter 10 Talking tothe Outside World 265
Linking to Other Wingz Spreadsheets 265
Exchanging Files With Other Programs 272
  Lotus 1-2-3 273
  SYLK 274
  DIF 275
  ASCII 275
Importing Graphics and Text 275
Using Wingz in a Network 276
Summary 277

Chapter 11 Programming in Hyperscript 279
What is Hyperscript? 280
  Direct Commands 280
  Learn Mode: Button Scripts 284
  Learn Mode: Sheet Scripts 287
  Learn Mode: Independent Scripts 288

Writing Scripts   289
Making Menus   294
  Menuitem Commands   295
Using Event Handlers   296
Sheet Events   297
Variables   300
Other Controls   302
  Slide Bar   302
  CTVALUE()   303
  Check Box   305
  Popup Menu   306
  List Box   308
  Radio Button   311
Loop Structures   313
Functions   316
Summary   318

Appendix: Macintosh Spreadsheet Feature Comparison   319

About the Authors   323

Index   325

FOREWORD

In the fall of 1986, a small development team returned from fall COMDEX more convinced than ever that windowing environments represented the future of applications software. They had already decided to build an advanced spreadsheet and returned to invest nine months in experimental development. But, it was not until they began using one of Apple's first Macintosh® II in early 1987 that they settled on the environment that would launch Wingz.

The team moved all development to the Macintosh II. Its rich graphical interface provided the windowing environment best suited to the developing spreadsheet. As work continued, the product which they had originally envisioned was redefined as a true graphic spreadsheet.

A demonstrable product was created by fall 1987, and the product was announced in January 1988. Momentum increased as the company began allocating resources to build recognition for the new product. Wingz was alive, but much work remained as the team continued to perfect the many unique concepts that lay beneath the implementation of Wingz.

Today, Wingz is the result of a dedicated team that insisted on quality even when it was not the expedient course to take.

Informix Software, Inc. would like to thank the authors and publisher of this premier book on Wingz for their hard work and devotion to detail in producing *Mastering Wingz*. The authors, Elna Tymes and Fred Davis, were wonderfully relentless in pursuit of an understanding of Wingz. And the publishers at Bantam, Jono Hardjowirogo and Kenzi Sugihara, were consistently patient in the face of our protracted development process. We appreciate their efforts and applaud this official introduction to Wingz.

> Michael J. Brown
> President, Informix Workstation Products Division
> Lenexa, Kansas

ACKNOWLEDGMENTS

This book was the product of the work of many people. We wish to acknowledge:

Bill Gladstone, superagent, who jumped on the project as soon as he heard about it.

Jono Hardjowirogo, the editor at Bantam who helped it all come together.

The Informix Product Support team for Wingz: Keith Brown, George Bingham, Fred Cunningham, Keith Goosey, Scott Hinrichs, and Jackie McKernan —incredibly dedicated and helpful people who helped track down problems with beta software and got back to us with answers, usually the same day. Definitely a model for how a product support team ought to work.

Kathleen Burnham and Corinne Smith, Informix public relations personnel assigned to Wingz, who supplied us with software, examples, and the names for the case studies, as well as helping us solve a number of other problems.

Steve Cloutier of Informix, for telling us about the Puerto Rico TV case study.

Rick Lucas, J.T. Keller, and Larry Horner for managing and presenting an eye-opening developer seminar on using HyperScript.

Charles Prael, for help in developing Chapter 8.

Bill Sanders, for doing the HyperScript chapter quickly and on time.

                                                                    Fred Davis

                                                                  Elna R. Tymes

                                                        Palo Alto, California

1

Introduction

You've done it. You've decided to join the forward-thinking group of spreadsheet users who recognize that it isn't enough to sift through, analyze, and display numbers in a spreadsheet—you need to present your data in a way that makes an impact on the person seeing the data, whether that person sees your data on a computer screen, on paper, or on a slide.

Wingz, the new spreadsheet program from Informix, Inc., has been deliberately placed in a new category—the presentation spreadsheet—to acknowledge that presentation of numbers requires the same kind of attention by tools usually associated with desktop publishing that presentation of words and pictures has earned in the last few years.

WHAT IS PRESENTATION SOFTWARE?

When desktop publishing was introduced, it broke through the previous division between people who created manuscripts, such as artists and writers, and people who produced finished documents, such as graphic artists, typesetters, and printers. Suddenly, the people who were directly in-

involved in the creation of text and pictures were also able to manipulate type size and fonts, and to work with details like shading and boxes, and page layout.

Once the business software community began to accept the Macintosh approach to working with information on a screen, software tools appeared that let you draw lines, curves, and shapes, that let you digitize and place pictures on a page, that let you combine pictures and words and numbers, and rearrange them as you need (see Figures 1-1–3).

The last few years have seen the introduction of a number of programs that incorporate features letting you mix text and graphics of all sorts. Many of them are called desktop publishing packages, but they have different combinations of features and are designed to do different things. Some of the packages calling themselves presentation software don't neatly fit into the desktop publishing category, either. So just what is this thing called a **presentation spreadsheet?**

Datapro Research Corporation, a leading computer market research company, groups presentation software into the following categories:

FIGURE 1-1 Text Produced by a Word Processor (c. 1982).

```
.pl 40
.lm 10
.op
```

The department has access to a lot of different computers, and a lot of software, so they tend to use some software to do the calculations, some to do the reports, and some to produce the graphs. Bill White has been deeply involved in translating the results of departmental studies into articles, complete with graphs and charts.

"When we first started getting into Macintosh software, we used Excel," White says. They didn't like the results when produced with Excel's graphics, so they used several other packages, including CricketGraph and some other graphics programs to make the

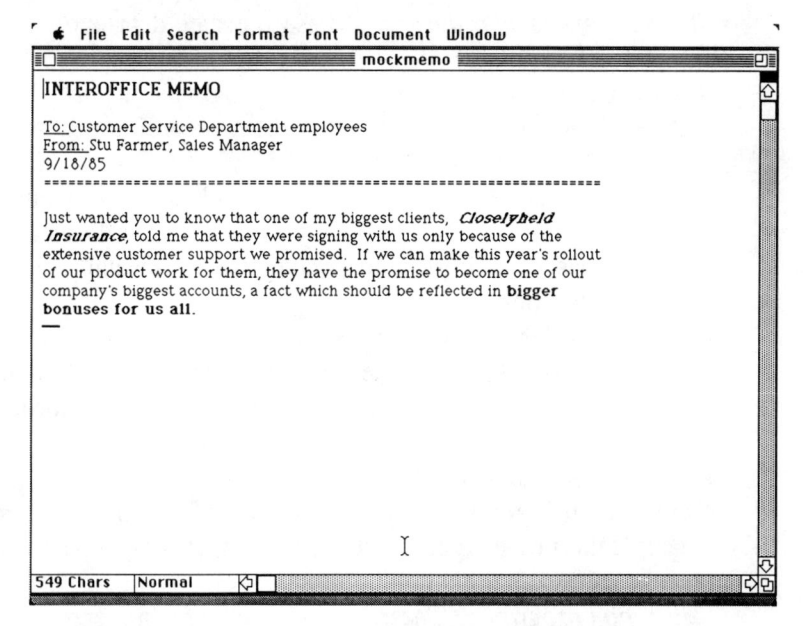

FIGURE 1-2 Same Text, Using Microsoft Word (c. 1985).

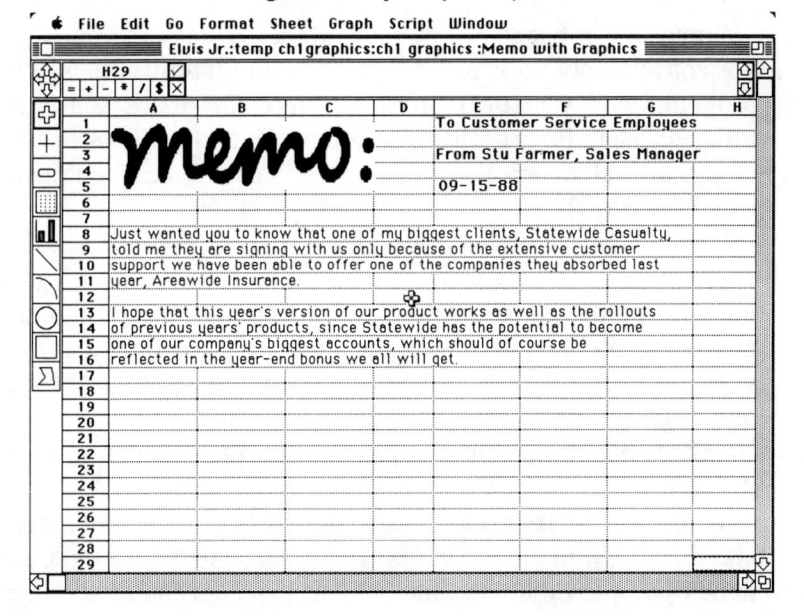

FIGURE 1-3 Text Augmented by Graphics (Created Elsewhere)

- *Business graphics programs*   These translate data into bar, pie, and line graphs and similar charts.
- *Paint programs*   These pixel-oriented programs, such as MacPaint, let you create images on-screen, and color them according to a series of options usually referred to as a palette.
- *Draw programs*   These programs are also pixel-oriented, but are concerned with images created by combining various standard objects: circles, rectangles, lines, etc. Editing with a draw program is usually easier than editing with a paint program.
- *CAD\CAM (Computer-Aided Design and Computer-Aided Manufacturing) programs*   These programs let designers, architects, and engineers describe an object, and rotate it so that different views appear on the screen.
- *Mapping programs*   These programs let you represent data geographically, usually on a U.S. map.
- *Statistical programs*   These primarily do statistical and mathematical manipulation of the data, and usually regard graphical presentation as a secondary benefit.
- *Animation programs*   These let you move graphic representations of data through a sequence of pictures, so that the elements you use appear to move.
- *Desktop publishing programs*   These let you incorporate text, pictures, and typographical devices into pages on the screen.

Wingz doesn't neatly fit into any of these categories, since its capabilities go considerably beyond the normal limitations of business graphics programs and statistical programs. It incorporates some of the object-oriented capabilities of the draw programs, and it allows the text–graphics–typographical incorporation features of many desktop publishing programs (see Figure 1-4).

Unlike many of the other programs that incorporate combinations of the features above, Wingz lets you produce three–dimensional graphics, allowing you to plot several data series over time, for instance, or add shading to an existing *X-Y* graph. Then, once you've got the graphic representation the way you want it, you can create the text to go with it, and format, size, and rearrange the text around the chart in whatever way works best, using standard word processing tools built into the program to create and place the text.

Wingz differs from most other spreadsheets on the market in its power and flexibility. In the Appendix, we present a feature comparison, originally done by Apple Computer, Inc., between Wingz and three other spreadsheet

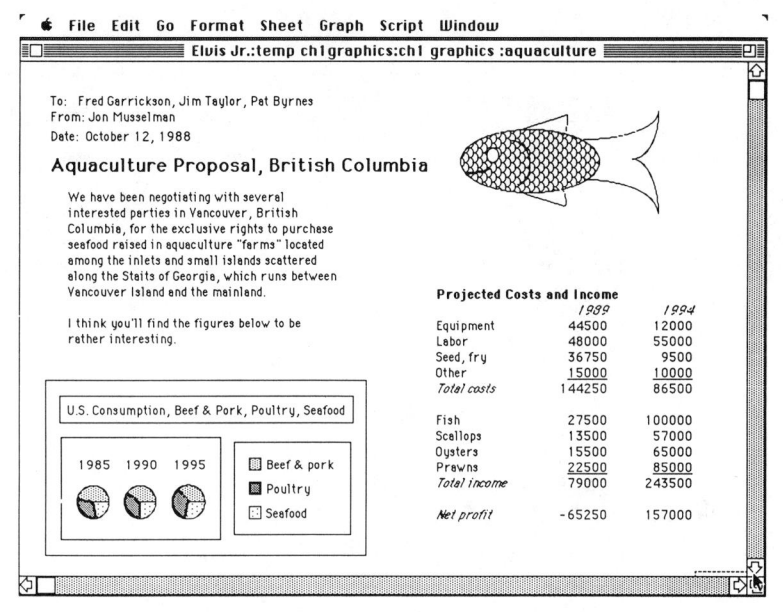

FIGURE 1-4 Wingz Document

packages for the Macintosh currently on the market. The comparison clearly shows that Wingz has features that make it superior among the spreadsheet programs.

But Wingz's strength goes beyond simple feature enumeration. Partly because of its graphic capabilities, partly because of the ease with which you can add text and other graphic images, and partly because it is simply a very powerful spreadsheet program, Wingz stands out as a leader in the new field of presentation spreadsheets.

WHAT CAN Wingz DO?

Probably the best way to illustrate how Wingz works is to demonstrate its abilities in a business situation. Let's suppose you have a product line you advertise through direct mail, and you pick target mailing areas by zip code. Your product line tends to appeal to higher income groups, particularly those without young children. You've been using some census data, with projections for 1992, to help pick target areas, and in one search you've collected census data for six specific zip code areas (see Figure 1-5).

6 Mastering Wingz

	A	B	C	D	E	F	G
1	Projected Household Income, by Zip Code, 1992						
2							
3		94306	94301	94022	94025	94040	94043
4	$0 - 7,499	529	412	302	1026	657	759
5	$7,500- 9,999	191	148	106	379	236	278
6	$10,000- 14,999	585	466	317	1004	694	696
7	$15,000- 24,999	1260	956	649	2253	1599	1860
8	$25,000- 34,999	1384	995	860	2320	1797	2239
9	$35,000- 49,999	1924	1275	1660	3323	2479	2846
10	$50,000- 74,999	2351	1337	3049	4015	2343	2366
11	over $75,000	3027	2184	8150	7984	2591	1607
12							
13	Total # households	11251	7773	15093	22303	12396	12651
14							
15	Projected Population, by Zip Code, 1992						
16		94306	94301	94022	94025	94040	94043
17	0-5	1074	596	1886	2721	1125	1973
18	6-13	1586	894	2705	3864	1636	2668
19	14-17	878	497	1640	2286	818	1334
20	18-24	1903	1176	4058	5116	1610	2501
21	25-34	3856	2170	6312	8272	4243	4225
22	35-44	5027	3279	4181	7511	5598	6865
23	45-54	3489	2451	6148	7184	3399	3474
24	55-64	2562	1623	5739	6204	2684	2029
25	65 and over	4026	3876	8321	11266	4447	2724
26							
27	Total population	24402	16562	40990	54424	25560	27793

FIGURE 1-5 Selected Census Data, Projected for 1992

The data for higher income groups for zip codes 94022 and 94025 look very promising, but it's difficult to tell how they relate to the whole. Wingz lets us quickly transform the data we're looking at into a bar chart (see Figure 1-6). It's obvious from inspecting the chart that the number of households in the highest income category is proportionally very high for the two zip codes we noted earlier.

But we're looking for households where there is a lot of discretionary income, not households with children. The population data for the six zip codes can also be depicted as a pie chart, which will represent proportional amounts of each category (see Figure 1-7).

If we analyze at the segments for the older three age groups, it's obvious that the population 45 and older makes up close to half the population of the 94022 group and the 94301 group, somewhat less but still better than a third of the 94025, 94306, and 94040 group, and about a quarter of the 94043 group.

Let's target the 94025 and 94022 groups in our presentation to management. Wingz lets us combine bar chart elements in a stack, so that we can look at sets of age groupings. In the one shown in Figure 1-8, for instance,

Introduction 7

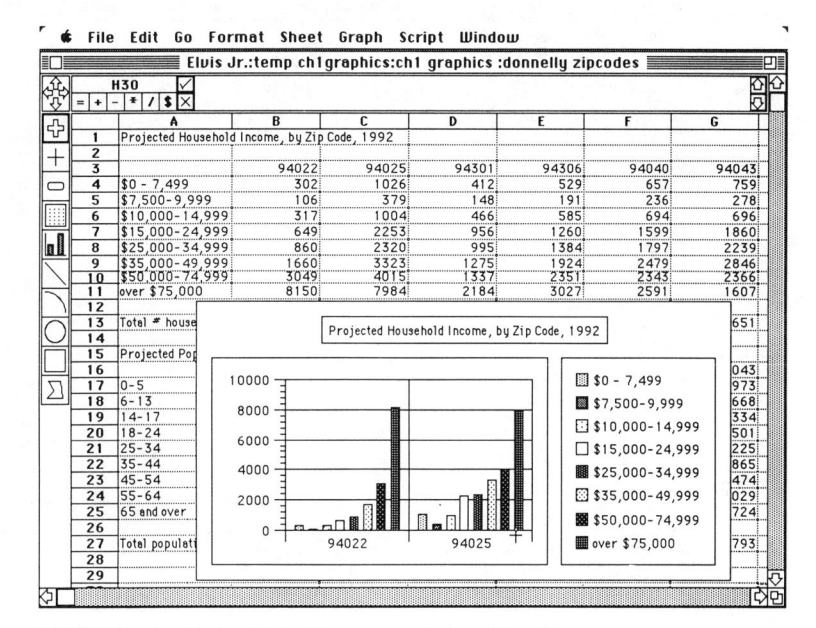

FIGURE 1-6 Same Data Represented as Bar Chart.

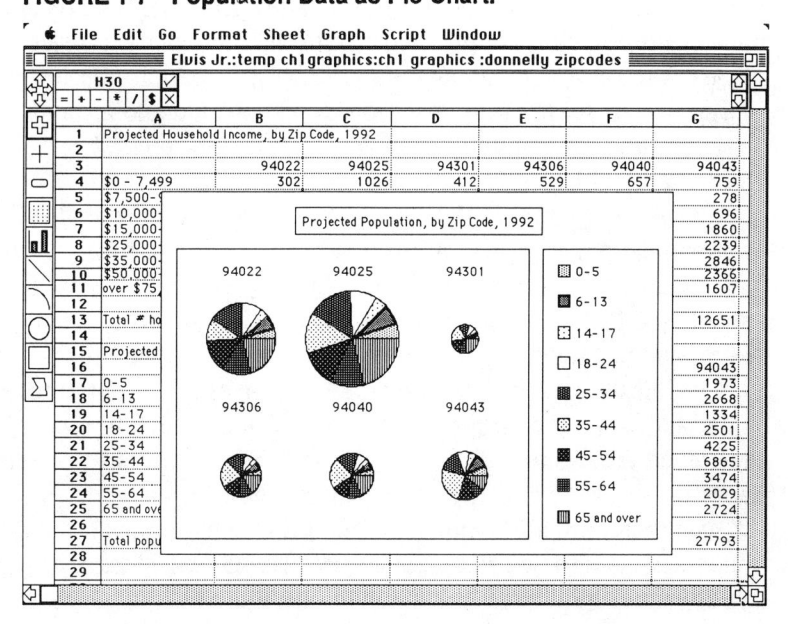

FIGURE 1-7 Population Data as Pie Chart.

8   Mastering Wingz

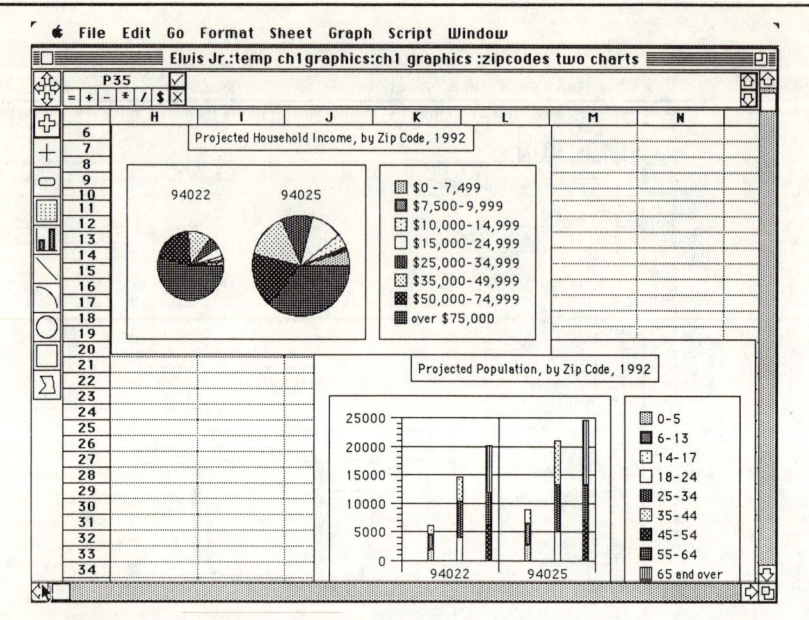

FIGURE 1-8   Income and Age Charts.

we've grouped the school-age set (0–5, 6–13, and 14–17), the child-bearing years (18–24, 25–34, and 35–44), and the older years (45–54, 55–64, and over 65). Our target population, the latter grouping, stands out.

When these data are presented with the income data, represented in a pie chart, we get some rather compelling information about the residents in these two areas (see Figure 1-8). We can now add text around the two charts, to explain what the numbers mean and make our pitch. Figure 1-9 shows the two charts with text.

But the text alone isn't enough. You'll need some headlines, and maybe an explanatory box indicating where the data came from. With the fonts, styles, and sizes available within Wingz, you can add these touches to your sheet (see Figure 1-10). You can also import graphics, such as a company logo, and use them on the presentation material (see Figure 1-11).

Graphics can also be added later on in the presentation, either drawn freehand with the graphics tools shown at the left side of the screen, retrieved from some previously saved file, or imported from some other application, such as a file of clip art images.

And that's not all Wingz lets you do! Our examples up to this point have been designed to be printed on a standard 8.5" x 11" sheet of paper. Suppose you wanted your presentation to be on the screen of a computer, and you

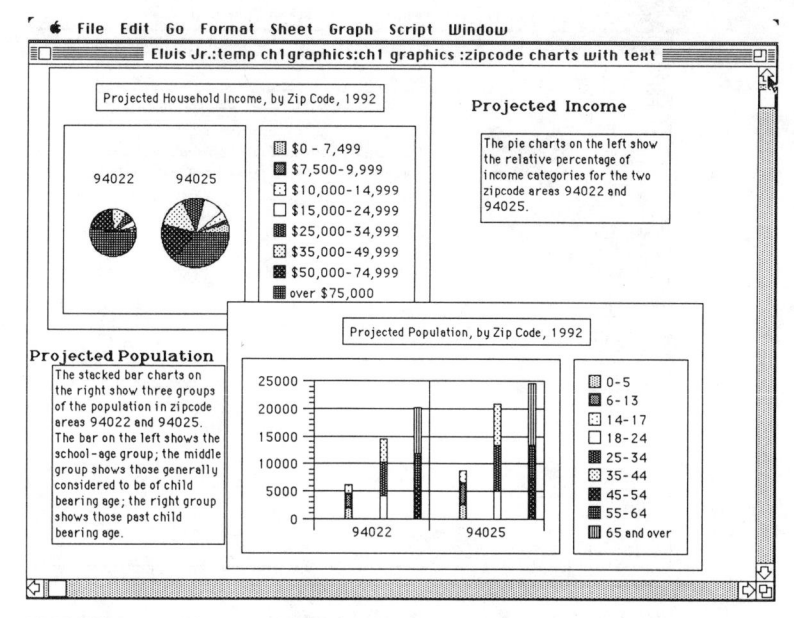

FIGURE 1-9 Charts with Text.

FIGURE 1-10 Edited Sheet.

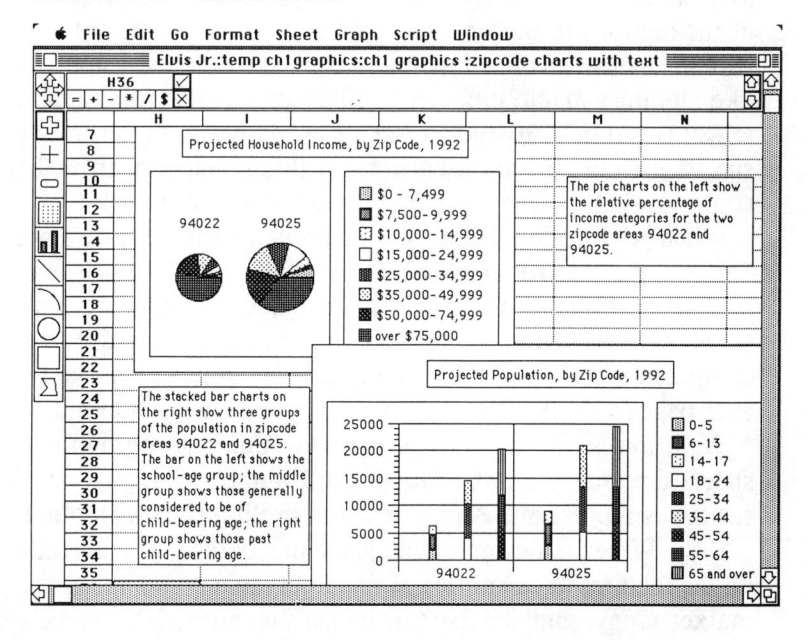

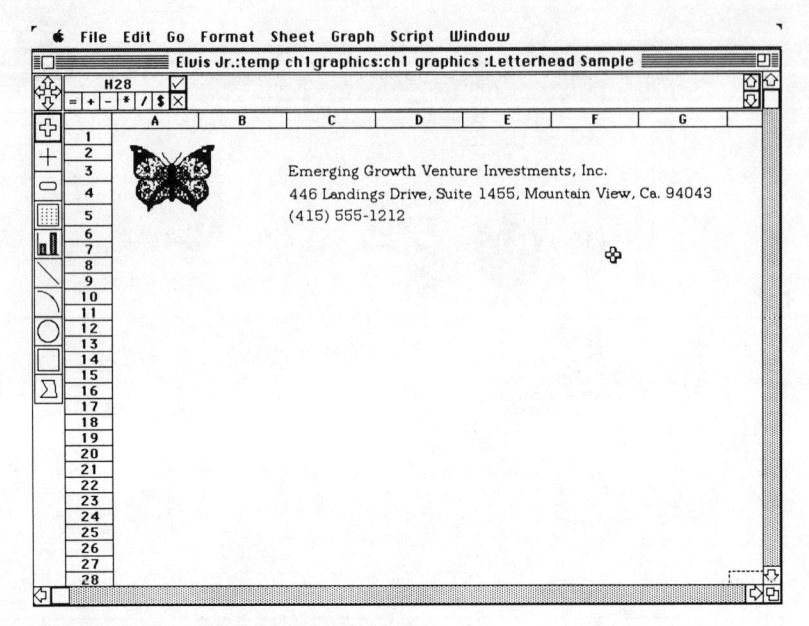

FIGURE 1-11 Sheet with Graphics.

wanted the user to be able to page back and forth through the material you've assembled. Wingz lets you set up a HyperScript file that attaches "scripts" of instructions to buttons you create on your screen. When the user clicks with the mouse on one of the buttons, the associated script is executed, much like running a macro program in other spreadsheet programs. The difference is that it can be constructed to be transparent to the user, who thinks he or she is just clicking on a button and things happen. In reality, your script controls what the user sees on the screen (see Figure 1-12).

When your reader clicks the Background button, for instance, your HyperScript set of instructions creates a screenful of background information, such as that shown in Figure 1-13. Selecting other buttons creates other screens, so that your reader can step through the entire presentation on a computer. Note that each screen can be distinct from the others, much as each page in a short presentation can contain different kinds of information.

Well, that's all very glitzy, you say. Color and graphics and script-run sheets are fine, but what about hard numbers? How does Wingz handle serious computation? And how about trading files with others?

Easy. Wingz is far more than just a pretty face. The spreadsheet itself has all the features of the most powerful personal computer spreadsheets on the market today, and then some. It has far more (303, to be exact) built-in

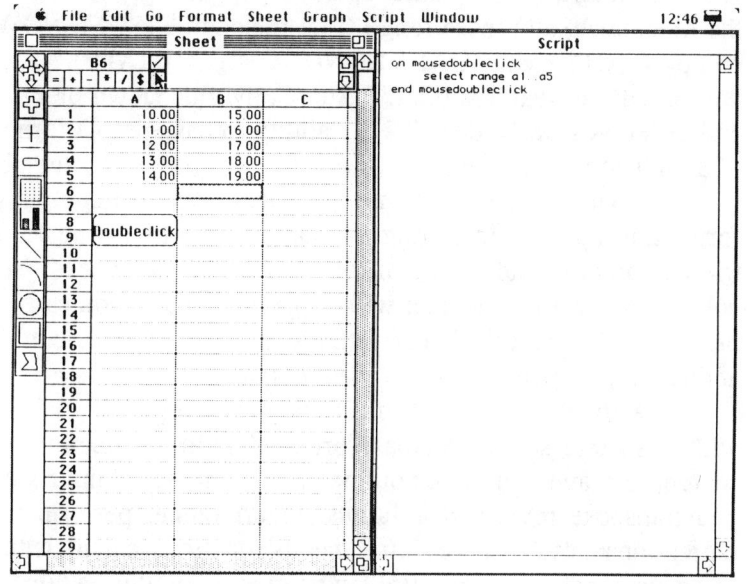

FIGURE 1-12 Sample Opening Script Screen

FIGURE 1-13 Background Information

functions than any of the other spreadsheet packages currently available for the Macintosh, and these range from the simple (SUM, NOW, INT) to the complex (CTERM, GOAL, BONDTYM, COLLATE). It allows all the normal editing features (Cut, Paste, Copy, Fill Down or Fill Right, Insert and Delete, Clear, Undo) plus the ability to paste into a formula the syntax of a built-in function. Figure 1-14 shows the Paste Formula Choice box.

Additionally, it lets you name cells or ranges, and apply a wide range of formatting options, including 14 number and time/date formats, four attribute formats, and precision up to 15 decimal places. You can freeze column or row titles, so that with large worksheets you can continue to see them while you scroll. You can enlarge or reduce the scale of the worksheet, and specify what features you want displayed.

The database portion of Wingz lets you manipulate your worksheet data with a special set of database-oriented built-in functions, and lets you search, sort, and rearrange your data. A special set of matrix commands lets you transpose rows and columns, invert range, perform multiple linear regression analysis, solve simultaneous equations, calculate the determinant of a square matrix, and multiply two ranges to produce a third. When you've

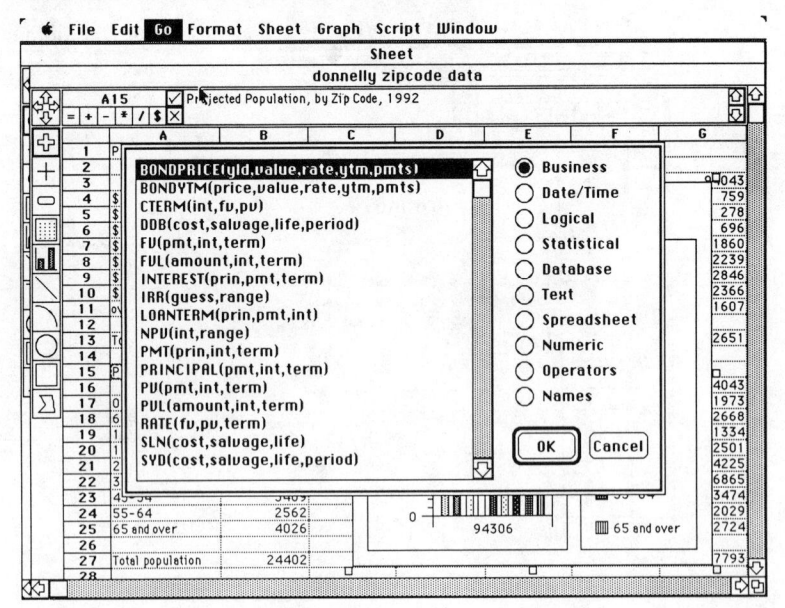

FIGURE 1-14 Paste Formula Choice Box.

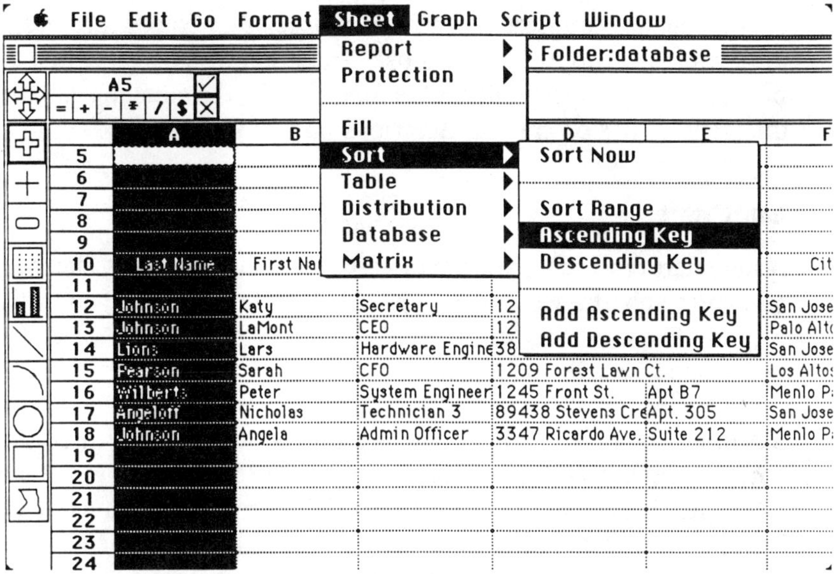

FIGURE 1-15 Sort Menu

manipulated your data to your satisfaction, you can produce a report, complete with headers and footers, with page breaks where you specify. Figure 1-15 shows the Wingz Sort menu.

Wingz can handle other files with ease. In addition to being able to trade Wingz files with other users in a network environment, you can also import and export files in other formats. Wingz can open and use files from Lotus 1–2–3, versions 1A and 2, and those written in SYLK, DIF, and ASCII formats. It can save files in the two Lotus formats, and in DIF and ASCII formats. A saved file can then be exported to another computer.

CHARTS

This section will devote itself to illustrating the twenty different kinds of charts you can produce with Wingz. It's important to understand how these work, and with what kind of data, so that you can use Wingz in a manner that's consistent with what you're trying to convey.

14 Mastering Wingz

If yours is a color system, Wingz uses color to display the different components of your graph. You can choose other colors for the elements, or mix your own, as well as choose background, axis, and line colors and patterns. If your system doesn't support color, the elements are displayed in different shades of gray or in various hatching patterns.

Bar Chart

A bar chart represents your data vertically, with the scale shown on the left side of the chart area. It's the default Wingz uses when you initially select a chart. The bar chart in Figure 1-16 shows the number of people in each age group in a selected zip code:

3D Bar Chart   A 3D bar chart represents your data as three-dimensional bars (see Figure 1-17). People tend to be very impressed with 3D bar charts, especially if they're in color. Be careful of having too much detail in a 3D bar chart, or it will lose its impact. You may also wish to rotate the chart, so that taller bars don't hide shorter bars.

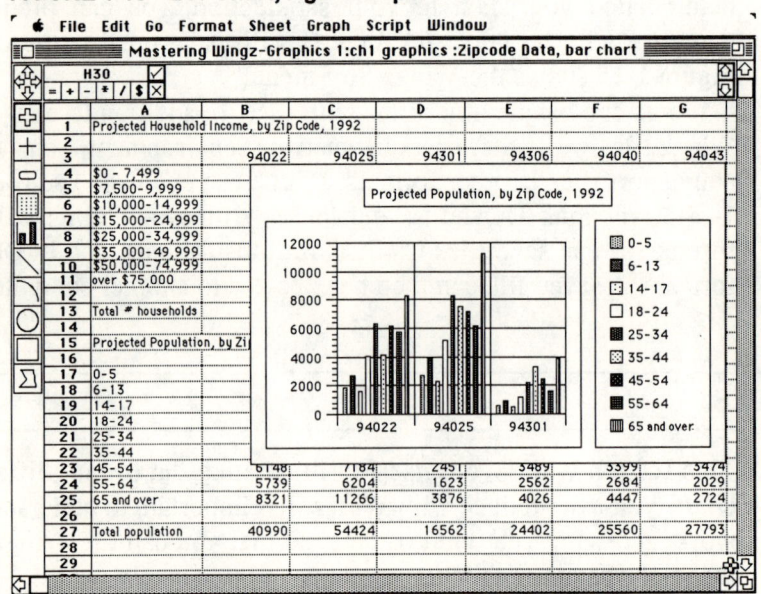

FIGURE 1-16   Bar Chart, Age Groups.

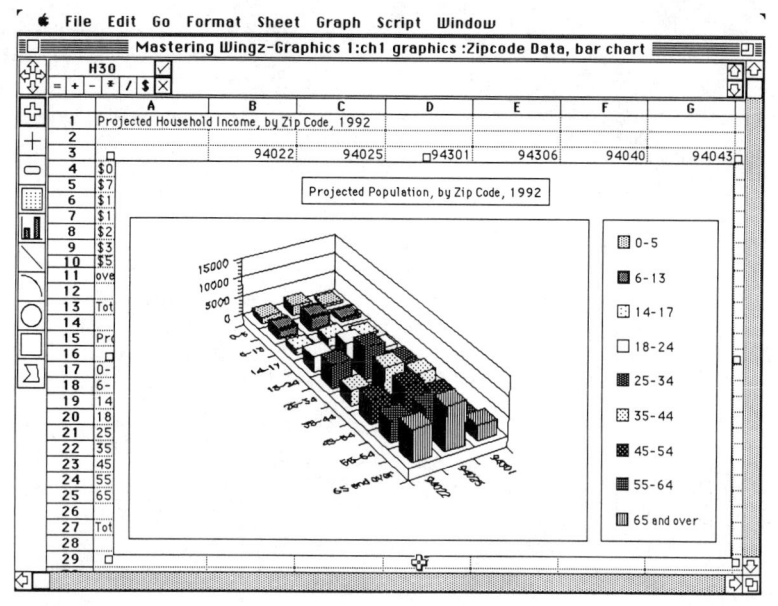

FIGURE 1-17 3D Bar Chart, Age Groups.

Because Wingz uses a bit-map mechanism to letter the division series labels and the items in the legend, the labels on a 3D bar chart may be difficult to read on the screen. However, when the chart is printed on a laser printer that uses Postscript or QuickDraw, the letters are far more legible.

Step Chart

A step chart is a bit like vertical bar chart, but all its bars are connected. Figure 1-18 shows a step chart of the same data we have used in the bar charts above. Step charts tend to be most useful when you would like to portray divisions of different sizes (in this case, the population of the three different zip code areas), but want to show the proportion of each series within the division.

3D Step Chart   You would think that a 3D step chart could easily use the same data as a 2D step chart. It doesn't quite work that way. Figure 1-19 shows the 3D step chart version of the data we've been using. As you can see, the individual series are linked, and are separated from adjacent series, implying a closer relationship than the age categories we've been using. A

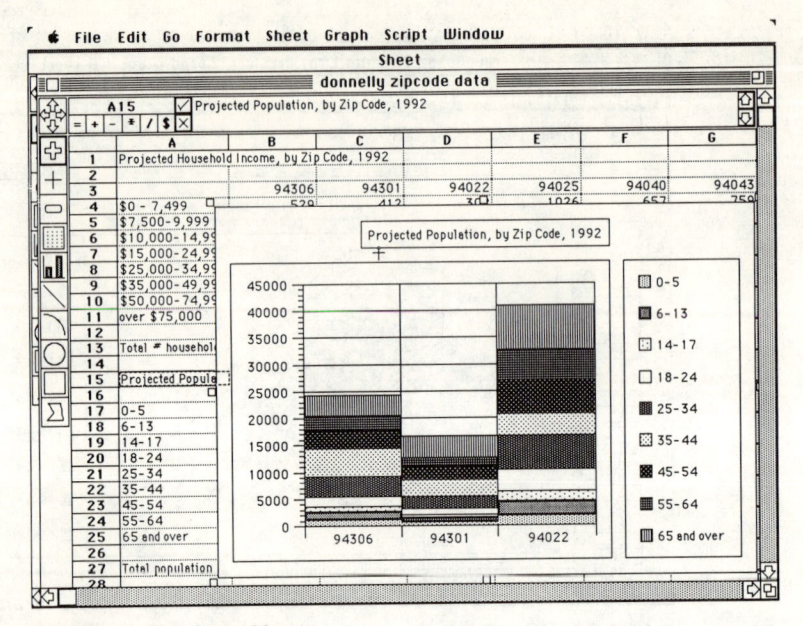

FIGURE 1-18   Step Chart.

better use of the 3D bar chart would be to illustrate the various departmental expenditures in an income statement (see Figure 1-20).

As you can quickly see, the Marketing, Administration, and R&D expenditures are each a separate series, tracked over time.

Horizontal Bar Chart

The horizontal bar chart is basically the vertical bar chart turned on its side. Figure 1-21 shows how the population data look as a horizontal bar chart. Horizontal bar charts lend themselves nicely to situations where you don't have the vertical room for a normal bar chart.

Pie Chart

Pie charts are another useful way of showing the different parts of a whole. When Wingz is using more than one division, it displays a pie chart for each division, sized proportionally (see Figure 1-22).

Introduction 17

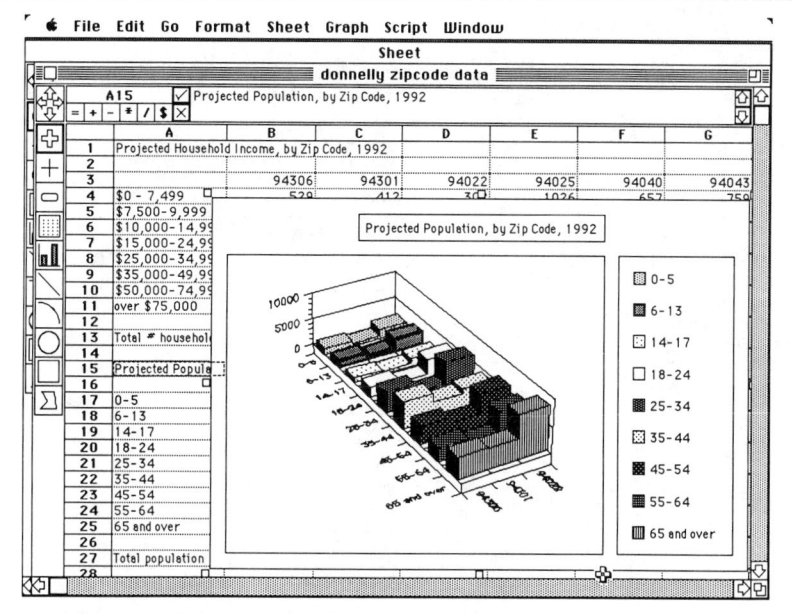

FIGURE 1-19 3D Step Chart.

FIGURE 1-20 Income Statement 3D Bar Chart.

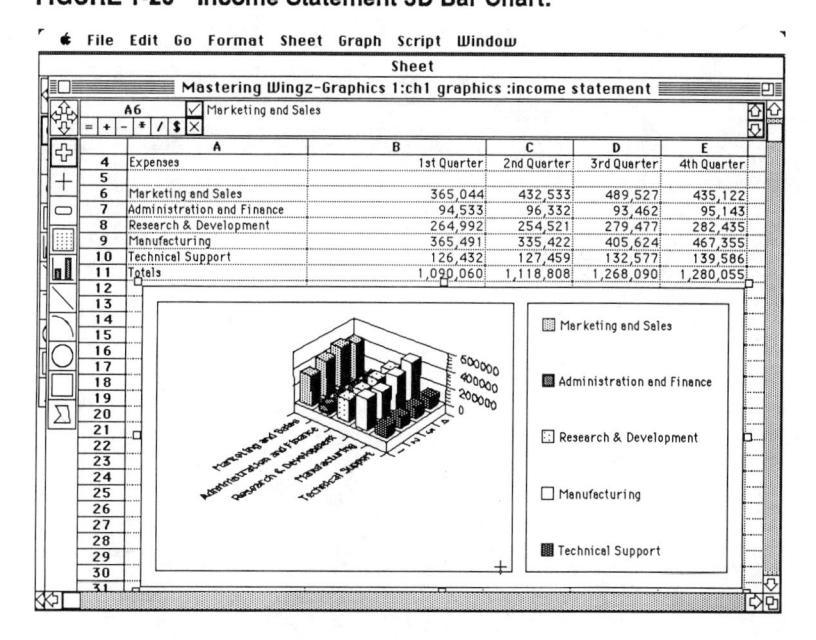

18 Mastering Wingz

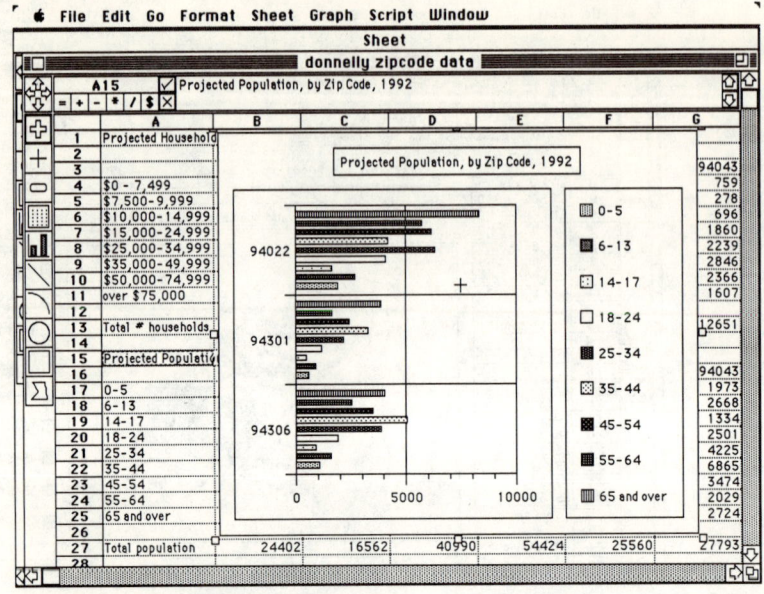

FIGURE 1-21   Horizontal Bar Chart

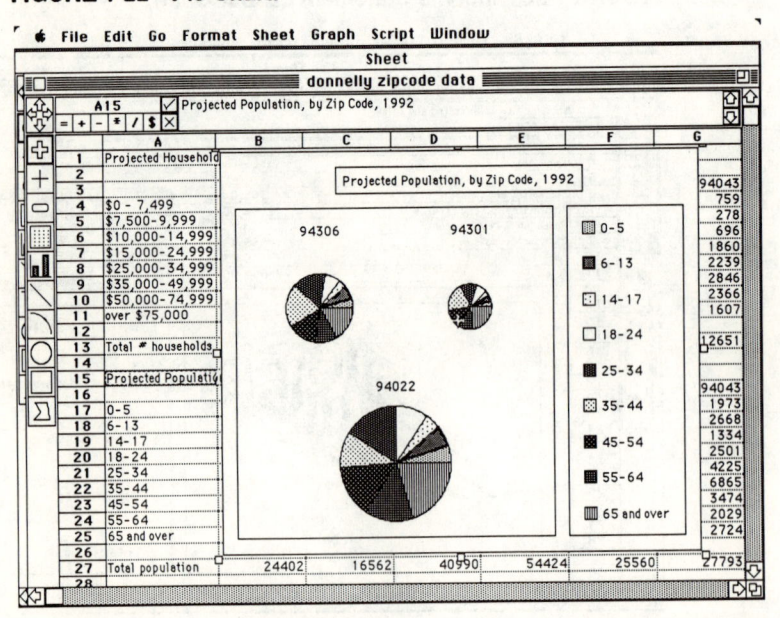

FIGURE 1-22   Pie Chart.

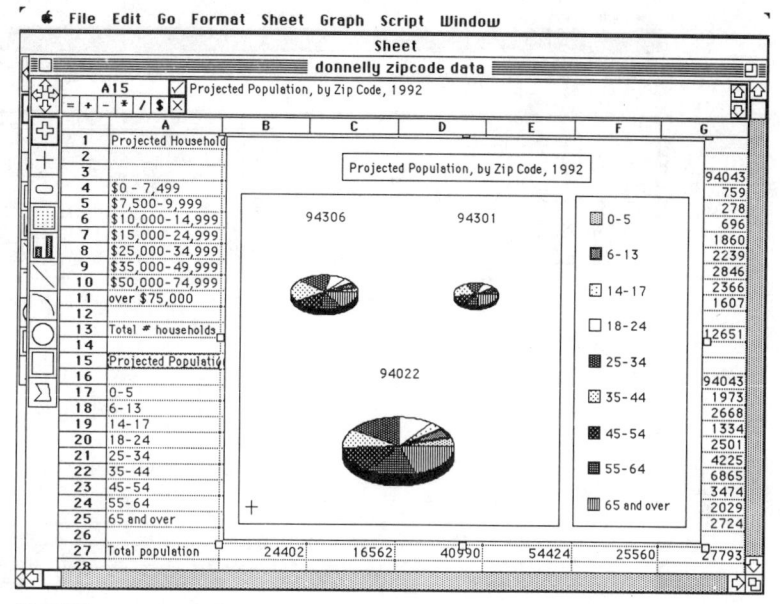

FIGURE 1-23 3D Pie Chart.

3D Pie Chart 3D pie charts are impressive ways to show data that are well represented in a pie chart (see Figure 1-23). The thickness of the "pie" is not, however, related to any data item.

Line Chart

Line charts are particularly good at showing progressions over time. Figure 1-24 shows expenses for five departments in a company, plotted over the four quarters of 1988. Notice that it's easier to track a path of rising expenses with a line chart. It's also easier to spot potential relationships between numbers: an increase in marketing and sales is followed, one quarter later, by an increase in manufacturing expenses, presumably as manufacturing gears up to produce the goods that were demanded as a result of increased marketing activity.

3D Line Chart A 3D line chart lets lines "float" in a three-dimensional cube, a technique that can be attention-getting (see Figure 1-25). However, you need to be sure your data are arranged in such a way that higher or more "forward" lines don't block lines that are lower or farther back.

20 Mastering Wingz

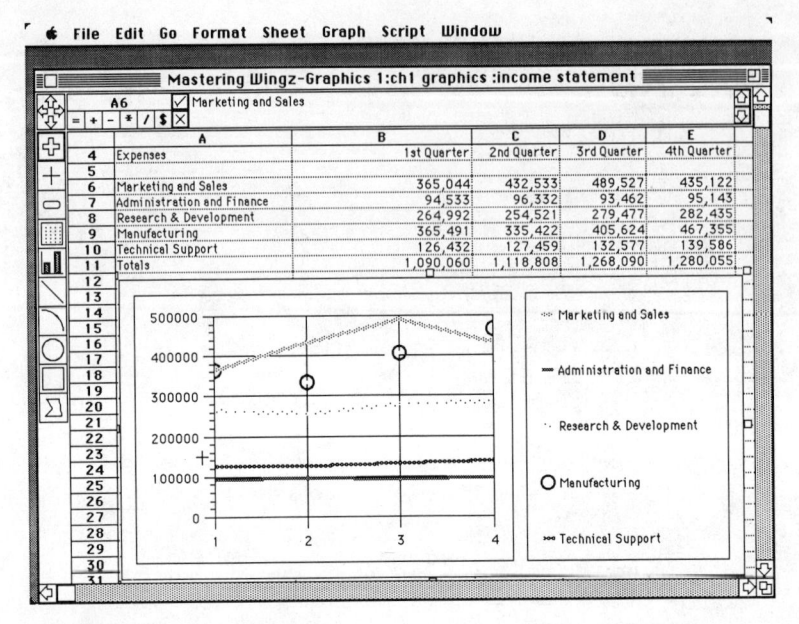

FIGURE 1-24   Line Chart.

FIGURE 1-25   3D Line Chart.

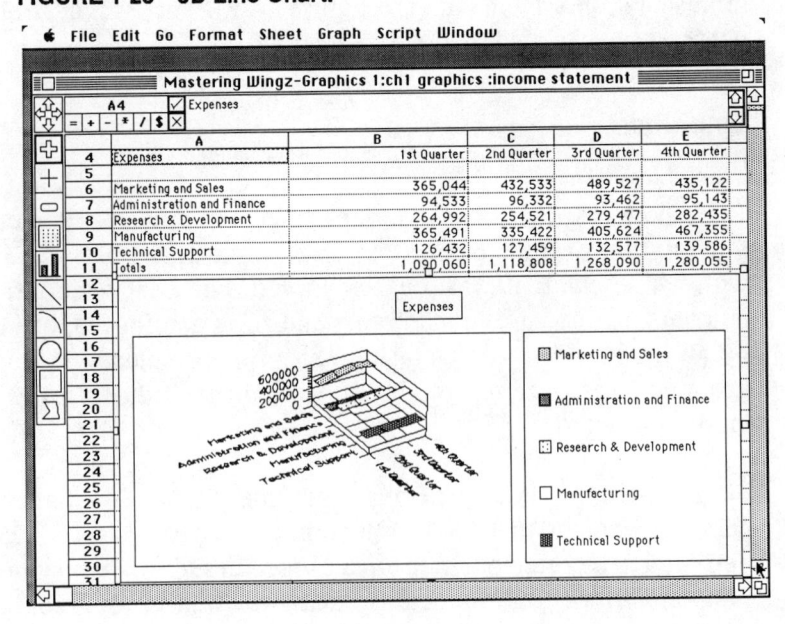

Layer Chart

A layer chart plots each category of expense atop another category, so that the topmost point for a division represents the total for that division. (see Figure 1-26). In this case, it's easy to see that total expenses for these divisions rose during the year, and to spot disproportionate rises.

If you compare the order of the series used in the line chart and the order used in the layer chart, you'll see that Wingz has rearranged the series. It plots the first series at the bottom, then the next on top of that, and so on, with the rightmost series at the top.

3D Layer Chart A 3D layer chart plots each division's numbers as if it were separate layer charts, starting at 0. It then arranges them, as irregular polygons, in series order (see Figure 1-27). As with the other 3D charts, it's important to recognize that smaller numbers will be represented by polygons that may be partially or completely hidden by polygons representing larger numbers. Such is the case in our example above. You can get around situations like this by arranging the numbers on your worksheet so that the

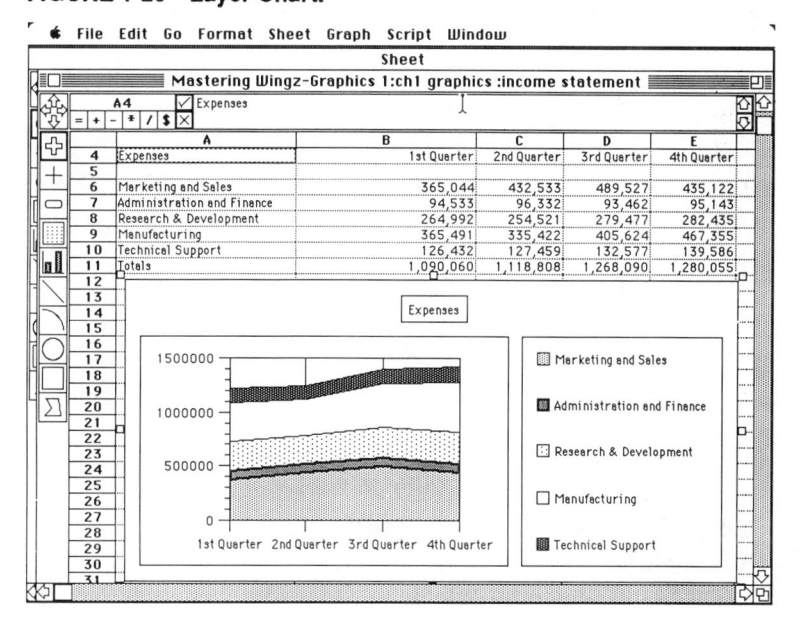

FIGURE 1-26 Layer Chart.

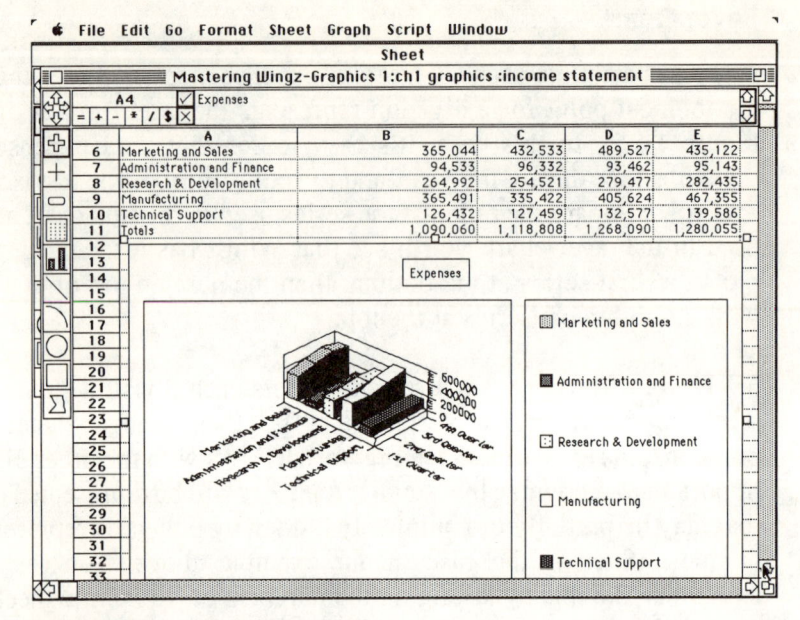

FIGURE 1-27 3D Layer Chart.

smaller numbers are in series toward the bottom of the sheet, and larger numbers are toward the top, or by rotating the chart.

Combination Chart

You may wish to use a combination chart to emphasize the performance of one group over the efforts of the others. Combination charts let you combine two or more types of charts in representing one set of data. Figure 1-28 shows an example of a bar chart combined with a line chart representation of the data for one group. Use combination graphs sparingly. The different element should be used primarily to emphasize something; if you combine too many elements, they'll lose their impact on the user.

3D Combination Chart A 3D combination chart is simply a 3D version of the combination chart shown above (see Figure 1-29). Just as a 3D bar chart is displayed a bit differently from the way a 2D bar chart is, so will a 3D combination chart be displayed differently from its 2D counterpart.

The warning about combining too many elements in a combination chart applies doubly to a 3D combination chart. The extra labels on axes, and the

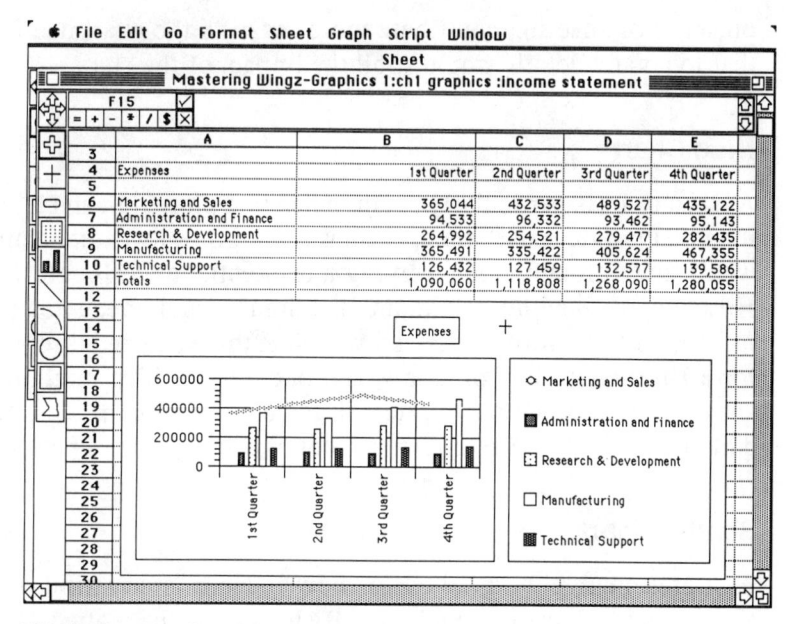

FIGURE 1-28 Combination Chart

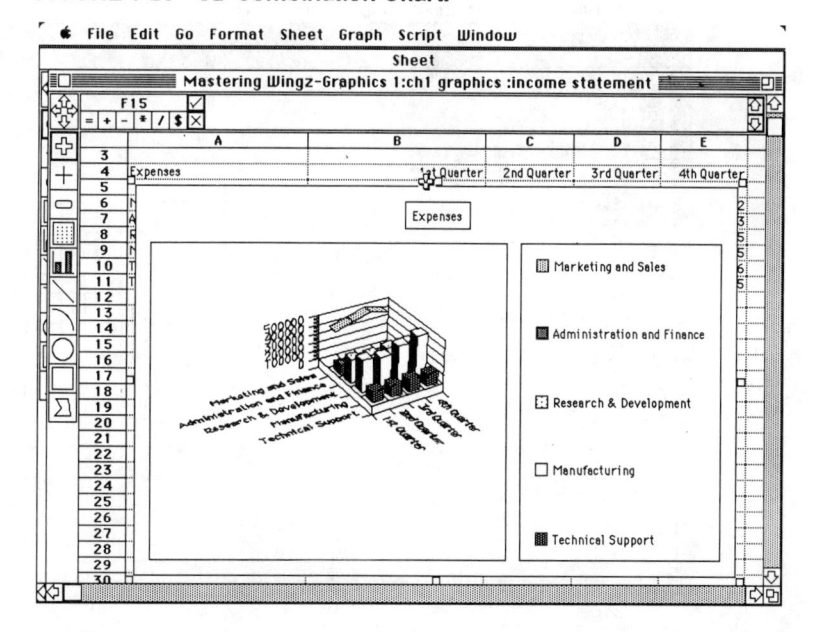

FIGURE 1-29 3D Combination Chart.

presence of shading, contribute more detail to the chart itself. You can see that too many details would spoil the impact of the chart.

HiLo Chart

A HiLo chart is particularly useful when you plot high and low points of an item that progress over time, such as stock prices, weather temperatures, or water flow through a pipe serving a residential area. Figure 1-30 depicts a HiLo chart showing minimum, maximum, and mean temperatures, by month, for a California coastal town. Note that you need three sets of figures for a HiLo chart: a high, a low, and one other, which might be a mean, as shown above, or a closing price, in the case of stock prices, or an average daily balance, if you're tracking account activity over a period of time.

Scatter Chart

A scatter chart is best suited to show if there is any kind of relationship among data points in a population. By looking at the plotted data points, you

FIGURE 1-30 HiLo Chart, Annual Temperature.

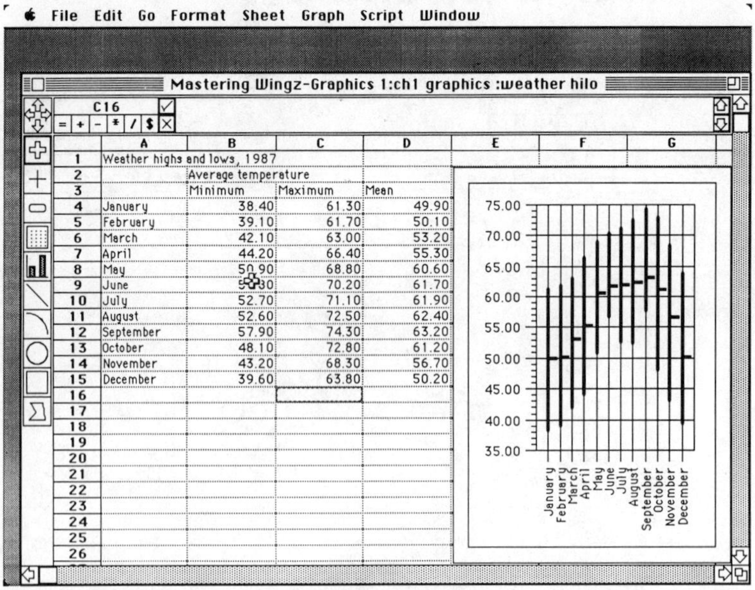

can tell if there is a positive relationship (the data points appear to fall in an upward path and to the right), a negative relationship (the data points appear to fall in a downward path and to the right), or no particular relationship (the data points are scattered with no discernible trend).

In the scatter chart shown in Figure 1-31, we've plotted the 1987 percent return to investors against the Fortune 500 rank for a number of companies in three industrial categories. We wanted to see if there was any discernible relationship between the return to investors and the Fortune 500 ranking. In this case, the closer to zero on the X-axis, the higher or more positive the Fortune 500 ranking, Thus a positive relationship would appear as a kind of diagonal band of data points, slanting down to the right. If there were a positive relationship between the two measurements, the companies with the lower number would have higher returns, and the companies with the higher number would have lower returns.

As you can see, most of the data points are scattered in no discernible pattern in the horizontal band between +50% and –50%, with some above that and two below that. We can conclude from the chart that there is no particular relationship between the two measurements.

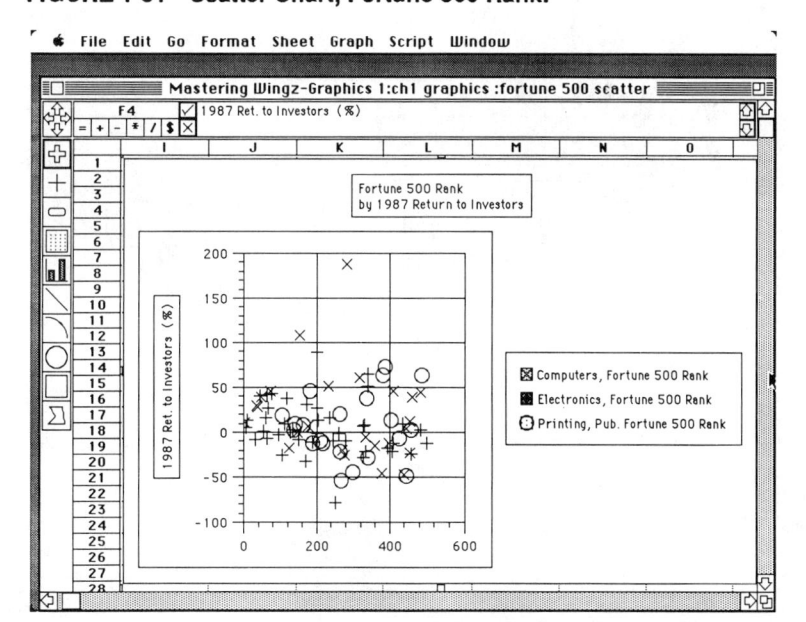

FIGURE 1-31 Scatter Chart, Fortune 500 Rank.

X-Y Chart

An *X-Y* chart is a form of scatter chart, but its data points are connected for visual impact (see Figure 1-32). The lines shown connect the data points in the sequence given in the worksheet, but don't necessarily mean any sort of progression from data point to data point. As with a scatter chart, if there is a positive or negative relationship between the data points, you should see a kind of trend line. This is NOT the same, however, as the line connecting the data points.

Polar Chart

Polar charts best show results of angular computation—for instance, situations where you're measuring sound or light levels as a function of distance and angle from a single source. The chart depicted in Figure 1-33 shows the result of one such set of calculations on a set of data measuring points of a specified distance (radius) and angle from the source point of sound coming from a high fidelity speaker.

FIGURE 1-32 XY Chart.

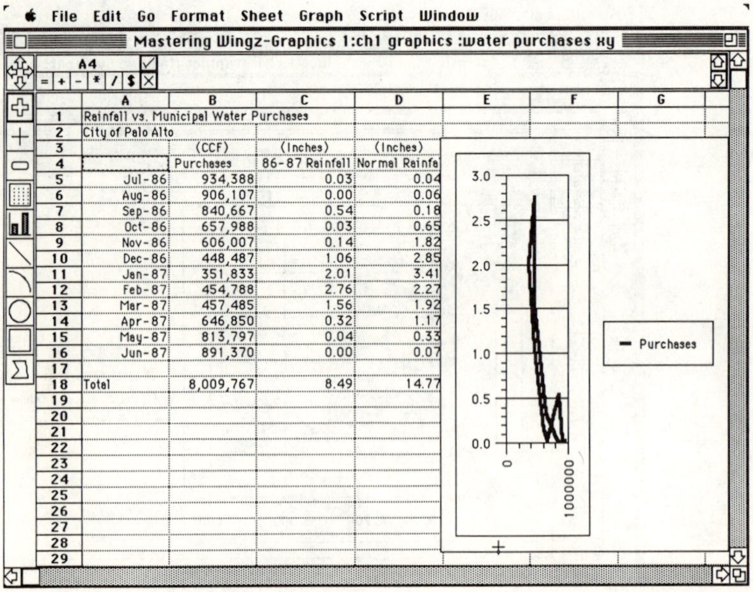

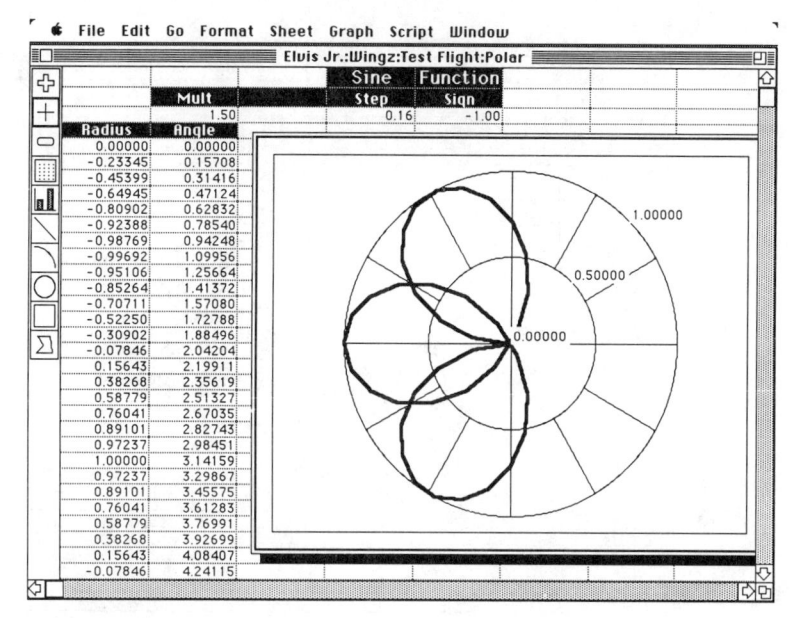

FIGURE 1-33 Polar Graph.

What does a graph like this show? In this case, the areas within the "petals" have acceptable sound levels, while the areas outside the "petals" have sound levels that are not acceptable.

Wireframe Chart

A wireframe chart is used to sketch the outlines of a three-dimensional shape whose definition lines are specified by the numbers it uses as x., y., and z-coordinates. The wireframe chart shown in Figure 1-34 was constructed as part of a demonstration in the Test Flight folder. You can rotate the graph so you can inspect it from different angles with the Graph 3D View command. The formula that constructed the chart is shown in the box at the top. The data it used in establishing wireframe coordinates for the chart are shown in Figure 1-35. Note that data is arranged for xy coordinates only.

Surface Chart

A surface chart is a filled-in three-dimensional representation of data represented as x, y, and z-coordinates (see Figure 1-36). Wingz arbitrarily assigns

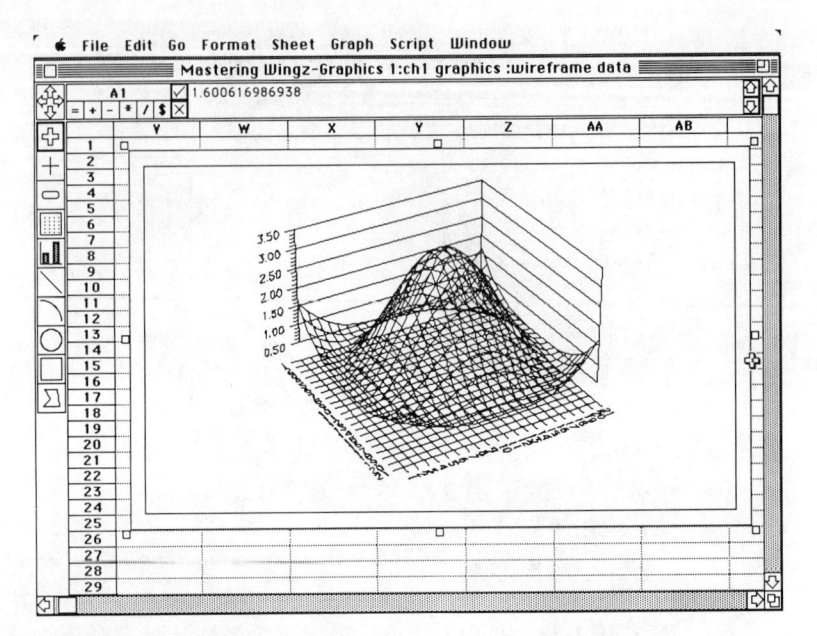

FIGURE 1-34 Wireframe Chart.

FIGURE 1-35 Wireframe Chart Data

colors (shades of gray, if yours isn't a color system) to what it considers reasonable "elevations," and displays the corresponding chart as bands of color. (You can get more "elevations" by hiding the Legend box and/or increasing the size of the graph. If you want to see a lot of "elevations"—as many colors as your computer can handle—use the Window Scale command to reduce the size of the worksheet cells, then increase the size of the graph box.)

The chart in Figure 1-36 was created from new data, and hence doesn't have the "buttons" that were created for the wireframe graph shown in Figure 1-34. However, the Graph 3D View command lets you rotate the graph and change its elevation and perspective, as you need.

Surface charts are particularly good at portraying topographic data, or data that need to be shown in three dimensions.

Contour Chart

A contour chart is merely a surface chart viewed from straight overhead, with no shading (Figure 1-37). Generally, Wingz assigns a larger number of colors (or shades of gray) to the "elevations," so that size of the graph isn't

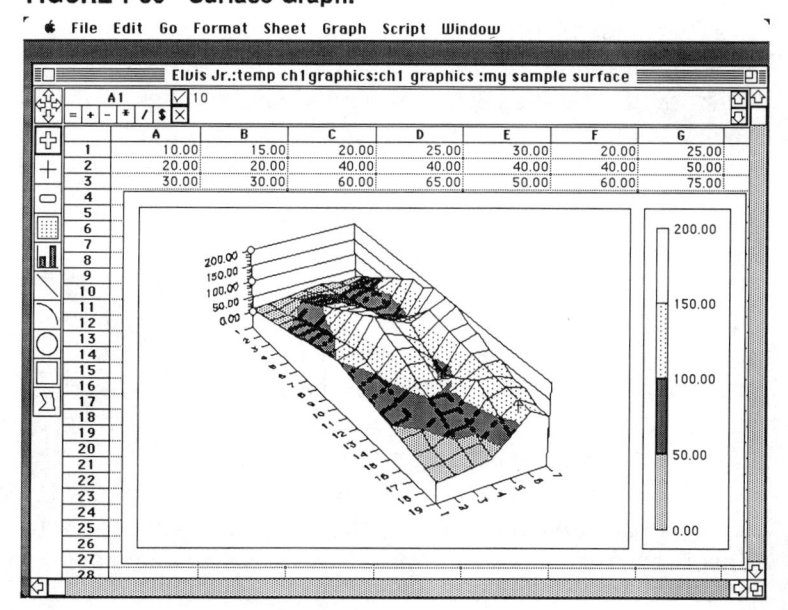

FIGURE 1-36 Surface Graph.

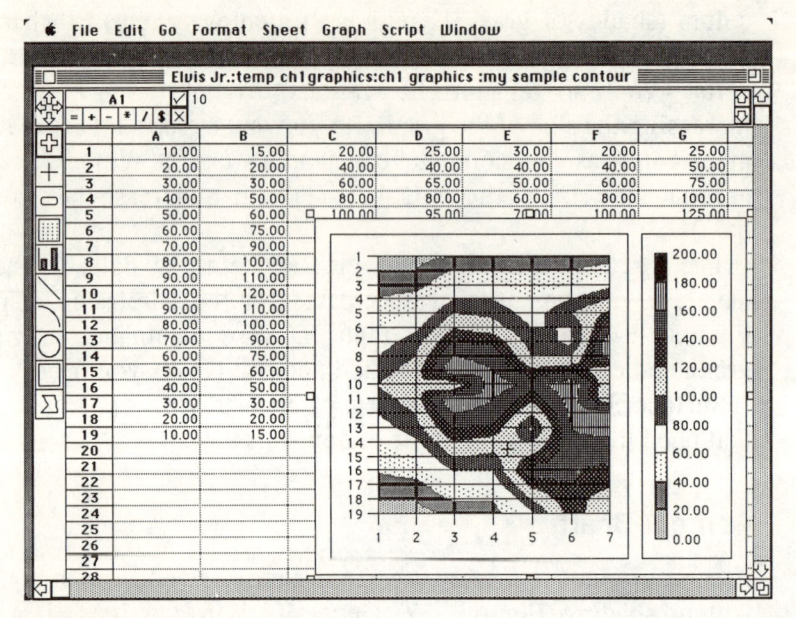

FIGURE 1-37 Contour Graph

as much a consideration. The graph in Figure 1-37 used the same data as were used for the surface graph in Figure 1-36. Note that the surface graph has four "elevations," while the contour graph has ten.

Contour graphs are frequently used to measure heat patterns in a solid (such as the relative heat of different parts of the body), or the intensity of something that can be measured numerically within three dimensions.

AUTOMATING YOUR WORK WITH HYPERSCRIPT

HyperScript, which is supplied with Wingz, is a powerful programming environment. More than a macro language, it is a high-level structured programming language. You use HyperScript to set up scripts of commands, functions, programming constructs, and event handlers that create or modify worksheets, or create or edit menus and dialog boxes.

Although you can create a script by typing it directly, HyperScript also comes with a **Learn mode**, which means that, when toggled, your steps on a worksheet are translated into HyperScript commands in an open script.

Scripts can be edited, formatted, and commented. When finished, a script is compiled, and any syntax errors are noted.

Scripts can perform three types of operations:

1. *HyperScript commands.* These are basically the equivalent of worksheet commands or other actions you could take on the worksheet:

SELECT RANGE B3..B9

PUT "HEADINGS" INTO B3..B9

TEXT STYLE "B"

ALIGN RIGHT

UNSELECT

2. *User-defined functions.* These are functions that you define and store, then reference with predefined arguments:

FUNCTION area(length,width)

RETURN length*width

END FUNCTION

3. *Events.* An event is something that the user does on a spreadsheet, or which otherwise happens on the spreadsheet. These events can include clicking or moving the mouse, opening or closing or recalculating a worksheet, as well as many other types of events. An event handler always has the following syntax:

ON [event]

    [perform actions]

END [event]

Scripts can respond to sheet activation or deactivation, sheet recalculation, mouse movement or clicking, screen repainting, idling, or error conditions. A script that handles events must be attached to the sheet, button, field, control, or dialog box involved.

We'll cover HyperScript in much more detail in Chapter 11.

SUMMARY

This chapter has briefly demonstrated some of the key features and benefits of Wingz, the new presentation spreadsheet from Informix. Further chapters in this book are designed to show you how to use Wingz in a business environment.

CASE STUDY 1:
Wingz in Environmental Study

Steven B. Johnson, Supervisor Hydrologist
James M. Montgomery, Consulting Engineers, Inc.
4525 S. Wasatch Blvd., Suite 200
Salt Lake City, Utah 84124

JMM is a nation-wide firm of approximately 1000 employees, including about 450 registered professional engineers and about 300 individuals with post-graduate degrees in various disciplines of environmental, civil, and sanitary engineering and related sciences. JMM's staff also includes hydrogeologists, toxicologists, soil scientists, geologists, and chemical, mechanical, structural, and electrical engineers.

The firm is a full-service architectural/environmental engineering firm with considerable experience in hazardous waste investigations, groundwater contamination studies, and remedial design. In addition, the firm provides laboratory services, health and safety planning, risk assessments, and studies in hydrology and geophysics.

JMM's staff routinely uses a Macintosh network to create print-ready graphics for reports, presentations, brochures, and marketing materials, as well as company forms, newsletters, overheads, and presentations of engineering and accounting data. Johnson's Salt Lake City office used Wingz to prepare graphics for a groundwater contamination study, in which they simulated the results of pumping groundwater from wells. When water is pumped from wells, the groundwater levels decline in the vicinity of the well. The amount of the decline depends on how much water is being pumped (discharge) and the ability of the rock or soil (aquifer) to transmit water.

Groundwater levels decline in direct proportion to the discharge of the pump, i.e., as the discharge increases, the water levels decline more. In the model they constructed, the worksheet calculates the groundwater level declines (called drawdowns) at each cell using the pumping rates and locations input by the user. Wingz then draws a contour map showing the calculated drawdowns.

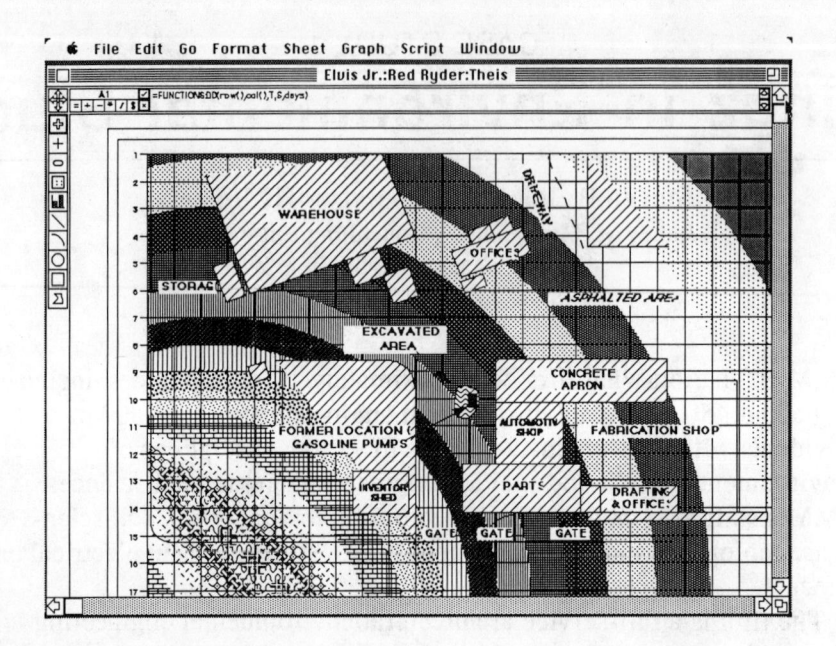

Drawdowns are calculated using the Theis (pronounced "Tice") equation, which is based on the analogy between heat flow and groundwater flow. It is also based on the assumption that the aquifer characteristics are uniform and infinite in extent.

The equation uses the following input factors:

- transmissivity: the ability of the aquifer to transmit water
- storage coefficient: the rate at which the aquifer releases water as the water level drops
- discharge: the amount of water being pumped
- distance from the pumping well
- elapsed time of pumping.

Using these variables, a function written in Hyperscript calculates the drawdown at each cell. The user can vary the transmissivity, storage coefficient and elapsed time with the number wheels (shown below), and the numbers and locations of the pumping wells are entered in a table on the worksheet. The location, duration of pumping and discharge of each well can be adjusted independently for each well.

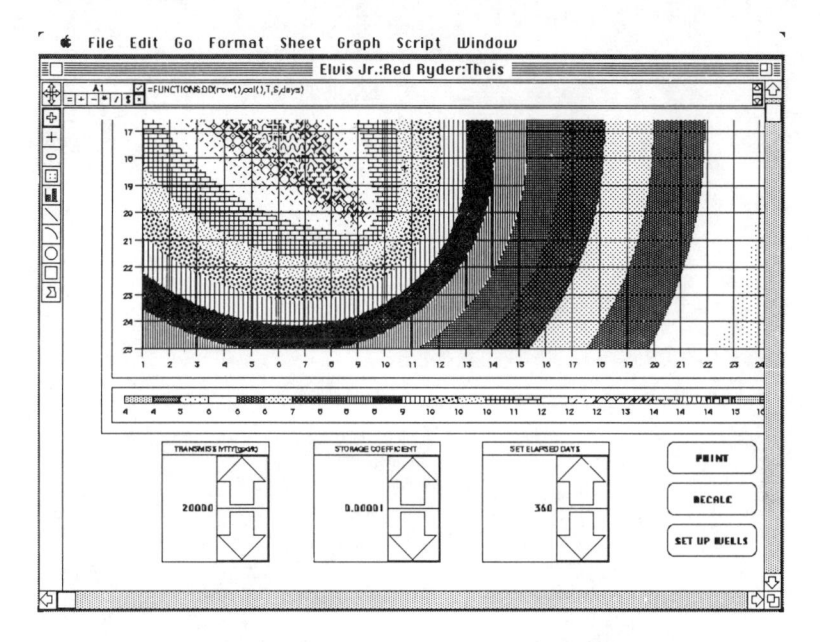

This model is used to estimate the impacts of pumping wells on nearby groundwater levels. Applications include determining if a new well might lower the water level in a nearby, existing well. The worksheet shows how far the new well should be installed to avoid affecting the existing well. The worksheet also can be used to simulate cleaning up groundwater by installing a series of pumps to intercept contamination. The worksheet can be used to test different well spacings and discharges to intercept all of the contamination.

Johnson feels *Wingz* is well suited for this application because it is easy to program. "The model can be set up quickly, and is easy to modify. A site map can be placed on top of the contour map, which creates a complete drawing. Finally, *Wingz* is very fast, so that recalculating a model of this size takes less than a minute," he comments.

2

Getting Started

Wingz runs on a Macintosh Plus, a Macintosh SE, or a Macintosh II. It operates under either a Macintosh operating system (Finder version 5.5 or later and System version 4.1 or later, or Multifinder) or A/UX—Apple version of the UNIX operating systems. You'll need 1 Mbyte of RAM to run Wingz; Wingz will address as much memory as is available on the system. If you're running Multifinder, you shoukd have 2 Mbytes of RAM. You'll need either a hard disk with 1.6 Mbytes of space, or two 800K floppy disks in order to run the on-line Help program and the tutorial.

You can use Wingz with either a monochrome or a color monitor. Wingz can detect color capability, and can use a large screen. Charts are portrayed in patterns if color is not available, or in color if it's available.

LOADING Wingz

Wingz comes on two diskettes. One contains the program and related files (labeled Program), and the other contains the online tutorial and help file (labelled Wingz Test Flight).

SE version." Use the version appropriate for your hardware. The disk labelled "Help and Examples" contains the online Help system. For hard disk users, copy these files into the same folder as the program files. The final disk, labelled "Test Flight," contains an interactive demonstration of the Wingz program.

You will want to make backup copies of the master diskettes. Initialize three blank 800K diskettes, and copy the Wingz files onto them. If you're using a Macintosh with two 800K disk drives, you may want to make another set of copies, to use as your working disks.

To start Wingz, turn on your Macintosh. Make sure you have a System folder in one of your disk drives, if you are starting from one of the 800K drives.

If you are using a hard disk, double click the hard disk icon, and click on the icon representing the Wingz folder. If you are using 800K disks, insert your working copy of the Wingz program disk in the second disk drive, and double click the progam disk icon, then click on the icon representing the Wingz program (see Figure 2-1).

When you double click the Wingz program icon, Wingz displays a new, untitled worksheet with all the tools and menus you need to get to work (see Figure 2-2).

GETTING HELP FAST

If you are using a hard disk, you can get immediate help from the Help file at any point, anywhere in your use of a Wingz spreadsheet, chart, or document. (If you're using a two-floppy system, you can't use the Wingz Help file.

As long as the Menu Bar is at the top of the screen, you can get to the Window menu. On it is the Help Window command. Choosing this command displays the opening Help box across the bottom half of your screen. (see Figure 2-3). (If you prefer seeing the Help screen side by side with your active worksheet, select Window Arrange. The Help text will wrap around to fit within the Help window.)

Note that you can search by topic, by keyword, or by command. To choose a general topic, click the Topic button, select the topic you want from the list, and click the Help bar. For instance, suppose you want more information

Getting Started 39

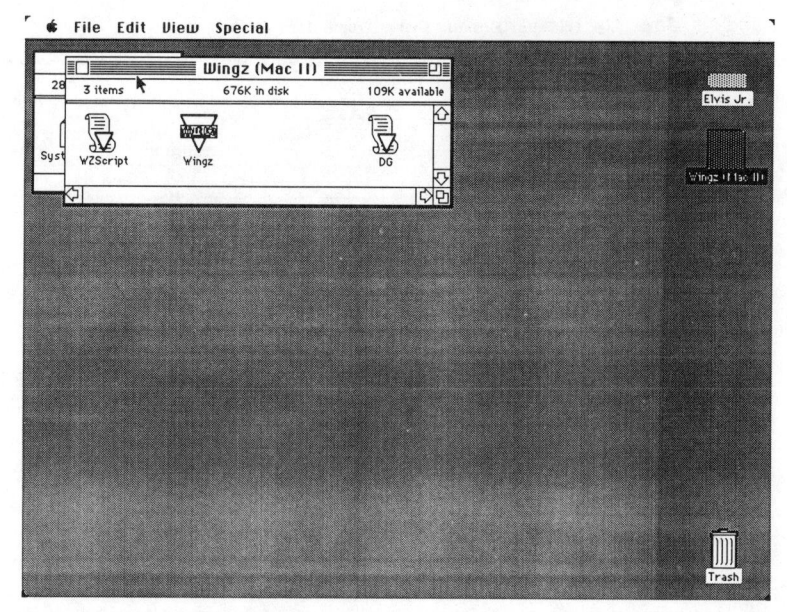

FIGURE 2-1   Wingz Folder.

FIGURE 2-2   Opening Worksheet.

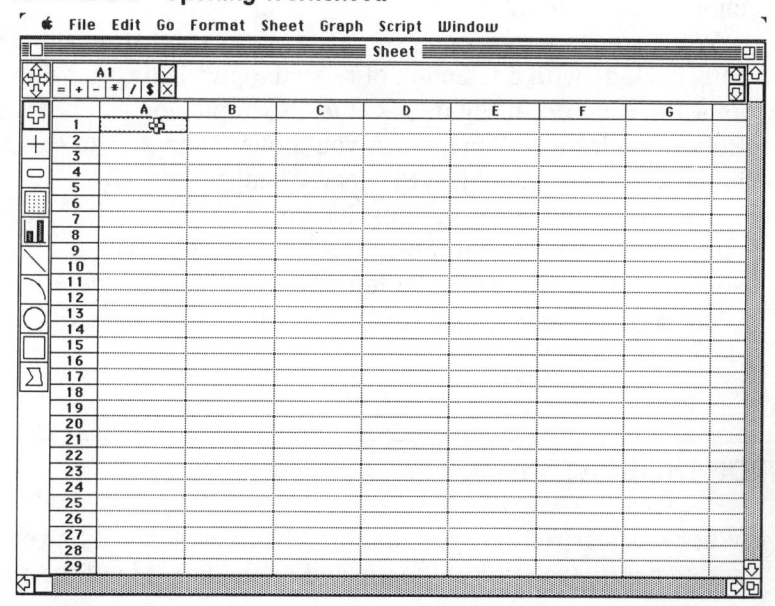

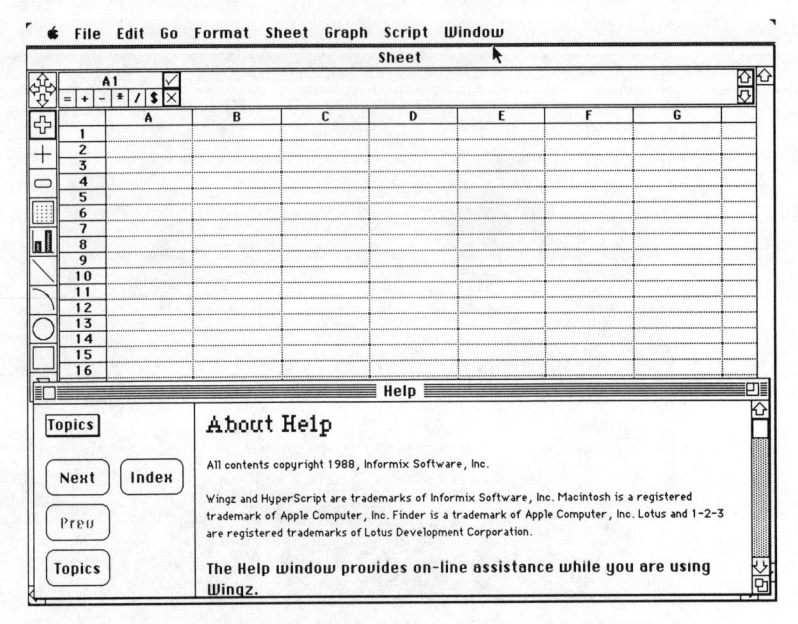

FIGURE 2-3 Opening Help Banner

about selecting an object. The Help topic window will help you with your choice (see Figure 2-4).

When you choose a topic, you get a brief explanation at the bottom of the screen, along with a selection of related topics in the pull-down menu in the upper left corner. In Figure 2-4, the only topic you can see is Select a Cell. Related topics are shown when you move the mouse to that bar and click, in this case Change Object Size and Change Field Size.

The Next and Prev buttons let you see the topics after and before, respectively, the current topic. The Topic button displays the list of topics you saw earlier. The Index button displays a list of keywords, each of which is contained in one or more of the topical explanations.

TOUR OF THE SCREEN

When you start Wingz, you first see a blank worksheet on your screen, with additional information at the top and on the left side of the sheet, as shown

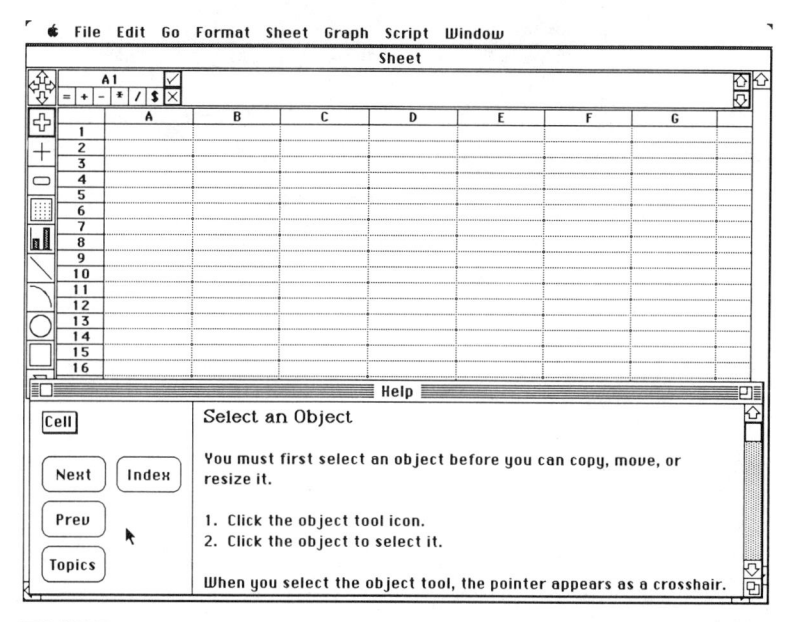

FIGURE 2-4 Help Topic Window, Selecting an Object or Text Field.

in Figure 2-2 above. This section will show you what each item of that information is, and how to use it.

The main body of the worksheet is a **standard spreadsheet**, ruled into **columns** and **rows**. Column headings are A, B, C, D, E, etc.; however, if you prefer the R1C1 format you can choose the column headings to be 1, 2, 3, 4, 5, etc. (Use the Column Heading command on the Window menu to use the R1C1 format if you don't want the A1 format.) Row labels are the numbers 1, 2, 3, 4, 5, etc., on the left side of the worksheet (see Figure 2-5)..

Each intersection of a row and a column is a **cell**, and each cell is referenced by its coordinates: the cell in the top left corner of the worksheet is referenced by its address of A1, and the cell in the third row and fifth column is referenced as E3.

The Menu Bar at the top of the screen contains the names of the menus, plus the Apple menu. Each of these refers to a pull-down menu, on which you'll find the commands we'll discuss a bit later in this chapter. The bar below the Menu Bar contains the file name of the current sheet, and on the left and right edges of this bar are the Close box, and the Zoom box. Just below the Zoom box are the arrows and Scroll box which let you move

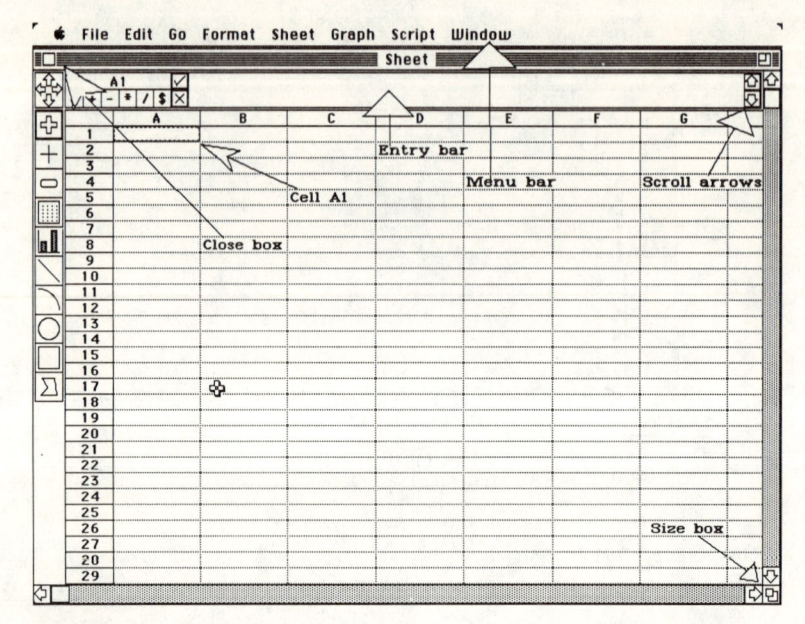

FIGURE 2-5 The Wingz Worksheet.

around a large worksheet. The Close box, Zoom box, arrows and Scroll box, and Size box in the bottom right corner are standard Macintosh devices.

Wingz has added a notice when you're using the Scroll bar: when you drag the Scroll box, Wingz displays a small box indicating where you are within the worksheet. The box disappears when you lift your finger from the mouse button.

The Wingz Navigation box and Toolbox appear on the left side of the screen (see Figure 2-6). The navigation arrows let you move to the next cell in that direction which borders a blank cell on your worksheet. The toolbox contains symbols for the tools you can use to create worksheets and charts, add or modify text, add buttons, and draw graphic items.

When you click the **worksheet tool** you're telling Wingz that it is to operate in worksheet mode: that the pointer is to move from cell to cell on the worksheet, or within the entry bar as you type things.

When you click the **object tool**, you're telling Wingz that what you're going to be manipulating next should be treated as an object—a data series, for instance, that you wish to use as a chart, or a figure you've drawn. To Wingz, an object is a chart, a text field, a graphic image, a button, etc. An

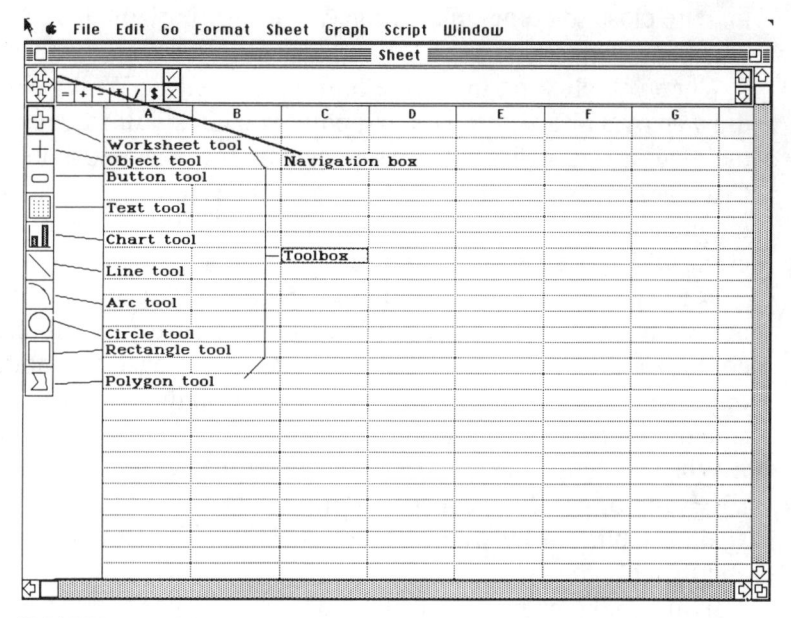

FIGURE 2-6 Wingz Navigation Box and Toolbox.

object can be selected, moved, changed in color or size, duplicated, or removed from the worksheet.

When you click on the **button tool**, Wingz lets you create a button.

When you click on the **text tool**, Wingz allows you to define a resizeable text window, known as a text field, on the worksheet. A text field is layered on top of the worksheet, and can appear with your data when you annotate the data in presentation form.

When you click on the **chart tool**, you're telling Wingz that you will be defining an area where a chart will be drawn with the data you've just selected. Wingz gives you a number of options about how to display your data (bar, pie, scatter, linear, etc.) as well as a number of customizing details from which to select.

When you click on the **line tool**, you're telling Wingz that you want to draw a straight line, beginning at the next point you click. You can draw a straight line anywhere on the worksheet, in text fields and charts, or over other graphic images.

When you click on the **arc tool**, you're telling Wingz that you want to draw an arc, beginning at the next point you click. You can change the shape of the arc by moving the mouse: you create a shallower arc with two points that are close to being on the same vertical or horizontal axis; a deeper arc, when two points are not on the same axis.

When you click on the **circle tool**, you're telling Wingz that you want to draw an oval or a circle. The first point you click will serve as an anchor for the oval or circle that will emerge as you drag the mouse in any direction. Circular shapes can range from perfect circles to wide or flat ovals, depending on where you move the mouse. When you release the mouse button, the circle will stay on your worksheet.

When you click the **rectangle tool**, you're telling Wingz that you want to draw a rectangle. When you first cick the mouse you will create the first corner of the rectangle; when you drag the mouse to another point the opposite corner of the rectangle will appear, so that you can create a perfect square or a rectangle of any dimension.

When you click the **poly tool**, you're telling Wingz that you want to draw a polygon or polyline, consisting of a series of connected lines from points again established by where you click the mouse. Double click to close or end the polygon.

In the next chapters, we'll show you how to enter data into your worksheet, transform data into eye-catching charts and graphs, add text and other graphic images, and use other tools to create presentation-quality worksheets.

3

Entering Data

The basic unit of a worksheet is a cell. It's the place where you enter and store data. A cell is located at the intersection of a row and a column. Since Wingz has a total of 32,768 columns, labeled as A through AVLH (A, B, C,...A; AA, AB, AC,...AZ; AAA, AAB, AAC, ...AAZ; AAAA, AAAB, AAAC...AAAZ; AABA...AVLH), and 32,768 rows, numbered 1 through 32768, simple multiplication shows that there are over a billion cells available in an Wingz worksheet. However, you'll see only some of them at any one time, through the "window" on your screen.

A cell is addressed by its row and column coordinates. The leftmost column is column A, the next is column B, and so forth, and the top row is 1, the next row is 2, and so on. The cell six columns from the left edge and nine rows down is known as F9.

CELLS AND RANGES

A new worksheet shows you 203 cells in which you can enter data, arranged in 7 columns and 29 rows (see Figure 3-1). Notice that the blank worksheet depending on your monitor.) Notice in the example that the blank worksheet also shows you part of column H. Given the default width of the columns, this is the way that the eighth column will look, regardless of whether there are data in it. If you change the width of any of the columns, of course, that will change what appears in your screen "window."

Another address style is permitted in Wingz: the R1C1 style. With this style, columns are addressed by number too, and an "R" is required before each row number and a "C" before each column number. You can choose this address style on the Windows menu at the Column Heading command.

Wingz allows three kinds of referencing: relative, absolute, and mixed. A **relative reference** is made to another cell a given number of rows and columns away from the current cell. It's the default, and is like telling someone the nearest gas station is three blocks to the right and one block up. When you type a formula or issue a command that uses a relative reference to identify another cell, the information in that original cell (D5, which used to be over three and up one, but is now E14) will be used, regardless of whether you insert or delete rows or columns.

An **absolute reference** is made to a specific cell. It will never change regardless of how much moving around occurs in the rest of the spreadsheet.

FIGURE 3-1 Blank Worksheet.

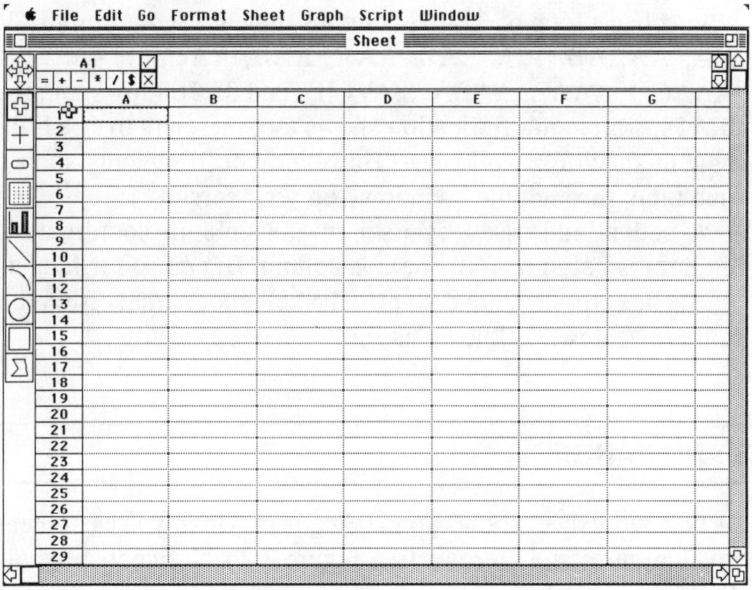

It's a bit like telling someone the gas station is at the intersection of Central Expressway and Rengstorff Avenue. An absolute reference is indicated by adding a dollar sign ($) in front of the column letter and row number. For instance, if you're sure you're never going to change the location of what's currently in B15, a formula in another cell might make an absolute reference to that cell by specifying B15.

Mixed references use both relative and absolute references. If you need to keep a row reference absolute, but the column reference relative, you may have a cell reference like C$7. An absolute column reference but relative row reference may look like $G15.

You can change from one type of reference to another in a formula in the current cell, by selecting the cell referenced in the entry bar and clicking the $ icon in the area next to the formula bar.

SELECTING

The **current** or **active cell,** the one where you can enter data, is indicated with a dashed-line border. Cell A1 in Figure 3-2 is the active cell. The border

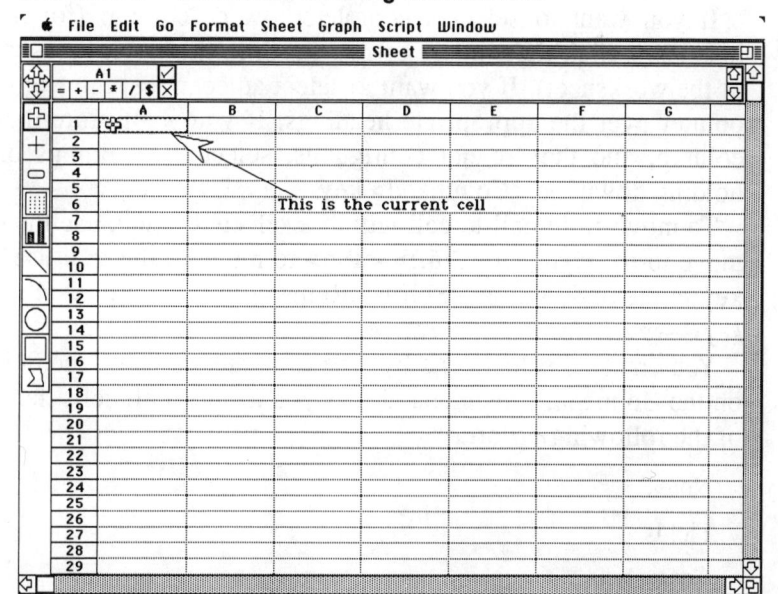

FIGURE 3-2   Worksheet Showing Current Cell.

indicates that the cell is selected, and its cell reference is displayed in the upper left portion of the entry bar near the top of the screen. To select a different cell, simply move the pointer and click on the cell you want.

You can select more than one cell—for copying or moving, for formatting, or for printing, for instance. If you select more than one cell, the first cell is considered the current cell, and the others are displayed in reverse-on-black.

A **range** consists of a group of cells, which are usually but not necessarily contiguous. Contiguous ranges are rectangles. You refer to a range by the cell references of its topmost and bottommost cells, e.g., B5..C15. To select a contiguous range, click the topmost cell (the anchor point) and drag the pointer to the bottommost cell. The desired cells are shown in black.

Noncontiguous ranges are referred to by cell references in sequence, separated by commas: B2..C5,E12..F15. To select a noncontiguous range, click and drag over the first range, hold down the <Command> key, then click and drag over the subsequent ranges.

To select a range that is larger than the current window, click the first cell in the range, move to the lower edge of the range, and hold down the shift key as you click the last cell. If you want to change the anchor point in a selected range, hold down the <Shift> key while you click the new anchor point. The new anchor point becomes the current cell, complete with dashed outline.

If you want to select a complete row or column (for formatting, for instance), click the column or row heading (in the upper edge or left edge of the worksheet). If you want to select adjacent columns or rows, drag the pointer over the appropriate headings. If you want more than one row or column, and they're not contiguous, select the columns or rows while holding down the <Command> key.

To move from cell to cell within a selected range, use the <Tab> key to move to the right, or <Shift> <Tab> to move to the left; use the <Return> key to move down, or <Shift> <Return> to move up. *Don't use the arrow keys—you'll deselect the range.*

You can also select cells by type of contents, using the Select command on the Go menu. This menu allows you to select all cells that meet any one of the following criteria:

    Notes

    Fields

    Controls

Graphics
Text Cells
Value Cells
Formula Cells
Error Cells
Locked Cells
Blank Cells
Heading
All Precedents
All Dependents
Direct Precedents
Direct Dependents
References to Blanks
Unreferenced Cells
Current Cell
Active Cells
Report Header
Report Footer
Report Border

Once selected, you can format them as a group, move them, protect them, or use other worksheet commands to manipulate them.

Entering Data

You enter data into a cell by typing, or using the pointer to select symbols or other information that you want. As you enter data, they appear in the entry bar at the top of the screen. Notice that the vertical bar moves when you type. Known as the insertion point, it indicates where the next character will go.

Once you press the <Return> key, whatever you typed will be entered into the current cell. If you don't want to enter your typing into a cell, click the Cancel icon . On an extended keyboard, use the <Esc> key(this is the x in a box).

You can enter up to 255 characters in one cell. If your entry is long, Wingz scrolls the contents of the entry bar, keeping the most recent characters in the bar. If the contents of a single cell don't fit in the width of that cell and are text, the contents will be displayed in adjacent cells so long as they don't also contain data. If the too wide contents are numeric data, Wingz displays a line of asterisks.

Text

To enter text into a cell, select a cell or cell range. (Remember, simply positioning the current cell somewhere amounts to selecting a single cell there.) Type the text, and press either <Return> or <Tab>. Pressing either key enters the text into the current cell; if you've selected a range, pressing the <Return> key moves the current cell down one row, and pressing the <Tab> key moves the current cell right one column.

Wingz lets you edit text, using the <Tab> key, Indent, Word Wrap, Search and Find. Text entries can include letters, numbers, and any of the special characters on your keyboard, in any combination. Examples: Price, JANUARY, 125 Elm Street. However, if what you enter is all numbers, Wingz considers it a numeric value. To keep it as text, precede the number string with a double quote mark: "415–555–1212.

Anything you enter as text can be used in a text formula. This means that you can search and sort it, as well as analyze its contents. (See Chapter 5, "Formulas and Functions," for more information about text formulas.)

Numbers

Numeric data can consist of integers, decimals, percentages, currency, and date and time values. In certain situations, numeric data can be considered to have logical values, too. (See below.)

When you type a number into a cell, Wingz recognizes it as a number if it's in one of the following formats:

Integer	314, -314
Decimal fraction	3.14, 0.314, -.314
Scientific notation	3.14e+01, 314E-03

Unless you enter a number in one of the above formats, Wingz thinks you've entered text.

However, you can include as a number any of the following characters:

( ) $ %

all of which are used to describe different kinds of numbers, or expressions that can be evaluated as numbers. You can use + or–- signs to indicate positive or negative values.Numeric data lend themselves easily to any of the formatting options Wingz offers. The same number can be represented a number of different ways. We'll look at formats in more detail in a bit.

Date and time values are a special form of numeric data. We'll also look at them shortly.

To enter numeric data in a cell, type the number. If it's a negative number, use a minus sign as the first character. Then press the <Return> or <Tab> key. Any of the formulas can be used with numeric data, except those that specifically refer to text. (If you use a text formula on numeric data, the formula may produce either no value, or a zero value.)

Once you've typed a number, its appearance will depend on how the cell into which it was entered was formatted. We'll look at the number format options available under Wingz shortly. With no formatting, Wingz assumes a General format, displaying numbers as accurately as possible, given the width of the cell and the number you entered. If you enter a number with a $ or %, the cell format will automatically be changed to reflect that. If you enter a date or time number in one of the appropriate date or time formats, the cell formatting is changed to reflect this.

Using Date and Time

Wingz uses a serial date/time number that's stored in your computer's memory to produce date and time information. What you see depends on how this number is formatted, but you can manipulate date and time information just as you would any other number.

The number assumes Day/Time 0 was midnight on December 30, 1899, with an increment of 1 for every day since then. The integer part of this number reflects the number of days; the decimal portion reflects the portion of 24 hours. For instance, 3 P.M. on September 6, 1988, would be stored internally as 32392.63.

You can enter the date and time in a number of formats. For instance, you can store the same date number in a cell using any of the following:

September 6, 1988

Sep-6–88

9/6/88

9–6–88

=DATE(88,09,06)

Because date and time are stored as a number, you can add dates or times, subtract them, and perform a number of other calculations with them. For instance, to determine the interval between two dates, use the DATE function and subtract the earlier date from the later one:

=DATE(88,9,12)-DATE(88,6,4)

Determining the interval between two times works the same way, except that it uses the TIME function:

=TIME(23,30,00)-TIME(6,55,30)

(You can also use the HOUR, MINUTE, and SECOND functions in the same way.)

Remember that the result of any such calculation will be expressed as a date/time serial number, unless you format the cell differently.

Logical Values

Wingz can manipulate logical values as well as text and numeric values. The logical values True and False indicate whether a con-dition exists. Wingz can evaluate an expression in terms of its truth, and store the result as a logical value. You can also use the functions =TRUE() or =FALSE() as to enter the value in a cell, and Wingz will treat what you enter as a logical value. Wingz also recognizes 1 and 0 as the logical values True and False, respectively.

Using Fill with Data

You don't have to enter all of your data, if you know that subsequent cells in a range will increase or decrease in regular increments.

Wingz' Fill command, on the Sheet menu, lets you fill a selected range of cells with numbers or dates. This is particularly useful if you're setting up a spreadsheet and want column or row labels in sequence.

The Fill command requires that the cells involved have been selected, and uses the value in the first of them as an indicator as to what type of values is to be stored. It increments that value by one for each subsequent selected cell. For instance, if you enter 1 in the first of five selected cells, and then use the Fill command, Wingz fills the other cells with 2.00, 3.00, 4.00, and 5.00, respectively. (It stores the value 1.00 in the first cell.)

If you want to try this with a date, type the formula

=NOW()

in the first cell of a five-cell range, select the range, format it in the MM-DD-YY format, then use the Fill command. If today's date is March 12, 1989, you'll see the values

03–12–89
03–13–89
03–14–89
03–15–89
03–16–89

in the selected cells.

You can also use this to create monthly column headings, which wind up being used frequently in budget spreadsheets. However, the procedure to create monthly budget headings is a little different from the one we used above.

Suppose you want to create monthly column headings for the current month and the next five months—six months in all. Here's how:

1. In the first cell, type the formula

=NOW()

What you'll see is the date/time serial number for right now. Don't worry about that—we'll change what you see in the next step.
2. Select all six column headings, the one with the current date/time serial number, and the five to the right.
3. Choose the Number command on the Format menu, and choose the Mon-YY option. Notice that instead of the serial number you now see the current month and year.
4. Since the range of cells is still selected, choose the Fill command on the Sheet menu (see Figure 3-3).

Oops! Since we didn't specify anything about how Wingz was to increment, the program assumed we wanted to increment just the serial number—which would mean that each increment would be one day. Hence we now have six columns, all headed with the current month and year.

We need to enter the month and year for the last cell in the range, so that Wingz can determine how to divide the intervening days and display them

FIGURE 3-3 One Result of the Fill Command.

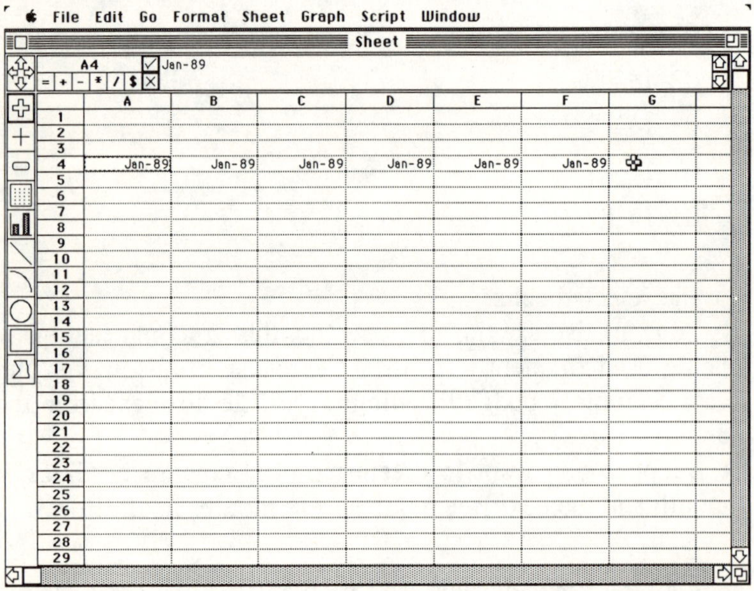

the way we want. Move the current cell to the last cell in the range, and enter the month and year for the sixth month from now. (Since it's already been formatted, Wingz translates what you enter to the format you selected.)

Next, go back and select the range again. Now choose the Fill command. Your column headings should look something like those in Figure 3-4.

That was pretty simple! How about some automatic entries for the sales figures? Let's see what happens if we assume that in six months, we'll triple sales. What would be the monthly increments? Again, we can't assume that the Fill command will do the incrementing right unless we specify both a beginning and an end value to the series.

Under the first of the column headings we created above, type a beginning value—say, 25000. Under the last of the column headings, type the figure that is three times that: 75000. Now select the range of cells that begins with the one containing 25000 and ends with the one containing 75000, and choose the Fill command (see Figure 3-5).

Wingz calculates the difference and inserts regularly incremented values—in this case, increasing sales by 10000 per month.

We'll look at other ways of creating data later in this chapter.

FIGURE 3-4 Column Headings, Fill Command.

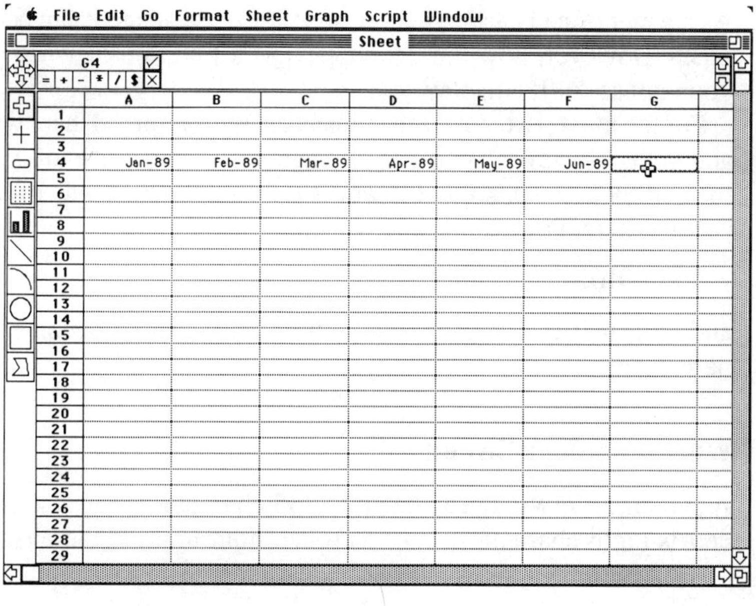

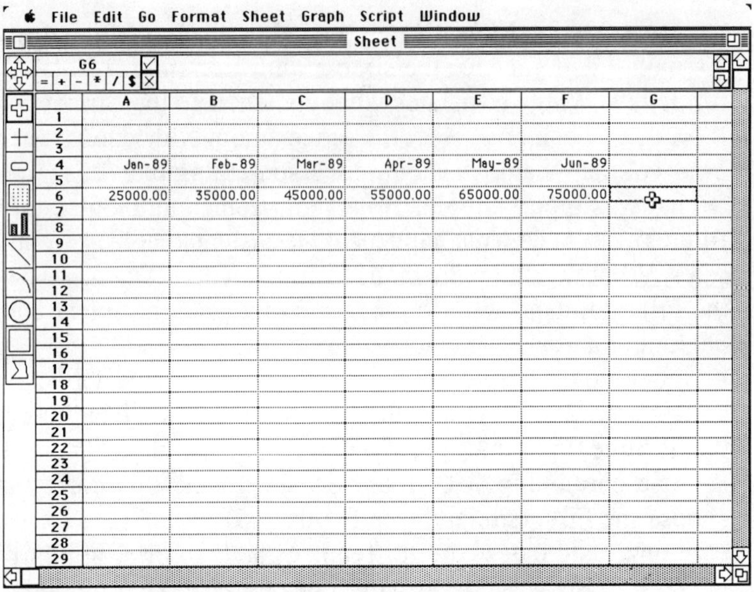

FIGURE 3-5 Data Created with Fill Command.

FORMATTING

As we mentioned earlier, data in an Wingz spreadsheet can be any of several types. However, how the data appear is a function of what kind of format you choose for its display.

For the most part, data you enter in an Wingz spreadsheet will be numbers and text. However, you can change the appearance of your data with formatting actions, so that it works only in certain kinds of operations and not in others. For instance, if you enter the number

1001001010

and format it as currency, that cell entry ceases to become available as a percentage.

What's Actually Stored

A cell entry in Wingz can be up to 255 characters. The standard width for a cell is eight characters, but a cell can hold more if the characters are any combination of letters and numbers (some letters take up less space than do numbers).

If you enter a number that's too big to fit in the cell, under the usual number formats, Wingz tries to convert it to scientific notation and display it that way. For instance, if you enter the number

123456

into a cell, you'll see that it just fits in a standard-width column. (Wingz uses the default format General and assumes you want two decimal places, displaying the value as 123456.00.) However, try entering the number

1234567

and what you'll see in the cell is **********. When you see that character string, Wingz tried to fit your number, with the format you are using, into the cell and has failed. What you'll see in the entry bar at the top of the screen, however, is exactly what you entered: 1234567.

If, on the other hand, you had formatted the cell into which you typed that number as Scientific, you'd find the notation 1.23e+06 in the cell where you typed the overlong number. As with other forms of notation, the actual number shows up in the entry bar, regardless of what appears in the cell.

These examples are typical of the way Wingz tries to display your data as you typed it, or as you formatted it, but uses a different method of displaying it if its original form doesn't fit the current cell limits. The actual contents of the cell are as you entered them, and that's what Wingz uses in formulas, functions, and other manipulations.

When Wingz manipulates your data—for instance, in a multiplication or division—the result may have more decimal places than either of the operands. Wingz will round off the result, where possible, so that it can be displayed in the appropriate cell.

However, you may wish to impose some of your own limits on this. For instance, if you've been calculating the amount of interest due on a loan with monthly payments, you're likely to come up with a result that has five or more decimals. Yet, you pay only in dollars and cents, expressed as $x.xx.

Rounding errors, small though they may be at any point, can cause problems in the long run. If you use the Precision command on the Format menu, you can choose the number of decimal places you want used in your calculations.

Format Options

Wingz lets you display your data and text in a variety of formats. You can also choose how text and data are aligned, specify the width of columns and the height of rows, choose font, font size, and style, specify how you want to use color, add borders or any of a number of styles of shading to cells, protect data in cells from accidentally being changed, or hide the cell altogether. Each of these options will be discussed in this section.

Number Formats

The Format Number command tells Wingz how you want to display numbers, dates, and time. You can choose from the 14 formats supplied with Wingz.

The Format Number command comes with a box showing your choices. Scroll down the list to pick the one you want to use. (The one in effect for the current cell has a checkmark beside it.)

Number formats include:

		Examples	
As typed	1	−1	.1
Fixed	1.000	−1.000	.100
Currency	$1.00	−$1.00	$0.10
Percent	100.00%	−100.00%	10.00%
Scientific	1.00e+00	−1.00e+00	1.00e-01
General	1	−1	0.1

Date and time formats include:

	Example
D-Mon-YY	15–Sep-88
D-Mon	15–Sep
Mon-YY	Sep-88
MM-DD-YY	09–15–88
MM-DD	Sep-15
HR:MN:SC AM	2:45:30 PM

HR:MN AM   4:55 PM
HR:MN:SC   16:55:15
HR:MN   16:55

To format a number, select the cell or cells you want formatted, choose Format Number, and select a format from the list shown. Scroll through the list of formats, selecting the one you want. When you let go of the pointer button, Wingz assigns the format to the cells selected. The format is then stored with the cell data.

Note: If your system can display colors, you can specify negative numbers in colors other than red, the default color where the format chosen uses a color. In addition to red, allowable colors are black, white, green, blue, yellow, magenta, and cyan, as well as custom colors you create. You can change these with the Color command on the Format menu. We'll discuss this in a bit.

Text Formats

You can type paragraphs into your worksheet and have them appear on a finished worksheet just as if you were using a word processor. Text can be formatted on your worksheet with some of the Format commands. Generally, questions about formatting text on a worksheet fall into two categories: alignment, and fonts and font sizes, both of which we'll discuss in more detail below.

Because you're in a worksheet, you can use many of the cell formatting techniques that are available—such as adding borders or shading, or changing the effective spacing of lines of text by changing the row height. Further, with a text box, you can type text into a part of your worksheet, within a screenful of numbers and formulas.

Alignment of Data and Text

Specific placement of the data or text in your cells is a function of alignment. You may want all your text to be **left-aligned**, which Wingz uses as a default. You may want all of your numbers **right-aligned**, which some number formats allow. You may want some data centered within a cell. All these options have to do with alignment.

Number formats dictate how a number is aligned, but generally numbers are right-aligned. However, if you have numbers with decimal places, you may find that the decimals are not aligned, since the numbers to the right of the decimal point will dictate where the decimal point appears.

For instance, look at the following column of numbers:

$125.66

5

23%

3.14159

2.01E+08

All of these are right-aligned numbers, a default used with all Wingz numbers unless you specify something else. To align the decimal points within a column of numbers, use the Format Numbers command, and pick formats with the same number of decimal places.

To align text, use the Format Align command and choose from the options in the box, as shown in Figure 3-6.

FIGURE 3-6 Format Align Options Box.

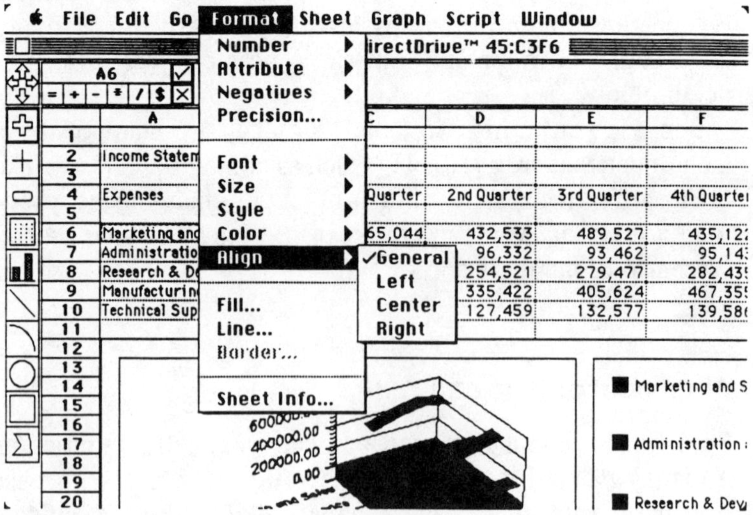

The Left, Right, and Center choices are obvious: text is either aligned at the left or the right edge of the cell or centered within the cell width. General alignment for text means that it is left aligned. Since it's a default value, it also means that any numbers are right-justified, and logical values and error messages are centered.

The Fill command on the Format menu lets you specify the color or pattern used as foreground or background for a selected range of the current spreadsheet.

Changing Column Width or Row Height

It may be necessary for you to change the width of a column, because a number can't be displayed in the format you've chosen, for instance. (You get ********** in the cell instead of numbers, for example.)

When you change the width of a cell, you change the width of all the other cells in that column, including any that may be hidden. To change the width of a cell, move the pointer so that it's in the area containing the column labels (A, B, C, and so on). Position the pointer so that it's right over the right edge of the column. Notice that it changes shape when it's over that edge (see Figure 3-7).

Click the pointer and move it to the right so that the column is as wide as you want it. When you release the pointer button, the column width will be reset, and the contents of every cell within that column will be readjusted to fit. If a value was originally too wide to fit the former width (it appeared as a string of ***'s), the new width can now accommodate the value so that it is displayed properly.

Use the same procedure to change the row height. Position the pointer over any of the lines between the row labels (1, 2, 3, and so on) on the left side of the worksheet. Drag the pointer until the row is the height you want, then release the button.

This option is also particularly useful when you're using different fonts, styles, and/or sizes for some of the characters on your worksheet. By changing the size of the cells, you can sometimes better display the contents.

You can have a column as wide as 255 characters, or as little as a fraction of one character. If you drag the column gridline to the left so that it overlays the next gridline, you'll in effect hide the column. You won't be able to enter data into it, because you won't be able to select them. However, any data already in cells in that column will still be there, where you can reference it and have it affected by any recalculation.

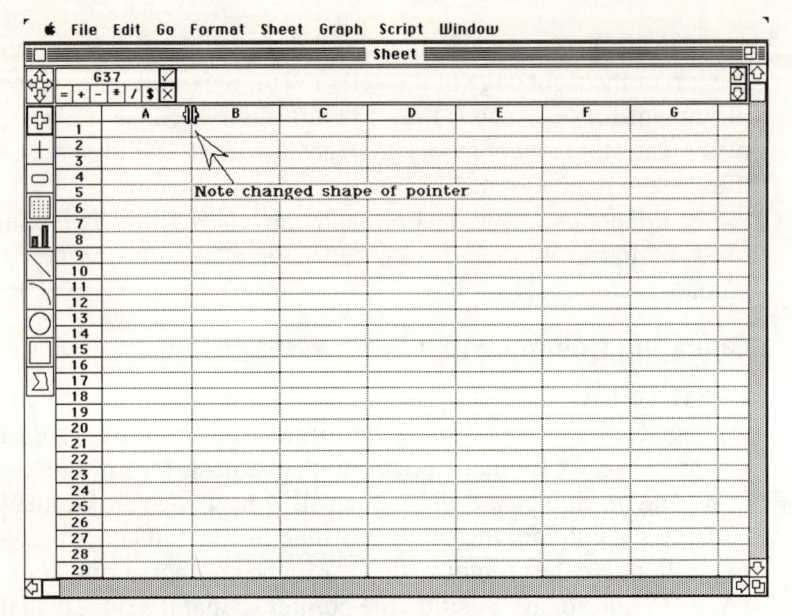

FIGURE 3-7 Pointer over Column Edge

Wingz's default typeface, size, and style is Helvetica 10 point plain; when we increased the type size of the data in one row to 14 points, and changed the row height to accommodate the new size, we got a screen like the one shown in Figure 3-8.

For instance, we chose to make the column headings of our sample worksheet 12 point, leaving the rest of the worksheet alone (Figure 3-9). Here's what it looked like after the row height and type size changes:

Note: if you change the row height in expectation of using a larger type size, allow for larger width of characters, too. If the larger characters don't fit in the existing column width, you'll see the standard ********** indicating that the data are too wide to fit the current column.

FORMULAS AND FUNCTIONS

Formulas are one of the ways you manipulate values in a spreadsheet. In Wingz, you enter them in the Formula Bar, with the first character being an = sign. You can use numeric, text, time/date, and logical formulas.

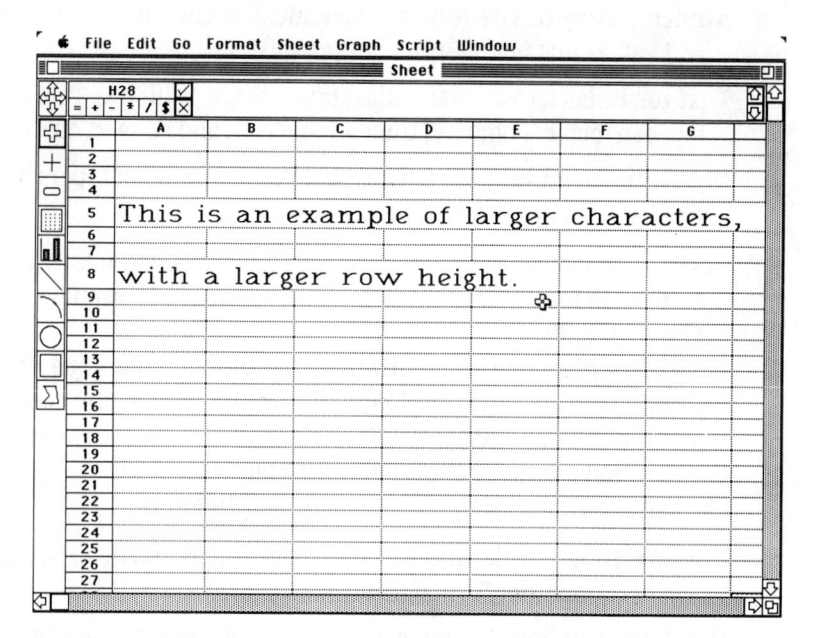

FIGURE 3-8 Larger Row Height, Larger Characters.

FIGURE 3-9 Worksheet with 12 point Column Headings.

Numeric formulas perform mathematical calculations, and use numbers and values that are interpreted as numbers.

Text formulas let you manipulate text strings. With this kind of formula, you can locate, compare, truncate, extract, and convert character strings.

Date/time formulas manipulate the date/time serial number and display the results in whatever format you've specified.

Logical formulas evaluate numeric values or text, and return a result based on the condition specified. The result of a logical formula is either 1.00 (True) or 0.00 (False).

Wingz has provided over 140 preprogrammed functions within the program. Functions are a standard kind of formula, which you can use anywhere in your spreadsheet that the formula is needed, simply by typing or pasting in the required syntax and plugging in your own data.

The functions are grouped by type of application:

Business functions let you calculate interest, principal, term, depreciation, and perform other financial calculations.

Database functions help you average, count, sum, and perform other statistical calculations on database information.

Date and time functions let you add or subtract time or dates, and manipulate the time/date serial number.

Logical functions let you check your data for logical values, such as whether there is a number or a character string in a cell, whether there's an error or a blank, or an exact match of something you specify. You can also use a logical function to place a logical value (True or False) into a cell.

Numeric functions let you perform a wide variety of mathematical operations on values. These include trigonometric and logarithmic functions, rounding, factorial, exponential, and others.

Spreadsheet functions let you determine cell locations, perform lookup table operations, find values in a list by indexing, and other cell manipulations.

Statistical functions let you perform a number of statistical manipulations on nondatabase data.

Text functions let you work with character strings, allowing you determine content, replace certain strings, truncate, add, or match strings of text.

We'll be looking in much greater detail at Wingz's formulas and functions in Chapter 4, "Formulas and Functions."

SUMMARY

This chapter has shown you how to enter data in Wingz. We have shown you about cells, ranges, selecting, text, numbers, date and time, formatting, and formulas and functions.

CASE STUDY 2:
Wingz in Physics Research

Bill White, Research Associate, Physics Dept.
Texas A & M University
College Station, Texas

The Physics Department at Texas A & M, like most university departments, generates papers for technical publications to show the results of some of their latest research. They sometimes face problems showing how sampling of test data fits a predicted pattern, since they frequently have very large samples to work with.

The department has access to a lot of different computers, and a lot of software, so they tend to use some software to do the calculations, some to do the reports, and some to produce the graphs. Bill White has been deeply involved in translating the results of departmental studies into articles, complete with graphs and charts.

"When we first started getting into Macintosh software, we used Excel," White says. They didn't like the results when produced with Excel's graphics, so they used several other packages, including CricketGraph and some other graphics programs to make the graphs look better.

"When I read about Wingz in MacWeek, I wrote to Informix and got on the beta test list. When the software arrived, I was able to get productive inside an hour. The scripts took a bit longer to learn, but it wasn't all that difficult."

Now that Wingz is a regular part of the department's software library, 80% of its use is for making graphs and plots. They also use it for general data reduction.

White used Wingz to display a quasicrystal chart. A quasicrystal is a solid state physics term that means that something exhibits some of the characteristics of a crystal, but it isn't a true crystal.

What the screen shows is a computer-generated simulation of what an electron microscope photographs of the quasicrystal icosahedral phase of Al-Li-Cu (aluminum, lithium, copper). The data is generated by theoretically determining the icosahedral phase structure and making a projection along the fivefold symmetry axis.

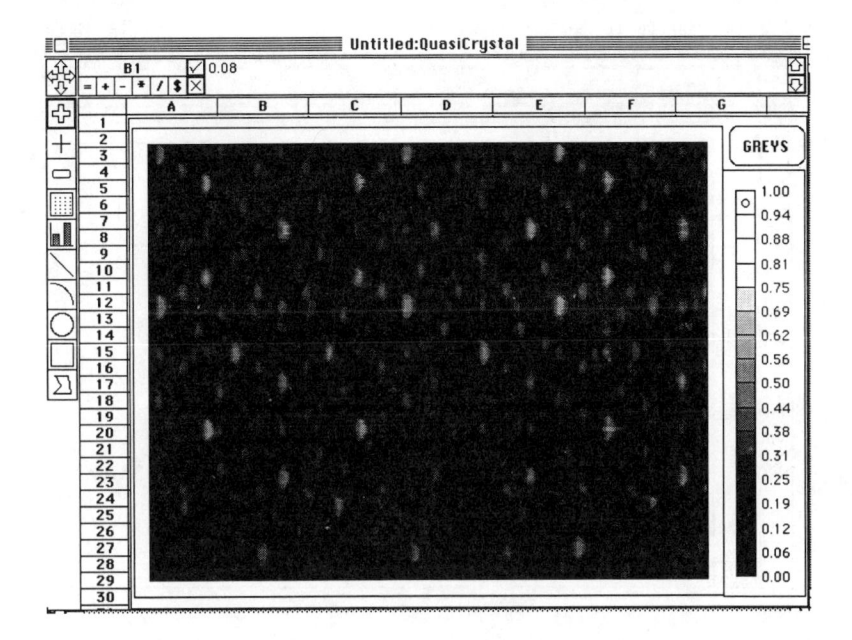

White added a color scale along the side, so that he could work with both color and shades of grey, depending on where he needed to use the graph. The "GREYS" button runs a script that remaps the graph in shades of grey.

White also used Wingz to chart theoretical calculations and experimental measurements for the scattering of 50 femtosecond laser pulses from a dielectric sphere

"The graph we wanted compared the real data against a theoretical curve generated by a Fortran program," says White. "The data used here is for a 50 femtosecond pulse, scattering from a 32.6 micron sphere. This data was recorded by an analog-to-digital board in a computer, then the two sets of data (real and projected) were normalized so that they had the same axes and the correct angular coordinates."

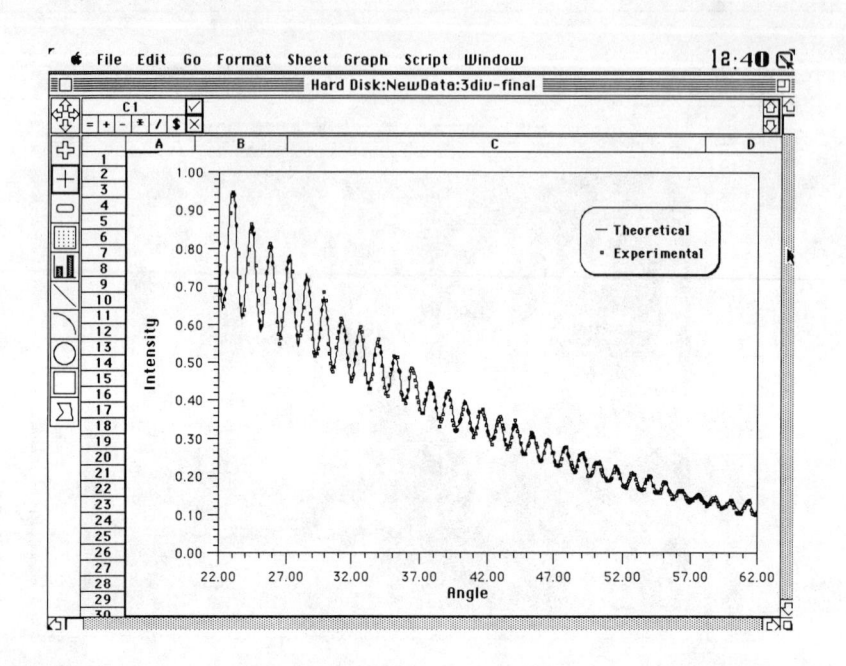

White remains impressed with Wingz and its ability to produce graphs from scientific data. "We're also really interested in some of the mathematical functions, because we do a lot of calculations with the data we get," he says.

4

Formulas and Functions

One of the most valuable features of a spreadsheet is its ability to use formulas to manipulate and reference values by location or name. Adding and subtracting values are nothing new to anyone who uses a checkbook. A spreadsheet like Wingz lets you set up a formula to reference these values by specific cell references (C35+F36) or by name (SALES-COSTS), and have the calculation done every time the formula is used, regardless of what values you've put in C35 or SALES or any of the other references.

This chapter will show you how to use formulas and functions within your spreadsheet.

ENTERING FORMULAS

Wingz recognizes a formula as a string of characters starting with an equals sign (=). When = is the first character in a cell, Wingz tries to evaluate the remainder of that entry as a mathematical expression that can include values, operators, cell references, names, and/or functions. If Wingz can evaluate these characters successfully, the result of the calculation appears in the cell. Otherwise, you'll see an error message.

Values can be constants that are entered with the formula, or ones that have been linked to previously defined cells. For instance, if you want to determine a monthly payment, but you're working with an annual interest rate that's already in cell E5, you can get the monthly interest rate by dividing that value by 12:

E5/12

In this example, both the value in E5 and 12 are considered constants, since both have been previously defined.

Operators come in five types: numeric, text, date/time, logical, and relational.

Numeric

+	Add
-	Subtract or negative
*	Multiply
/	Divide
%	Percent
^	Exponential

Note that the first four of these operators appear as icons in the entry bar. This enables you to click them on as you're constructing a formula.

There are a large number of numeric functions built into Wingz, allowing you to build complex formulas with ease.

Text

& The ampersand is the only text operator. It joins two or more text values, creating a new text value. For instance, if you want to join a first name and a last name as a new text value, the formula ="Jane "&"Farrell" produces the new text value "Jane Farrell."

Text strings are defined by enclosing characters within double quote marks: "This is a text string." "A56+B45" is also a text string, not a numeric formula.

Date/Time
Date and time operations use the date/time constant as if it were any other number. It can be formatted to reflect a number of forms, but can be added, subtracted, multiplied, or divided the same way any other number is handled.

Logical
AND   "True" if both operands are true
OR   "True" if either operand is true
NOT   "True" if the operand is false

Relational
    =   Equal
    <   Less than
    <=   Less than or equal to
    >   Greater than
    >=   Greater than or equal to
    <>   Not equal to

A relational operator compares values on either side of the operator, and produces the logical value "True" or "False." The formula

    =Netsales<10000

evaluates whatever is currently in the cell named Netsales, and compares it with 10000. If the value in Netsales is greater than 10000, the formula produces the value "True" or 1; if not, it produces the value "False" or 0.

Wingz has five types of expressions: numeric, text, logical, item list, and range.

Numeric expressions are evaluated in terms of their numeric value. They may be formatted in different ways and have different precisions.

Text expressions work on text strings, and do not perform any numeric or other form of evaluation.

Logical expressions evaluate the relative truth of two expressions of the same type, using one or more of the logical operators, and return either 1 (TRUE) or 0 (FALSE).

Item lists are sets of cell or range references and appropriate expressions, used as arguments in a function. Items are usually separated by commas.

Ranges refer to one or more cells, and can be identified either by the cell coordinates (either A1 or R1C1 format) or by range name.

Wingz evaluates the operators in a formula according to the following priorities:

inches, mils, points, decipoints, millimeters

negative, positive

* and /

+ and −

= > >= < <= <>

NOT

&, AND, OR

To change this order, group your values in parentheses. Wingz evaluates what's in the parentheses first, going from the innermost set to the outermost set; it then uses those values to calculate the rest of the formula.

You can use absolute, relative, or mixed cell references. D5 is an absolute column and row reference to cell D5. E15 is a relative reference, which shifts when used in a formula if Move, Insert, or Delete operations change the current location of the cell or cells involved. A mixed reference is one where either the column or row reference is absolute, and the other is relative: with $D49 no matter what else you do on the worksheet, the value you're after will always be in column D, but the row number may change.

WHAT'S A FUNCTION?

Functions are formula shortcuts. Wingz comes with over 140 different built-in worksheet formulas, or functions, which you can use if you also supply the necessary data in the required format. We'll discuss each of them later in this chapter. (Wingz also has a number of HyperScript functions. These will be discussed in detail in Chapter 11.)

Note: Since functions are denoted by a text string, such as WEEKDAY or MATCH, be careful to not use the name of a function as the name of a cell or cell range.

Some of the functions supplied with Wingz, such as SUM, VARIANCE, and PMT, are standard forms of a mathematical formula you could type. However, there are other functions, such as IF, CHOOSE, and HLOOKUP, that would be difficult, if impossible, to type in a single cell since they involve some programming or multiple steps. Some, such as IRR, involve many iterations of a test calculation, something that's impossible to do in a single cell.

Functions have a particular syntax: you have to enter the name of the function and the data that go with it in a particular order, punctuated properly. Most of Wingz's functions enclose the associated data in parentheses, like this:

=SUM(C5..D11)

The left parenthesis must immediately follow the function name. If you put a space between the function name and the left parenthesis, or for that matter any inappropriate character, Wingz will display an error message. There must be a corresponding right parenthesis at the end of the arguments, or Wingz will display another error message.

What's inside the parentheses is called

arguments

Most of the functions have one or more of them. They tell Wingz which cells or values the function is to act upon. In the sample function above, Wingz is being told to total the values it finds in all the cells from C5 through D11.

Suppose your worksheet looks like the one depicted in Figure 4-1.

Wingz adds the values in the range like this:

50+100+125+150+125+135+75+200+205+201+220+210+217+215

and comes up with a total of 2228. The values A4..G5 are considered an argument. If you were to specify more than one cell range, you'd need to separate the ranges with commas:

=SUM(A4..G5,A11..F11)

To indicate arguments with Wingz functions, use a comma to separate the arguments.

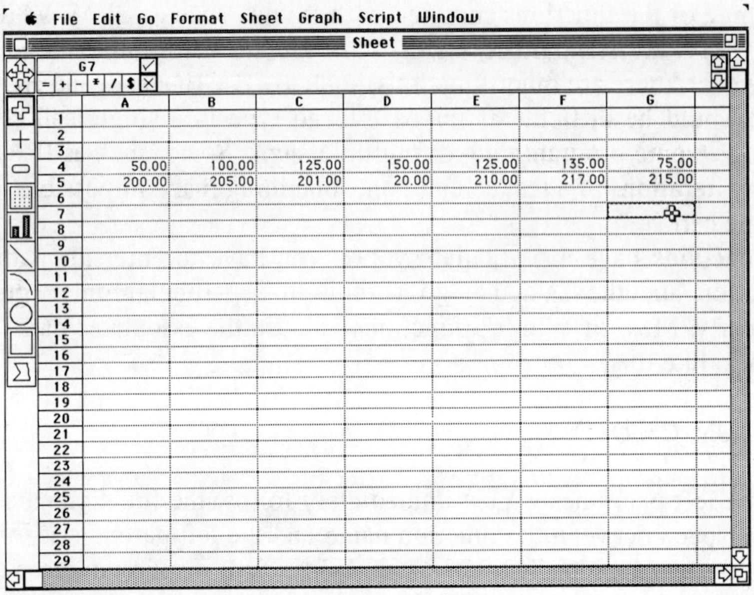

74 Mastering Wingz

FIGURE 4-1 Sample Worksheet.

Some functions let you use more than one kind of value as arguments. The SUM function lets you also use numbers or even text as arguments. Here's an example using numbers:

=SUM(5,10,15,20,25)

Wingz adds the numbers indicated and displays the result, 75, in the cell where you typed the function. In this particular function, you can combine cell addresses and numbers, as well as other values, and get a numeric total. Later in this chapter we'll go into more detail about what kind of arguments are used with each function.

When typing the functions and their arguments, you can use uppercase or lowercase letters, or mix them. Wingz doesn't distinguish case in functions.

It's important to type the correct number of arguments for any function you use. If a function requires three arguments, for example, and you supply only two, Wingz will return an error message.

PASTING FUNCTIONS

Unlike a lot of other spreadsheet programs, Wingz makes typing a function name easier by giving you a Paste Formula command on the Go menu. When you select the cell or cells where you want a particular formula to go, and choose the Paste Formula command, Wingz shows you a list of all the built-in functions (see Figure 4-2).

Select the category you want, and then the function you want, and choose the OK button. Wingz pastes the formula, complete with reminders about the arguments needed for the function in the formula bar. Position the I-bar and backspace over the argument description when you've typed the value that belongs there, or double click the word and start typing. When the formula appears as it should, complete with arguments, press the <Return> key. The formula is then stored in the cell or cells you selected.

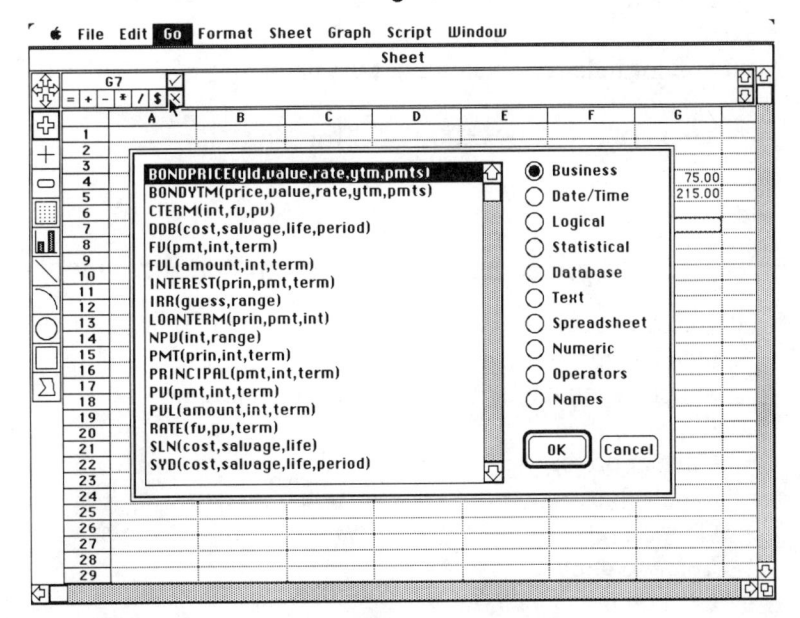

FIGURE 4-2 Paste Formula Dialog Box.

EXPLANATION OF FUNCTIONS

In each of the function explanations in the remainder of this chapter, you'll find the function name along with the arguments it needs, a brief definition, and an explanation that includes some examples of how to use the function.

BUSINESS FUNCTIONS

BONDPRICE(yield,value,rate,yearstomaturity,payments)

The BONDPRICE function calculates the current price of a bond where the parameters shown are specified.

Suppose you have the following information about a bond:

Listed yield to maturity:	9.5%
Face value:	$500
Coupon rate:	8%
Years to maturity:	7
Coupon payments/yr:	2

The formula for calculating this, using the BONDPRICE function, is

=BONDPRICE(.095,500,.08,7,2) or $462.28.

BONDYTM(price,value,rate,yearstomaturity,payments)

BONDYTM calculates the yield to maturity of a bond where the parameters shown are specified.

Suppose you have the following information:

Current price:	$875
Face value:	$1000
Coupon rate:	9%
Years to maturity:	5
Coupon payments/yr:	2

The formula for calculating the yield to maturity, using the BONDYTM function, is

=BONDYTM(875,1000,.09,5,2) or 0.12.

CTERM(rate,futurevalue,presentvalue)

The CTERM function calculates the number of compounding periods it will take for the amount you specify as presentvalue to grow to the amount in futurevalue, assuming a periodic interest rate. For example, you have a $10,000 to invest, and you want it to grow to $15,000. You assume that you can get 7.5% per year on your investment. How long will it take for you to reach your goal?

The formula for determining this is:

CTERM(.075/12,15000,10000) or 65.08

Note that the interest rate has to be specified as the periodic interest rate. That is if you want the number of months, you'll have to specify interest in a monthly figure (hence, the .075/12 value). The number of periods returned by the function, here 65.08, translates to about five and a half years.

DDB(cost,salvage,life,period)

The DDB function calculates depreciation by the Double-Declining Balance method. You have to specify the original cost, what you think you might get as salvage value for the item at the end of its depreciable life, the number of years of its depreciable life, and the year number for which you want to figure **depreciation**. Depreciation helps you determine the book value of an item, where book value is defined as the original cost of an asset minus the depreciation taken over the intervening period.

This is one of the methods that accelerates depreciation so that more depreciation is written off during the early periods of an item's useful life, and less later on. For example, if you're interested in the current depreciation amount for a truck you purchased five years ago for $12,500, with a useful life of eight years and a probable salvage value of $2,500, the function would be stated thus:

=DDB(12500,2500,8,5) = 988.77

Prior years' depreciation would be:

Year 1 3125.00
Year 2 2343.75
Year 3 1757.81
Year 4 1318.36

FV(payment,interest,term)

The FV function calculates the future value of a series of payments that have a regular payment amount, a periodic interest rate, over a specified period of time.

Suppose you plan on taking regular monthly deductions from your paycheck, and putting them in a company credit union account that pays 7.5% annually. How much will you have at the end of two years if your monthly deductions are $50?

The equation for this is:

=FV(50,.075/12,24) = 1290.34

FVL(payment,interest,term)

The FVL function substitutes a lump sum payment for the string of regular payments you use with the FV function. It calculates the amount the lump sum will grow to, if it earns the interest rate specified for the specified amount of time. For instance, you get a lump sum payment of $42,000 from your retirement plan when you leave one company and join another. The new company has a different plan, but you can invest your previous proceeds in a special retirement fund at your bank, and the fund pays 9.6% annually. You plan on retiring in 12 years. How much will be in this fund?

The formula for determining this is:

=FVL(42000,.096,12) = 126175.76

(Note that, since we stated the period in years, we could also state the interest rate as an annual rate.)

INTEREST(principal,payment,term)

The INTEREST function determines the interest rate for an investment of a specified principal, which is to be repaid in fixed payments over a certain period of time.

In selling your house, a prospective buyer makes you an offer whereby you'd take back a second deed of trust for $20,000, with payments of $425.00 per month for five years. What rate of interest would you be getting?

Using the INTEREST function, you determine:

=INTEREST(20000,425,5)*12 = 0.10

(We multiplied the results by 12 because the monthly payment of 425 as a parameter in this equation yields a monthly interest rate, and we wanted an annual rate.)

IRR(guess,range)

Internal Rate of Return, or IRR calculates an approximate rate of return on an investment that consists of an initial payment and a series of cash flows. The Internal Rate of Return is the discount rate at which the present value of the cash flow equals the value of the investment. Put another way, it calculates the discount rate for which the net present value of a series of cash flows equals zero.

The IRR is calculated by iterative guesses, which you help by specifying guess. Wingz uses 20 automatic recalculations to come up with the most accurate result it can. What you specify in range is where the cash flows are located, including the initial payment. This initial payment must be negative, since it is assumed to be what you paid out as an investment. The subsequent cash flows can be positive or negative, in any order. Blank cells in the range are assumed to contain 0.0.

For instance, suppose you're thinking of buying a small rental house. The down payment and closing costs will run you about $25,000 and you can rent the house for a net profit of $65 per month, after paying the mortgage, taxes, and insurance. You plan to sell the house in three years, realizing a profit of $55,000. What will be your Internal Rate of Return?

You've arranged your spreadsheet so that the projected income and expenses are in annual columns, in Figure 4-3. The formula for determining the Internal Rate of Return for the above situation is:

=IRR(.5, B9..D9) = .56

LOANTERM(principal,payment,interest)

The LOANTERM function gives the term over which equal payments must be made in order to earn the specified interest on the principal. This LOANTERM function is particularly useful when you evaluate loan options where the term is negotiable—for example, a car loan, where you can choose between 24-, 36-, 48-, and 60-month terms. If you know how much you can afford in payments, and you know how much the amount of the loan will be, you can experiment with different rates of interest, using the LOANTERM function to see what the interest rates will do to the term of the loan.

FIGURE 4-3 Income/Expense Spreadsheet.

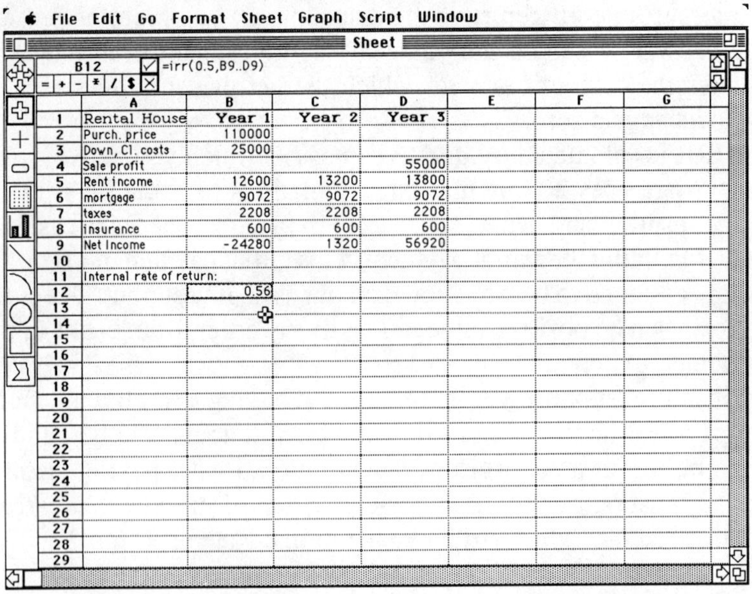

	A	B	C	D
1	Rental House	Year 1	Year 2	Year 3
2	Purch. price	110000		
3	Down, Cl. costs	25000		
4	Sale profit			55000
5	Rent income	12600	13200	13800
6	mortgage	9072	9072	9072
7	taxes	2208	2208	2208
8	insurance	600	600	600
9	Net Income	-24280	1320	56920
10				
11	Internal rate of return:			
12		0.56		

The LOANTERM function is probably also useful in calculating how long you'll have to wait for your money if someone makes you an offer where the principal, payments, and interest rate are specified, a situation that sometimes happens in real estate financing.

NPV(interest,payments)

The Net Present Value function, or NPV, calculates the value of a series of cash flows payments, if discounted at a specified interest rate. The payments don't have to be equal, but they do need to be in a series of cells that can be specified as a range.

Net Present Value is a basic financial function that can give you the value of money that will be received in the future. The value that is returned is the amount of principal that would have to be invested, at the specified interest rate, in order to generate the cash flows indicated. The Net Present Value of an investment is today's value of a series of future cashflows, both positive and negative. It assumes that the rate you specify is what you might have received for a competing investment, or for the rate of inflation. This is not the same as an interest rate, which compounds growth on a regular basis.

Net Present Value lets you compare dissimilar investments that provide future cashflows, taking into account factors that could influence what you might otherwise earn over equivalent periods.

In the computation of Net Present Value, the interest is removed from a future amount to arrive at the initial amount invested. The process of reducing future values to present values is called **discounting**, and for that reason, net present value is sometimes called a **discounted value**. The interest to be subtracted is called the **discount**, and the rate of interest is called the **discount rate**. It is this discount rate you specify in a net present value function.

For example, let's assume that you're faced with the awesome fact that you're going to have to fork out at least $7500 each year for college tuition money and other expenses for your son or daughter for a minimum of four years, and that expenses will grow by $500 each year. How much do you need to have stashed away at the beginning of your offspring's freshman year?

You can evaluate this one in two different ways: in one scenario, you quit contributing to the lump sum at the beginning of college; in the second, you continue to put money into the pot, adding to the amount that's still there.

82 Mastering Wingz

Let's assume that you can earn an even 10% on your money, and that any unused funds will accrue interest at that rate. This is the discount rate, and the value we'll use for interest. Let's also assume that the money will be drawn at the beginning of each of the school years. Using Wingz, you also have to assume that the lump sum will earn a full 10% interest just before the first withdrawal.

Arrange your cash outflows in a range, like the one shown in Figure 4-4. (This example assumes that you're through putting money into the pot when school starts. If you want to consider the second option mentioned above, adjust the cash flows so that they reflect the difference between what you put in and what gets drawn out.)

The Net Present Value function is formulated as follows:

=NPV(.10,A6..D6) = 25963.05

Thus if you have $25,963.05 invested somewhere at the beginning of the school term, in an account drawing 10% annual interest, you'll be able to deal with the college expenses as shown.

FIGURE 4-4 College Expenses.

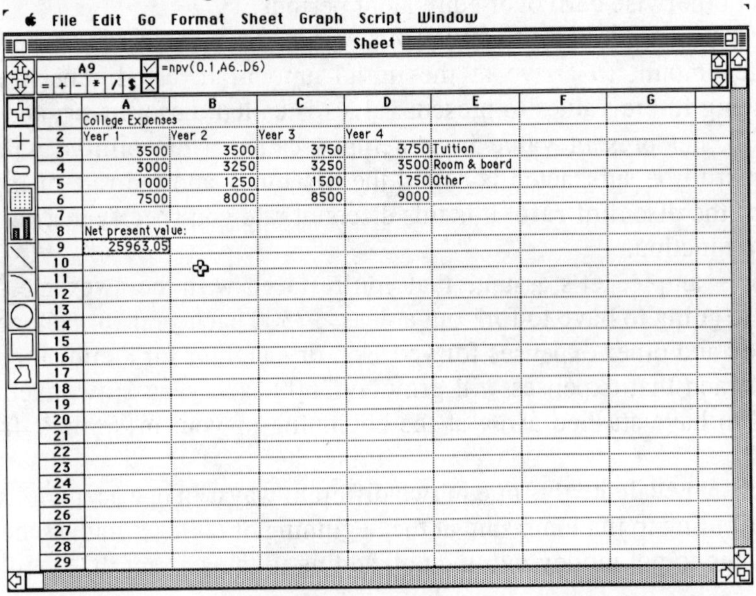

	A	B	C	D	E
1	College Expenses				
2	Year 1	Year 2	Year 3	Year 4	
3	3500	3500	3750	3750	Tuition
4	3000	3250	3250	3500	Room & board
5	1000	1250	1500	1750	Other
6	7500	8000	8500	9000	
7					
8	Net present value:				
9	25963.05				

A9 =npv(0.1,A6..D6)

You could also express the formula this way:

=NPV(0.1,7500,8000,8500,9000)

and you'd get the same answer.

Note: Wingz assumes that the interest you're using is an annual rate, and that cashflows are annual. If you use any other term for cashflows, Wingz assumes that the interest given is the monthly rate. Therefore, if you're using irregular cashflows, arrange them in a row by month, with a 0 value where there is no cashflow, and use a monthly interest rate in the formula.

PMT(principal,interest,term)

The PMT function calculates the payment you need to make in order to pay off a loan, given the principal, interest, and term. You can use this function whenever you're thinking about paying for something over time, whether that be a house, a car, or some other purchase that involves a loan. You can also use this to determine how much you'll be receiving on a periodic basis if you loan money to someone on specific terms.

Examples:

PMT(100000,.0975,25) =

PRINCIPAL(payment,rate,term)

The PRINCIPAL function gives you the ability to compute the total amount of principal paid, given the payments you make over a specified term at the specified interest rate.

Lots of people trade in a car when they buy another, and frequently the older car isn't fully paid off. The PRINCIPAL function can help you determine how much principal has been paid, of the original amount owed. (There may be other factors in a payoff, however; frequently there is a prepayment penalty, or some fine print that specifies how much interest must be paid if the contract is paid off early.)

Let's assume you want to trade your old car in on a new one, but the original loan was for five years, and there is still money due on it. How much remains to be paid on the old car? To determine the principal paid after 29 months on a loan of $7500, if the payments were $177.50 a month, and the loan was at 18% annual interest, use this function:

=PRINCIPAL(177.50,.18/12,29) = 4149.25

Thus, you will have to pay off $3350.75 in principal ($7500 − $4149.25) when you acquire the new car.

PV (payment,interest,term)

The PV function determines the present value of an annuity, or regular series or cashflows, at a constant rate of interest over a specified number of periods. For example, let's say you're approached by a broker who is offering you a limited partnership interest that will pay you $500 a month for 5 years. You can invest these payments and get 8% on your money. The cost of the partnership interest is $20,000. Should you buy an interest?
The PV function tells you:

=PV(500,.08/12,5*12)= -24659.22

The negative result means money you'd pay out now in order to get the annuity specified. Since the broker is asking $20,000 as the price, it sounds like a good deal.

PVL(payment,interest,term)

Like the PV function, PVL determines the present value of cash flow that will arrive in the future. However, the difference between PV and PVL is that PVL looks at the effect if there is a lump sum payment, rather than a series of payments. For instance, suppose your son approaches you for a loan of $5000, indicating that he'll pay you back in a year in a lump sum of $5500, with interest at 12%. What's the present value of his promise?
The function

=PVL(5500,.12,1) = 4910.71

In other words, given what he's willing to pay, your $5000 would be worth some $90 less than the bank would say it was worth. Well, it was a nice try on his part. You may want to ask him to rethink his offer.

RATE (fv,pv,term)

The rate function gives you the interest rate returned on an investment. RATE is similar to IRR in that it returns an interest rate. However, while IRR works with cashflows, RATE looks at both present value and future value.

Like IRR, RATE is an iterative calculation. Wingz tries up to 20 guesses at a solution. For instance, let's say you've borrowed $15000 from your parents to complete the downpayment for a house. You've promised to pay them $25000 in five years, because you think that your house will rise in value far more than that, and you'll be able either to sell it or refinance and to pay your parents out of the proceeds. What implicit rate of interest have you agreed to? The RATE function tells you:

=RATE(25000,15000,5)=0.11, the annual interest rate

SLN(cost,salvage,life,period

The SLN function computes the amount of straight line depreciation for an asset. **Straight line depreciation** is the simplest and most commonly used form of depreciation. It assumes that an item depreciates in linear fashion, with equal amounts of value lost each year of its useful life.

Suppose you own a rental property, and you've purchased a new washer and dryer for it. Because it's considered "business equipment" for tax purposes, you can depreciate it and deduct the depreciation when you compute your taxes. To make things easier, you decide to use straight line depreciation. The appliances cost you $780, and you expect them to last five years, after which time you can probably get $100 for them when you trade them in on newer models.

The SLN function to tell you how much you'll be able to deduct for them each year is:

=SLN(780,100,5,1)=136

SYD(cost,salvage,life,period)

The SYD function computers the amount of depreciation for an asset using the sum-of-the-years'-digits method. SYD is a form of depreciation that results in more depreciation in the earlier years of an item's useful life, and less toward the end. Because each period's depreciation will differ, SYD has you specify the period for which you want to determine the amount of depreciation. If you're looking for an annual amount, specify the year number of the item's life. (Be sure to use the same unit for both life and period.)

For instance, you've bought a truck for $15,000 that has a useful life of 10 years, and you estimate a salvage value of $1000. Using the SYD method, how much depreciation can you take in the first year?

=SYD(15000,1000,10,1)=2645.45

Note: When preparing to calculate depreciation, it's wise to compare what the different methods will produce for you. For instance, for the same truck compare the depreciation amounts if you use the Double Declining Balance method with those if you use the Straight Line method:

=DDB(15000,1000,10,1)=3000

=SLN(15000,1000,10,1)=1400

In this case, you'll get more depreciation the first year using the Double Declining Balance method. However, you may want to weigh your decision in terms of how much depreciation you'll get in subsequent years.

TERM(payment,interest,fv)

The TERM function lets you know how long you're going to have to make a series of payments in order to amass the specified future value, assuming that the investment is earning the specified interest rate.

Let's reconsider that college fund. In the discussion under Net Present Value, we determined that you'd need the sum of $25,963.05 salted away in order to meet the college expenses you predicted. Now let's assume you could afford to put $250 a month into such a fund, which would pay 10% annual interest. How long would you have to keep up the payments? The function to do that is:

=TERM(250,.10/12,25963.05) = 75.13

The answer is expressed in the number of months, since you entered $250 as the monthly payment and 10% interest as a monthly interest rate. That translates to six years and a bit over three months.

DATE/TIME FUNCTIONS

Wingz stores date and time values as numbers. Date are stored as an integer from 1 to 109574, representing the dates in sequence from January 1, 1900, through December 31, 2199. Time is stored as a decimal fraction, from 0 through 0.9999, representing each second from 0:00:00 (midnight) to 23:59:59 (one second before midnight). Date and time calculations are performed on this serial number, much as if it were any other integer or decimal number. What you see in a cell, however, depends on what function you use and how the cell is formatted.

ADATE(datenumber,picture)

The ADATE funcion converts the datenumber specified into text, in the following form:

"month day, year"

You can specify the format in which you want to see the text in the argument picture, using the appropriate combination of the following indicators:

d	A one- or two-digit number representing the day of the month (for example, 3, 27).
dd	Two digits representing the day of the month (for example, 03, 27).
day	The full-text version of the day name (Monday).
dy	The abbreviated text version of the day name (for example, Mon).
m	A one- or two-digit number representing the month of the year (for example, 5, 12).
mm	Two digits representing the month of the year (for example, 05, 10).
month	The full-text version of the month name (March).
mon	The abbreviated version of the month name (for example, Sep).
y	The one- or two-digit number representing the year (for example, 1 for 2001; 89 for 1989).
yy	The two-digit number representing the year (for example, 01 for 1002; 89 for 1989).
yyyy	The four-digit number representing the year (for example, 1989).

ADDDAYS (datenumber,days)

The ADDDAYS function (yes, there are three D's) adds the specified number of days to the given datenumber. You can use a negative number for days; if you do, the number of days will be subtracted.

Examples: Used with no formatting, ADDDAYS works just like another number formula:

=ADDDAYS(15633,39) = 15672.00

However, you can format the cell in which you use the formula so that it displays the information in a date format:

=ADDDAYS(15633,39) = 11–27–42

ADDHOURS(datenumber,hours)

The ADDHOURS function adds the number of hours you specify to the date number you give. If you use a negative value for hours, that number of hours will be subtracted from the time number.

You can format the cell in which you place the formula so that the result you see is in one of the time formats, rather than as the date/time serial number.

Example:

=ADDHOURS(123.45678) = 123.87

However, if formatted with the HH:MM AM format, the result looks like this:

=ADDHOURS(123.45678,10) = 08:57 PM

ADDMINUTES(datenumber,minutes)

ADDMINUTES works like ADDHOURS in that it adds the number of minutes you specify in minutes to the datenumber you specify. If minutes is a negative value, that value is subtracted from datenumber.

ADDMONTHS(datenumber,months)

ADDMONTHS works like ADDDAYS in that it adds the number of months you specify in months to the timenumber you specify. If months is a negative value, that value is subtracted from timenumber.

ADDSECONDS

ADDSECONDS works like ADDHOURS and ADDMINUTES in that it adds the number of seconds you specify in seconds to the datenumber you specify. If seconds is a negative value, that value is subtracted from datenumber.

ADDYEARS(datenumber,years)

ADDYEARS works like ADDDAYS and ADDMONTHS in that it adds the number of years you specify in years to the datenumber you specify. If years is a negative value, that value is subtracted from namenumber.

ATIME(datenumber,picture)

ATIME converts the number of minutes you specify in datenumber to time in an AM/PM form, depending on the format you specify in picture. If minutes is a positive number, the number is added to the beginning of the day (12:00 AM); if it's a negative number, it's subtracted.

The value specified for picture must be in the form "hh:mm:sc" or the form "hh:mm:sc AM." If you use a single letter for any of these values (for example, h:mm:s) that letter will appear as text along with the number of minutes. If you leave off the AM or PM, it will not appear in the cell.

CMONTH(month)

CMONTH converts the month specified to the corresponding name of the month. For example, CMONTH(5) returns the value May.

CWEEKDAY(weekday)

CWEEKDAY converts the number of the day given in weekday to the corresponding name of the day. For example, CWEEKDAY(4) returns Wednesday.

DATE(year,month,day)

DATE returns the date/time serial number of date specified.

When you specify the date in the format shown, Wingz stores the serial number corresponding to that date in the cell. For example, if you specify =DATE(88,1,1) Wingz returns the serial number 32143.00. However, if you specify anything other than a two-digit year value, Wingz assumes it is referring to the literal year (100 is the year 100, 2000 is the year 2000, and so on) and calculates the serial number accordingly. Wingz assumes that a two-digit number refers to a year from 1900 through 1999.

What you see in the cell depends on the format of the cell. You may see 01/01/88, or 01–Jan-1988 or the serial number, depending on the format.

Examples:

=DATE(88,06,01) = 32295

=DATE(2000,01,01) = 36526

DATEVALUE(datestring)

DATEVALUE returns the date/time serial number corresponding to the value you specify in datestring. DATEVALUE differs from DATE in that you enter text rather than numbers as the argument. Like DATE, DATEVALUE needs a date from January 1, 1900 to December 31, 2199. You can use any of Wingz's date formats:

"November 15, 1988"

"Nov 15, 1988"

"Nov 15 88"

"15 Nov 1988"

"11–15–88"

"11.15.88"

"11/15/88"

Formulas and Functions 91

Examples:

=DATEVALUE("01/01/88")=32143
=DATEVALUE("01.01.2000")=36526

DAY(datenumber)

DAY returns the day of the month equivalent to the datenumber you specify. DAY converts the datenumber you give into a date, paring off the month and year information and returning only the number representing the day.
Examples:

=DAY(5) = 5
=DAY(32237) = 4

DAYNAME(datenumber)

DAYNAME returns the name of the day corresponding to the number you specify in datenumber. DAYNAME works much like DAY, in that it pares off the month and year information. Unlike DAY, however, it returns the name of the day, rather than its number.
Examples:

=DAYNAME(5) = Thursday
=DAYNAME(32237) = Monday

HOUR(datenumber)

HOUR returns the hour of the day equivalent to datenumber. The value given in datenumber must be a decimal number (the integer portion is regarded as a date value, and is ignored). HOUR converts datenumber into the hour of the day, paring off any information about minutes and seconds. The hour is in a 24–hour clock, ranging from 0 (midnight) to 23 (11 PM).

You may also wish to use TIMEVALUE within the HOUR function to get the hour portion of a string that is in one of the time formats.
Examples:

=HOUR(.5) = 12
=HOUR(1357.13579) = 3
=HOUR(TIMEVALUE("9:15")) = 9

MINUTE(datenumber)

MINUTE returns the minute of the hour equivalent to datenumber. The value given in datenumber must be a decimal number (the integer portion is regarded as a date value, and is ignored). MINUTE converts the time serial number you give into the minute of the hour involved, paring off any information about hours and seconds.

You can also enter the argument as text, such as "20:15:00" or "8:15:00 PM" or one of the other acceptable time formats if you use the TIMEVALUE function within the MINUTE function.
Examples:

=MINUTE(1.5)=0

=MINUTE(0.01)=14

=MINUTE("2:35:52 PM")=35

MONTH(datenumber)

MONTH returns the number of the month of the year equivalent to datenumber. MONTH converts the number you give as datenumber into the number corresponding to the equivalent month of the year (1-12). You can also specify a text form of the date if you also use the DATEVALUE function with the MONTH function.
Examples:

=MONTH(12345) = 10

=MONTH(7531) = 8

=MONTH(DATEVALUE("01–Jan-1988")) = 1

MONTHNAME(datenumber)

MONTHNAME works like DAYNAME, in that it in that it pares off the day and year information. Unlike MONTH, it returns the name of the day, rather than its number.

Examples:

=MONTHNAME(34) = February

=MONTHNAME(31860) = March

NOW()

NOW returns the date/time number equivalent to the current date and time. NOW lets you insert the current date and time into your worksheet. What Wingz reports is the serial number for both date and time, in the form 11111.11111. To use the serial number in one of the time or date formats, format the cell appropriately.

If you want just the current date, use the INT function with NOW; if you want just the current time, use the MOD function (see the examples below).

Note: The parentheses are required, even though they contain no arguments.

Examples:

=NOW() = 32420.51

=INT(NOW()) = 32420

=MOD(NOW(),1) = 0.51

SECOND(datenumber)

SECOND returns the equivalent in seconds of datenumber.

SECOND converts the time serial number you give into the second of the hour involved, paring off any information about hours and minutes.

You can also enter the argument as text, such as "20:15:00" or "8:15:00 PM" or one of the other acceptable time formats, providing you use the TIMEVALUE function with the SECOND function.

Examples:

=SECOND(.007) = 4
=SECOND(32445.007) = 5
=SECOND(TIMEVALUE("1:52:27")) = 27

TIME(hour,minute,second)

TIME returns the serial number corresponding to the time specified. The TIME function translates the time you enter into the corresponding time serial number. The time entered can be positive or negative. You can also enter time as text, provided it's used with the TIMEVALUE function.

Examples:

=TIME(12,0,0) = 0.5
=TIME(19,45,15) = 0.82
=TIME(16,48,0)-TIME(12,0,0) = 0.2

TIMEVALUE(timestring)

TIMEVALUE returns the timenumber corresponding to timestring. Like DATEVALUE, TIMEVALUE translates the value specified in timestring into an equivalent time serial number. The value in timestring can be in any of the Wingz time formats.

Examples:

=TIMEVALUE("2:24 AM") = 0.1
=TIMEVALUE("7:15:45 PM") = 0.80213

YEAR(datenumber)

YEAR returns the year equivalent to datenumber. YEAR converts the serial number you give into the number corresponding to the equivalent year, from

1900 to 2199. If you use the DATEVALUE function, you can also enter the argument as text, such as "4–15–1988" or "15–Apr-1988."
Examples:

=YEAR(29747) = 1981

=YEAR((DATEVALUE("15–Apr-1988")) = 1988

LOGICAL FUNCTIONS

Wingz' logical functions are concerned with the logical values TRUE and FALSE. Usually the function is involved in a test as to whether a condition exists, but many of the logical functions simply return values.

FALSE()

FALSE returns the logical value FALSE. FALSE is frequently used in IF or conditional formulas, where it's important to recognize that a false condition is one of the potential results. The logical zero it returns is the same as a numeric zero.

Note: The parentheses are required, even if they contain no argument.
Example:

=FALSE() = 0

IF(condition,x,y)

The IF function tests condition, and returns TRUE if condition is true, FALSE if it is false. IF is used to make conditional tests of cell values and formulas. If condition is evaluated as true, the next argument is used; if condition is evaluated as false, the last argument is used.

The x and y values can be numbers or text. If the arguments are numbers, the appropriate number is returned after the test. If the arguments are text, text is returned.

You can nest IF functions as arguments, permitting you to construct some fairly elaborate conditional tests.

Examples:

IF(E7>E6,5,10) = 5 if the value in E7 is greater than the value in E6; otherwise it returns 10

IF(A1=0,"We've got a problem",A1) puts the text string "We've got a problem" in the active cell; otherwise it stores whatever is in A1 in the active cell

ISBLANK(x)

ISBLANK returns TRUE if the cell or range is blank. ISBLANK tests a cell or range to see whether it is blank. If the cell or range is blank, it returns TRUE; otherwise it returns FALSE.

Examples:

If C5 contains 0, =ISBLANK(C5) = FALSE

If C5 contains "TRUE", =ISBLANK(C5) = FALSE

If C5 is blank, =ISBLANK(C5) = TRUE

ISERR(x)

ISERR returns TRUE if the cell or range you specify returns an error upon calculation. If the specified cell or range does not return an error, ISERR returns FALSE.

Example:

=ISERR(F17) returns FALSE (0) when F17 is blank

ISNA(x)

ISNAreturns TRUE if the cell 9or range you specify contains the value "N/A." ISNA looks specifically for the error value N/A. This is useful when checking for errors as a result of earlier calculations.

Example:

=ISNA(D42) = FALSE if D42 contains the error value ERR or the values $750 or TRUE.

ISNUMBER(x)

ISNUMBER returns TRUE if x is a number. ISNUMBER checks x for the presence of a number, and returns a TRUE if it is there, or a FALSE if it finds anything else. The value x can be a text string, a numeric expression, or any valid cell reference.
Examples:

=ISNUMBER(B35) = TRUE if B35 contains a number

=ISNUMBER(B35) = FALSE if B35 contains TRUE

ISRANGE(x)

ISRANGE returns TRUE if x is a valid range reference. ISRANGE checks x for the presence of a valid range reference, and returns a TRUE if it is, or a FALSE if it finds anything else. The value x must be a text string.
Example:

=ISRANGE("Salary") = TRUE if Salary is a range name

ISSTRING(x)

ISSTRING returns TRUE if x is a text string. ISSTRING checks x for the presence of a text string, and returns a TRUE if it finds a text string, or a FALSE if it finds anything else. The value specified as x can be a text string, a numeric expression, or any valid cell reference.
Example:

=ISSTRING(F12) = TRUE if F12 contains "Mary Smith"

TRUE()

TRUE returns the logical value TRUE. TRUE, like FALSE, is frequently used in IF or conditional formulas, where it's important to recognize that a true condition is one of the potential results. The logical one it returns is the same as a numeric one.

Note: The parentheses are required, even if they contain no argument.

Example:

=TRUE() = TRUE

STATISTICAL FUNCTIONS

AVG(itemlist)

AVG calculates the average of numbers given as arguments. AVG calculates the average of the values specified as number1, number2, ... , etc. Each of the arguments can be numbers, or ranges that contain numbers. Arguments containing text or blanks are ignored.

Examples

=AVERAGE(2,6,10)=6

=AVERAGE(A4..A8)=15 if cells A4 through A8 contain the values 11, 13, 15, 17, and 19.

COUNT(itemlist)

COUNT counts the numbers in itemlist. COUNT determines how many values are in itemlist. The arguments in itemlist can be cell references or ranges, numbers, empty cells, logical values, or text. However, any cell containing a blank is ignored.

Examples:

=COUNT(D5..D6) = 2 (assuming D5 and D6 contain numbers)

=COUNT(D1,D5..D7) = 4 (assuming all four cells contain acceptable values)

=COUNT(0.5,FALSE,"six",25,3.143159) = 5

MAX(itemlist)

MAX determines the largest number in itemlist. MAX gives you the largest numeric value in the list of arguments. The arguments in itemlist can be

numbers, empty cells, logical values, or text representations of numbers. However, any text strings or blanks in the list are assigned a value of zero.
Examples:

=MAX(15,2,19,8,11) = 19

=MAX(C5..C9,22,B4..B8) = 35 if B4..B8 contains the series 31, 31, 33, 34, and 35 and C5..C9 contains the series 5, 10, 15, 20, and 25.

MIN(itemlist)

MIN determines the smallest number in itemlist. MIN gives you the smallest numeric value in the list of arguments. The same limitations about arguments that were true for MAX also apply to MIN.
Examples:

=MIN(15,2,19,8,11) = 2

=MIN(C5..C9,22,B4..B8) = 5 if B4..B8 contains the series 31, 31, 33, 34, and 35 and C5..C9 contains the series 5, 10, 15, 20, and 25.

STD(itemlist)

STD calculates the standard devision of a population based on the entire population given in itemlist. A **standard deviation** of a list of values is the square root of the variance of all those values from the average. STD is used to test the reliability of that average as representative: the more the individual values vary from that average, the higher the value STD returns. Conversely, the less the individual values vary from that average, the lower the STD value and hence the more reliable the mean is likely to be.

In a normally distributed population, 68% of all data points fall within one standard deviation from the mean (plus one standard deviation and minus one standard deviation, where the single largest number of values is assumed to be at the mean). Normal distribution also assumes that about 95% of the data points fall within two standard deviations.

The values given in the arguments should be numbers; text or blanks in a cell are ignored.

Example: Assume you have the following complete "population" or all the data points there are for this calculation:

	F	G	H	I	J
Row 27	141	150	137	153	145

The function =STD(F27..J27) = 5.81

STDEV(itemlist)

STDEV calculates an estimate of the standard devision of a population, given sample specified in itemlist.

Note: Use STDEV if the numbers you're using as arguments represent a sample of the population. If the numbers represent the entire population, use STD.

Example: Suppose you have cell values as follows:

	A	B	C	D	E
Row 16	241	198	203	247	225

The function =STDEV(A47..E47) = 21.96

SUM(itemlist)

SUM calculates the sum of the numbers given in itemlist. SUM adds up all the values either shown or referenced. Arguments that are numbers or logical values are considered. Logical values are considered to have a +1 value if True, or a 0 value if False. Text and blanks are ignored.

Examples:

=SUM(A5..A15)= the total of all values in cells A5 through A15.

=SUM(25,B9..D11,"three")= the total of the 25 plus the contents of B9 through D11.

SUMSQ(itemlist)

SUMSQ calculates the sum of the squares of the numbers in itemlist. The sum of the squares of numbers is useful in a number of different statistical calculations, including linear regression. The SUMSQ function lets you determine that quickly, using a list of numbers identified in itemlist.

Example: If you have the numbers 1, 2, 3, 4, and 5 in a row, you could calculate the sum of their squares as follows:

=SUMSQ(A10..E10) = 55

VAR(itemlist)
VARIANCE(itemlist)

VAR calculates the variance of a population based on the entire population, which is listed in itemlist. VARIANCE calculates an estimate of the variance of a population based on the sample given in itemlist.

Variance is another of the standard measures of reliability of a set of data. It is the square of the standard deviation from the mean, and measures how much data points vary from the mean value. The higher the figure, the more nearly random the sample is likely to be. (See the discussion about deviation from the mean under STD.)

The arguments in itemlist for VAR and VARIANCE must have at least two entries. All text or empty cell values are ignored.

Note: VAR assumes that its arguments represent the entire population. If your data are a sample of the population, use VARIANCE.

Suppose you have the student test scores that are shown in Figure 4-5. You'd like to know if the test was reasonable, and you're willing to say that it was reasonable if the test scores follow a normal distribution. A "normal" distribution would mean that about two thirds of the test scores will be grouped within plus and minus one standard deviation from the mean.

A large standard deviation, and hence a large variance, means that scores are widely scattered. A smaller standard deviation and a smaller variance mean that scores are closer together, your goal if the test was a reasonable test of what students had learned, other things being equal.

The function =VARIANCE(D3..D20) lets you determine whether the test scores for Period 3 fell into a normal pattern. VARIANCE, remember, works on a sample of the population, not the population as a whole. The function =VAR(B3..F20) gives you a look at the distribution for the entire population. The answer, 73-78, indicates that your test was somewhat skewed toward the higher numbers. The result, 69.21 indicates the test was probably reasonable, but only as a single sampling.

```
                    test scores
   B24      =var(B3..F20)
=  +  -  *  /  $  X
        A           B         C         D         E         F         G
 1  Test Scores: Winter Quarter
 2                Period 1  Period 2  Period 3  Period 4  Period 5
 3  Anderson, Jo      67        72        74        75        79
 4  Berens, Bill      91        96        95        99        97
 5  Caccielli, Ann    94        91        93        90        92
 6  Dohrmen, Glen     88        82        83        87        89
 7  Evans, James      81        85        84        86        85
 8  Fairchild, Bob    74        72        77        79        79
 9  Garcia, Janice    90        88        92        93        94
10  Hanamoto, Jan     99       100       100       100       100
11  Inglis, Doris    100        97        99       100       100
12  Jackson, Dan      65        73        76        78        81
13  Kirshner, Hal    100       100       100       100       100
14  Lemmon, Jon       97        98        99        98        99
15  McCann, Jim       92        95        91        94        92
16  Norris, Marsh     83        89        88        87        89
17  Ohara, Kim        85        96        90        92        93
18  Porter, Hank      94        87        90        91        89
19  Quentin, Ross     79        85        81        82        84
20  Roberts, Rick     81        86        87        89        88
21
22  Variance:       69.21
23
24  PVariance:      73.78
25
```

Figure 4-5 Sample Test Scores

DATABASE FUNCTIONS

The database functions are roughly equivalent to their counterpart statistical functions. For instance, DAVG returns an average of values defined in a database; AVG returns an average of values defined in its argument list. DCOUNT counts the number of items in a particular area of the database; COUNT counts the number of items defined in its argument list.

Each of the database functions has the same type of arguments. The database range (input) must include all the database records and their field names. The offset column (offset) is the column number containing the field you want to work with, and is determined by counting from the leftmost column of the database: the first column of the database range is field 0, the second column is field 1, and so forth. The Criteria Range, a separate area of the database, must use the same field names as the database range, with the criteria shown directly below each field name.

For further discussion of the database capabilities of Wingz, see Chapter 8.

DAVG(input,offset,criteria)

DAVG calculates the average of the values in the offset column (offset) of the database range (input) that meet the criteria specified in the criterion range (criteria).

Example: Assume you have a database in A1 through F15, with the criteria in A17 through F19. The function

=DAVG(A1..F15,3,A17..F19)

averages the values in column D (which is field 3, since column A is field 0) of the database range A1 through F15, which meet the criteria that are specified in A17 through F19.

DCOUNT(input,offset,criteria)

DCOUNT counts the nonblank cells in the offset column (offset) of the database range (input) that meet the criteria specified in the criterion range (criteria).

DMAX(input,offset,criteria)

DMAX determines the maximum numeric value in the offset column (offset) of the database range (input) that meets the criteria specified in the criterion range (criteria).

DMIN(input,offset,criteria)

DMIN determines the minimum numeric value in the offset column (offset) of the database range (input) that meets the criteria specified in the criterion range (criteria).

DSTD(input,offset,criteria)

DSTD determines population standard deviation for values in the offset column (offset) of the database range (input) that meet the criteria specified in the criterion range (criteria).

DSTDEV(input,offset,criteria)

DSTDEV determines the estimate of a standard deviation for the sample shown in the offset column (offset) of the database range (input) that meets the criteria specified in the criterion range (criteria).

DSUM(input,offset,criteria)

DSUM calculates the total of the values in the offset column (offset) of the database range (input) that meet the criteria specified in the criterion range (criteria).

DSUMSQ(input,offset,criteria)

DSUMSQ calculates the sum of the squares of the values in the offset column (offset) of the database range (input) that meet the criteria specified in the criterion range (criteria).

DVAR(input,offset,criteria)

DVAR calculates the variance for the entire population shown in the offset column (offset) of the database range (input) that meet the criteria specified in the criterion range (criteria).

DVARIANCE(input,offset,criteria)

DVARIANCE calculates the statistical variance for the values in the offset column (offset) of the database range (input) that meet the criteria specified in the criterion range (criteria).

TEXT FUNCTIONS

CHAR(x)

CHAR returns the text character corresponding to the ASCII code you specify as the argument x. The code can be from 1 to 255. See the ASCII chart in Appendix B.

Examples:

=CHAR(72)=H

=CHAR(52)=4

=CHAR(35)=#

CODE(text)

CODE returns the ASCII character that is equivalent to the first character in text. CODE is the inverse of CHAR.
Example:

CODE("Animal")=65

COLLATE(text1,text2)

COLLATE compares two text strings, specified as text1 and text2, to a collation table that is internal to Wingz, and returns −1 if text1 is greater than text2, 1 if text2 is greater than text1, and 0 if the two text strings are equal.

The table used by COLLATE is a sorting sequence used when sorting or merging alphabetic characters. It is not the same as the ASCII table, since it does not distinguish between upper- and lowercase letters, between accented and unaccented letters, or between punctuaion symbols. The collation table assigns weights to the letters A (low) to Z (high), followed by the numbers zero (low) to 9 (high).
Examples:

COLLATE("A","a") = 0

COLLATE("A","B") = -1

COLLATE("B","a") = 1

COLLATE("a","4") = -1

CONTAINS(textsearch,text)

CONTAINS looks through searchtext for text, and returns a 1 if the text string includes the characters specified in text, or a zero if text is not found within searchtext. The value specified in searchtext can be text, numbers, or cell references, but text and numbers must be enclosed in double quotes. Spaces in text cause an error message.

CONTAINS is case sensitive, meaning that text must be entered in the appropriate combination of upper and lowercase letters. You may not use the wildcard characters * and ? within text, since Wingz considers them literal characters.

Examples:

=SEARCH("11223344556677889900","5") = 1

=SEARCH("April","i") = 1

CURRENCY(x)

CURRENCY reformats the number you specify as x into a currency value, with the appropriate currency symbol and two decimal places. The number can be any positive or negative number or numeric expression, or 0.
Examples:

=CURRENCY(543.21) = $543.21

=CURRENCY(543.21–246.88) = $296.33

=CURRENCY(987654321e-2) = $9,876,543.21

EXACT(text1,text2)

EXACT tests to see if text1 and text2 are exactly the same. EXACT returns the value TRUE if text1 and text2 are exactly the same. If they're not identical, EXACT returns the value FALSE.

The arguments text1 and text2 must be text values, or references to text values.
Examples:

=EXACT("this","this") = TRUE

=EXACT("this","that") = FALSE

=EXACT("This","this") = FALSE

FIND(searchtext,text,start)

FIND allows you to search a specified set of text (searchtext), beginning at the start character position, for a specific character string (text), and returns the character position within searchtext at which text first occurs. (The first character of searchtext is character 1. However, the number you specify as start starts with 0 for the first character in searchtext, 1 for the second, etc.)

The text to be searched is specified as searchtext, and may be the name of a cell containing text. You indicate what you want to find as text. FIND is case sensitive, and you may not use wildcard characters in text.

Examples:

=FIND("Ampersand","A",0) = 1

=FIND("Ampersand","a",6) = 7

=FIND("Ampersand","and",1) = 7

=FIND(D5,"and",5) = 7 where cell D5 contains the text "Ampersand"

LEFT(text,n)

LEFTextracts the leftmost *n* characters of text. LEFT counts the characters in text and copies the leftmost *n* characters of them into the current cell.
Examples:

=LEFT("Paul Gauguin",6) = "Paul G"

=LEFT("80386–inspired architecture",5) = "80386"

=LEFT(A42,7) = "FY 1988" if A42 contained the text string "FY 1988: 3rd Quarter"

LENGTH(text)

LENGTH measures the length of text and returns the number of characters it finds. LENGTH is particularly useful when you prepare to insert text of uncertain length into some other cell. In some of these cases, it may be useful to widen the cell width to accommodate the full length of text string.

Examples:

=LENGTH("Mendocino") = 9

=LENGTH(Name) = 25 if the first cell of the range named Name has text that is 25 characters wide

LOWER(text)

LOWER converts text to all lowercase. LOWER is the opposite of UPPER, in that LOWER makes all characters in text lowercase, whereas UPPER capitalizes all letters in the specified text.

Examples:

=LOWER("JANUARY") = january

=LOWER("First Friday") = first friday

=LOWER(B37) = prices if cell B37 contains "Prices"

MATCH(text,searchtext,start)

MATCH looks for the character string specified as text with the character string searchtext, starting at character position start. MATCH lets you pinpoint a specific text string, and returns the character number within the specified text where it was found. The text string you're after is text, and the text you want to search is searchtext.

MATCH is case sensitive, meaning that text must be entered in the appropriate combination of upper- and lowercase letters. The wildcards * and ? are not recognized as operators, but as text to be matched.

Examples:

=MATCH("5","0123456789",1) = 6

=MATCH("i","April",1) = 4

=MATCH("tart","false start",2) = 8

MID(text,start,n)

MID extracts *n* of characters from text, starting at character position start. MID allows you to copy a specified number of characters from text, beginning wherever you specify within the text string. If start is greater than the length of text, the result is "", the empty text value.

MID can be useful in a situation where some other manipulation has removed all spaces from text, and now you need some of the characters from within that compacted text.

Examples:

=MID("Here'sasampleofcompactedtext",8,6) = "sample"

=MID("4007 Hall Blvd. NE",6,20) = "Hall Blvd. NE"

N(range)

N returns the numeric value of the upper left cell in range.
Example:

=N(Costs) = 4452 if the range named Costs has the figure 4452 in its upper left cell

NFORMAT(number,format)

NFORMAT puts number in a cell and assigns a format and attributes to it, depending on the sum of the formats and attributes chosen from the list below:

0	General
16	Fixed
22	Currency
48	Percent
64	Scientific
80	Date 1: "D-MON-YY"
96	Date 2: "D-Mon"
112	Date 3: "Mon-YY"
128	Date 4: "MM-DD-YY"
144	Date 5: "MM-DD"
160	Time 1: "HR:MN:SC:AM"
176	Time 2: "HR"MN AM"
192	Time 3: "HM:MN"SC"
208	Time 4: "HH:MN"

110 Mastering Wingz

   256   Parentheses
   512   Comma
   1024   Hide Zero

You specify more than one format attribute by adding the code numbers for the attributes you want: if you want to use Fixed and Parentheses, for instance, add their attribute code numbers: 16 + 256 = 272. If you want to use Currency and uae commas, add the code numbers: 32 + 512 = 544.

Don't use more than one date format, or one time format.

PROPER(text)

PROPER Converts text to initial capitals. PROPER capitalizes all text strings it finds in text. It considers anything that follows a space or punctuation to be a text string.

Examples:

=PROPER("JAN FEB MAR APR") = "Jan Feb Mar Apr"

=PROPER("It's a boy!") = "It'S A Boy!"

REPEAT(text,n)

REPEAT repeats text, the text string you specify, n number of times. REPEAT allows you to repeat a character or set of characters the number of times you specify.

Examples:

REPEAT("^-^ ",4) = "^-^ ^-^ ^-^ ^-^ "

REPEAT("phth",5) = "phthphthphthphthphth"

REPLACE(text,start,n,newtext)

REPLACE replaces *n* number of characters in text with newtext, starting at character position start. REPLACE allows you selectively to replace characters in text. You have to specify how many characters from the beginning of text for the operation to start, and how many characters are to be replaced.

Examples:

=REPLACE("Proj. Mgr: Linda Smith",12,11,"Duc Ng") ="Proj. Mgr: Duc Ng"

=REPLACE("Review 12/1/87",8,7,"6/1/88") = "Review 6/1/88"

RIGHT(text,n)

RIGHT returns the rightmost *n* characters in text. RIGHT counts the characters in text, and copies the rightmost n of them into the current cell.

Examples:

= RIGHT("George O'Keeffe",8)

= "O'Keeffe"

=RIGHT("432SheratonLane,Overton,CA95977",5)

= "95977"

S(range)

S returns the contents of the upper left cell of range as text.
Example:

S(E22..G25) = "July 15, 1990" if cell E22 contains the date July 15, 1990

STR(x,n)
STRING(x,n)

STR and STRING return *x*, the numerical value you specify, as a text string. The number *n* is the numer of significant digits to be returned. The difference between STR and STRING is that with STR, the argument *n* is optional; with STRING, the *n* is required.

Examples:

=STR(54321) = "54321"

=STRING(54321,2) = "543.21"

=STR(10000) = "10000"

=STRING(10000,4) = "1.0000"

TRIM(text)

TRIM removes spaces from text. TRIM compacts a text string, leaving only one space between words. It also removes any leading and trailing spaces.
Examples:

=TRIM("123 4567 8998") = "123 4567 8998"

=TRIM(" 125 Cherry Ave. ") = "125 Cherry Ave."

UPPER(text)

UPPER converts text to uppercase letters. UPPER converts all of the text you enter or reference as an argument to uppercase letters. It's the inverse of LOWER.
Examples:

=UPPER("September") = "SEPTEMBER"

=UPPER(C5) = "TOTAL AMOUNT DUE" if C5 contained the text "Total Amount Due"

VALUE(text)

VALUE converts text to a number.

VALUE translates a text representation of a number to its numeric value. It works on any of the number, date, or time formats recognized by Wingz. However, conversion stops at the first character that can't be interpreted as part of a number.
Examples:

=VALUE("November 15, 1988")=11/15/1988

VALUE("15:58:00")-VALUE("11:10:00")=0.2, the serial number equivalent to 4 hours, 48 minutes.

SPREADSHEET FUNCTIONS

CELL()

CELL returns the contents of the current cell. Its primary use is with other functions, notably the FIND function, which allows you to define a logical expression. CELL is useful to search for particular information.

If the current cell contains a formula, CELL returns the results of the formula, not the formula itself.

Examples:

=CELL() = $42.50 if that's the contents of the current cell

=CELL() = November 15, 1988 if the contents of the current cell contains the formula NOW() and today is Nov. 15, 1988

CELLTEXT(cell)

CELLTEXT is like CELL, in that it returns the contents of a cell. However, unlike CELL, you can specify a cell other than the current one with CELLTEXT. Also, CELLTEXT returns the information as text.

You can specify a single cell or cell range as the argument with CELLTEXT; however, what will appear in the current cell is only the contents of the first cell in the given range.

Examples:

=CELLTEXT(A5) = "Prices" if cell A5 contains the text Prices
=CELLTEXT(B42..B45) = "March" if the range contains text as follows:

	B
42	March
43	April
44	May
45	June

CHOOSE(n,itemlist)

CHOOSE uses the number you specify as *n* to select a value from itemlist. CHOOSE works somewhat like the LOOKUP functions, except that CHOOSE works with any of the values referenced in the itemlist, rather than just those arranged in table form.

The first item in the list has a reference value of 0, the second has a value of 1, the third has a value of 2, etc. If *n* is negative or greater than one less than the number of items in the list, you'll get an error message.

The arguments for CHOOSE can be range references as well as individual values. These allow you some interesting possibilities for calculations:

=SUM(CHOOSE(Offset,C5:C9,D5:D9,E5:E9))

lets you sum the results of one of the three ranges shown, depending on whether the named cell Offset contains a 0, 1, or 2.

You can also use CHOOSE in a macro with GOTOs as the value arguments. For instance, you could use the following functions in a macro:

=CHOOSE(Counter,GOTO(First),GOTO(Second),GOTO(Third))
Examples:

=CHOOSE(A5,"Pass","Fail","Conditional")="Pass" if A5 contains 0
=SUM(D23:CHOOSE(F2,D32,D36,D40))=SUM(D23:D40) if F2 contains 2

COL()

COL returns the column number or letter(s) of the columns specified in range. If there is more than one column involved in range, Wingz will return all the column numbers or letters. If you are using the A1 naming convention, you'll see the column letters; if you are using the R1C1 naming convention, you'll see column numbers.

Example:

COL(A5:D16) = A,B,C,D

COLOF(range)

COLOF returns the column number of the first column in the range specified.
Examples:

=COLOF(B5..J14)=2
=COLOF(AC34..AZ34)=29

COLS(range)

COLS returns the number of columns specified in range.
Examples:

=COLS(D5) = 1
=COLS(D5:G20) = 4

ERR()

The ERR function returns the value ERR. It's usually used in tests of certain conditions, such as in an IF function, when it's necessary to report an error condition.

Note: Wingz uses the Macintosh System Error notation to report an error where this function is used. Consult your Macintosh system documentation for other error numbers and explanations.
Examples:

=ERR() = ERR26

=IF(A15>0,A15,ERR()) = whatever is in A15 if it's a positive value, otherwise it returns ERR26

HLOOKUP(x,range,row)

HLOOKUP finds a value in a column labeled *x* of the table defined by Range down the number of rows specified by Row, and returns the value it finds there. The functions HLOOKUP and VLOOKUP let Wingz find values from a table in much the same way you scan a table. HLOOKUP assumes the values in the top row of the table are stored in ascending order from left to right in two or more rows; VLOOKUP assumes the values in the leftmost column of the table are stored in ascending order from top to bottom in two or more columns.

With HLOOKUP, Wingz scans the top row of table, looking for the last value that equals or doesn't exceed *x*. Having found that, it drops down the number of rows indicated in Offset, and returns the value it finds there.

HLOOKUP lends itself nicely to dealing with tax tables. For instance, suppose you wanted to determine the amount of straight-line depreciation for property, using a table that shows the percentages for properties with various standard useful lives. Below is such a tax table:

Depreciation rate for recovery period, by years

	A	B	C	D	E	F	G
10		3	5	7	10	15	20
11	1	33.33%	20.00%	14.29%	10.00%	5.00%	3.75%
12	2	44.45%	32.00%	24.49%	18.00%	9.50%	7.219%
13	3	14.81%	19.20%	17.49%	14.40%	8.55%	6.677%

where rows 11 through 13 are for years 1, 2, and 3 in each category. If you wanted to determine the depreciation for an item with a 7–year life, in its third year, the HLOOKUP function to do this would look like this:

=HLOOKUP(7,AB10:AG13,3)=17.49%

and depreciation for the second year of an item with a 15–year life would look like this:

=HLOOKUP(15,A10:G13,2)=9.50%

INDEX(range,column,row)

INDEX works a bit like HLOOKUP and VLOOKUP, in that it considers the indicated range to be a table, and returns a value indicated by the other two arguments. The difference is that INDEX lets you specify by number which column and which row contains the cell whose contents you're after.

As with the LOOKUP functions, the column and row arguments are counted from the top left edge of the table, not from the edges of the worksheet. 1 is the top row within the range, regardless of its actual row number, 2 is the second row, etc. The same principle is used to number

columns within a range: 1 is the leftmost column within the range, 2 is the second column, etc.
Example:

Suppose you have the following table listing, among other things, various types of lettuce seeds for your nursery. It's keyed to a stock number as follows:

	A	B	C
35	Simpson	1.85	B-59535
36	Royal Oak Leaf	2.10	B-58982
37	Buttercrunch	1.95	B-59543
38	Great Lakes	1.95	B-59550
40	White Cos	1.95	B-59014
41	Ruby	1.95	B-59048
42	Tango	2.10	B-59600
43	Arugula	1.00	B-59128

To obtain the stock number of White Cos seeds, the INDEX function would look like this:

=INDEX(A35:C42,5,3) = "B-59014"

INDIRECT(text)

INDIRECT evaluates the text you give, and returns what it finds. This function is particularly useful when you need to find the contents of a cell where you need to make an indirect reference to it.
Examples:

=INDIRECT("Costs") = Costs

=INDIRECT(4*C2) = 96 if C2 contains 24

=INDIRECT(G34) = $502.35 if G34 contains the cell reference D25, and D25 contains $502.35

MAKECELL(column,row)

MAKECELL creates as text the cell reference corresponding to the numbers you specify for column and row. While row numbers are acceptable, no matter which cell naming convention you're using, you must specify the desired column by number, not letter.

You can also make indirect references to the column and row numbers.
Examples:

=MAKECELL(5,2) = E2

=MAKECELL(Offset+5,4) = F4 when the cell named Offset contains 2

MAKERANGE(column1,row1,column2,row2)

MAKERANGE lets you denote a range by specifying the numbers of its topmost and bottommost rows (row1 and row2, respectively), and leftmost and rightmost columns (column1 and column2, respectively).

As with MAKECELL, rows and columns must be specified by number, not with the A1 cell-naming convention.
Example:

=MAKERANGE(5,8,7,8) = r5c7..r8c8

NA()

NA returns the value N/A wherever it is used. N/A (Not Available) is used to indicate that a cell's value has not yet been calculated. All cells that reference a cell containing the N/A value will themselves have the value N/A.

RANGE(text)

RANGE returns True (1) if text is a valid range reference, or False (0) if it is not.
Examples:

=RANGE(G4..H8) = 1.00

=RANGE(Master) = 1.00 if Master is a range name

=RANGE("Master") = 0 because "Master" is text

ROW()

ROW returns the row number of the cell in which the formula containing ROW() is located.

ROWOF(range)

ROWOF returns the row number of the first row in the range specified. Examples:

    =ROWOF(B5..J14)=5
    =ROWOF(AC34..AZ34)=34

ROWS(range)

ROWS returns the number of rows in range.
Example:

    =ROWS(S35..T39) = 5

VLOOKUP(x,range,column)

VLOOKUP finds a value in the first column of the table defined in range that does not exceed x, then returns the value in that row that is the specified number of columns to the right. VLOOKUP inspects the first column of range for a value that is less than or equal to x. It then indexes over the specified number of columns and returns the value it finds there.

Like HLOOKUP, VLOOKUP lends itself nicely to tax table work. For instance, suppose you want the program to determine your tax based on your taxable income and status. (You actually could use Wingz to determine tax amounts, using the current year's tax tables from the appropriate IRS document and a combination of lookup functions and mathematical operations.) A portion of a tax table might look like the one at the top of the following page.

A VLOOKUP function to determine the tax for a single taxpayer with a taxable income of $30,335 would look like this:

    =VLOOKUP(30225,A10:E19,4) = 5373

	A	B	C	D	E
		Single	Mar/joint	Mar/sep.	Head hshld
10	30050	6363	4647	7054	5317
11	30100	6380	4661	7071	5331
12	30150	6398	4675	7089	5345
13	30200	6415	4689	7106	5359
14	30250	6433	4703	7124	5373
15	30300	6450	4717	7141	5387
16	30350	6468	4731	7159	5401
17	30400	6485	4745	7176	5415
18	30450	503	4759	7194	5429
19	30500	6520	4773	7211	5443

NUMERIC FUNCTIONS

ABS(x)

The ABS function returns the absolute value of number, which is the value of a number without its sign.
Examples:

=ABS(3) = 3

=ABS(-3) = 3

ACOS(x)

ACOS returns the trigonometric arc cosine of the number you specify. The arc cosine of a number is the angle in radians whose cosine is the number. The number you specify must be between -1 and 1.
Examples:

=ACOS(-0.5) = 2.09

=ACOS(1) = 0

=ACOS(0) = 1.57

ACOSH(x)

ACOSH returns the hyperbolic arc cosine of the number you specify. The number you specify must be 1 or greater. The result will be a nonnegative value.

Examples:

=ACOSH(1) = 0.00
=ACOSH(2) = 1.32

ASIN(x)

ASIN returns the trigonometric arc sine of the number you specify. The arc sine of a number is the angle in radians whose sine is the number. The number you specify must be between -1 and 1.

Examples:

=ASIN(0) = 0.00
=ASIN(1) = 1.57

ASINH(x)

ASINH returns the hyperbolic arc sine of the number you specify. The number you specify is given in radians, and can be any value or numeric expression.

Examples:

=ASINH(1) = 0.88
=ASINH(0) = 0.00

ATAN(x)

ATAN rturns the trigonometric arc tangent of the number you specify. The arc tangent of an angle is the angle in radians whose tangent is the number given.

Examples:

=ATAN(1) =0.79
=ATAN(0) = 0

ATANH(x)

ATANH returns the hyperbolic arc tangent of the number you specify. The value specified as x can be any number between but not including -1 and 1.
Examples:

=ATANH(.5) = 0.55
=ATANH(-.25) = -0.26

ATAN2(x,y)

ATAN2 returns the arctangent of point defined by xnumber and ynumber. ATAN2 determines the arc tangent of the angle represented by the angle represented by the x-axis and a line drawn from the point of coordinates xnumber and ynumber to the zero point on both axes. The result is an angle in radians. A positive result is a counterclockwise angle from the x-axis; a negative result is a clockwise angle.
Examples:

=ATAN2(1,2) = 1.107149
=ATAN2(-5,10) = 2.034444
=ATAN2(-1,-1)*180/PI() = 135 degrees

COS(x)

The COS function returns the trigonometric cosine of the value you specify in radians, where x is an angle ranging from -1 to 1.
Examples:

=COS(1) = 0.54
=COS(0) = 1.00
=COS(60*PI()/180) = 0.50

COSH(x)

The COSH function returns the hyperbolic cosine of the value you specify in radians, where x is any positive or negative number or 0.

Examples:

=COSH(0) = 1.00

=COSH(.24) = 1.03

DEGREES(radians)

The DEGREES function converts the number you specify from radians to degrees.
Examples:

=DEGREES(180) = 3.14

=DEGREES(90) = 1.57

E()

The E function returns the value of e, 2.7182818. It's used as a constant in logarithmic expressions.

EXP(x)

The EXP function returns the constant e ($e = 2.718 \ldots$) to the power of the number specified as x.

The constant e, 2.71828182845904, is the base of the natural logarithm. The EXP function calculates e raised to the power of the number you specify. (To calculate powers of other bases, use the ^ to indicate exponentiation.)

EXP is the inverse of LN, the natural log of number.
Example:

=EXP(1) = 2.71828182845904

EXPONENTIAL(x)

The EXPONENTIAL function selects a random number from an exponential distribution that uses the mean specified as *x*part. For example, EXPONENTIAL(10) returns a random positive number, and EXPONENTIAL(-1) returns a random negative number.

FACTORIAL(x)

The factorial of a number is equivalent to:

(number)*(number-1)*(number-2)*...*(number-n)

where (number-n)=1. Number should be an integer, or the noninteger part is truncated.

Examples:

=FACTORIAL(1) = 1
=FACTORIAL(2.5) = 2
=FACTORIAL(4) = 24

GOAL(initial,result,formula)
GUESS()

You use GOAL and GUESS when you're trying to find a value for a term in an equation that will make the equation true. The formula can be as simple as $X + 2 = 5$ or as complex as a some financial computation involving many iterations. You use GUESS as part of formula within GOAL.

To use GOAL, specify a formula with an unknown term, represented by GUESS, the desired result (what would be on the right side of the equation, such as GUESS ^ 3 = 9), and an initial estimate as to what GUESS will be. Using your initial estimate, GOAL calculates the formula and compares it with your initial estimate. It recalculates up to 20 times, trying to reach the same result twice or until two successive calculations differ by less than 0.0000001.

It's important to make your initial estimate as close as you can to what you expect the result to be for GUESS, or what you get after 20 calculations may differ too much from your estimate and hence not be very useful. Rather than specify very small numbers in the arguments, use the numbers you want multiplied by some large constant, such as 1000. Because of the nature of the calculations, more accurate results happen when you work with larger numbers. When GOAL has finished calculating, you can then divide the result by your large constant.

Example:

GOAL(2.5,216,6^GUESS()) = 3.00

INT(x)

The INT function returns the number you specify rounded down to the nearest integer. INT shaves off the decimal or fractional part of number, and leaves the integer part. It rounds the number to the nearest integer.

Examples:

=INT(3.14159)=3

=INT(4*B55)= the integer portion of the result of multiplying the contents of B55 times 4.

LN(x)

LN returns the natural logarithm of the number you specify, using the mathematical constant e as a base. The number you specify as x must be positive. LN is the inverse of the EXP function.

Examples:

=LN(100) = 4.61

=LN(2.7182818) = 1.00

=LN(EXP(4)) = 4.00

LOG

LOG returns the base 10 logarithm of a number you specify.

LOGN(x,logbase)

LOGN(x,logbase) returns the logarithm of the number you specify, in the base you specify as logbase. Both LOG and LOGN return the logarithm of the number you specify. Because you omit the base with the LOG function, Wingz assumes it to be 10, and the result is the same as if you had used the LOGN function and specified logbase as 10.

Examples:

=LOG(10) = 1.00

=LOGN(10,10) = 1.00

=LOG(86,2.7182828) = 4.45

MOD(x,y)

MOD returns the remainder of x divided by y. MOD evaluates the formula number/divisor, where divisor is any number other than zero, and returns the remainder (modulus). The result has the same sign as divisor. If divisor is zero, you'll get an error message.
Examples:

=MOD(8,2) = 0 (8/2 has no remainder)

=MOD(7/2) = 1.00

=MOD(3,-2) = 1.00

=MOD(-3,2) = –1.00

NORMAL(x)

NORMAL selects a random number from a normal distribution, based on a standard deviation you specify as *x*.
Example:

=NORMAL(3.55) = -2.14

PI()

PI returns the number 3.14159265358979, rounded to the format used in that cell. The parentheses are required.

=PI() = 3.14159

RADIANS(degrees)

RADIANS converts the number you specify as degrees to radians.
Examples:

=RADIANS(45) = 2578.31

=RADIANS(25) = 12891.55

RAND()

RAND returns a random number between 0 and 1.

ROUND(x,n)

ROUND returns the number you specify as *x*, rounded off to *n* number of decimal places.
Examples:

=ROUND(3.14159,2) = 3.14
=ROUND(.55903534,1) = .6

SIGN(number)

SIGN returns a number with the same sign as number. If you specify a positive number as number, SIGN returns 1. If you specify a negative number, SIGN returns −1. If you specify 0, SIGN returns 0.
  You can also specify a numeric expression as number.
Examples:

=SIGN(54678) = 1
=SIGN(-3.112) = -1
=SIGN(0) = 0

=SIGN(54–60) = -1 SIN(x)

The SIN function returns the trigonometric sine of the value you specify in radians, where *x* is an angle.
Examples:

=SIN(0.5) = 0.48
=SIN(1) = 0.84

SINH(x)

The SINH function returns the hyperbolic sine of the value you specify, which can be any positive or negative number or 0 value.

Examples:

=SINH(.5) = 0.52
=SINH(1) = 1.18

SQRT(x)

SQRT calculates the square root of the number you specify as x. (x must be greater than 0.)

Examples:

=SQRT(5.44) = 2.33
=SQRT(43229) = 207.92

TAN(x)

TAN returns the tangent of the value you specify in radians, where x *for example is an angle.*
Examples:

=TAN(4) = 1.16
=TAN(0) = 0
=TAN(45*PI()/180) = 1 (the tangent of 45 degrees)

TANH(x)

The TANH function returns the hyperbolic tangent of the number you specify, where the number can be any value expressed in radians.
Examples:

=TANH(2) =0.96
=TANH(-1.5) = -0.91

UNIFORM(x)

UNIFORM returns a number selected randomly from between 0 and the number you specify as x.

OPERATORS

Wingz recognizes the following operators or symbols in calculating the results of a formula. Where there are two or more operators in a formula, and parentheses *do not* enclose an operation, they are processed in the following order. (Portions of a formula that are enclosed in parentheses are calculated first, then normal calculation order is used.)

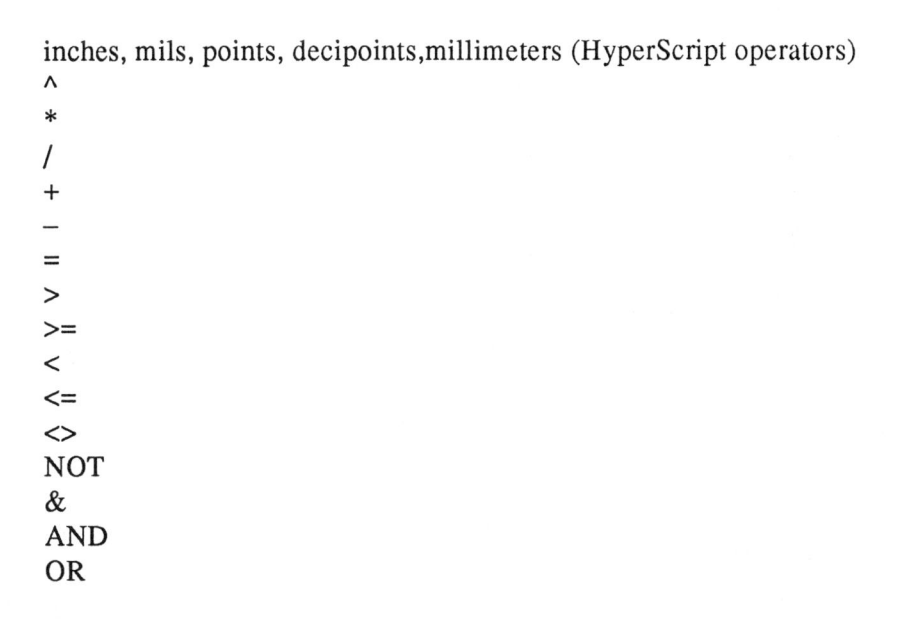

inches, mils, points, decipoints, millimeters (HyperScript operators)
^
*
/
+
−
=
>
>=
<
<=
<>
NOT
&
AND
OR

OTHER FUNCTIONS

There are hundreds of other functions available with the HyperScript language, falling into general categories COLOR, ENVIRONMENT, CONTROL, and MISCELLANEOUS. Users can create custom functions with the HyperScript language.

We'll look at using HyperScript in Chapter 11.

5

Charts and Graphs

The single most impressive aspect of Wingz is its handling of charts and graphs. You can get your data displayed in any of 20 different chart types. And in dazzling color, if your Macintosh is enabled for color graphics. Given Wingz' presentation capabilities, you can use your data to create impressive charts and graphs, in three dimensions if appropriate, and insert them in a page of text, along with pictures or drawings to help explain your point.

Data are more meaningful to a wider spectrum of people if it's presented graphically. The introduction of the Macintosh, with its icon and graphics orientation, was based in part on the premise that people made meaningful decisions about information presented in pictures, as well as words and numbers. *USA Today*, the national daily newspaper, has demonstrated that a significant percentage of the population chooses a news environment where information is presented graphically. National television networks have discovered that comparative information, such as that originally arranged in a table, is better communicated with graphic images than with "talking heads."

On a smaller scale, the tools associated with desktop publishing suddenly made it possible for even the smallest of organizations to produce professional-looking newsletters, memos, and reports. These desktop publishing tools allowed people quickly and easily to integrate words and graphics in a way that really communicated.

In terms of development philosophy, Wingz is firmly a part of the desktop publishing environment. Its ability to create sharp, multidimensional charts and graphs surpasses the graphing abilities of any other Macintosh spreadsheet program on the market today.

This chapter will show you how to translate your data into graphs, and will give you some ideas about which types of graphs are appropriate for different kinds of data.

DIVISIONS AND SERIES

When you create a chart or graph, you work with divisions and series. **Divisions** are the columns of data that are frequently displayed in bar or stacked bar form. **Series** are often represented as lines, pie slices, bars, or points in a scattergram. You select the range of cells containing the data that will be made into your chart. Once selected, those data will always be reflected in the chart. If you change or move the data, or insert or delete anything, the chart will also change.

CREATING A CHART

Let's illustrate this with some data. We used some U.S. Census projections for a few selected zip codes, and created the following chart shown by Figure 5-4. We'll use these data to create several new charts.

First, select the data. Let's look at the income projections for some of the zip codes. To keep things simple, let's use just the first three columns of data, for zip codes 94306, 94301, and 94302.

First step: Select the data. We want the row labels in column A, rows 4 through 11, and the corresponding data in rows B, C, and D. Notice that we're not selecting the column headings in row 3—we'll deal with that in a moment. To select the data, position the mouse pointer in A4, click and drag the mouse so that A4 through D11 is highlighted (see Figure 5-3).

Charts and Graphs 133

	A	B	C	D	E	F	G
1	Projected Household Income, by Zip Code, 1992						
2							
3		94306	94301	94022	94025	94040	94043
4	$0 - 7,499	529	412	302	1026	657	759
5	$7,500-9,999	191	148	106	379	236	278
6	$10,000-14,999	585	466	317	1004	694	696
7	$15,000-24,999	1260	956	649	2253	1599	1860
8	$25,000-34,999	1384	995	860	2320	1797	2239
9	$35,000-49,999	1924	1275	1660	3323	2479	2846
10	$50,000-74,999	2351	1337	3049	4015	2343	2366
11	over $75,000	3027	2184	8150	7984	2591	1607
12							
13	Total # households	11251	7773	15093	22303	12396	12651
14							
15	Projected Population, by Zip Code, 1992						
16		94306	94301	94022	94025	94040	94043
17	0-5	1074	596	1886	2721	1125	1973
18	6-13	1586	894	2705	3864	1636	2668
19	14-17	878	497	1640	2286	818	1334
20	18-24	1903	1176	4058	5116	1610	2501
21	25-34	3856	2170	6312	8272	4243	4225
22	35-44	5027	3279	4181	7511	5598	6865
23	45-54	3489	2451	6148	7184	3399	3474
24	55-64	2562	1623	5739	6204	2684	2029
25	65 and over	4026	3876	8321	11266	4447	2724
26							
27	Total population	24402	16562	40990	54424	25560	27793

FIGURE 5-1   Projected Income and Population, 1992.

FIGURE 5-2   Highlighted Block

	A	B	C	D	E	F	G
1	Projected Household Income, by Zip Code, 1992						
2							
3		94306	94301	94022	94025	94040	94043
4	$0 - 7,499	529	412	302	1026	657	759
5	$7,500-9,999	191	148	106	379	236	278
6	$10,000-14,999	585	466	317	1004	694	696
7	$15,000-24,999	1260	956	649	2253	1599	1860
8	$25,000-34,999	1384	995	860	2320	1797	2239
9	$35,000-49,999	1924	1275	1660	3323	2479	2846
10	$50,000-74,999	2351	1337	3049	4015	2343	2366
11	over $75,000	3027	2184	8150	7984	2591	1607
12							
13	Total # households	11251	7773	15093	22303	12396	12651
14							
15	Projected Population, by Zip Code, 1992						
16		94306	94301	94022	94025	94040	94043
17	0-5	1074	596	1886	2721	1125	1973
18	6-13	1586	894	2705	3864	1636	2668
19	14-17	878	497	1640	2286	818	1334
20	18-24	1903	1176	4058	5116	1610	2501
21	25-34	3856	2170	6312	8272	4243	4225
22	35-44	5027	3279	4181	7511	5598	6865
23	45-54	3489	2451	6148	7184	3399	3474
24	55-64	2562	1623	5739	6204	2684	2029
25	65 and over	4026	3876	8321	11266	4447	2724
26							
27	Total population	24402	16562	40990	54424	25560	27793

Second step: Choose the chart tool, on the left side of the screen (see Figure 5-3).

Third step: Draw a chart window on your screen. This is the window in which your chart will appear, and it will overlay any other data. It won't destroy what's under it, and in fact will be stored separately but as a related item. Start with the pointer somewhere below the income data—we used the left side of cell A13—and click and drag the mouse so that you sketch a box outlined with a dashed line. Make sure your box is big enough to hold the graph and the legend.

Wingz displays a bar graph, in color if your computer has it (see Figure 5-4). Wingz has used the row labels on the left as labels for the series, and displays them in the legend on the right side of the window. Wingz has also scaled the graph to reflect the data proportionally, and displays its scale on the left.

Notice that, because we choose no column heading, there are no labels under the *x* axis showing what each of the divisions means. If you had chosen A3 as the starting cell in your selected range, you'd wind up with the zip

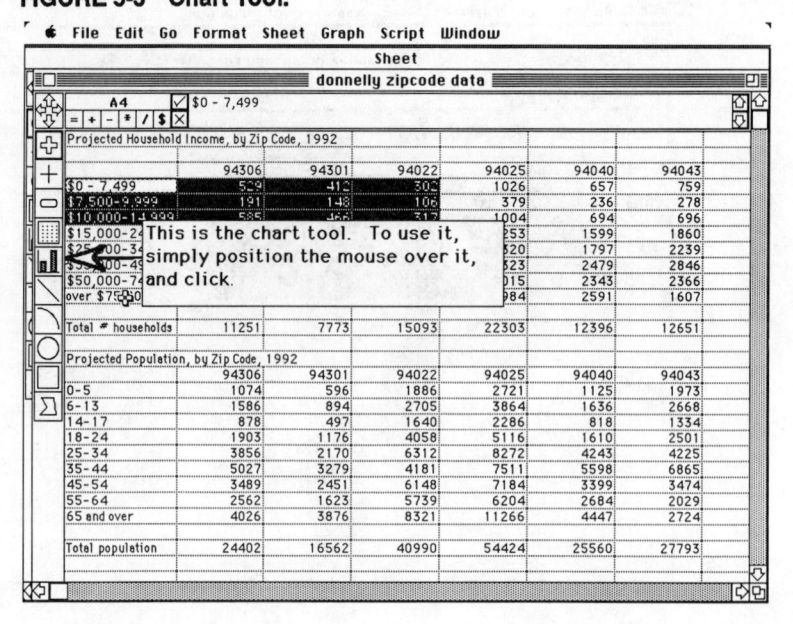

FIGURE 5-3   Chart Tool.

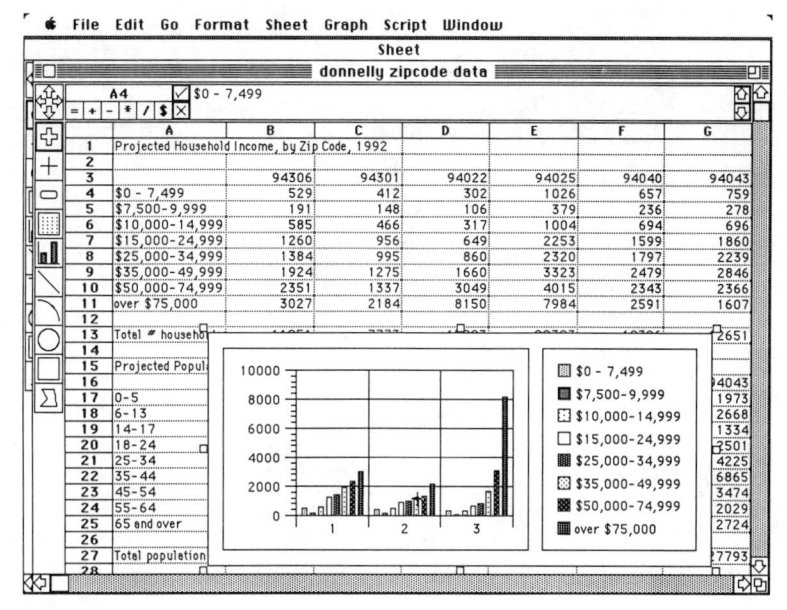

FIGURE 5-4 Initial Bar Graph.

codes as an element of data. We'll use the zip codes figure in a bit, after looking at some other elements.

Wingz also used its default form, the bar graph. You may use instead any of the other 19 graph forms available when you look at the Graph Gallery command. For instance, Figure 5-5 shows how the same data look as a line graph. Obviously, this form doesn't reflect what you want this graph to portray. What about a pie chart? As we can see from Figure 5-6, it looks reasonably good. We may want to use this form later on, after we add more data. But for now let's look at another possibility, the horizontal bar graph, shown in Figure 5-7.

Wingz also offers some three-dimensional options, which can make striking presentations. Figure 5-8 shows what the data look like using the 3D Bar option. This also has possibilities, but at the moment it doesn't appear to be the best way to portray our data. Let's go back to the Bar graph.

We still need to label the *x* axis of the graph. However, if we try to use numeric data, Wingz will try to graph it. Division labels need to be alphabetic data. In order to get that, we need to convert the zip codes to

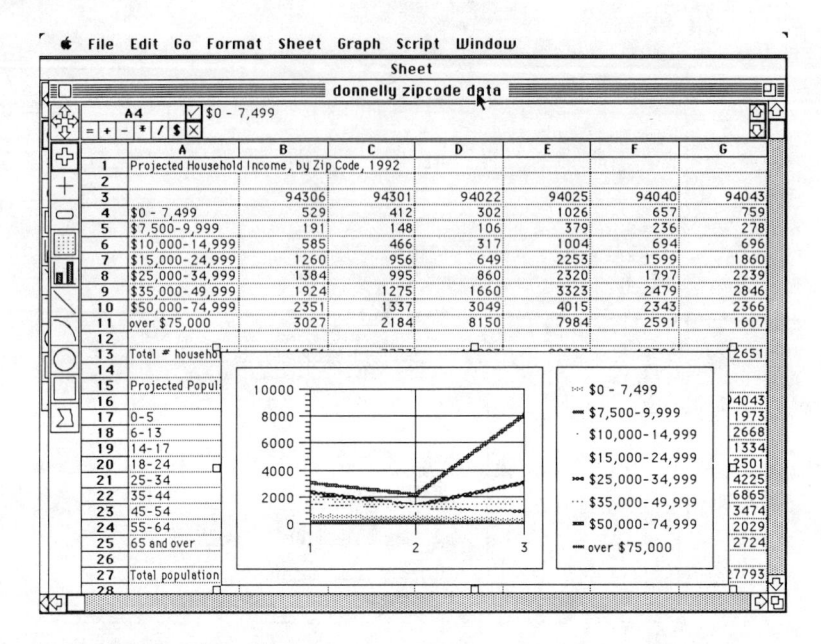

FIGURE 5-5 Line Graph.

FIGURE 5-6 Pie Chart.

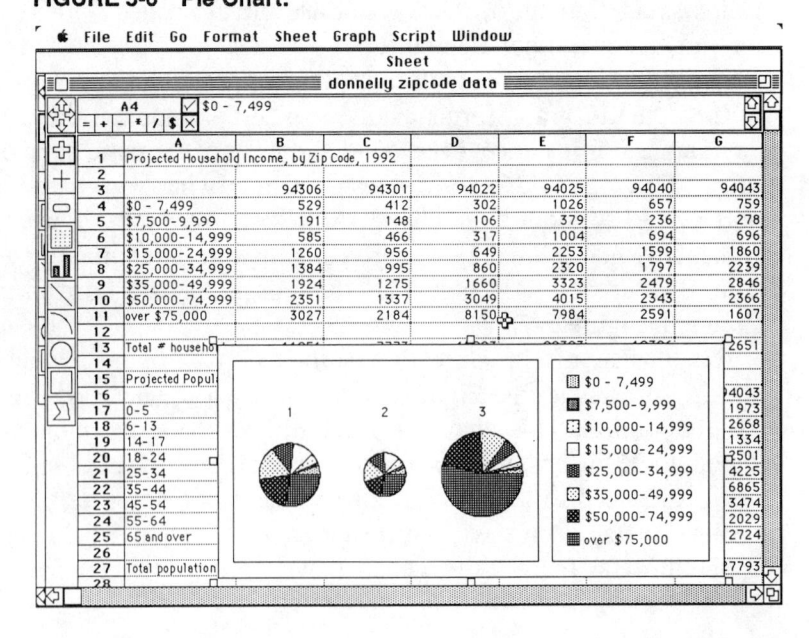

Charts and Graphs   137

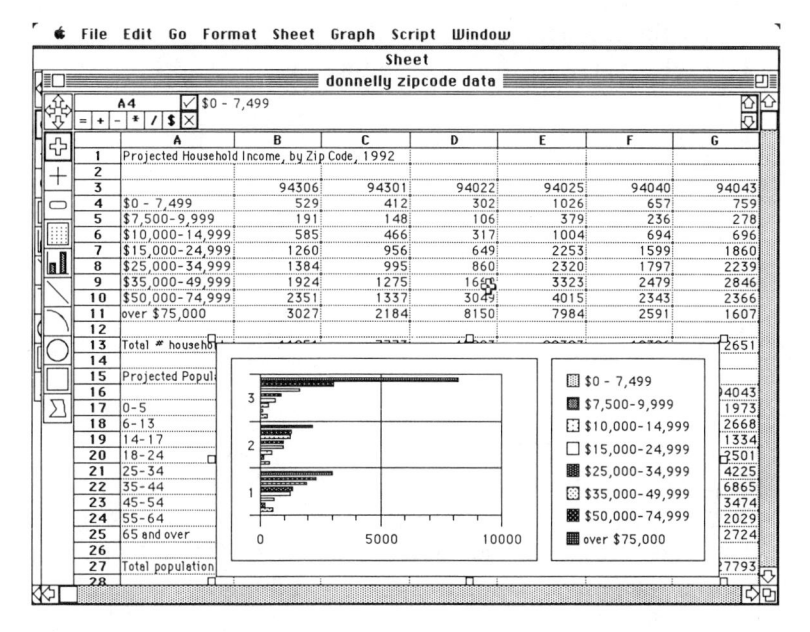

FIGURE 5-7   Horizontal Bar Graph.

FIGURE 5-8   3D Bar Graph.

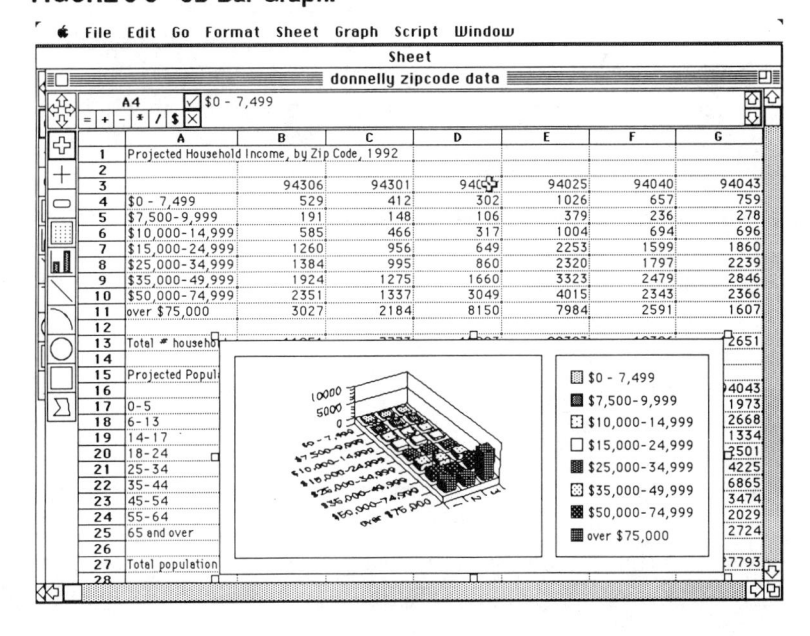

alphabetic data. One way to do that is to edit the contents of each of the zip code cells, using the String command:

=STR(94306)

makes the numeric data into a character string. Repeat the process for each of the zip codes. (You may wish to go back and use the Format Align command to right align the number, once it has become a string.) Note that Wingz regards dates and times as alphabetic data, in this case, so that whenever you use them as column labels, you won't have to make this adjustment.

We're going to make the zip codes into a division label, used on the *x*-axis. Click the worksheet tool, then position the mouse pointer on the *x*-axis of the chart, and click. You'll see a series of open circles to indicate that the axis has been selected. Then press the <Command> key (the one with the Apple symbol), and select the cells with the zip codes corresponding to the data we've used (B3 through D3). Finally, choose the Graph General command, and when the submenu appears, choose Division Label Range. As soon as you release the mouse button, the zip codes appear as the *x*-axis labels for your graph.

You need a title for your graph. Click on the upper portion of the graph to select the graph (it's shown with squares at the corners and along the edges when selected), hold down the <Command> key and select A1, the cell with the title. Then choose the Graph Title command, and the Title Range option. When you release the mouse button, your graph now has a title (see Figure 5-9).

This particular graph lends itself nicely to three-dimensional representation. Choose the 3D Bar option on the Gallery command. We saw it before, shown in Figure 5-9 above. To transform your bar graph into a 3D bar graph, simply choose the 3D Bar option on the Graph Gallery command. Let's experiment a bit with it.

As it's currently drawn, it's a small graph, somewhat difficult to see. Since we won't lose any data by making the graph bigger, and we don't need to see the data on the spreadsheet for now, we can enlarge the graph window.

If the small squares outlining the window aren't visible, click in the graph window to select it. Position the mouse carefully in the next step—it affects how Wingz moves the window. If you click in the upper right corner of the window (but inside the window), you'll be able to drag the entire window up and to the right, but not change its relative size. If you click in any of the

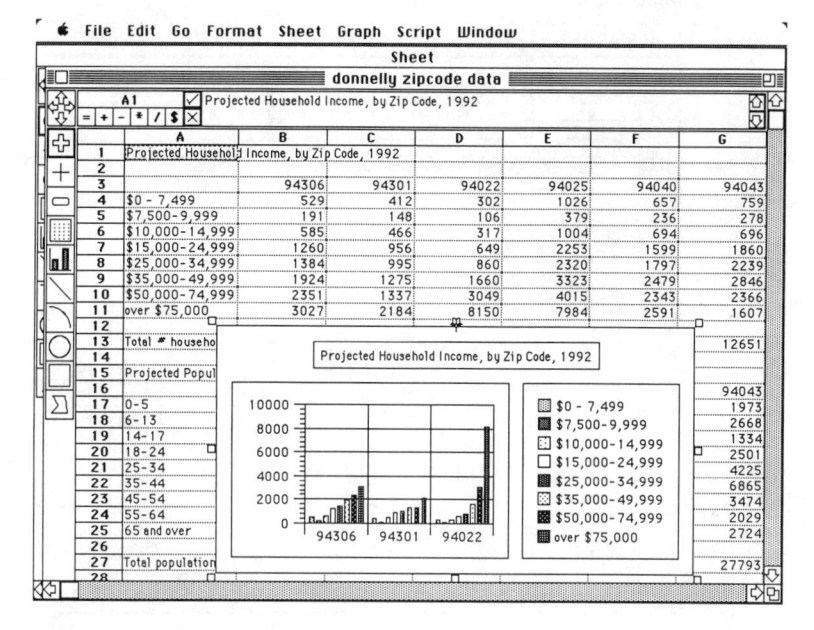

FIGURE 5-9 Bar Graph with Title.

small squares at the window's edge, you'll be able to drag that border (or borders, if you click in a corner box) so that it changes the relative size of the window. In this case, to make the window larger click in the upper right square and drag up and to the right. Notice that the entire graph is redrawn when you release the mouse button, and it's bigger (see Figure 5-10).

Some of the boxes are still difficult to see. They'd be easier to see if we could rotate the graph. You can do that with the View option on the Graph 3D Info command. When you choose that option, you're shown a dialog box that lets you choose the perspective of the box containing your graph (see Figure 5-11). The cube shows you the current perspective. The slide bars at the bottom and left side let you change that perspective: the bottom slide bar lets you tilt the chart forward and backward, and the left side bar lets you rotate the chart. The Vanishing X and Vanishing Y number bars let you determine the point on the "horizon" toward which the lines on the chart converge. The Distance number bar lets you control the perspective; lower numbers mean greater perspective.

It's difficult to see the "over $75,000" cubes in the current perspective. Let's change the perspective by adjusting the rotation. Slide the pointer to

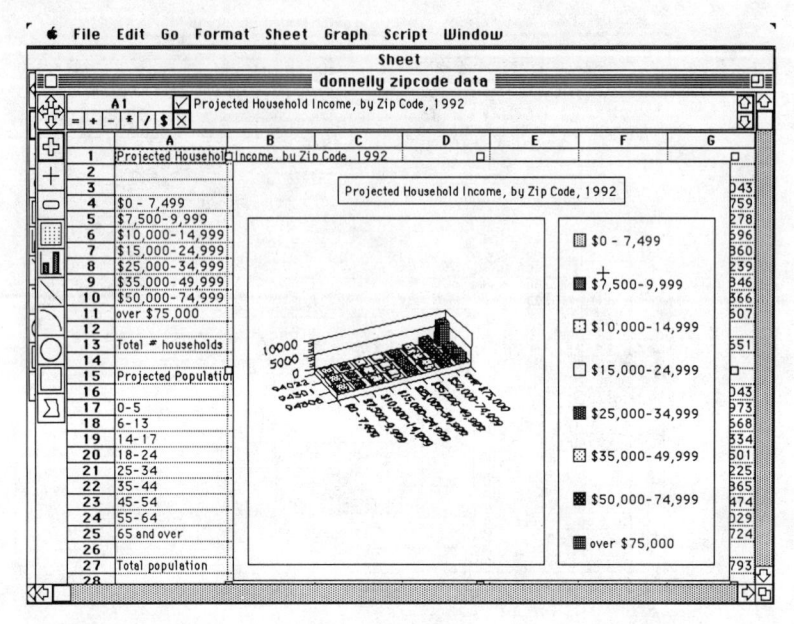

FIGURE 5-10   Enlarged Graph Window.

FIGURE 5-11   3D View Dialog Box.

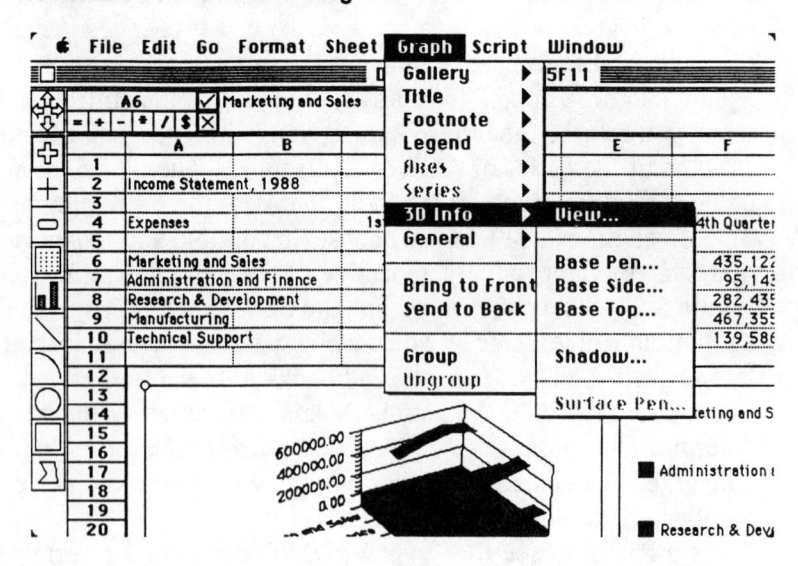

about 60 on the rotation scale. Then choose the OK button. Figure 5-12 shows the chart as it now looks. You can fine-tune your chart by changing the appearance of objects on the base, or the shadows on the data elements.

- Change the border of the base by choosing the Base Pen option on the Graph 3D Info command, then choosing the line width, color, and pattern. Be careful in doing this—patterned lines can clutter your chart and interfere with what your chart is trying to communicate.
- Change the side of the base (both visible sides) by choosing the Base Side option on the Graph 3D command, and choosing the color and pattern you want.
- Change the grid lines on the top side of the base by choosing the Surface Pen option on the Graph 3D command, then choosing the line width, color, and pattern you want. Again, be careful that the pattern you choose isn't going to clutter the overall impact of your chart.

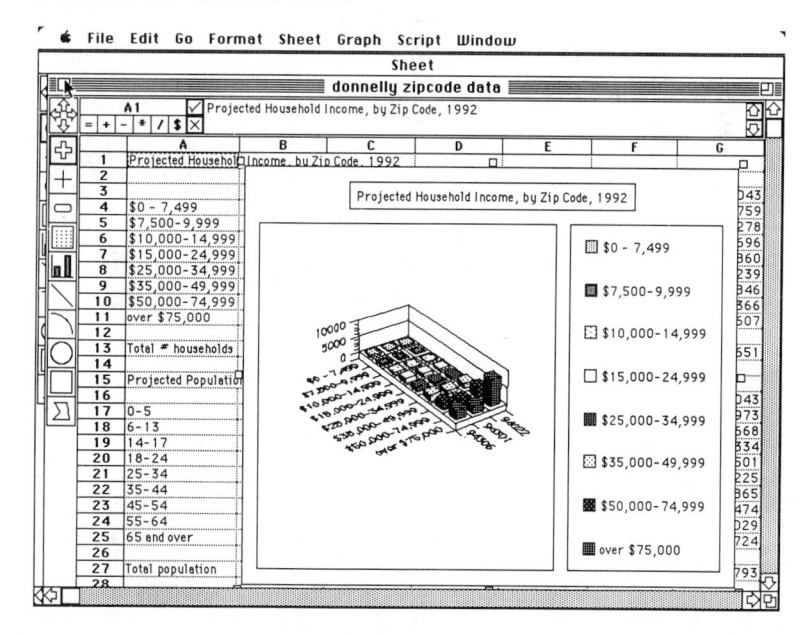

FIGURE 5-12   Rotated Chart.

- Change the shadowing of the bars by choosing the Shadow option on the Graph 3D command, then picking the color and pattern, and the shadow strength. The lower the number, the lighter the shadow.

TAILORING YOUR CHARTS

Wingz provides a very large number of other options for manipulating and changing how your data are displayed. We'll look at them in this section.

Titles

To add a title to your chart, the chart must be set for Automatic Layout.

If you want to change the contents of the title on your chart, you need to make sure the new contents also comes from the worksheet. Type what you want in a spreadsheet cell, then select both the chart and the cell (as described above), and choose the Graph Title command, Title Range option. These steps change the contents of the chart title box.

You can add color to the title box, or, by selecting the appropriate cells on the workshhet, change the font, size, or style of the letters, with the Format commands. You can move the title to the right, left, or center of the window containing the chart, or you can hide the title. Select the appropriate option on the Graph Title command.

Legends

A legend is the explanation of what the data series mean. In the example shown in Figure 5-13, the legend is on the bottom of the chart window. The default position of the legend is on the right (see Figure 5-12), but you can reposition it on the left, at the bottom (as shown), or at the top. You can also hide it, the same way you can hide a title. All these are options available with the Graph Title command.

Footnotes

You can add explanatory footnotes to your charts. As with a title or the legend, the contents of the footnote must be text already on a worksheet. To add a footnote, select the cell containing the text, click the object tool, hold

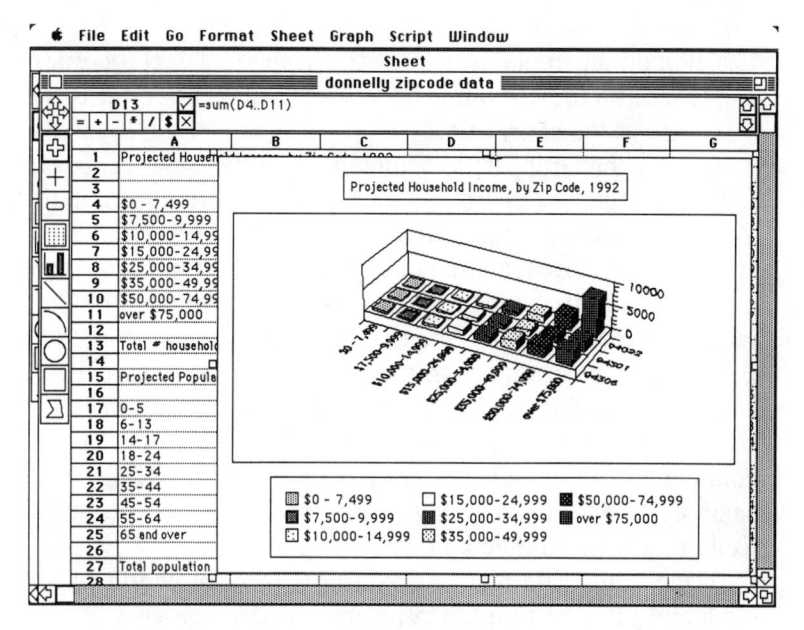

FIGURE 5-13 Chart with Legend at Bottom.

down the <Command> key, and select the chart. Then choose Footnote Range from the Graph Footnote command.

Text used for a footnote must be defined and formatted in a worksheet cell or range, and must not exceed 255 characters. If text is in a range, it must be in a single row or column, and the contents of each cell will be on a separate line in the footnote. If the amount of text is too big to fit within the chart, Wingz displays only that which fits. You can display the rest of the footnote by resizing the chart.

As with the title, you can add color to your footnote, or, by selecting the appropriate cells on the worksheet, change the font, size, or style of the characters. You can also move the footnote to the left, right, or center of the chart, and you can hide the footnote, all with the options available on the Graph Footnote command.

Chart, Division, and Series Ranges and Labels

You use text from the worksheet to create various labels on your chart. Earlier, we showed you how to create a title for the chart we've been developing as a sample in this chapter. To repeat the steps:

1. Click on the upper portion of the graph to select the graph.
2. Hold down the <Command> key and select the cell with the text you want to use as the chart title.
3. Choose the Graph Title command, and the Title Range option.

To add a title to a chart, you must put the chart in Automatic Layout mode. You can change the font, size, or style of the text you use for the title, by changing the corresponding cell on the worksheet. If you want to change the text itself, edit the worksheet cell just as you would normally—any changes made to the cell used for the title will show up in the chart title as well.

You can reposition the title anywhere on your chart. Its default position is centered, at the top. To move the title to the right or left, also at the top, simply choose the Title Right or Title Left option on the Graph Title command. You can also hide the title, using the Hide Title option on the same command. (To display it after hiding it, choose the Title Left, Title Center, or Title Right command.)

To move the title manually, turn off the Automatic Layout option, then click and drag the title to the position where you want it.

We also showed you, in the sample chart we constructed earlier, how to label the divisions shown on the x-axis. To summarize:

1. On the worksheet, select the range of cells containing the labels you want to use to label the divisions.
2. Click the object tool, hold down the <Command> tool, and select the chart.
3. Choose the Division Label Range option on the Graph General command.

Now, suppose you want to label each of the series elements, as seen in Figure 5-14. Select one or more of the series in your chart's legend. (Hold down the <Command> key to select more than one.) Choose the Label option on the Graph Series command. The dialog box shown in Figure 5-15 now appears. To put the labels at the top of each of the elements, as we did in Figure 5-15, we chose the Exterior button in the Display box, and the Value button in the Type box.

Be careful when you use series labels in your charts. In a smaller chart, they tend to clutter the appearance of your data elements. The labels are displayed horizontally and may overlap each other, especially in a smaller chart. Ask yourself whether your reader can get the impression you really

Charts and Graphs 145

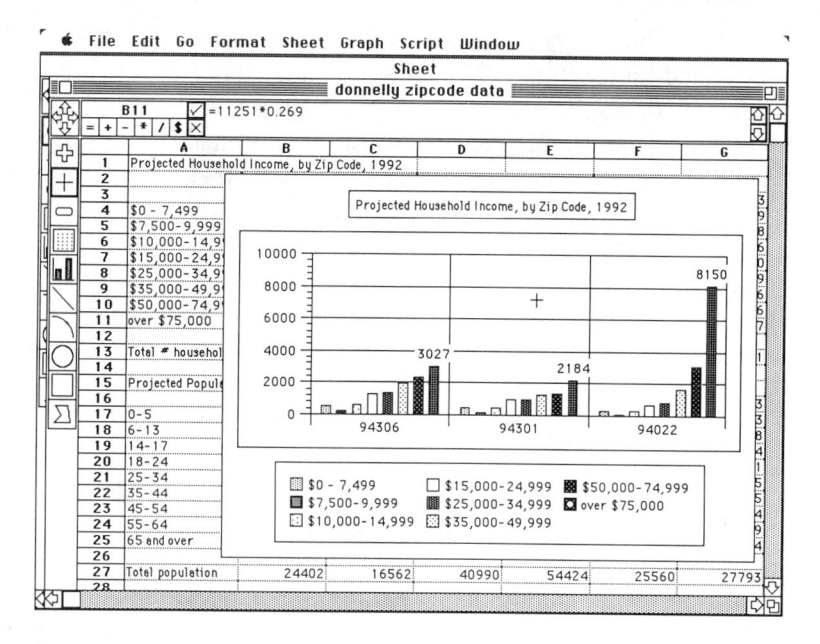

FIGURE 5-14 Bar Chart with Data Series Labelled.

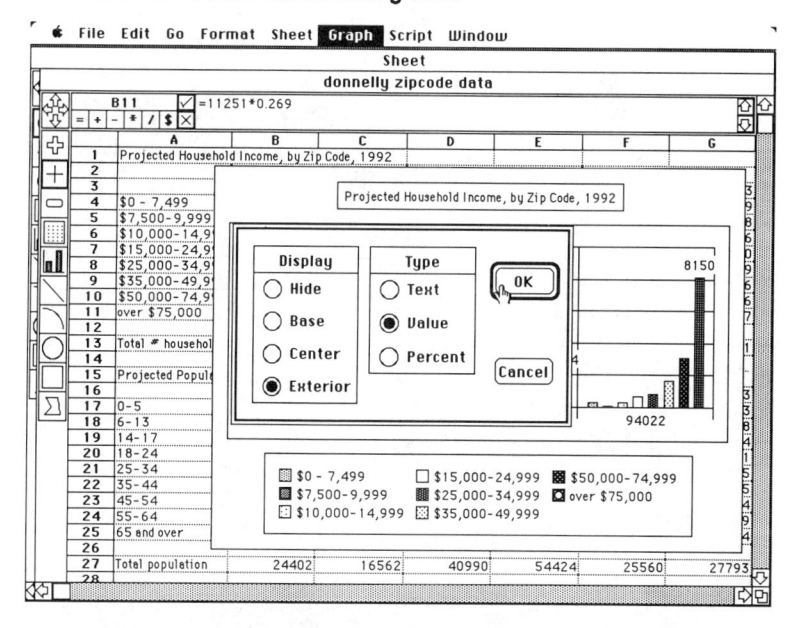

FIGURE 5-15 Series Label Dialog Box.

want by inferring the values from the scale shown with the chart; you may not need the numbers displayed as series labels.

You can also use symbols to mark data points. These work particularly well in a line graph, where you want to emphasize each of the data points, without necessarily show a value for each (see Figure 5-16). To show data points with symbols, select one of the series in the Legend box. Choose the Symbols option on the Graph series command. You'll see a dialog box like the one shown in Figure 5-17. Pick the line weight, color, and symbol type you want for this series, and specify a point size (for the symbol) in the Size box. Then click the OK bar. Repeat the procedure for each of your series.

Working with Axes

You can also specify a title for an axis. Again, the text for the title must already exist as text within a worksheet cell. Follow these steps:

1. Select the cell containing the text you want to use.

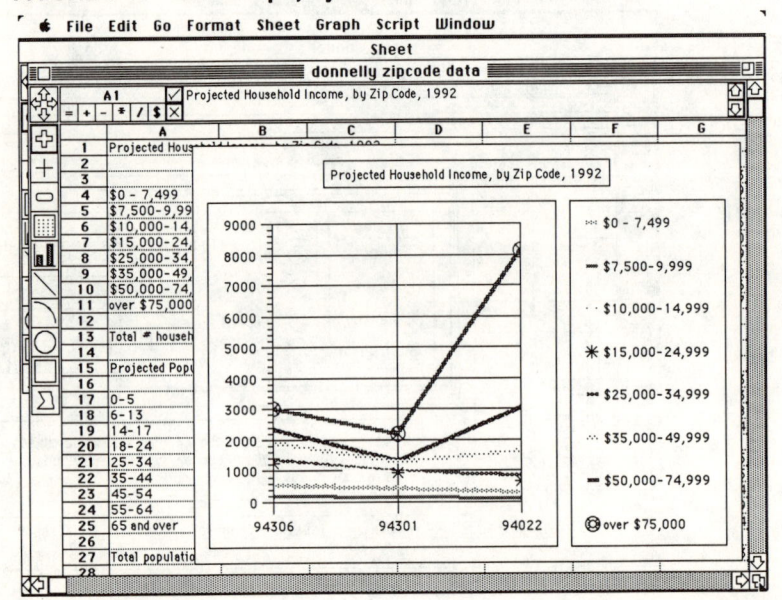

FIGURE 5-16 Line Graph, Symbols at Series Data Points.

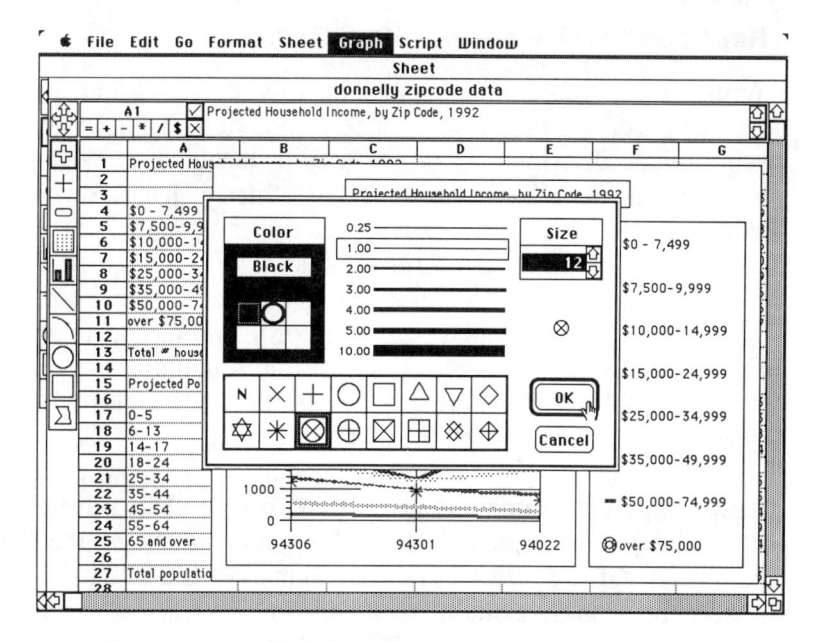

FIGURE 5-17 Data Series Symbols Dialog Box.

2. Select the object tool, hold down the <Command> tool, and select the axis.
3. Choose the Title Range option on the Graph Axes command.

You may also wish to rotate the axis title 90 degrees. Do this by selecting the axis, and choosing the Rotate Title option on the Graph Axes command. You may not like the result you get when you rotate the title, since it can have significant results on the size of the rest of your chart. If you find you don't like the looks of the chart with a rotated title, simply repeat the steps to rotate the title back into its previous position.

You can also change the scaling on any of your chart's axes. Wingz scales them automatically. The Log Scale option on the Graph Axes command lets you specify logarithmic values. The Linear Scale option, which Wingz uses as a default, lets you show values on a linear scale. The Percent Scale option lets you display the values as a percent of the largest value in the series. The Scale Info option lets you manually scale the axis, so that you can specify the maximum and minimum scale values, and the major and minor units of measure.

Repositioning Elements in Your Chart

Within limits, you can move elements of your chart around within the chart window. You cannot, for instance, reposition the individual pies representing data divisions, as Wingz lays them out. However, you can move whatever in your chart window can be defined by handles when it's selected. You can also, for example, explode a series in a pie chart, or stack a bar chart series, or combine certain forms of charts.

One common application of the ability to move things occurs when you're getting ready to add explanatory text, or to add a chart to an existing page of text. Wingz automatically positions the actual chart, legend, and title in ways that balance the three elements in the rectangular window you drew when you first constructed the chart.

You can choose to move these elements on your own, but to do so, you have to deselect Automatic Layout. With your chart selected (the handles are visible), choose the Automatic Layout command on the Graph General command. (If it doesn't have a checkmark beside it, it has already been deselected. The checkmark means it is in effect.)

Once Automatic Layout is off, you'll notice that each element of the chart has its own set of handles. Use these to reposition an element, change its size, or even move it outside the chart window. For instance, you may have a chart with a title and a legend, but you don't want the title the way the chart displays it, preferring rather to incorporate the title in a text reference. You can move it off the page, or even delete it. Or suppose you have two charts you want displayed on a page, side by side, each using the same legend. As Wingz constructs a chart, each will have its own legend. You don't need two legends—you can use this manual positioning to move one legend off the page, and arrange the two charts beside each other (see Figure 5-18).

Stacked charts are another kind of manual positioning of chart elements. When Wingz constructs a stacked chart (called Step), it stacks the data for each series element in a division, one on top of another, so that the total is the sum of the values for the division. In our population data, a stack would represent the total number of people in each zip code (see Figure 5-19). This arrangement is useful, if there's some sort of equality in the way the series are constructed. But in our population data, most of the adults were counted by 10-year age groups, while people under 25 were counted in different groups: 0–5, 6–13, 14–17, and 18–25.

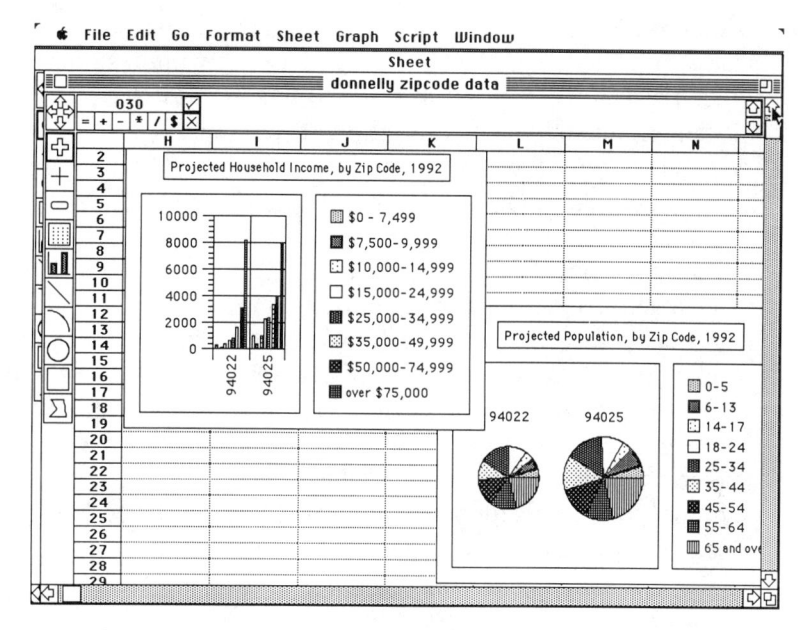

FIGURE 5-18 Side by Side Charts.

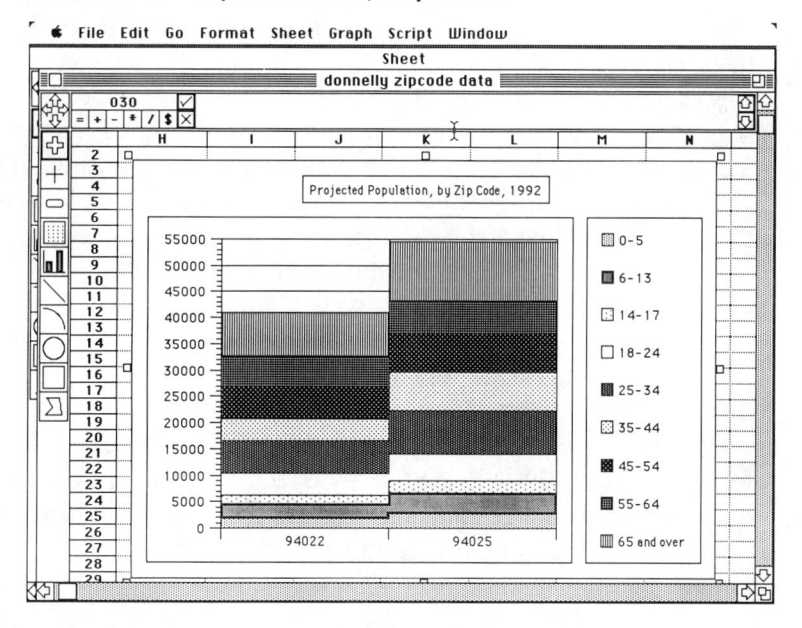

FIGURE 5-19 Population Data, Step Chart.

Suppose we are interested in a bar chart that looks primarily at population groups from 18 up, and we are only marginally interested in the population under 18, which can be stacked in a single bar. Can we portray this? Indeed we can. To do so, we need to follow these steps:

1. Select the chart. On the Graph Galley command, choose the Combination option.
2. Select a series. In this case, select the 0–5 group in the Legend box. Then choose the Combination... option on the Graph Series command.
3. A dialog box appears (see Figure 5-20). Choose the Bar chart button, click the Stack box, and click the arrow so that 3 appears in the Column box. (This will stack the three groups in the column currently holding the data for the 14–17 group.) Then click the OK bar.
4. Repeat steps 2 and 3 above for the 6–13, and 14–17 groups. When you're done, the three groups should appear as a stacked bar, and your chart should look like the one depicted in Figure 5-21.

You can use the same procedure with different groupings. For instance, suppose you wanted to portray the population data we used above in four groups: 0–24, 25–44, 45–64, and over 65. (These are groups that might reflect children and young adults, adults of child-bearing age, empty-nesters, and seniors.) Figure 5-22 shows what a chart might look like, using the same data as above.

Sometimes you want to make a point by showing one or more exploded segments in a pie chart. You can do that with Wingz. Figure 5-23 depicts a pie chart showing the population data we've been working with.

If you remember the income data on these two zip codes, you know that these two area have a very high percentage of the population with incomes over $75,000. Yet a very respectable percentage of the population here is in the 25–34 age group, when incomes theoretically should be lower. While these data don't allow you directly to correlate the income of this age group, it might be of interest to someone interested in some targeted mailing to see this group in an exploded pie chart (see Figure 5-24).

How do you explode a section of a pie chart? Select the series you want to explode from those listed in the Legend box. Choose the Explode option on the Graph Series command. To return the pie slice to its normal position, simply choose the Explode option a second time.

Charts and Graphs 151

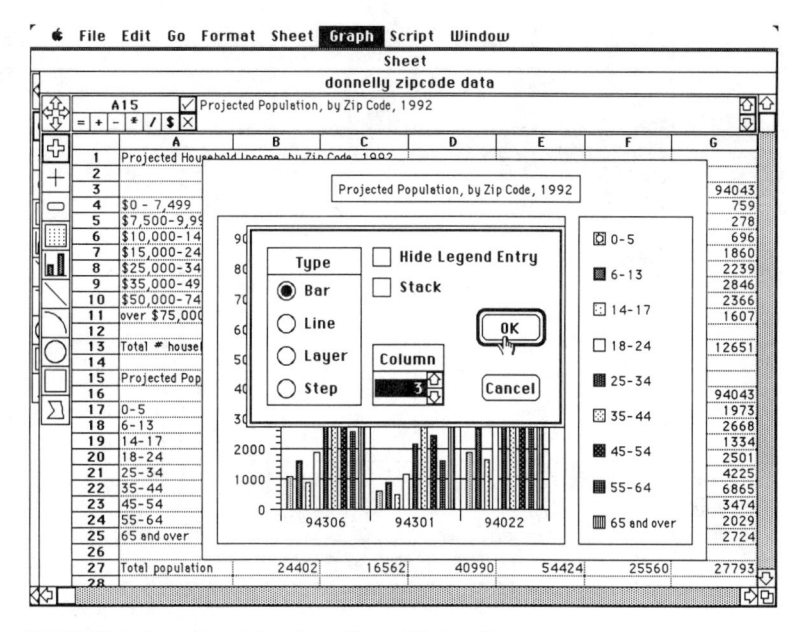

FIGURE 5-20 Combination Chart Dialog Box.

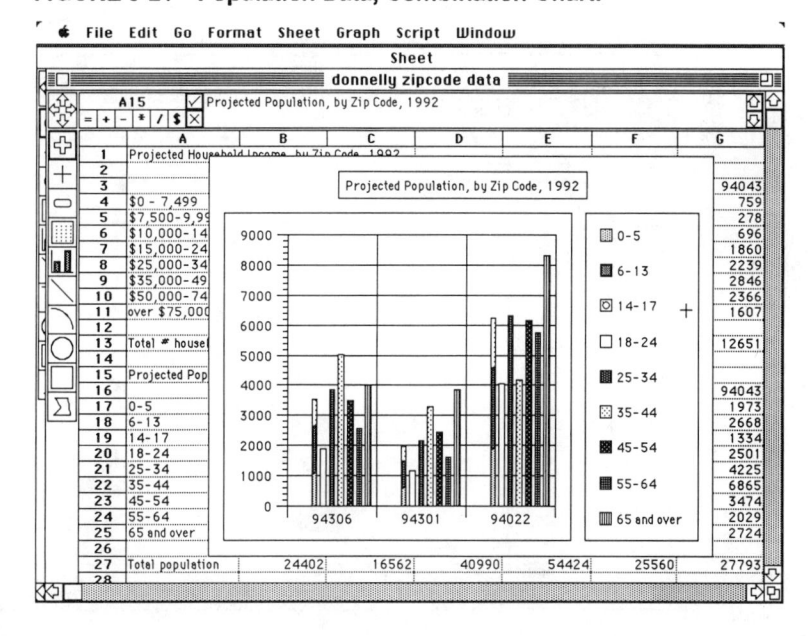

FIGURE 5-21 Population Data, Combination Chart.

152 Mastering Wingz

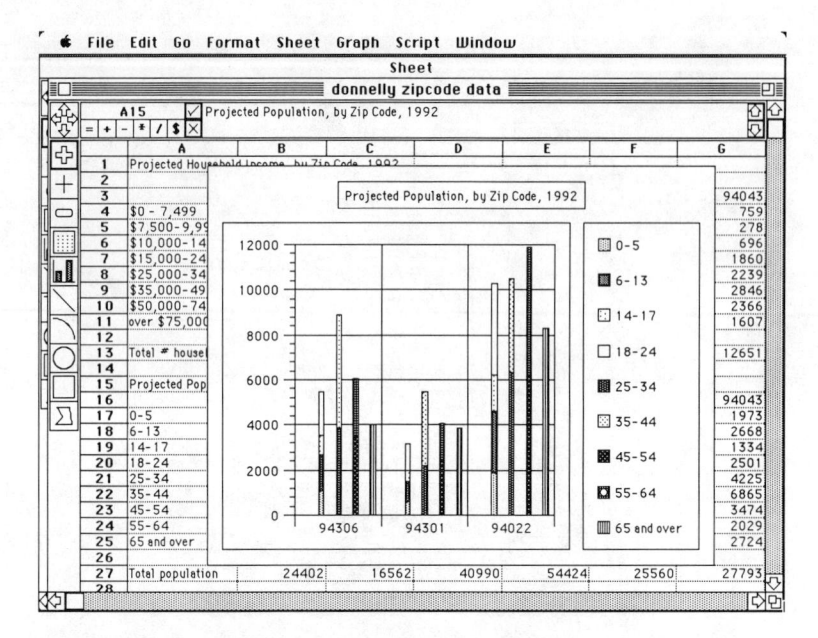

FIGURE 5-22 Population Data, Revised Groups.

FIGURE 5-23 Population Data, Pie Chart.

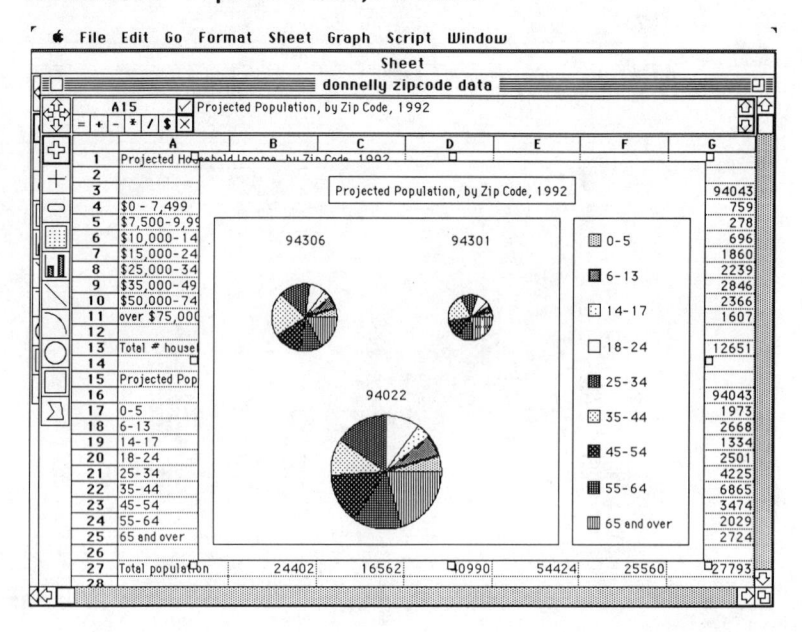

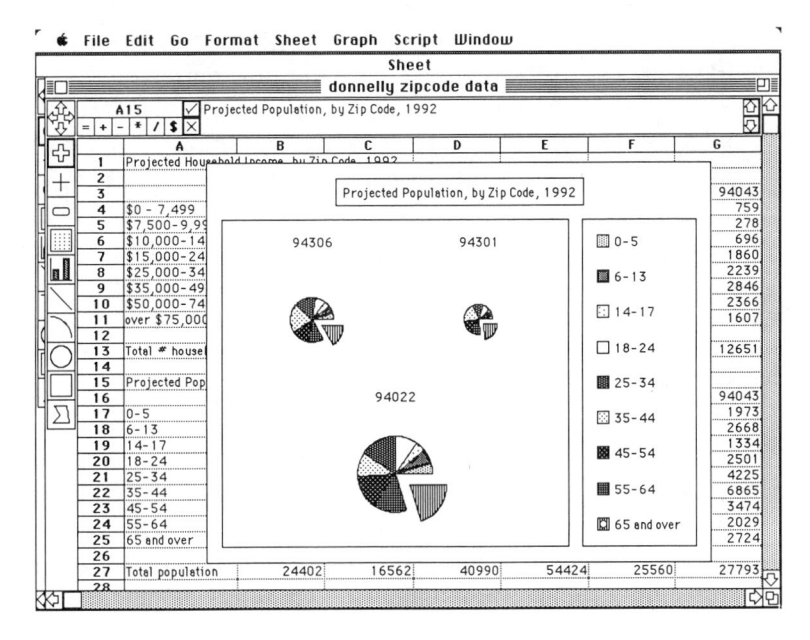

FIGURE 5-24 Population Data, Exploded Pie Chart.

OBJECTS

To Wingz, an object is anything created with the button tool, the text tool, the chart tool, or the drawing tools. Objects can be selected, moved, changed in color, pattern, or size, duplicated, and removed.

To create an object, click the appropriate tool for what you want to do, position the pointer where you want the object to appear, hold down the mouse button and drag to draw the object, then release the button. We did this earlier when we formed the window in which the chart appeared.

An object can be a block of data, a word within a text string, a paragraph or set of text, a line, a complete graph, or a drawing. (We'll show you how to draw, with related object tools, later in this chapter.) An object is usually defined by small circles or squares when it's selected. These small circles or squares are called "handles" since they're used to drag the objects around the screen.

When you create an object, you can go on to create an additional object of the same type by pressing the <Shift> key, then using the mouse to draw the subsequent object. If you want your object to align with gridlines on the worksheet, hold down the <Command> key while you drag.

You can move and position an object anywhere on your worksheet, and you can combine different types of objects on the same screen. When you save the file containing your objects, Wingz will save both what you see on the screen and any data underneath the objects that may overlay it.

You use the object tool to select objects or parts of objects. When you select the object tool, the pointer changes from whatever you were using to a crosshair. To select an object, click the object tool, then click inside the border of the item you want to treat as an object. To select more than one object, click the object tool, hold down the <Command> key, then click each object you want. To declare them as a group, with all the objects selected, choose the Group command on the Graph menu. (To ungroup the objects, select the group and choose the Ungroup command.) When you've selected more than one object, they're treated as a group, and you can move them, resize them, copy them, or manipulate them as if they were a single object.

Adding and Removing Data Elements

Once Wingz has arranged your data in chart form, you can't rearrange individual data elements. You have to go back out to the worksheet and select a new data range in order to add a new chart element. However, working with data series (rows) differs from working with data divisions (columns). For instance, let's add data to our chart—the data for zip code 94025. If you explore the Graph General command's submenu, you'll see the only option that has to do with data divisions is the Division Label Range. You're interested in adding an entire column of data, and there isn't another command on the Graph menu that covers this.

You change the range by going back out to the worksheet, and selecting the divisions you want this time. Click the worksheet tool, then select the range you want to chart. Click the object tool, hold down the <Command> key and select the chart. Now choose the Chart Range option on the Graph General command. Figure 5-25 shows your chart with the new range.

Changing a data series requires a different procedure. You add a data series by copying one of the existing series to the same chart, and then modifying what it defines. For instance, Figure 5-26 shows a portion of the worksheet we worked with earlier, with population projections for the same zip codes: And

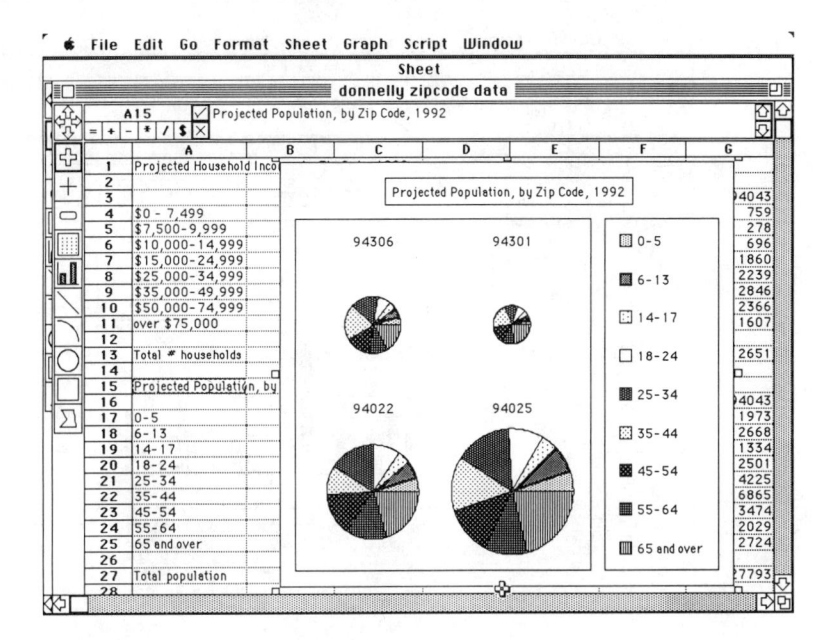

FIGURE 5-25 Chart with New Range.

FIGURE 5-26 Population Worksheet.

156 Mastering Wingz

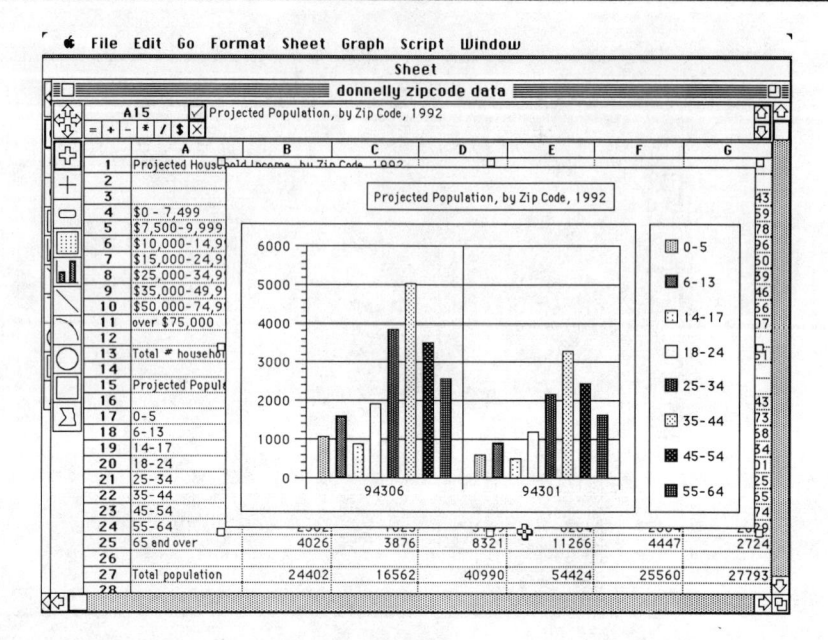

FIGURE 5-27 **Population Bar Graph.**

Figure 5-27 is a bar graph showing the population for two of the zip code areas, minus the "over 65" population.

To add the "over 65" data for the two areas, follow this procedure:

1. Select an existing series in the legend. The new series will be added next to it. We clicked on the "55–64" series.
2. Choose the Add Series option on the Graph Series command. Notice that there's a new item in the Legend box, labeled with the text that was just below the "55–64" label.
3. On the worksheet, select the range you want to use for the series. Select only the data, not the row label. In this case, we've selected B25 and C25.
4. Click the object tool. Then hold down the <Command> key and select the series in the Legend box that will be used to display the new data. In this case, select the "over 65" box. Then choose the Range Command or the Graph Series Menu.

The graph now reflects the new data series, as seen in Figure 5-28.

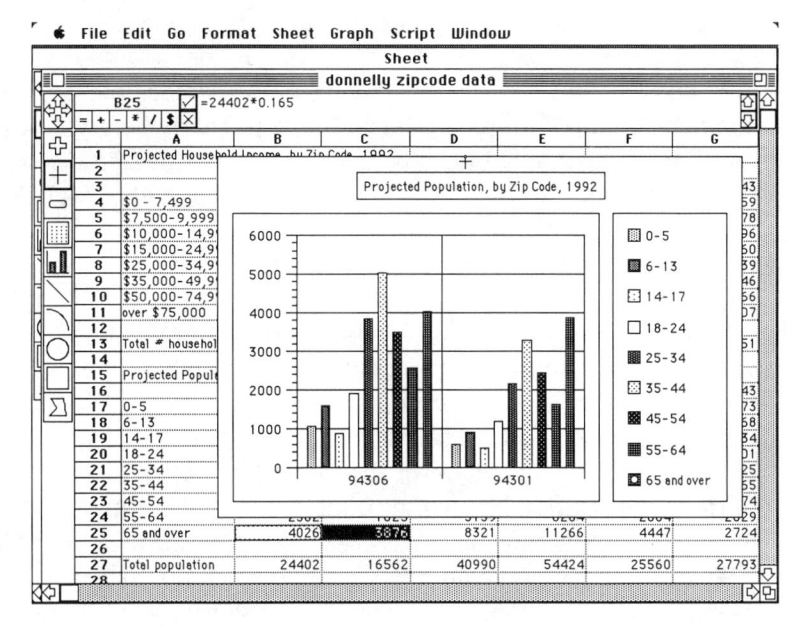

FIGURE 5-28 Population Bar Graph with New Data.

Removing a data series is a lot easier than changing one. On the Legend box, select the series. Then select the Delete Series option on the Graph Series command. The graph reflects the new configuration.

You can also hide data series on a chart. Select the series you want to hide by clicking on its box in the Legend box, then choose the Hide option on the Graph Series command. The element for that series disappears from the graph, as does its item in the Legend box. To see it again, choose the Show All Series option on the Graph Series command.

COPYING OR MOVING OBJECTS

Copying or moving objects generally works the same way as copying or moving data on a worksheet. However, for either copying or moving to work on objects, you have to deselect the Automatic Layout option on the Graph General command. (To turn off Automatic Layout, select the entire chart, then choose Automatic Layout on the Graph General command. If it's selected, Automatic Layout has a checkmark beside it. If it's deselected, the checkmark isn't there.)

To copy an object, click the object tool, select the object, choose the Copy command on the Edit menu, position the pointer where you want the object copied (which can be either in the current chart window or anywhere else on your worksheet, including a new chart window) and click, and choose the Paste command on the Edit menu. If you paste an object over something else, the object hides what's under it, much as the top item in a stack hides what's under it.

To move an object, click the object tool, select the object, choose the Cut command from the Edit menu, select the cell where you want to place the object, and choose the Paste command. When moving a chart, click at the edge of the window containing the chart, not within a portion of the chart itself, such as the legend or the drawn portion. Also, be sure not to click one of the handles around the window, or you'll be dragging the anchor point of the window to its new location, resizing the window in the process.

You can also remove an object. To do so, simply select it, and press the <Delete> key. Or choose the Clear command from the Edit menu. Like most actions, you can reverse the removal action by immediately choosing the Edit Undo command. If you want to remove an object from the screen but to save it on the Clipboard, choose the Cut command instead of Clear.

CHANGING COLORS AND PATTERNS

Wingz lets you use color and patterns with your spreadsheet and with your charts. If your system hardware allows it, you can display your work in a wide variety of colors. Solid colors and patterns can be combined to produce striking results. You can even blend your own colors.

Presentation graphics includes the assumption that your information can be presented on-screen, as well as in slides and overhead transparencies, and on paper. With a color system, you can create powerful on-screen messages that effectively communicate what your data are portraying.

Initially, Wingz presents your spreadsheet data in black and white. If you have a color system, graphs are presented in color. You can choose to apply color and/or patterns to any part of your screen, as you work with an integrated presentation. To use color and patterns, you apply them where you want them: lines, solid objects, borders around solid objects, and worksheet cells.

If you have a black-and-white printer, such as an Apple LaserWriter, solid colors will appear as shades of gray. Be sure you choose the Black & White Output in the Output box of the Page Setup command. Otherwise, red, green, blue, and black will be printed as black, and yellow, magenta, and cyan will be printed as white.

Let's try a few things with an existing chart. If you haven't already done so, reconstruct the chart shown in Figure 5-29 (or one similar). To apply a color or pattern, we have to select an object. In this case, let's work with the Legend box. Click in the Legend box so that you see the small circles, or handles, around the Legend box.

While some of the commands on the Graph menu add color and patterns to a selected object, let's look at other options first. Three of the commands that deal with color and patterns are on the Format menu.

The Fill... command lets you fill an existing space with color and/or pattern. With the Legend box selected, choose the Format Fill... command.

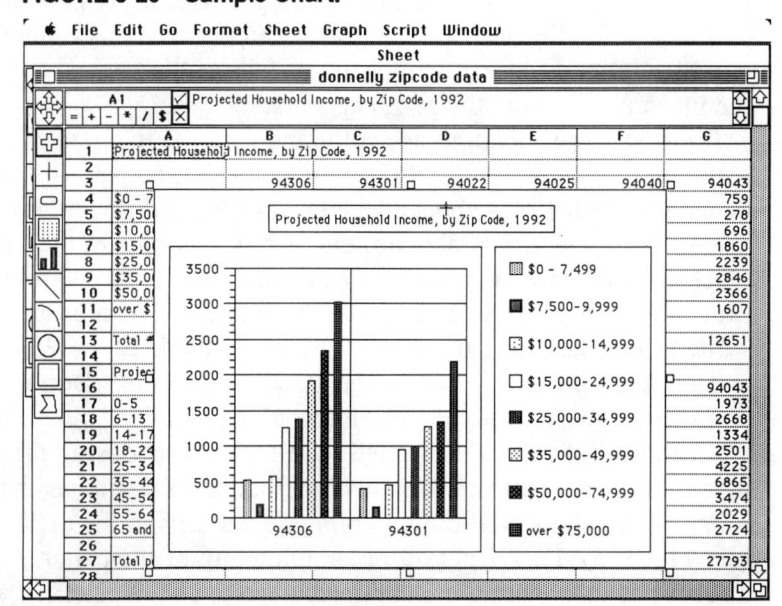

FIGURE 5-29   Sample Chart.

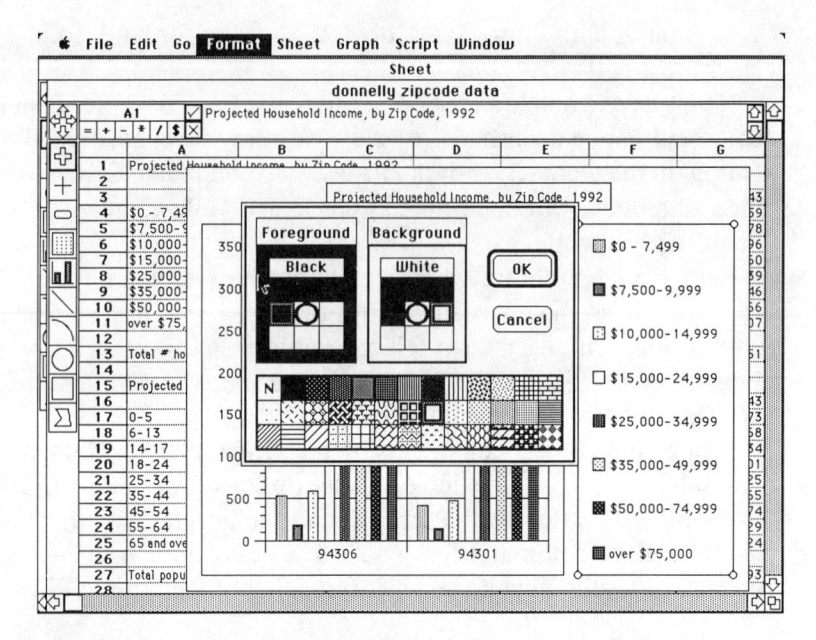

FIGURE 5-30 Fill... Dialog Box.

Figure 5-30 shows the dialog box. The patterns at the bottom are patterns that will be applied to either the foreground or the background of whatever you select. In this case, it will be the surface of the Legend box, upon which the information about the graph appears.

The best way to learn to use color and patterns in charts and graphs is to experiment with them. The N box indicates that no pattern is chosen. How the rest of the patterns appear depends on what you do with the Foreground and Background boxes above them. As shown above, the default selects black as the foreground color, and white as the background color. To illustrate what color selection will do, move the pointer and click on the white box in the Foreground box (on the right side of the Foreground box), and click on the black box in the Background box. (Don't click the OK button until you're ready to use what you've chosen in your graph. However, you can change how the selected item looks by choosing the Fill... command again and using a different combination of colors and patterns.)

When you choose different colors, the patterns in the dialog box change (see Figure 5-31). When you're applying any of the patterns to a box that already has information in it, be careful not to pick a pattern that is too busy

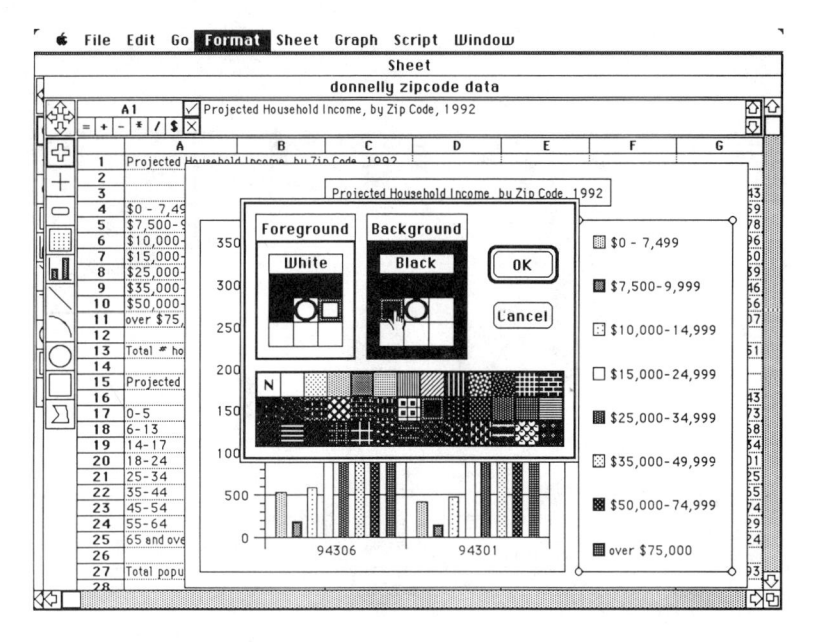

FIGURE 5-31 Fill... Dialog Box with Foreground and Background Changed.

FIGURE 5-32 Legend Box with Pattern Applied.

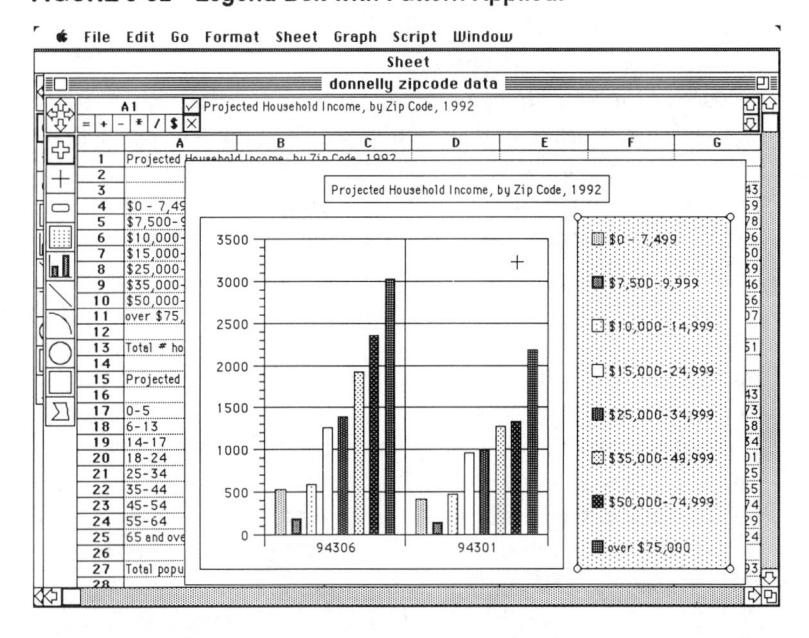

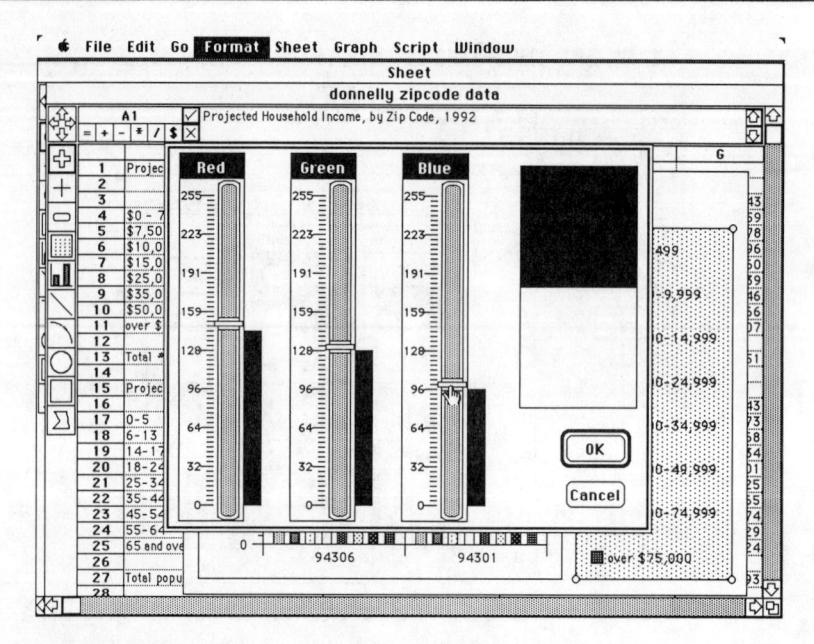

FIGURE 5-33   Color Picker Dialog Box.

or too dark, or you'll obscure the information. Figure 5-32 shows how the Legend box looks with one of the patterns.

With color, you also can change how the patterns appear. Experiment with the different colors that are shown. (If you don't have a color screen, the colors will appear as shades of gray.) The center button in the middle of the Foreground and Background color boxes lets you choose a custom color. When you choose this button, you get another kind of dialog box (see Figure 5-33).

Each bar has a slide, which you move with the pointer to blend a custom color. The box in the upper right has two parts: the bottom part shows the present color of the selected object, and the top part shows the new color that you're blending. As you move the three sliders, you can see the color of the lower box change. When you get the color you want, click the OK button, and you'll be returned to the Color and Pattern dialog box. This custom color will be applied as either foreground or background color, depending on which you've chosen, and in the pattern you've picked, when you choose the OK button on this dialog box.

You can also use the Fill... command to change the color or pattern of any of the series on your chart. Just select the series you want in the Legend box, and choose from the options on the Fill dialog box.

Now let's look at one of the other color options on the Format menu: the Line... command. This one applies the same color and pattern options to the outline of the Legend box. (If you were working with another kind of object, the options would be applied to anything that Wingz could recognize as a line.)

When you choose the Line... command, you see a dialog box, as shown in Figure 5-34). This time, there are also some options about line width. The default line width, .25 pica (72 picas = 1 inch), is shown in a rectangle. You can choose the width of the line in the selected object, in this case the line around the Legend box.

The width can be expressed as a solid line, as it currently exists, or you can apply any of the colors and/or patterns in the dialog box. Experiment with the patterns and colors, by clicking on some combination of them. You'll see samples in the line width area of what the patterns will look like,

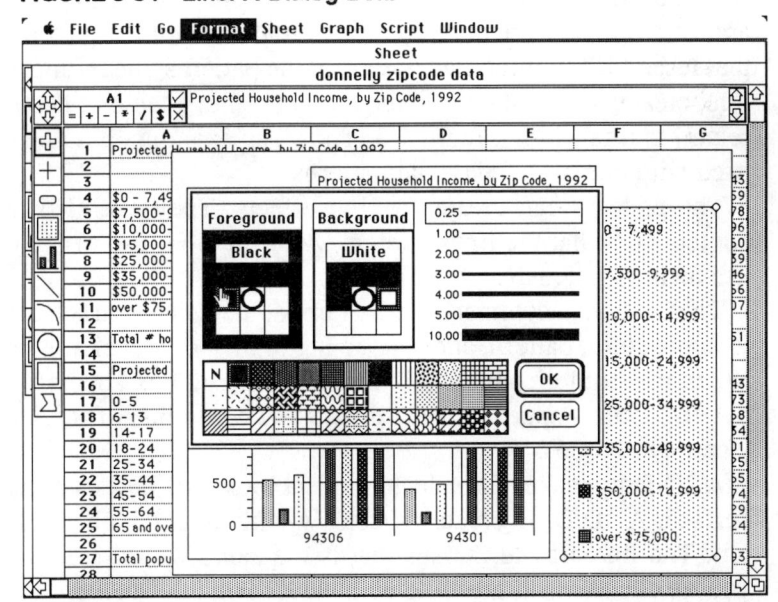

FIGURE 5-34 Line... Dialog Box.

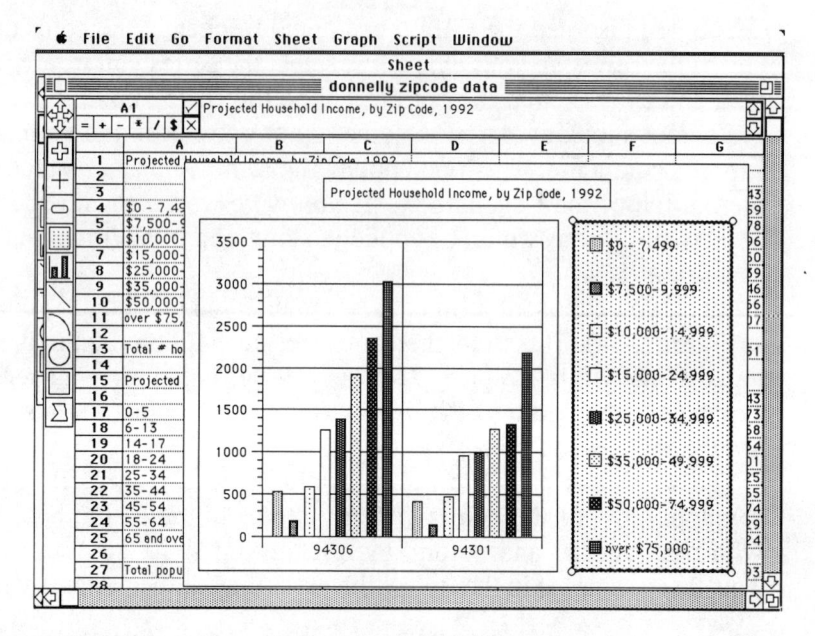

FIGURE 5-35 Legend Box with Altered Line Width.

with the various line widths. Note that the horizontal line patterns generally appear as single horizontal lines, and that some of the patterns create a line that resembles railroad tracks. One of the patterns, the leftmost in the second line, creates a line of dots—frequently used in a table of contents—without regard to line width. Figure 5-35 shows an example of a line width of 3.00, used with one of the diagonal patterns.

The patterns can create striking effects. They can also overpower the contents of what the lines contain. As with other use of color and pattern, use them judiciously.

The Border... command on the Format menu lets you select how you want to apply color, pattern, and shadowing to the borders of any selected object. When the Border command is chosen, a dialog box appears. The color and pattern options appear grayed until you choose one of the Shadow options (see Figure 5-36).

A 2D Drop makes the selected object look as if it casts a shadow on a flat surface. A 3D Drop creates a shadow with an equivalent border around it, too. The line around the shadow is the same width, color, and pattern as you've chosen with the Line command. The 2D Drop option also lets you

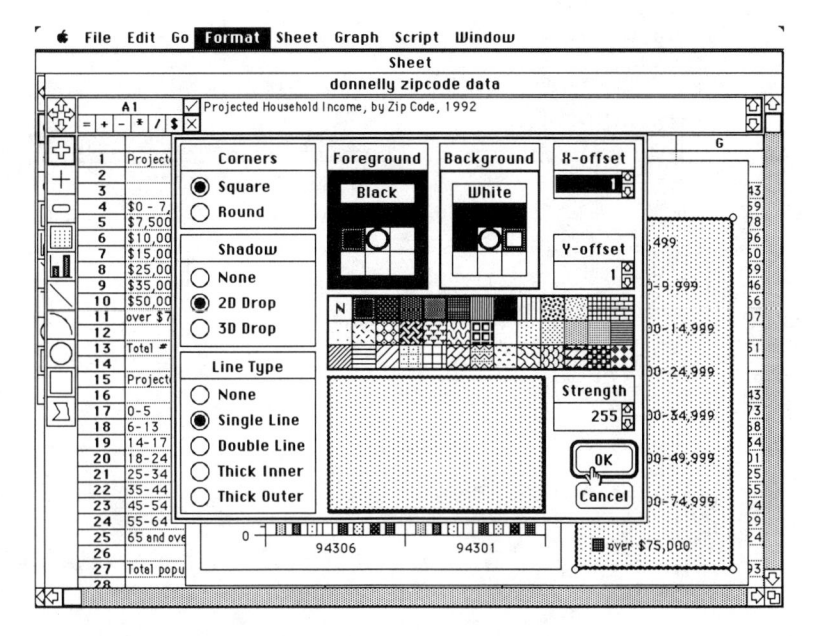

FIGURE 5-36 Border Command Dialog Box.

choose the visual strength of the shadow, which is indicated by the number in the Strength dial. The default number, 255, creates a black shadow. Lower numbers create shadows in shades of gray. If a color is in use, the number refers to the color intensity used for the shadow. The Strength dial is not an option when you've chosen a 3D shadow—it appears grayed.

How big and where your shadow appears are dictated by the two offset dials in the upper right corner of the dialog box. A number in the X-offset dial indicates how far to the right (positive number) or left (negative number) of the selected object the shadow is to appear; the number in the Y-offset dial indicates how far up (positive number) or down (negative number) from the current position of the selected object the shadow appears.

The options in the Line Type box indicate how the line around your object appears: as a single or double line, or if a double line, with a thicker inner or outer line. (If you choose neither of these, the lines are of equal weight.) A set of border options that includes round corners, a 2D drop, X- and Y-offsets of 10, a single line, and a strength of 255 creates a border effect like the one shown in Figure 5-37.

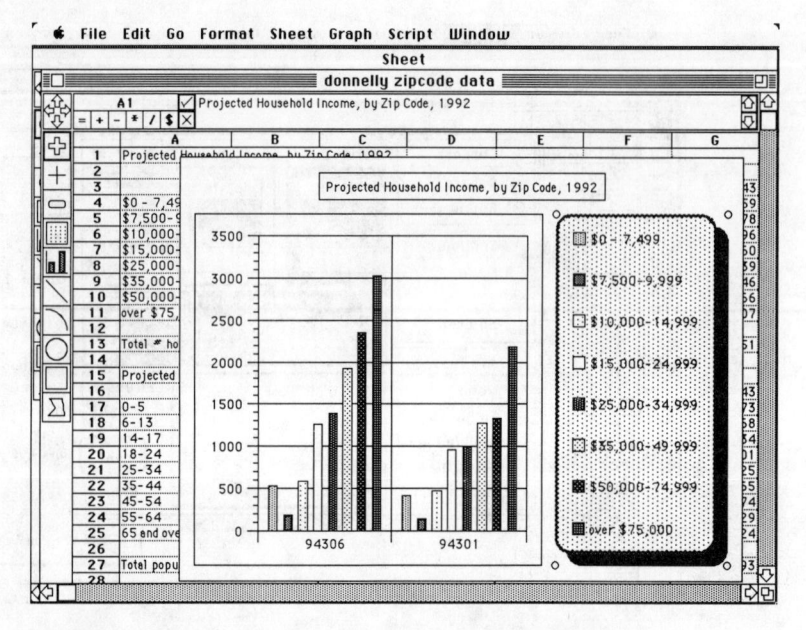

FIGURE 5-37 Legend Box with Border and Shadow.

Two more options for applying color and patterns to your chart are the Plot Interior Brush and the Plot Interior Pen options on the Graph General command. The Interior Brush option lets you apply color and patterns to the area on which your graph is plotted, and the Interior Pen option lets you change the color, pattern, and width of the top and right lines that define the plot area. (The left and bottom lines are not affected; the left line is a scale, and the bottom line is used for the division labels.)

You can also change the color and pattern of the grid lines on your chart. Choose Major Grid or Minor Grid on the Graph Axes command, then choose the options you want from the dialog box.

DRAWING AND WORKING WITH GRAPHICS

You can draw shapes with Wingz, and resize and reposition them, adding color and patterns just as you did with charts. You can also import scanned

Charts and Graphs 167

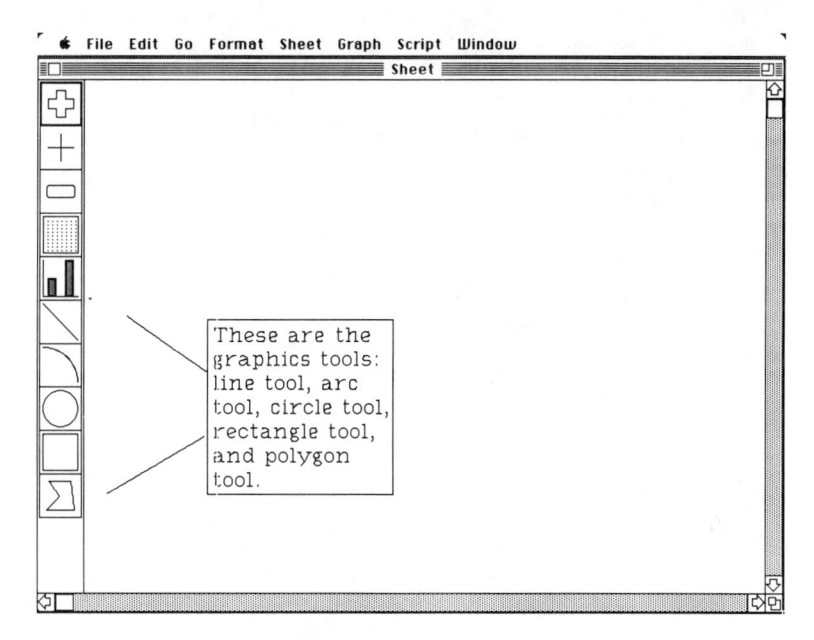

FIGURE 5-38 Drawing Tools.

photographs or illustrations from other applications, and use them in a Wingz document. Drawings and scanned pictures are considered objects, just like charts, worksheet cells, and text blocks. Thus they're eligible for all the options available for anything that can be considered an object.

Wingz' drawing tools and techniques are very reminiscent of Mac-Draw™), and an experienced Macintosh user will find it easy to learn how to use the Wingz drawing tools. These tools are shown in Figure 5-38. Click one of these tools to draw the kind of object you want. To enclose a drawing in a border, make the drawing, then draw a rectangle (pick a border style, if you want), and drag the drawing into the rectangle.

If you're just starting to work with graphics, it's a good idea to draw on the worksheet grid. It helps you align parts of your drawing and keep them in proportion. After you're comfortable with drawing, you can turn off the grid.

To draw a straight line, click the line tool, position the pointer where you want to begin the line, and drag the pointer to the end of the line. When you release the pointer, it becomes a selected object, and you can add color or a pattern to it, or change its width. This is the procedure for any object you

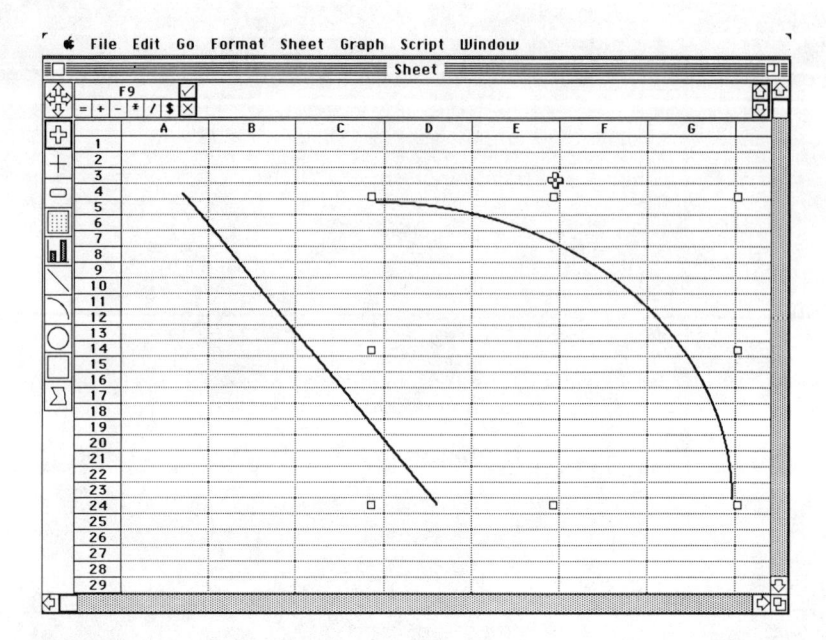

FIGURE 5-39 Line and Arc.

draw: when you release the pointer, the object is selected, and you can then apply color or patterns, or change the width of the lines involved. To draw an arc, click the arc tool, position the pointer where you want to begin the arc, and drag the pointer. Notice that Wingz creates a single arc of any curvature, wherever you drag the pointer. You can change the size of the arc by dragging one of the handles. Figure 5-39 shows a line and an arc in this manner.

To draw a circle or an oval, click the circle tool, position the pointer where you want the shape to being, and drag the pointer. If you drag the pointer in equal increments on an imaginary *x-y* axis, you'll create a circle; the farther you go, the bigger the circle. If you drag the pointer farther in one dimension than in another, you'll create an oval. To draw a rectangle or square, click on the rectangle tool, position the pointer where you want the shape to begin, and drag the pointer. As with the circle tool, dragging in equal increments on an imaginary *x-y* axis creates a square; unequal increments create a rectangle. The circle, oval, square, and rectangle in Figure 5-40 were drawn in this way.

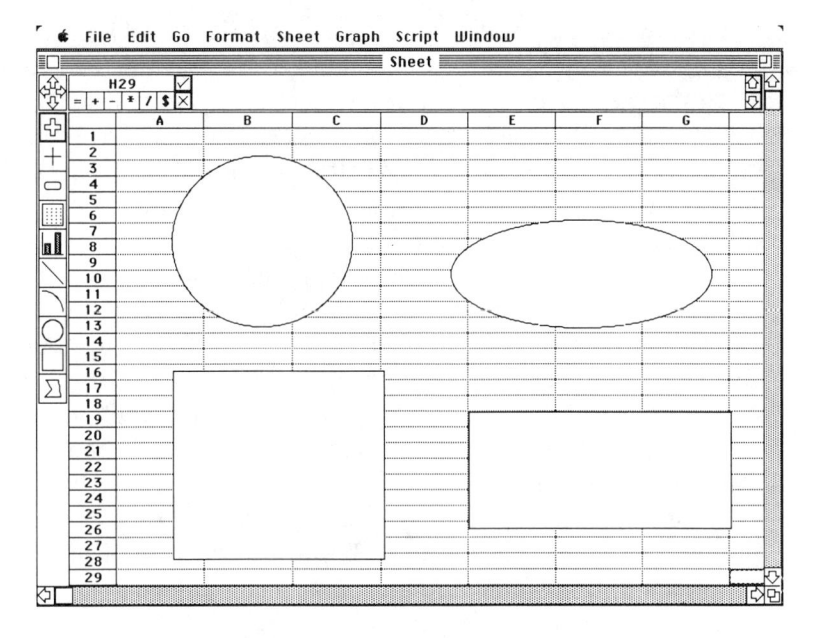

FIGURE 5-40 Circle, Oval, Square and Rectangle.

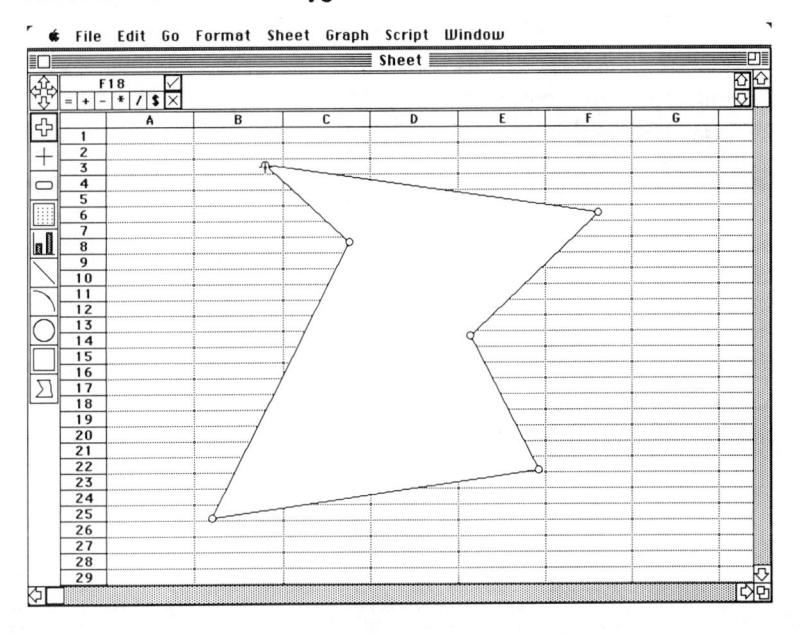

FIGURE 5-41 Closed Polygon.

170   Mastering Wingz

To draw an open or closed polygon (see Figure 5-41), click the poly tool, position the pointer where you want to begin drawing, and click the mouse. Drag the pointer to the first corner and click the mouse. Drag to the next counter, and click, and repeat the process until you have reached the point where you want to stop. If you've drawn a closed polygon, click once where the beginning and ending lines meet; if you've drawn an open shape, double click at the end of the last line.

Any polygon must contain at least three points. You can reshape the polygon by clicking on one of the handles, and dragging the handle so that the shape changes. You can add a handle to a polygon by double clicking on the edge or the line; this handle can then be used to create another corner.

The Format menu contains an extra command when you have created a polygon, the Polygon Info... command. When you choose this command, you see the dialog box depicted in Figure 5-42. If you've drawn a closed polygon, you can open it by choosing the Polyline button. Wingz then eliminates the last line you drew. If you've drawn an open polygon, you can

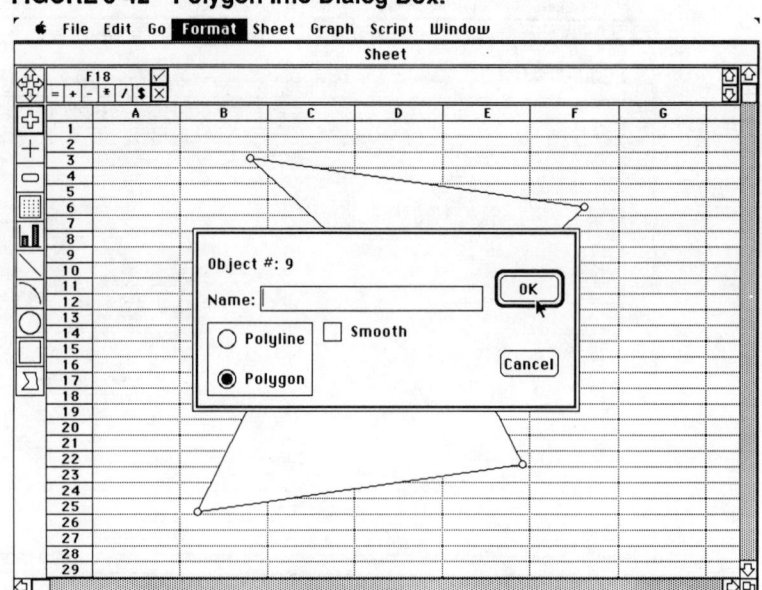

FIGURE 5-42   Polygon Info Dialog Box.

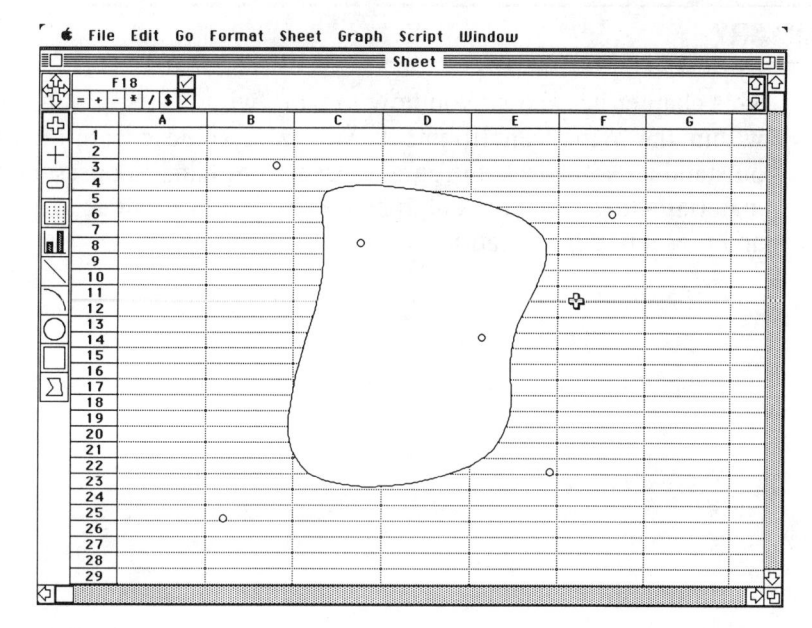

FIGURE 5-43 Smoothed Polygon.

close it by choosing the Polygon button. Wingz adds a line across the opening.

If you click the Smooth box, Wingz smooths the angles in your polygon, and creates a slightly different shape. Figure 5-43 shows what it did with the polygon we created in Figure 5-42. Note that the dialog box also lets you name the object, so that you can retrieve it and use it elsewhere. Wingz automatically assigns each object a reference number, which you can use instead of the name. Names and reference numbers are useful when you work with HyperScripts.

To import a picture from another application, cut or copy the image to the Clipboard, open the Wingz worksheet and select the cell where you want the image to go, and then choose the Edit Paste command. Once the image appears on your screen, you can move or modify it just as you can any other object.

SUMMARY

This chapter has shown you how to work with charts, graphs, and drawing within the Wingz environment. Wingz' graphic capabilities make it an outstanding spreadsheet program, capable of handling presentation-quality material and giving you a high degree of flexibility in choosing, arranging, and presenting information.

CASE STUDY 3:
Wingz in Investment Banking

Larry Schmittinger, vice president and branch manager
Wheat First Securities, Inc.
Norfolk, Virginia
804-625-4281

Wheat First Securities is a regional investment brokerage firm on the East Coast, and has been in business since 1934. Currently, the firm has 92 offices and about 750 brokers.

Schmittinger first saw Wingz demonstrated at a Macintosh user's group, and has since acquired his own copy. He's impressed.

"The investment industry has mainstreamed computers into our business. Most of them, however, are dumb terminals. So many brokers have brought personal computers into the office to help them manage client portfolios, maintain client databases, and do a lot of other things."

He thinks Wingz is particularly useful when doing presentation graphics.

"In an investment firm, where you're dealing with clients on a daily basis, who do not have the subject knowledge and the expertise that you have, it's nice to be able to show them a concept graphically (a picture's worth a thousand words). The graph may have a bigger an impact on them than if you just showed them numbers on a spreadsheet. With the click of a mouse you can convert the spreadsheet on your screen to a bar chart, showing their portfolio distribution.

"In our business, when you're dealing with a portfolio of securities, one security (a stock, for instance) will sometimes grow to a much larger position than is perhaps prudent for someone to have—one stock may represent 33% or more of that whole portfolio, and that's too large. You can show the client numbers, but that won't have as much impact as a bar chart that shows them him one security that's way out of proportion to the rest of the portfolio. If that one security goes down, that takes a large part of the net worth of the portfolio with it.

"When any one part of the portfolio goes over 10–12%, I like to talk to the client, and ask them about proportions. That's the kind of thing I'd show them on computer, with the numbers representing their current position. With a click of the mouse, I can show them a chart representing relative positions.

"Wingz is definitely going to give me a competitive edge over another broker who serves his clients only with number-based spreadsheets."

6

Changing Your Mind

Once you have data entered in a spreadsheet, you frequently find that you need to arrange them differently—changing this value or that, displaying it differently, moving it around, or in some way putting it somewhere other than where or how you first placed it.

Wingz offers a number of ways to let you change your mind and experiment with how you present your data. Wingz' orientation as a presentation spreadsheet allows it to include a number of tools that let you modify your original data: you can experiment with different types of graphs, with shading, with color and patterns, with borders, and with added text in different type sizes and fonts, so that you create the kind of environment in which your data carry the impact you want.

The **Edit menu** contains a number of commands that help you manipulate existing data (see Figure 6-1):

The **Undo command** lets you reverse the effects of the just-prior command.

The **Cut command** specifies that selected cells will be moved when you choose the Edit Paste command. The cells disappear from the worksheet

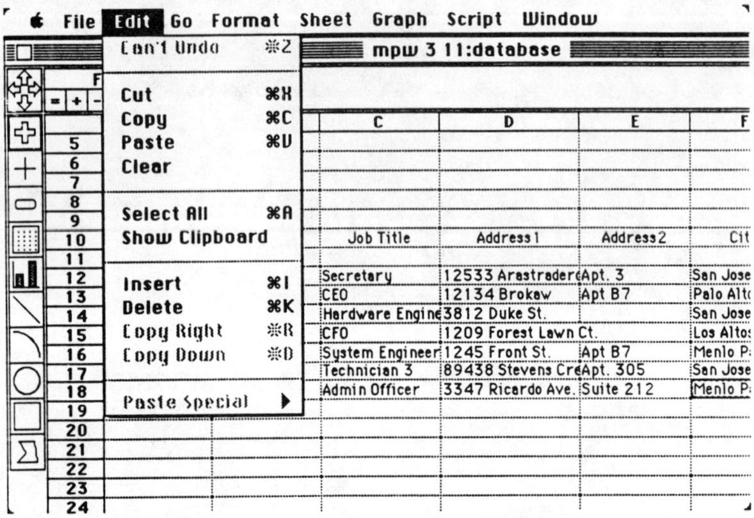

176 Mastering Wingz

FIGURE 6-1 Edit Menu.

when you choose the Cut command, and are stored on the Clipboard. (You can see what's there at any time by choosing the Show Clipboard command.)

The **Copy command** specifies that selected cells will be copied when you choose the Edit Paste or the Edit Paste Special command. The cells selected are also stored on the Clipboard, but unlike the Cut command, they don't disappear from the worksheet.

The **Paste command** moves or copies the selection of cells you have identified with the Cut or Copy command.

The **Clear command** removes data, formulas, or both from the current document.

The **Select All command** selects all the cells in the worksheet, so that you can make a universal change to cells—such as changing the type style, size, or font.

The **Show Clipboard command** displays the current contents of the Clipboard in the bottom portion of your screen. The Clipboard overlays the current worksheet (see Figure 6-2).

The **Insert... command** inserts a blank cell, range of cells, row, or column into the worksheet, and shifts selected cells to make room for the

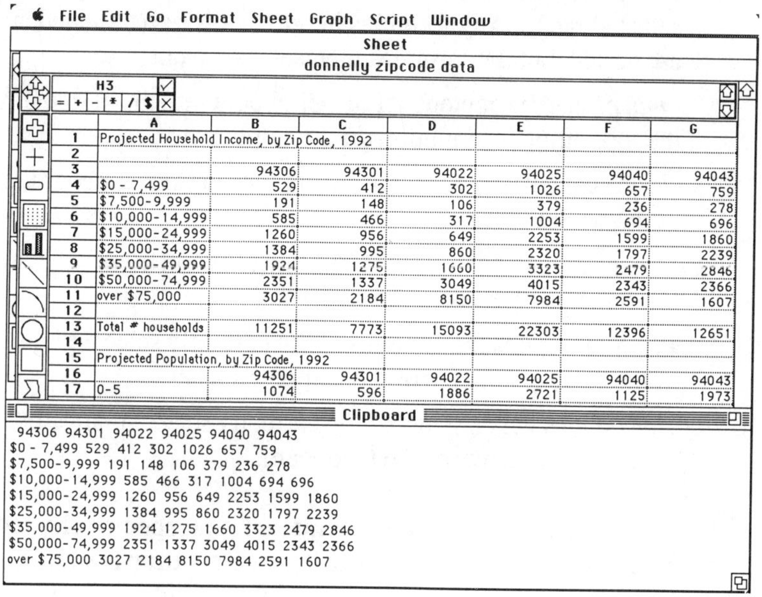

FIGURE 6-2 Clipboard.

new cells. When you select Insert without specifying a complete row or column, Wingz inserts a cell or range of cells equivalent to what you've selected, moving over and/or down the selected cells. If you want to insert a row, select the row label and a new row will be inserted above the current row; if you want to insert a column, select the column label and a new column will be inserted to the right of the selected column.

The **Delete...command** removes the selected cells from the worksheet and shifts other cells to close up the space.

The **Copy Right command** copies the contents and formats of the cells in the leftmost column of selected cells into the rest of the columns in the selected cells, overwriting anything that's there.

The **Copy Down command** copies the contents and formats of the cells in the top row of selected cells into the rest of the rows in the selection, overwriting anything that's there.

The **Paste Special command** pastes the contents of the Clipboard into cells you select, with the following forms of manipulation:

Values pastes the values of the cells currently in the Clipboard into the selected range. Any formulas in those cells are evaluated and the results are pasted, but the formulas themselves are not.

Format pastes the contents of the Clipboard into the selected range, using the formatting information on the Clipboard.

Add adds the values of the current contents of the Clipboard to the contents of the selected range.

Subtract subtracts the values of the current contents of the Clipboard from the contents of the selected range.

Multiply multiplies the contents of the currently selected range by the values of the current contents of the Clipboard.

Divide divides the contents of the currently selected range by the values of the current contents of the Clipboard.

The commands of the **Go menu** are not specifically concerned with editing. However, they let you specify recalculation methods, use predefined function templates, find or select specified kinds of information for incorporation in what you're working on, and use previously named blocks of data, functions, or formulas within formulas you're constructing:

The **Recalc command** results in the immediate recalculation of the entire worksheet, including all formulas and charts.

The **Recalc Info command** lets you determine the circumstances under which recalculation will take place. You can specify the timing (Automatic or Manual) and order (Natural, Row, or Column) of recalculation, as well as how many times the worksheet is to be recalculated under certain test conditions (Iteration).

The **Paste Formula command** displays a list of built-in function templates, operators, and current range names, allowing you to select one that will be pasted into whatever is in the formula bar.

The **Find command** lets you search through the worksheet for text strings, values, cells, or criteria that you specify as a formula, and moves the active cell to the first occurrence of a match.

The **Select command** lets you select all cells that fit the criteria you specify. The criteria can be:

Notes

text fields (Fields)

buttons (Controls)

objects (Graphics)

Text Cells

Value Cells (selects all cells containing numbers, including those formatted as dates)

Formula Cells

Error Cells

Locked Cells

Blank Cells

Headings

All Precedents

All Dependents

Direct Precedents

Direct Dependents

References to Blanks

Unreferenced Cells

Current Cell

Active Cells (selects range containing all data and objects in the worksheet—used with Report Print Range command)

Report Header

Report Footer

Report Border

The **Name command** lists all names you've used for cell and range names. Once you choose a name, that cell, or the upper left cell of that range, becomes the active cell.

The **Define Name command** assigns, deletes, or changes a name for a cell or cell range.

The **Create Names command** lets you name selected rows or columns of data by using the text at the left edge or top, respectively, of the range.

The **Remove Names command** lets you selectively delete the names currently in use for cells and ranges.

Most of the menu items listed above can be used with shortcut keys, which are shown next to the command when the menu appears on the screen.

A REMINDER ABOUT SELECTING

When you want to change an item, you first need to select the cells involved first. You select one or more cells by highlighting. Selecting on a worksheet was discussed in Chapter 3. When you've selected a cell, its contents appear in the formula bar at the top of the screen. To edit the contents within a cell, move the vertical bar so that it's positioned just to the right of whatever you want to delete, or at the point you want to insert new material.

To delete characters from within a cell, once you have the vertical bar correctly positioned, use the Delete key to backspace over the characters you want to remove. To insert characters within a cell, position the vertical bar where you want the characters to go, and either type the characters, select what you want from the operators at the left side of the formula bar, or use one of the commands to help you select the function, name, or data you want.

AND A REMINDER ABOUT UNDO

In the subsequent pages, you're likely to be given several examples that you can try on your Macintosh. To reassure yourself that you won't crash the program, keep in mind the Undo command on the Edit menu. This command will let you reverse whatever action you last took; for example, you can get back that range of data you just deleted, or take back out the cells you just inserted which caused everything else to move around.

The Undo command works only on the action taken just prior to pressing the <Return> key, not on any actions before that. You get one reprieve, not an unlimited amount of them.

REMOVING DATA: CLEARING AND DELETING

Like most worksheet programs, Wingz makes a distinction between deleting something and clearing it. When you delete something, Wingz removes the contents of the cell or cells, as well as the cell itself, and adjusts the cells around it to fill up the space. When you clear something, only the contents of the cell is removed. Let's use a simple example to demonstrate the difference.

On a blank Wingz worksheet, enter the following:

    Cell A1   2
    A2   2
    A3   =A1+A2
    B1   3
    B2   3
    B3   =B1+B2

When you press the <Enter> key after typing the formula for A3, you'll find the value 4.00 in cell A3 and if you check B3 after typing the formula you'll see 6.00. (see Figure 6-3). Now click on cell A2 to make it the active cell, and choose the Edit Clear command. This command removes the data in cell A2, but leaves the cell otherwise intact. (You can use an alternate method: click on A2, then press the Delete key. This action also clears the contents of the selected cell.)

Notice that the value in cell A3 is now 2.00. If you click on A3, you'll see that the formula is intact, and that the evaluation of the formula is accurate: 2 + (blank) = 2.

Now click on cell A2 again, and retype the 2. As soon as you press the <Return> key, your worksheet looks like the original example shown above.

To demonstrate the difference between the two commands, click again on A2, and this time choose the Edit Delete command. Again the 2 disappears from cell A2, but this time, the value from B2 is moved over. If you click on A3, you'll see that the formula is the same. (see Figure 6-4). What has happened is that when cell A2 was deleted, any cells to the right move over to close up the space.

(To restore the just-prior condition of your example, choose the Edit Undo command. If you have not pressed any other keys in the meantime, the Undo command will put A2 and its contents back where they were. If anything else has been typed, you'll see a "Can't Undo" message.)

As a general rule, the Clear command is better for removing data from cells when there's any suspicion that the addresses of those cells might be

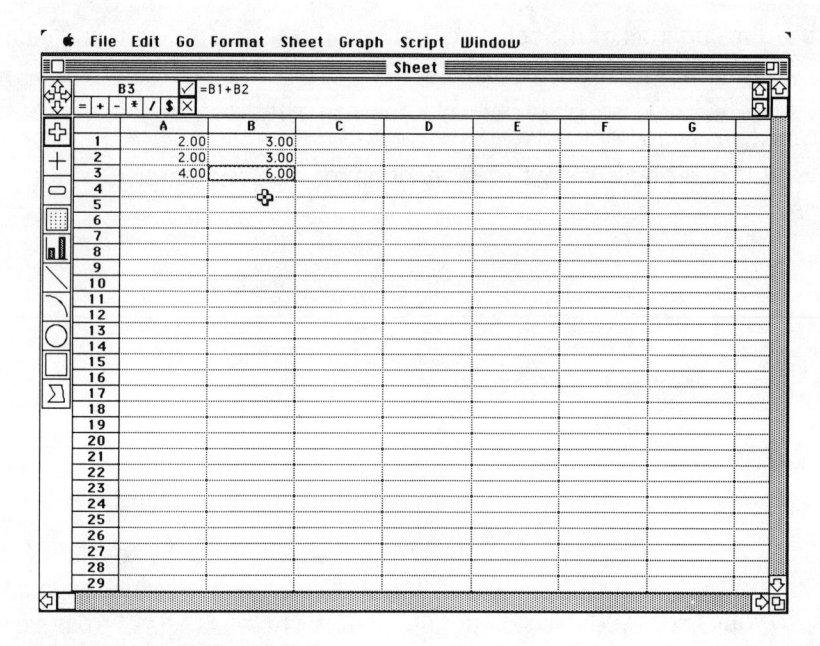

FIGURE 6-3 Original Data.

FIGURE 6-4 Data Deleted.

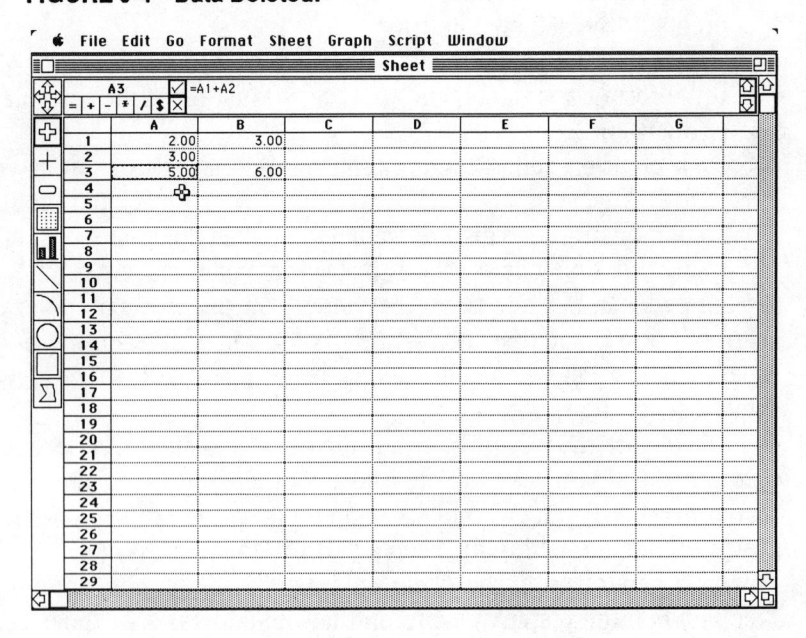

Changing Your Mind 183

used as part of formulas in other cells. The Delete command is better for completely wiping out whole rows or columns or for removing one or more cells so that Wingz can shift other cells around to fill in the space. To delete a row or column, select the row or column (by clicking in the row or column heading), and choose Edit Delete. Wingz automatically moves the remaining rows or columns to fill in the space.

INSERTING

As we pointed out above, Wingz has two different concepts of inserting: inserting within a cell, and inserting within the worksheet.

Inserting within a cell means that you can choose where, within a cell's contents, new data is to be inserted. When you are typing new data into a cell, you'll notice the blinking vertical line, which indicates where new data will go next. Normally this is to the right of the last character entered. However, if you want to insert one or more characters somewhere in the line of characters you've already typed, you can: simply use your mouse to position the I-bar where you want to insert the characters, and click. The blinking vertical bar now appears where you put the I-bar, and anything you type will be inserted at this point.

Inserting within a worksheet is done with the Edit Insert command, which lets you insert one or more blank cells, columns, or rows into an existing worksheet. To insert one or more blank cells, select the area where you want the new cells inserted. Choose the Edit Insert command, and the existing cells, complete with data, formats, and formulas, will be moved to the right to make room for the new blank cells.

For instance, let's look at a projected income statement showing monthly assumptions about income and expenses (see Figure 6-5). Suppose we wanted to change this, to add three-month summaries. What would happen to the rest of the spreadsheet?

Before we start, we should understand that the Undo command works with Insert as well as with Delete. So if we make a mistake and want to undo the Insert command, we can do this easily.

Now, let's insert a new column after the March figures, one which can hold the quarterly summary figures. We'll look at the new column's impact after we get it in place. To insert the new column, position the cursor in the column heading for column E, and click. This selects all of column E. With

	A	B	C	D	E	F	G
1	Projected Income and Expenses, 1989						
2							
3							
4		January	February	March	April	May	June	July
5	Income						
6	Product sales	150000	180000	216000	216000	259200	311040
7	Service	35000	38500	42350	42350	46585	51244
8	Training	100000	125000	156250	156250	195312	244141
9							
10	Total income	285000	343500	414600	414600	501098	606424
11							
12	Expenses						
13	Salaries	125000	150000	175000	200000	225000	250000
14	Payroll taxes	37500	45000	52500	60000	67500	75000
15	Rent	13200	13200	13200	13200	13200	13200
16	Utilities	3500	3850	3500	3250	3250	3000
17	Equipment	15000	18000	21600	21600	25920	31104
18	Supplies	5000	5000	6000	6000	7500	7500
19	Advertising	15000	25000	20000	30000	25000	30000
20	Training	17500	16000	17500	17000	18000	18000
21							
22	Total expenses	231700	276050	309300	351050	385370	427804
23							
24	Net Income	53300	67450	105300	63550	115728	178620

FIGURE 6-5   Income Statement, Monthly Figures.

the column highlighted, choose the Edit Insert command. Since you selected the entire column, Wingz moves everything to the right, leaving you with a blank column E. Now you have a spreadsheet like the one in Figure 6-6. If you want to take out the newly inserted column, before you type anything else choose the Edit Undo command. The blank column will disappear and the rest of the worksheet will shift back to the left.

However, we assume that you're interested in adding quarterly summary figures. To do that, add a formula like this one:

=SUM(B3..D3)

to each cell in column E where there should be a summary number. We'll show you how to do that quickly in the section where we explain copying, later in this chapter. For now, just type the formula into the appropriate cells.

We should, however, point out one of the effects of inserting blank cells, whether they are single cells, ranges, or whole columns or rows. Suppose that this spreadsheet were a full-year income statement, and had year-end summary figures in the column following the December figures. Chances

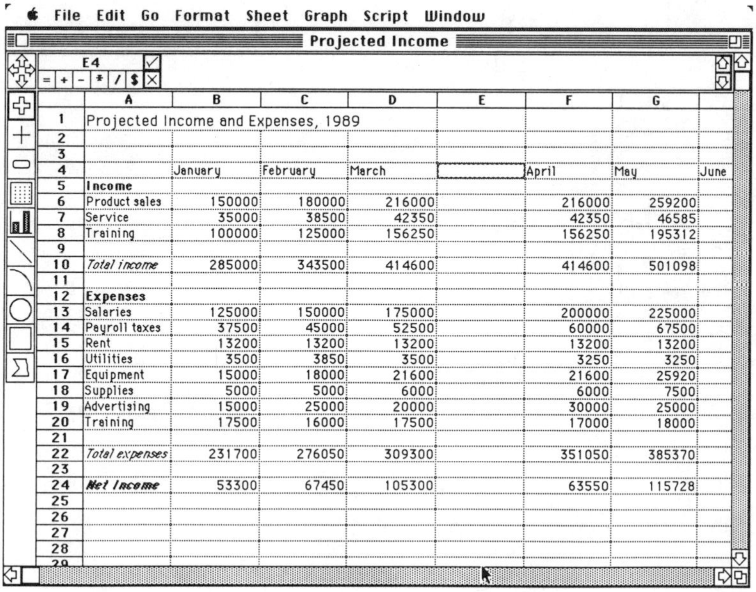

FIGURE 6-6 Income Statement with Column Inserted.

are the formula to add up those figures would have been a SUM function, perhaps

=SUM(B7..M7)

which would be a summary figure for Total Income. This is the formula that appears in the example below when the active cell is in Row 7 of that summary column (see Figure 6-7).

When inserting a column, Wingz automatically adjusts any such formulas to the right of the inserted column to allow for the new locations. However, Wingz also assumes that the newly inserted column contains data that should be added in, and hence would modify the function to read:

=SUM(B7:N7)

Notice that this is exactly what's happened in our example (see Figure 6-8).

186 Mastering Wingz

	H	I	J	K	L	M	N
1							
2							
3							
4	July	August	September	October	November	December	Annual Total
5							
6	311040	373248	447898	537477	644973	773967	4289802
7	51244	56368	62005	68205	75026	82528	633560
8	244141	305176	381470	476837	596046	745058	3606540
9							
10	606424	734792	891372	1082519	1316045	1601553	8535002
11							
12							
13	275000	300000	325000	350000	375000	400000	3150000
14	82500	90000	97500	105000	112500	120000	945000
15	13200	13200	13200	13200	13200	13200	158400
16	3000	3000	3250	3250	3500	3500	39850
17	31104	37325	44790	53748	64497	77397	428980
18	7000	7000	8000	8000	7500	7500	82000
19	20000	25000	35000	35000	30000	35000	325000
20	17500	16500	21000	20000	23000	21000	223000
21							
22	449304	492025	547740	588198	629197	677597	5352230
23							
24	157120	242767	343632	494322	686847	923957	3182772

FIGURE 6-7 Summary Column before Insert.

FIGURE 6-8 Summary Column after Insert.

	I	J	K	L	M	N	O
1							
2							
3							
4	July	August	September	October	November	December	Annual Total
5							
6	373248	447898	537477	644973	773967	928760	5038563
7	56368	62005	68205	75026	82528	90781	692941
8	305176	381470	476837	596046	745058	931323	4412863
9							
10	734792	891372	1082519	1316045	1601553	1950864	10142367
11							
12							
13	275000	300000	325000	350000	375000	400000	3150000
14	82500	90000	97500	105000	112500	120000	945000
15	13200	13200	13200	13200	13200	13200	158400
16	3000	3000	3250	3250	3500	3500	39850
17	37325	44790	53748	64497	77397	92876	503856
18	7000	7000	8000	8000	7500	7500	82000
19	20000	25000	35000	35000	30000	35000	325000
20	17500	16500	21000	20000	23000	21000	223000
21							
22	455525	499490	556698	598947	642097	693076	5427106
23							
24	279267	391882	525822	717097	959457	1257788	4715260

Unfortunately, that's not what you meant to happen. You're adding together the monthly figures for January, February, and March to produce the quarterly summary figures in Column E, and then adding those same three sets of monthly data along with the first quarter summary figures to the data in the remaining nine columns to get an annual total. Correct this by modifying the year-end formulas to add only the monthly figures (=SUM(B7..D7)+SUM(F7..H7)+...), or add the four quarterly summary figures (if you also insert columns for summaries for the second, third, and fourth quarters).

CUT AND PASTE: MOVING, COPYING, AND THE CLIPBOARD

You can move cells around on your worksheet, transferring entire blocks of calculations to other locations on your worksheet. You can also copy cells containing formulas or values to other locations. In both cases, the cell references will automatically adjust to reflect the new locations.

Moving is done by selecting the cells involved, then using the Cut and Paste commands; copying is done by selecting the cells, then using the Copy command. However, there are other kinds of copying (Copy Right and Copy Down) and some specialized Paste actions (Paste Special) that let you do some of these things very efficiently. We'll look at both kinds of operations in this section.

When you move a set of cells, you remove them from one location and put them in another location—as if you were literally cutting out the block of cells, moving them to a new location, and pasting them in place there. Because this analogy is so easy for most people to grasp, the designers of Wingz used the Cut and Paste commands to accomplish the tasks involved in moving cells.

To illustrate how you can move cells, let's move some cells around a small sample worksheet. Figure 6-9 is an example of a worksheet on which we can practice. The Net Sales, Total Expenses, and Net Income cells contain formulas as follows:

Net Sales	=B3–B4
Total Expenses	=SUM(B9..B14)
Net Income	=B6–B16

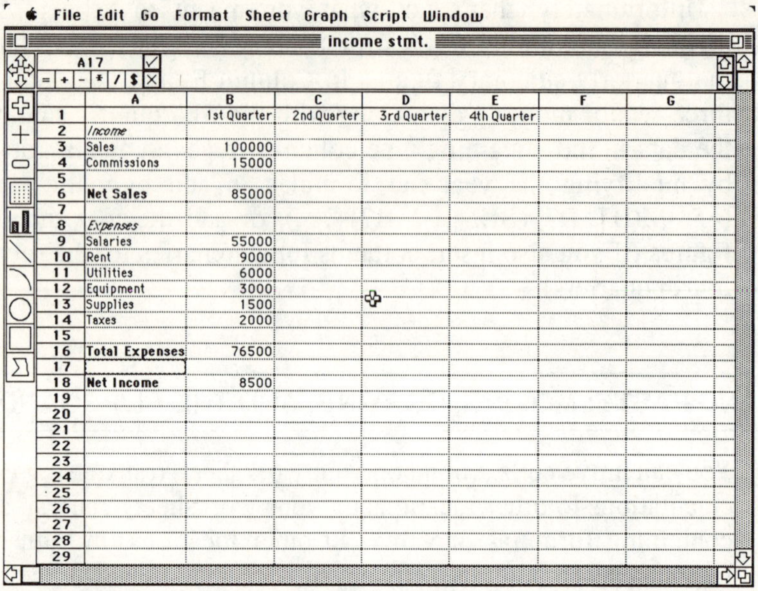

188   Mastering Wingz

FIGURE 6-9 Sample Worksheet.

(You can devise your own worksheet to follow this exercise; be sure to put in a few formulas so that you can see how the move and copy operations handle the references.)

Those cells that are to be involved in a Move or Copy operation must first be selected. Let's use the expense figures, just to illustrate how this works. Select all of the expenses, from B9 to B16 (see Figure 6-10).

With the cells selected, choose the Edit Cut command. Notice that the data disappear from the worksheet, but that the selected cells remain highlighted. Where did the data go?

It's all safe, on the Clipboard. If you want to verify that, select the Edit Show Clipboard command. You'll find the current contents of the Clipboard in the bottom portion of your screen (see Figure 6-11). Now move the cursor to some other location in the worksheet—for instance, one column to the right. When you're where you want the new cells moved, choose the Edit Paste command. (You can also use the shortcut key shown beside the Paste command on the Edit menu.) The data you cut now appear in its new location.

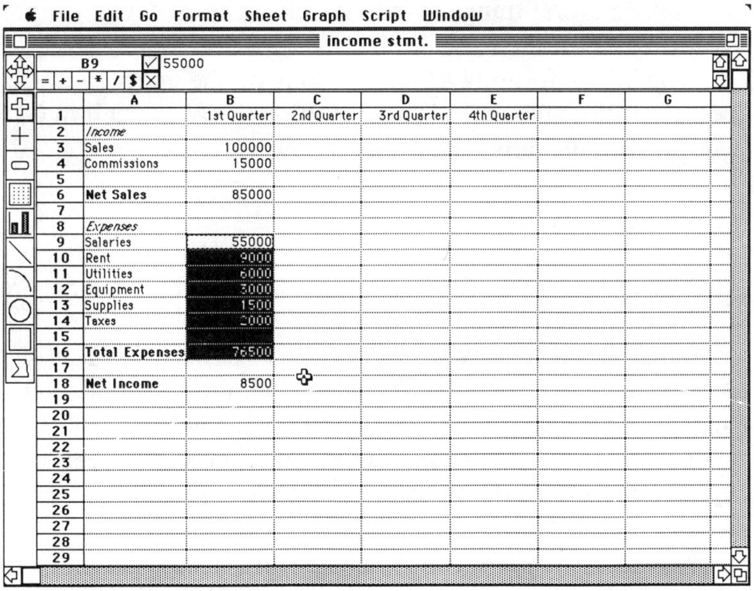

FIGURE 6-10 Selected Cells, Sample Worksheet.

FIGURE 6-11 Clipboard with Cut Data.

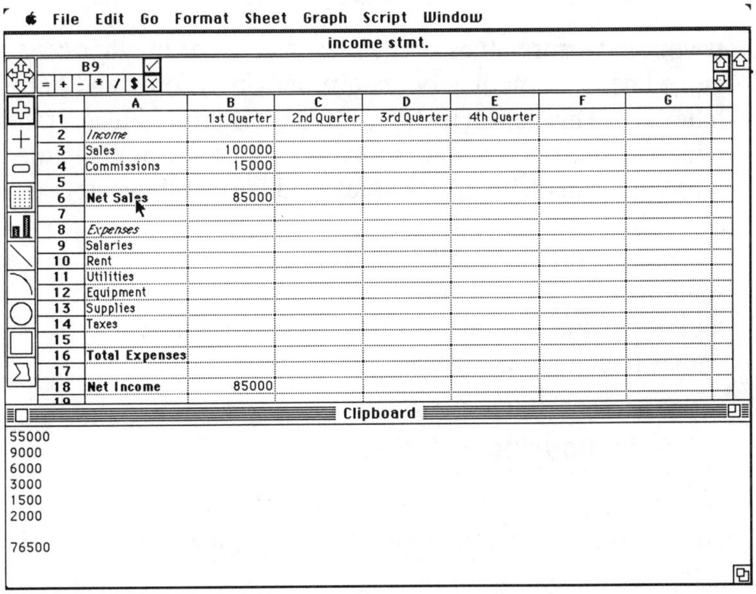

Notice several things about the cells in their new locations:

1. The SUM formula at the bottom of the range now reflects the new location of the cells. If you position the active cell in C16, you find that the formula now reads

   =SUM(C9..C14)

2. The formula in B18 reflects the new location, too, it now reads =B6–C16.

Wingz automatically adjust references to the moved cells. Any references within the moved area to other cells within the moved area still designate the same cells, although the cell addresses will be different. References to cells outside the moved area will be the same. However, references to cells in the area where the moved area was pasted will now produce erroneous values.

You can also move cells from one worksheet to another with the same Cut and Paste commands. However, note that references in the current worksheet to the area that is moved to another worksheet will produce an error in the current worksheet once the cells are moved.

What To Do When Things Go Wrong

If you find error values in the moved cells, or in other cells referencing the moved cells, immediately choose the Undo command before pressing any other key. This action restores all to their prior values. If you don't want to undo the entire Move operation, use the Find command on the Go menu to locate the cells with error values, and correct them so that they refer to the cells you want.

Just to assure yourself that everything works as we described, move the same block back to its original location. You can doublecheck yourself by looking at the formulas in B14 and B16—after the move, they'll reflect values in column B, instead of column C.

A Simple Copying Exercise

How is copying different from moving? Copying lets you duplicate cells in another location, without moving the original cells.

Let's start with something simple, however. With the sample worksheet on your screen, select the Expenses cells again (B9 through B6). Instead of choosing the Edit Cut command, choose Edit Copy.

Move the cursor to a new location—cell C9, for instance. When the cursor is pointing to the top cell in the area where you want the cells copied, choose the Edit Paste command. The selected cells are now duplicated in the new location (see Figure 6-12).

There are differences between the results of the Move and the Copy operations. While a Move operation results in adjustment of relative cell references, any references within the copied area to cells outside the copied area will not be to the same cells, but rather to cells in the equivalent position relative to the original copied formula.

For instance, suppose the figure in B13 were not a number, but a formula reflecting a percentage of commissions:

=200+0.15*B4

FIGURE 6-12 Sample Worksheet, Copied Cells.

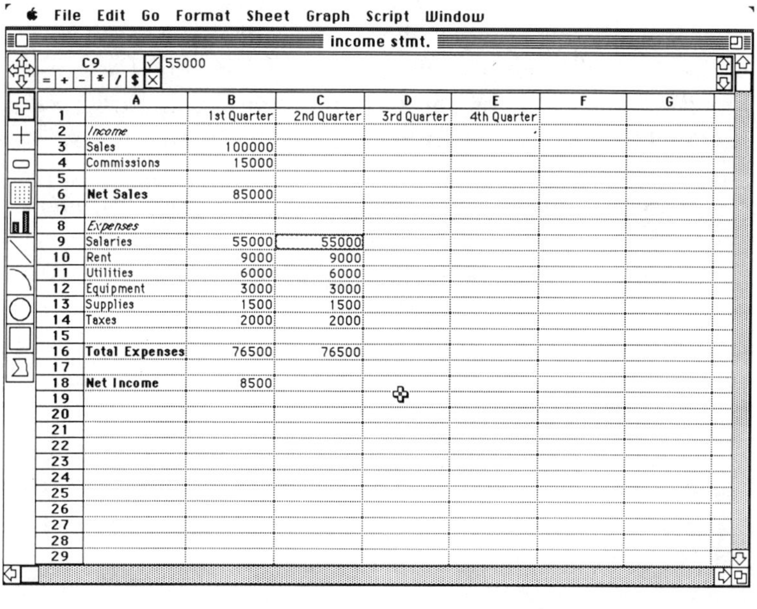

When the expenses figures are all moved, but not the income figures, this formula remains the same, still referencing B4. When the expenses figures are copied to a new location, however, such as we did with the figures in Figure 6-12, the formula refers to the equivalent location above, and becomes

=200+0.15*C4

Notice also that, once the cells have been copied, the copied cells remain highlighted until you move the active cell. Thus you could copy the same set of cells anywhere else on the worksheet—or even to another worksheet—with the same procedure. (If you copy to another worksheet, use the Edit Paste command.)

Using Copy Right or Copy Down

If you want to put the same formula or values in several adjacent cells (for instance, you will use the same formulas to compute total income, total expenses, and net income when doing a 12-month income statement), use the Edit Copy Right or Edit Copy Down commands. They work a bit differently from the normal Edit Copy command.

Instead of selecting just the cell or cells you want to copy, select both the source and destination cells. In the example below, we're going to copy the formula for Net Sales into the 11 columns to the right, so that as data get entered for sales and commissions for each month, the same formula can be used to compute Net Sales. Notice that we've selected row 6, columns B through J on this screen. (We've actually selected through column M, but these are more columns than can be shown on our screen.)

To copy the formula in B6 into the cells to the right, once the cells have been selected choose the Edit Copy Right command. The formula is copied, and at this point each of the destination cells shows a value of 0. If you check on the contents of these cells, you'll see that the formula is there; because there are no values in the rows above it, its current evaluation is 0.

Edit Copy Down works the same way. Select the source and destination cells (destination cells must be adjacent to the source cell) and choose the command. The contents of the source cell now appear in all the destination cells.

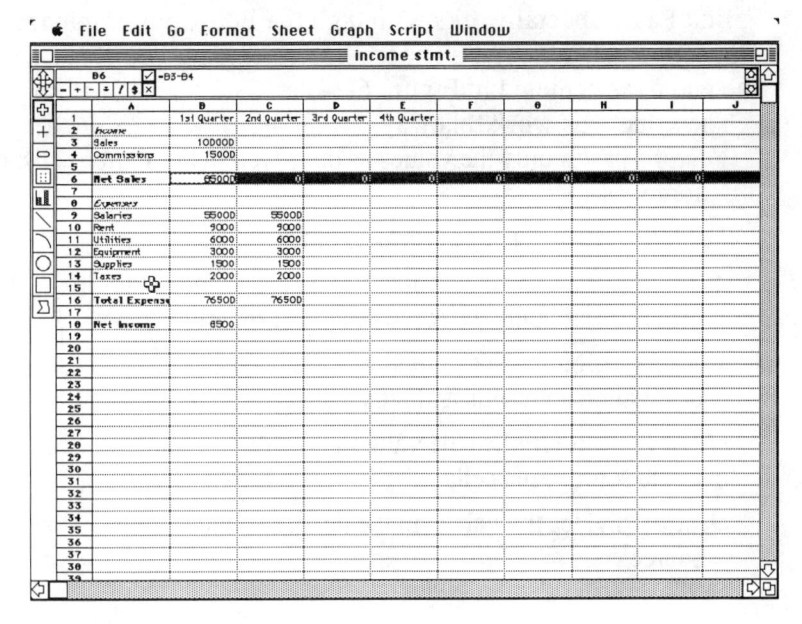

FIGURE 6-13 Copied Cells.

Copying Specific Cell or Data Attributes

Wingz broadens the definition of copying to allow you to selectively to copy data or formulas, or to combine the contents of the copied cells with those already there, to copy all or part of a predesigned function into whatever is currently in the formula bar, to copy names or opertions into a formula, or to copy data and formats from one chart to another.

The Edit Paste Special menu lets you choose whether you want to copy values only or formulas, and to manipulate copied data. The area you select for pasting should be the same size and shape as the area you're copying from. If the destination area is bigger, Wingz will repeat the copied cells as many times as will fit. If it's smaller, Wingz will copy as much as will fit and ignore the rest. As with the other Paste command, you can use the source cells as often as you like, since they're stored on the Clipboard and available for numerous Paste operations until something else gets put on the Clipboard as a result of another Cut or Copy command.

Edit Paste Special works with both the Edit Copy command and the Edit Cut command. When you choose this command, you'll see an extension of the menu, as depicted in Figure 6-14).

The selections work this way:

Values   pastes only the values as displayed in the source cells; disregards formulas

Formats   pastes only the formats of the selected cells

Add   adds the contents of the source cells to the values in the destination area cells and puts the results in the destination area

Subtract   subtracts the contents of the source cells from the values in the destination area cells and puts the results in the destination area

Multiply   multiplies the values in the destination area cells by the values of the source area cells

Divide   divides the values in the destination area cells by the values in the source cells

FIGURE 6-14   Edit Paste Special Menu.

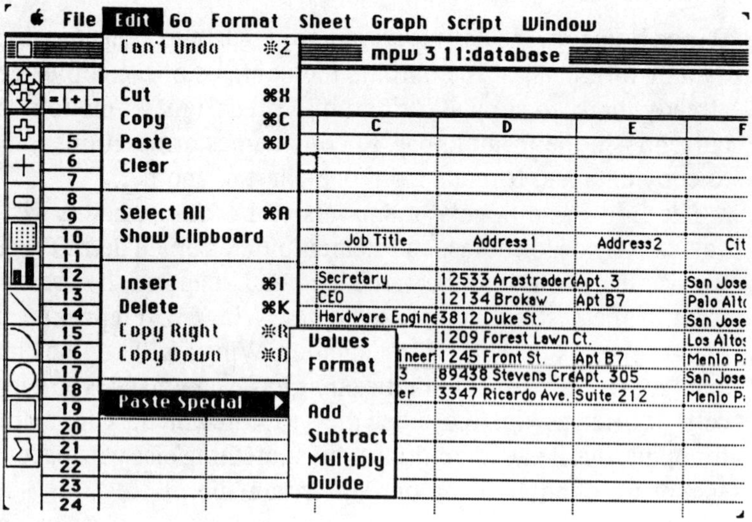

Copying Into the Entry Bar

You can use the Edit Copy and Edit Paste commands to save time when you're constructing long formulas or labels.

You may need to duplicate a label or a particularly intricate set of characters within a formula (when you're constructing a set of nested IF statements, for instance). When typing something like this in the Entry Bar, type the characters you want to copy and any others up to the point where you need the duplicated character string. Next, select the characters you want to copy (click and drag the mouse over the characters so that they're highlighted). Choose the Edit Copy command, move the insertion point in the Entry Bar to the point where you want to use the copied characters, and choose Edit Paste. The characters now also appear at the new location.

Copying Names or Functions Into a Formula

The Paste Formula and Name commands on the Go menu let you paste existing names and predefined functions or formulas into the formula bar, so that you don't have to be as concerned about accuracy or spelling.

The Name command is particularly useful if you're working on a large worksheet and can't remember either the address of a particular cell, or what it is named. When you choose the Name command, and names are already defined, a box will appear showing all the currently defined names in use for this worksheet. (If no names have been defined, the Name command is grayed.)

To use one of the names in a formula, activate the Entry Bar and identify the insertion point where you want the name to go. Then choose the Name command, and when you see the list of existing names, choose the name you want to use. The name is pasted at the insertion point.

The Paste Formula command works pretty much the same way. A dialog box appears, showing templates for all of the functions, listed by category. Choose the category button you want, then scroll through the list of functions until you find the name of the function you want, and choose it. The template is pasted into the Formula Bar (see Figure 6-15). You still need to edit the template, adding values for the arguments suggested.

Suppose you can't remember the arguments for a Net Present Value function, but you want to use it in a formula. With the Formula Bar active, choose the Paste Formula command on the Go menu, then in the Formula dialog box choose the Business button, then scroll through the list till

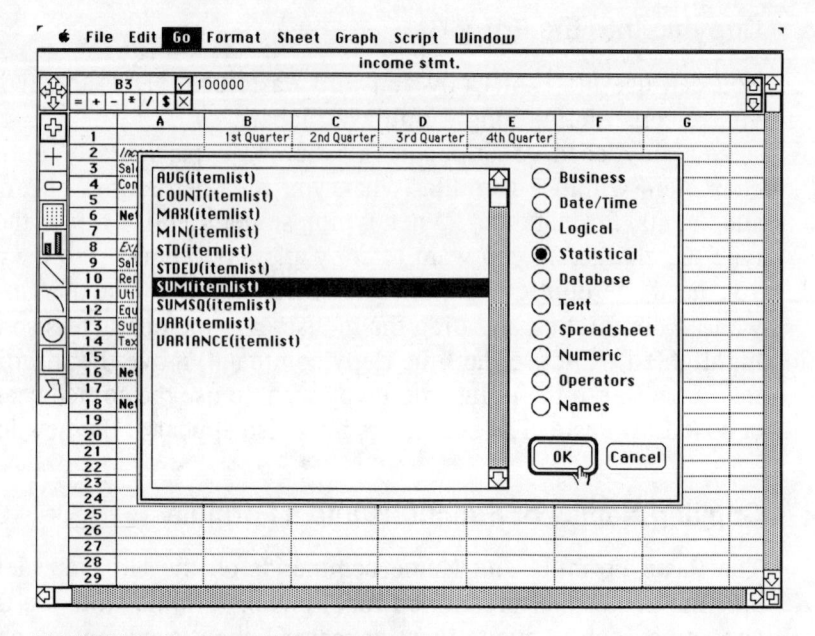

FIGURE 6-15 Paste Formula Box.

NPV(int,range) is highlighted. When you choose the OK button, the NPV function appears at the insertion point in the Entry Bar, followed by the arguments:

NPV(int,range)

Move the Insertion Bar to the first letter in Int and type the interest rate. (You'll need to delete the letters Int.) Leave the comma in place, and move the insertion point to the next word that describes an argument, in this case Range, and type the reference that belongs here, deleting the word Range. Leave the right parenthesis in place. When you press the <Return> key, Wingz either accepts what you've done with the function, or tells you that there is an error.

Copying Objects

You can use the Edit Copy, Cut, and Paste commands to copy objects from one chart to another, or from a chart to one or more worksheets. You use the Edit menu commands only after you've identified the objects with the object tool. Remember, objects can consist of charts, text fields, or graphic images you've drawn. Let's look at an example that will give you some ideas how to manipulate objects, using the Copy, Cut, and Move commands.

Let's start with a blank worksheet. We've entered some numbers to show you the monthly sales by product (see Figure 6-16).This report is going to go out to the divisional salespeople, who need to note that sales for Product A have slipped dramatically in the last month. A bolt of lightning ought to call their attention to this fact. But how do you get a bolt of lightning onto a spreadsheet?

Wingz lets you do just that. First, let's move the figures down several rows, so that we have more room for anything else we want to add (see Figure 6-17). Next, we need to draw the lightning bolt. To draw the one we have shown here, choose the poly tool, and then position the mouse in an unused area of the worksheet, and click. This will be the starting point of the polygon, and is marked by a small circle.

Each time you move the mouse, you'll be drawing a line. You can adjust the line any way you like, but it will stop at the point where you click again,

FIGURE 6-16 Sample Sales Figures.

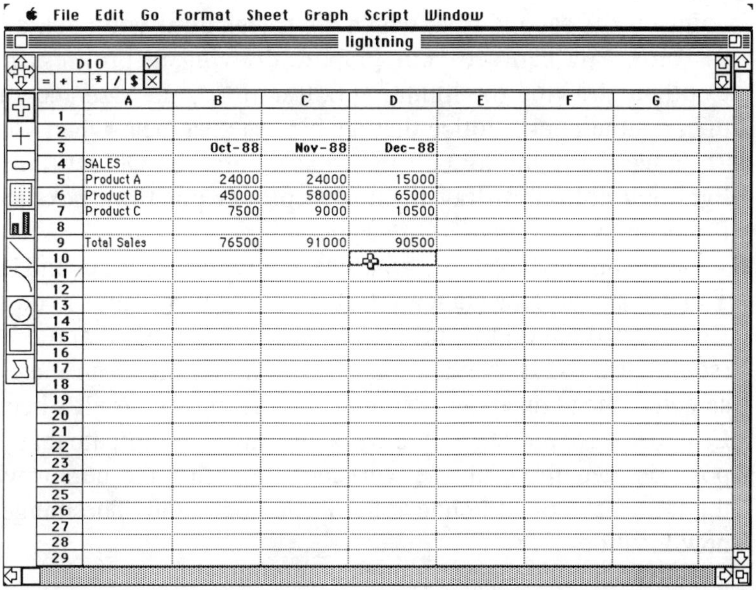

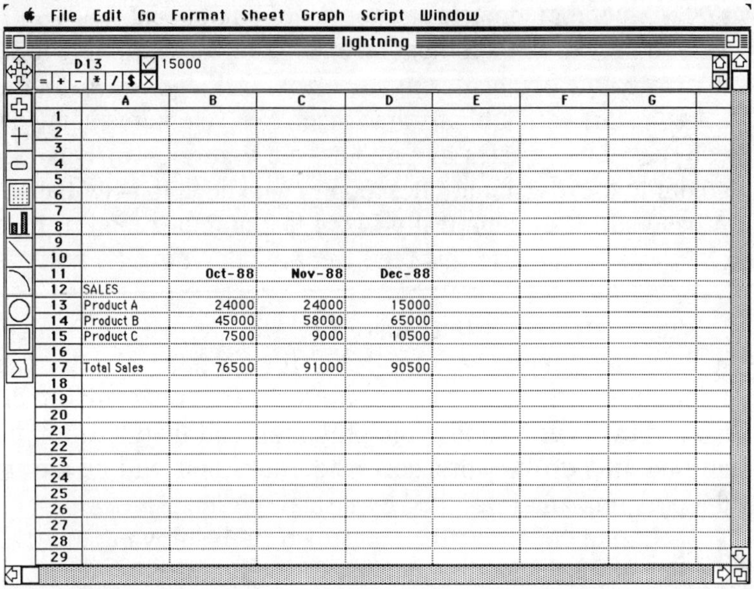

FIGURE 6-17 Sample Sales Figures, Repositioned.

with another small circle. That second point will also serve as the starting point for the second line, which continues until you click a third time, and so forth. You can see your graphic drawing in progress in Figure 6-18. Continue drawing the lightning bolt until it's the size and shape you want, then double click. Notice that the circles disappear when you double click. To move the lightning bolt into place, click the Object tool, then click the lightning bolt, and drag it into the proper position, next to the low sales figure for March.

What you've done is the graphical equivalent of a Cut and Paste operation. You can also use the standard Cut and Paste commands to do the same thing. Click anywhere on the image, to create a rectangle marked by small circles (see Figure 6-19). Next, choose the Cut command on the Edit menu. The selected image disappears from your screen, because it's been moved to the Clipboard. Now click on the worksheet tool, to indicate that you're about to position something on the worksheet. Position the cursor where you want the image to go, and choose the Paste command. The image appears in its new location.

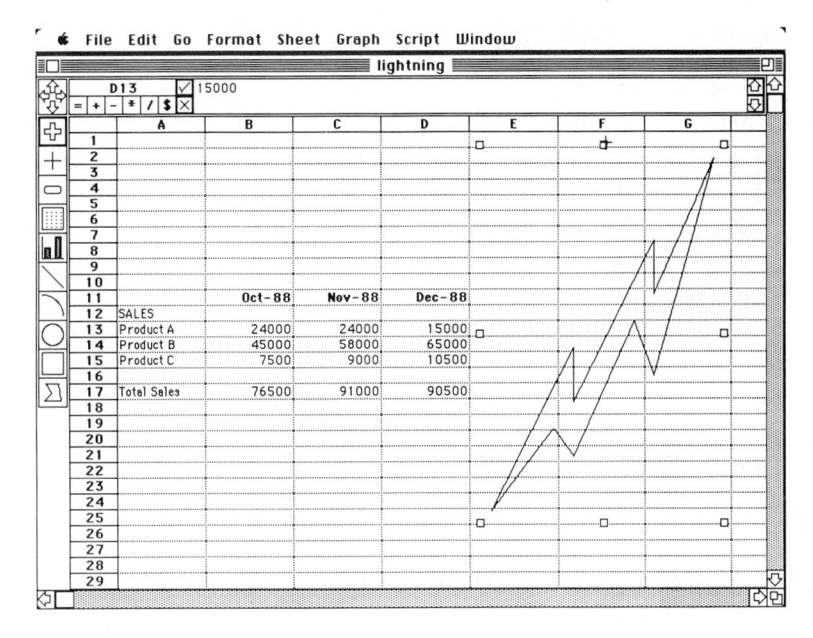

FIGURE 6-18 Graphic Drawing in Progress.

FIGURE 6-19 Selected Object.

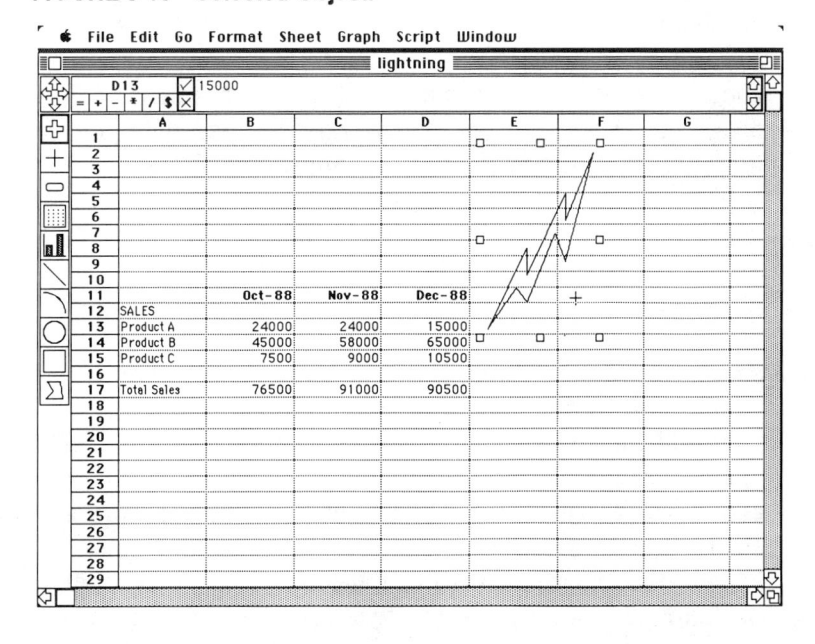

Copying and Moving Text Boxes

We showed you in Chapter 5 on Charts and Graphs how to add text to your charts. It's a simple matter to move the text boxes anywhere you need to place them, and to move them between charts and worksheets. Moving text boxes is like moving any other object: you declare the box to be an object, using the Object tool. Then you select it by clicking on the box, which turns on the open boxes surrounding the text box. Once these are on, simply drag the box to its new position.

You can also copy the box, once it's been selected as an object, using the Copy and Paste commands. However, before you choose the Paste command, be sure you've selected the Worksheet tool, so that you can pick a cell location where the box is to be pasted. You won't be able to use the Paste command unless the Worksheet tool is active.

BORDERS, PATTERNS, AND COLOR

You can add borders to data, a text field, a control box, or a chart. You can also add borders to chart titles, footnotes, legends, and plots, and you can change the color, pattern, or width of lines that define an object, such as a graphic image.

You can get a number of different effects, depending on the option you choose and how it's combined with other options. The Format Line command , used when a cell is currently selected, lets you specify how the gridlines on your worksheet are to appear. For instance, the gridlines in the worksheet you first see are 0.25 mm. wide. If you'd like them to be bolder, you can choose that option with the Line... command (see Figure 6-20). The dialog box that appears on your screen lets you specify how wide you want the gridlines, and whether you want a color and/or pattern in the background or foreground (see Figure 6-21). The area on the right, which shows the various options for lines, indicates how wide the gridlines will be for the entire worksheet. Notice in Figure 6-19 that one choice made all of the gridlines the same size.

The Foreground and Background boxes on the left show the selection of colors possible with your equipment. The square indicates which color (or shade of gray, if your equipment can't show color) is currently chosen. In Figure 4-20 above, the squares indicate that the foreground is black and the background is white, thus whatever pattern is chosen for the gridlines will

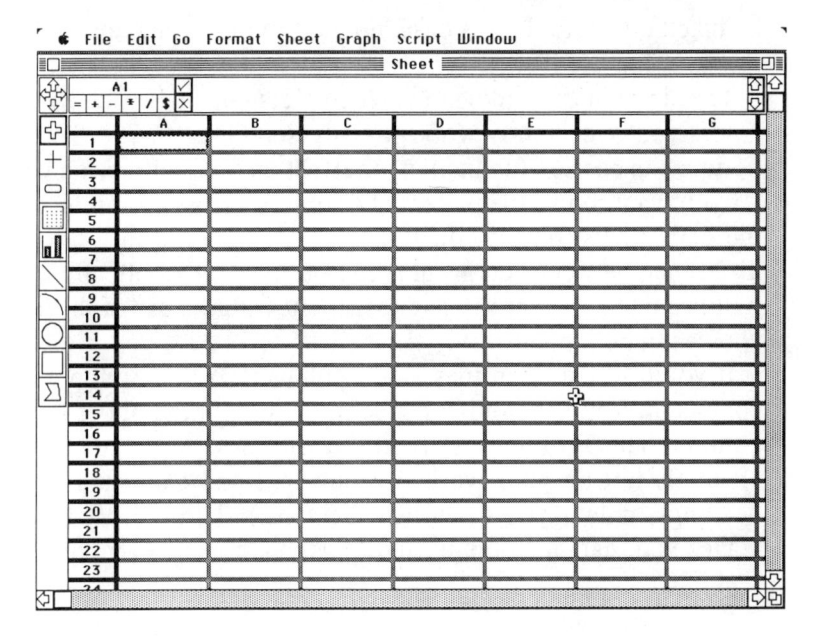

FIGURE 6-20 Worksheet with 4.00 Gridlines.

FIGURE 6-21 Line Dialog Box.

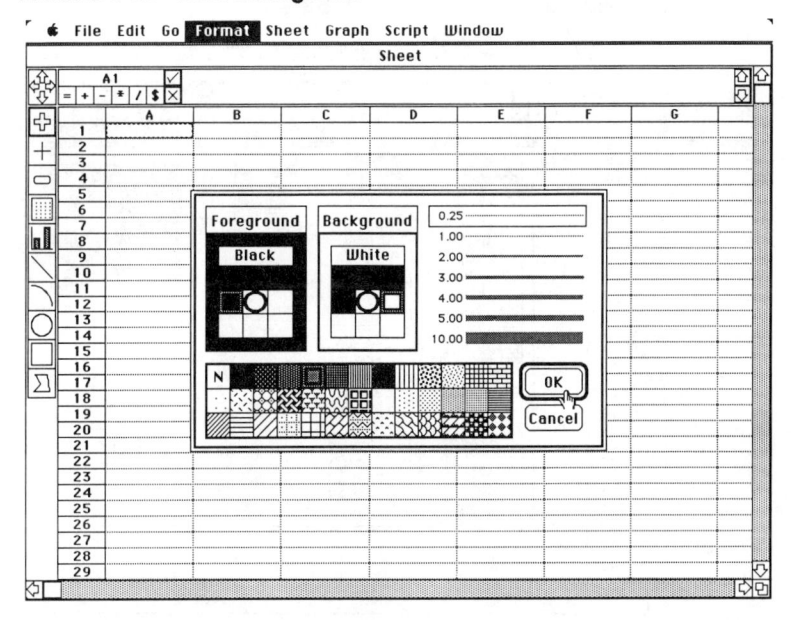

be black on white. In this case, no pattern has been chosen, and a 0.25 mm. line is being used.

The circle in the middle of each box lets you make fine adjustments to the colors you're currently working with (see Figure 6-22). The patterns at the bottom can be used for an all over effect on the gridlines on your worksheet. (If you want to use the patterns within the cells, or on selected cells, select the cells or the object you want, and choose the Fill... command.) The difference between foreground and background application of the patterns will become apparent if you experiment with the use of the black and white choices in both boxes.

If you'd like no gridlines at all, you can get that option with the Line... command. You need only choose the N box in the upper left corner of the patterns. This action turns off all the gridlines. When you turn off gridlines, all that's left on your worksheet are text and data (and row and column headings, unless you've turned them off). Turning off the gridlines still leaves your data in columns and rows, but makes it look less like a spread-

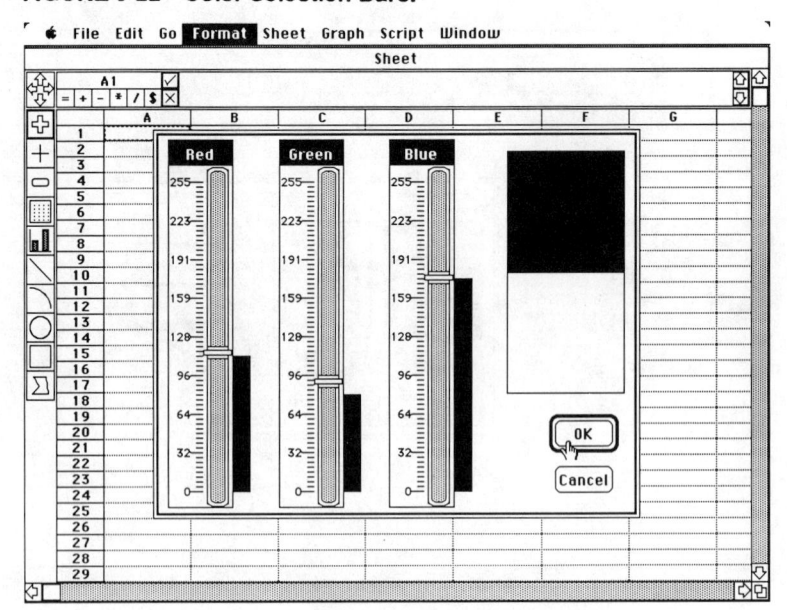

FIGURE 6-22 Color Selection Bars.

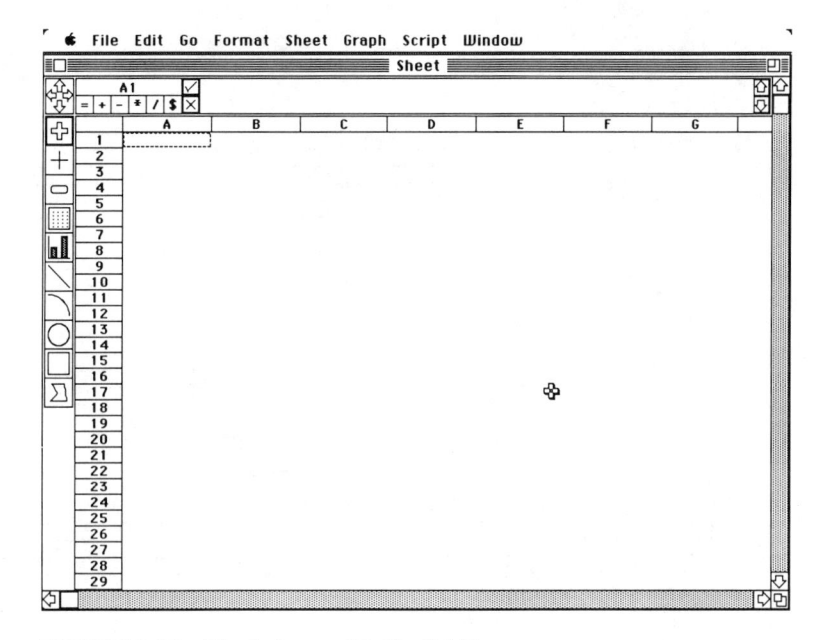

FIGURE 6-23 Worksheet with No Gridlines.

sheet. Figure 6-23 is an example of what our sample worksheet, complete with text, now looks like with no gridlines:

To use colors, lines, or patterns in the worksheet, in selected portions of it, or within graphic images, use the Fill... command. For instance, we have created a patterned border around a set of numbers by selecting the cells around the numbers, choosing the Fill... command, and selecting a pattern (see Figure 6-24).

You can also use the patterns to create shapes with different degrees of shading. Note that you'll have to create a shape, then apply color and/or pattern to it. Unfortunatley, Wingz doesn't recognize as a shape or object something you've drawn with the line tool—any enclosed shape must be drawn with the circle, square, or polygon tool. We drew the box shown in Figure 6-25 with the box and polygon tools.

You can put borders around any rectangular shape with the Border command on the Format menu. (The Border command isn't available unless you've selected a rectangular object—it doesn't work with any cell or any other shape.) When you've selected a rectangle or button, the Border command shows you a set of choices (see Figure 6-26). The Foreground,

204　Mastering Wingz

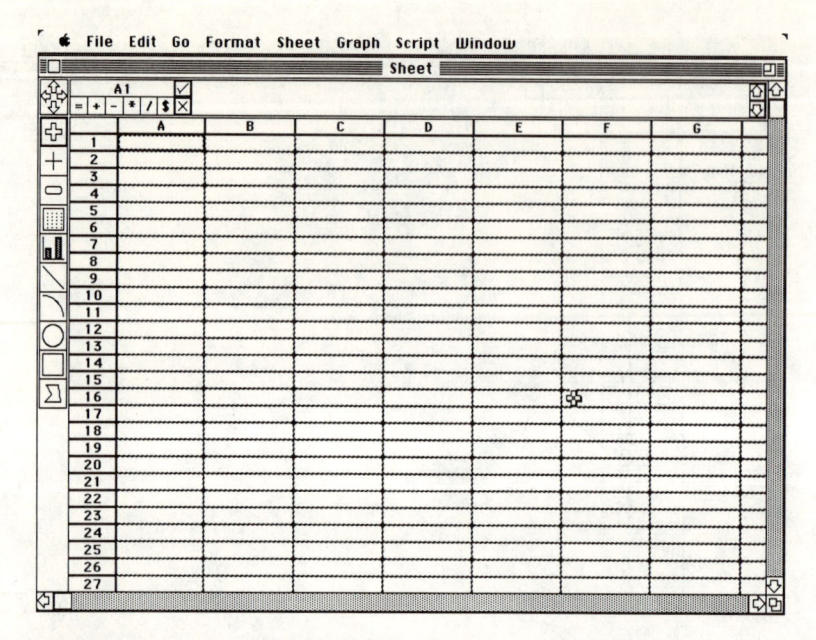

FIGURE 6-24 **Patterned Border Created with Fill Command.**

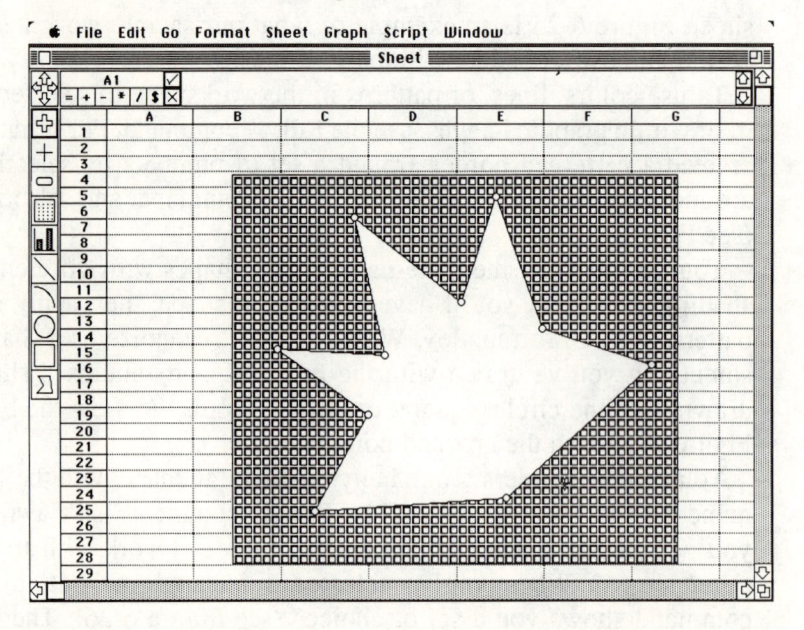

FIlGURE 6–25 **Patterned Figure**

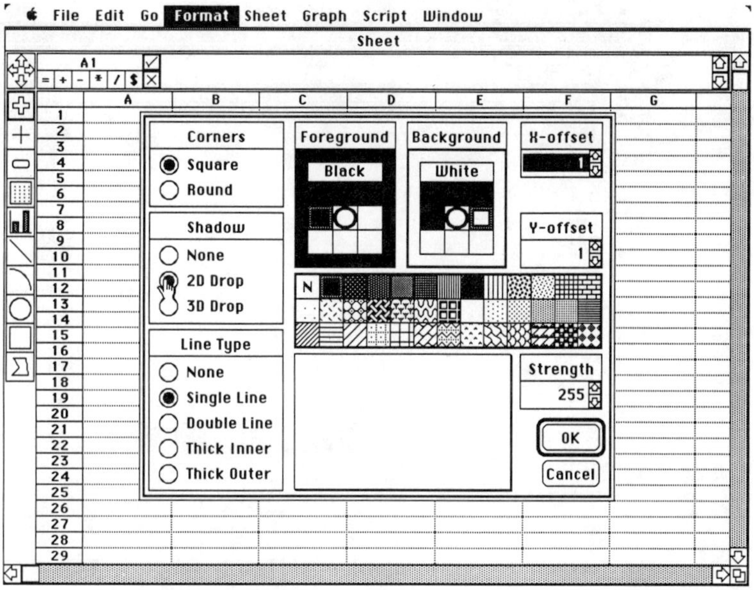

FIGURE 6-26 Border Dialog Box.

Background, Offset, Pattern, and Strength boxes appear grayed until you choose either the 2D Drop or 3D Drop Shadow choices. With the Border Command, we created the shadow effect shown in Figure 6-27, using a 2D Drop, X and Y offsets of 20, and choosing rounded corners and thick outer lines, along with a patterned shadow.

ADDING TEXT TO YOUR WORKSHEET

You can add a text field anywhere on your worksheet. You do so by creating a text box (using the text field tool to draw the box) wherever you want to place the text. Text fields can be useful when you're constructing a fairly elaborate worksheet, and need reminders about why a particular formula was used, or what assumptions have been used. They're also very helpful when more than one person is developing a worksheet, and a trail needs to be left as to what variables are being used for specific purposes, and what names are being used.

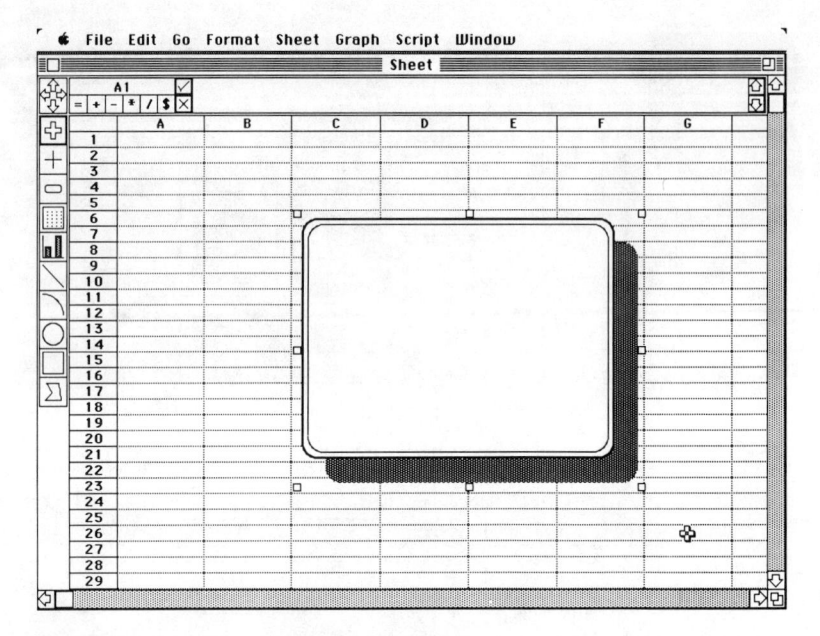

FIGURE 6-27 Sample Border on a Box.

However, in a presentation spreadsheet, and Wingz is such, you use text fields to put any sentences or phrases that explain the numbers and/or graphs that appear on the same page. Since a text field responds to many of the editing controls you have with a word processor on the Macintosh, you have a great deal of freedom to format what appears in a text field as you want. Figure 6-28 shows an example of a text field that helps give meaning to the numbers appearing on the same page.

You create text fields with the text tool. This changes the cursor to a box-drawing tool. The point where you next click the mouse will be the upper left corner of the text field. Drag the mouse to create the size and shape box you want (see Figure 6-29).

Once you release the mouse, you'll have the outline of your text field, with the pointer indicating where characters you type will be placed. Any text you type will automatically be wrapped around so that lines fit within the box. If you change the size of the type, the lines will be adjusted again so that they fit within the box.

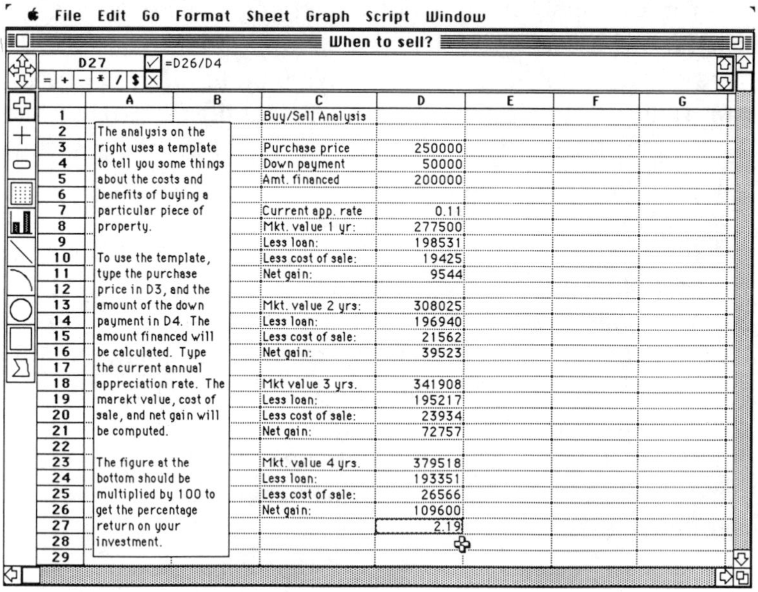

FIGURE 6-28 Sample Text Field.

FIGURE 6-29 Initial Text Field.

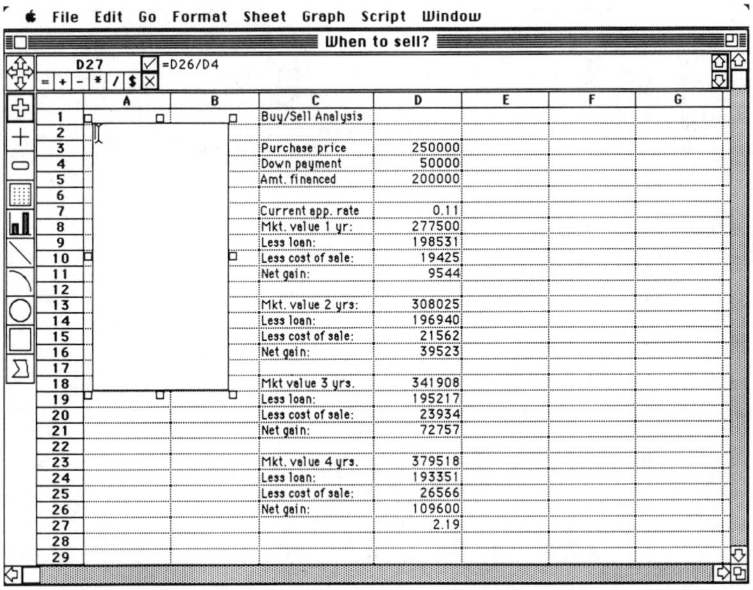

You can apply many word processing functions to text fields: you can insert and delete characters, words, lines, or paragraphs; you can copy or move when. You can turn Word Wrap on or off; you can align it to the left or right or center it. You can set margins and tabs, line spacing, and paragraph indentations. You can use any of the fonts, styles, or sizes listed in the Format menu, and you can use color with individual characters or the entire text box. If you have a lot of text, you can add a Scroll bar to the text field so that you can move up and down the text field with ease.

Like other objects, text within the text field needs to be selected before it can be manipulated. To select something within a text field, click the worksheet tool, then click in front of whatever you want to change, and drag the mouse so that the item is highlighted. Then choose the appropriate command or commands.

To set margins, tabs, or indentations in a text field, select the text field, and choose Field Info on the Format menu. You'll see a box like like the one in Figure 6-30.

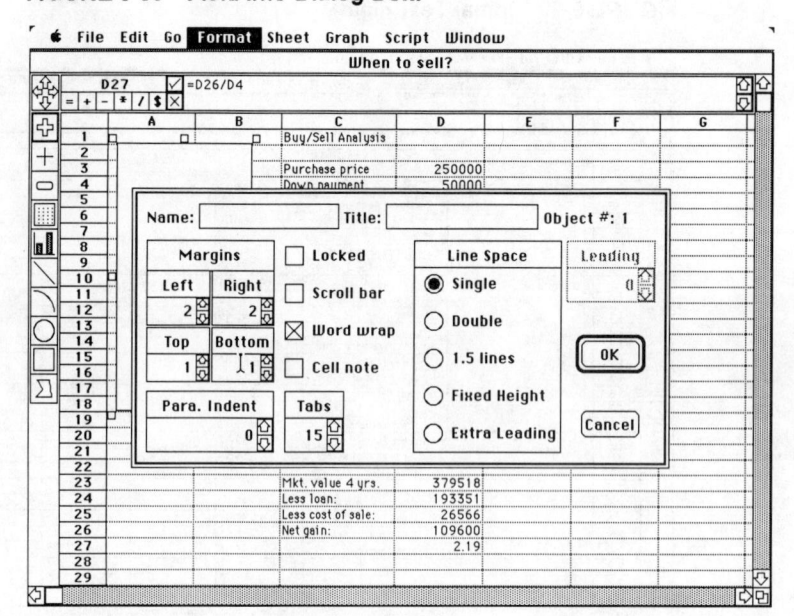

FIGURE 6-30 Field Info Dialog Box.

To change margins, indicate in points (72 points = 1 inch) you want as top, bottom, left, and right margins as measured from the edge of the box. To change tabs, use the Scroll box to indicate how many points the cursor should jump each time the <Tab> key is pressed. To change paragraph indentation, use the Scroll box to indicate how many points you want paragraphs indented. (Indents apply to all text in the current box.) To change line spacing, select the appropriate entry in the Line Space box.

Use the same Field Info dialog box to lock the text field (it can be read but not modified), to add or delete a Scroll bar, or to turn Word Wrap on or off.

A **cell note** is a text field under a different name. The difference is useful when you want to hide some fields but show others with the Show command on the Window menu (see Figure 6-31). You edit a note the same way you edit text in a text box. You can use the Select command on the Go menu to select all the notes in the current document, and the Find command to find which cell note contains a particular character string.

You can remove a note can be removed by selecting the cell involved using the worksheet tool, so that the cell note appears, then clicking within it so

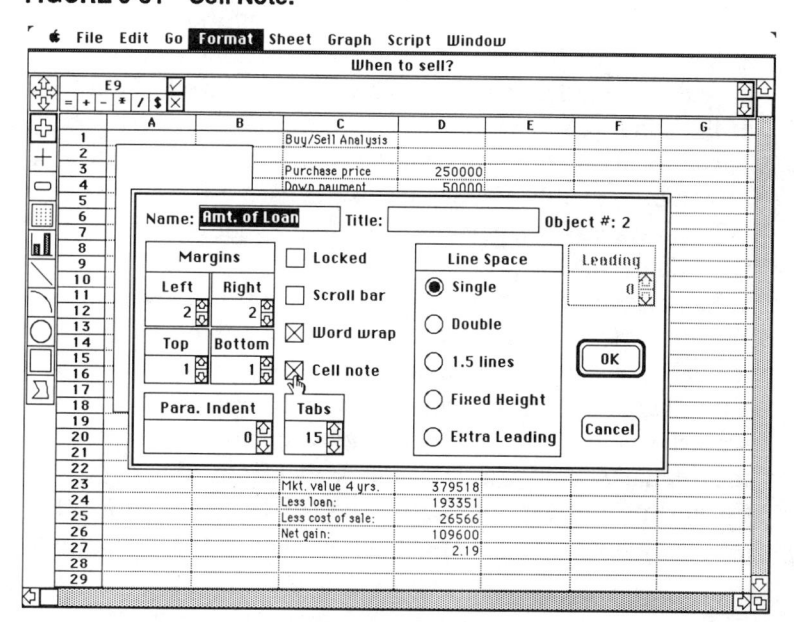

FIGURE 6-31 Cell Note.

that the small squares around it appear. Once the note has been thus selected, use the Edit Clear command. You may need to repeat the process using the Object tool in order to get the Edit Clear command to work.

USING WINDOWS

Windowing lets you have more than one document active and accessible on your screen. One of the more obvious examples is that you can have both a worksheet and a related set of charts accessible on your screen. Another example is that you can have several related worksheets on your screen, so that you can accurately pass data from one to another. A third example is that you can open multiple windows into a single very large worksheet.

The **New Window command** creates an additional window for the currently active document. This lets you look at two or more sections of the same document at once, a useful tool when you're working on a large spreadsheet and can't remember how certain cells or cell ranges are arranged.

A new window created with the New Window command simply overlays the previous window, but with the same data showing. Unless there are many windows, the filename for each of the windows thus created will be visible as a line above the one in front of it. Each new window of the same file will have the same filename, but each will be followed by a colon and the number of the window.

The **Arrange Windows** command rearranges the windows currently open in Wingz so that the available space is used effectively. For instance, Figure 6-32 shows an arrangement when two windows are open, and Figure 6-33 shows one when four windows are open.

You can also use the windows concept to copy data to and from other Wingz worksheet files. The other file simply needs to be an open file, that is it will appear on your screen as just another window. Move back and forth between the open files by selecting the appropriate filename (open Wingz worksheets are listed on the Window menu). The window associated with the filename you select becomes the front window, or currently active document. You can then copy data from one file to another the same way you copy data from one place to another in the current worksheet, except

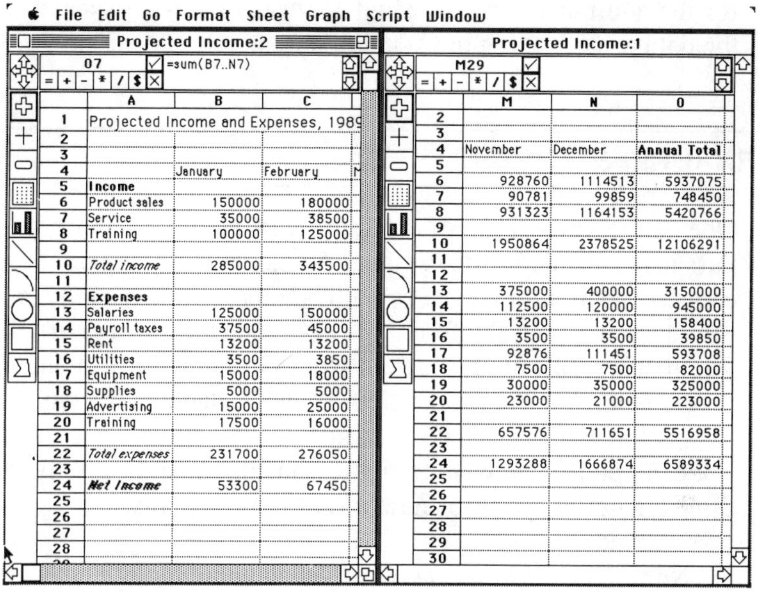

Changing Your Mind 211

FIGURE 6-32 Two Windows After Arranging.

FIGURE 6-33 Four Windows After Arranging.

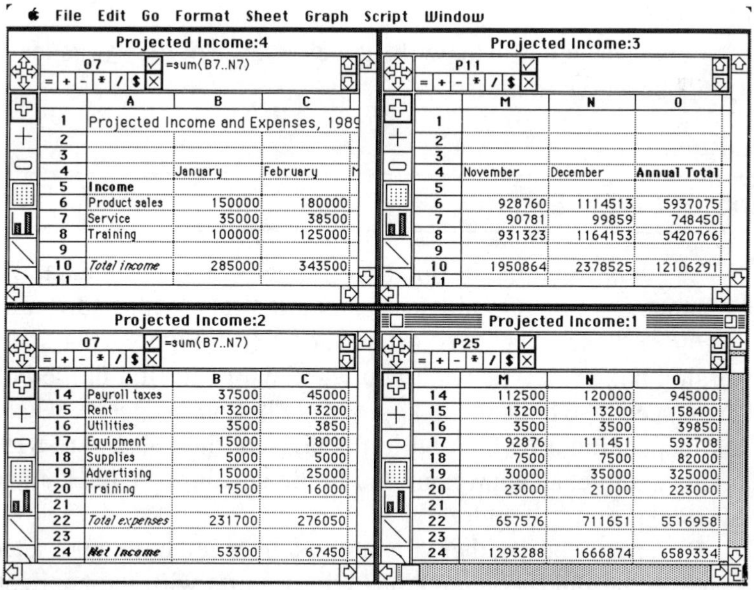

for the additional step of bringing forward the worksheet where you want the data pasted, using the Window menu.

EXTERNAL REFERENCES

One of the advantages of working with multiple windows is that you can pass data back and forth, without necessarily moving or copying them. You can use data stored in a cell on another worksheet by making the cell reference an external reference. This action tells Wingz that the cell or range you're after isn't on the current worksheet—that it's on another one.

An external reference consists of the filename of the worksheet, followed by a colon and the cell coordinates of the cell or range on that worksheet. For example, if you were trying to consolidate the monthly sales figures for three territories, your formula might look like this:

=North:C7+Midwest:C7+West:C7

In this case, the value in the active cell in the current worksheet will be the sum of the value in C7 on the worksheet named "North," plus the value in C7 on the worksheet "Midwest," plus the value in C7 on the worksheet "West."

For the calculation to work, however, each of the worksheets so referenced must be active in memory.

FINDING SPECIFIC DATA

Wingz lets you quickly find specific cells or specific data, with the Find... command on the Go menu. You can instruct Wingz to find specific text, a value, a formula, a set of criteria, or a cell. Figure 6-34 shows the Find... dialog box. You type what you want Wingz to find in the box on the right. You need also choose the appropriate button to specify what type of data it is; depending on which button is chosen, the characters S15 could be text (for example, an apartment number in an address), the name of a value or a formula, or a cell address.

Regardless of whether you have a single cell or a range selected when you choose the Find... command, Wingz starts with the next cell and looks to

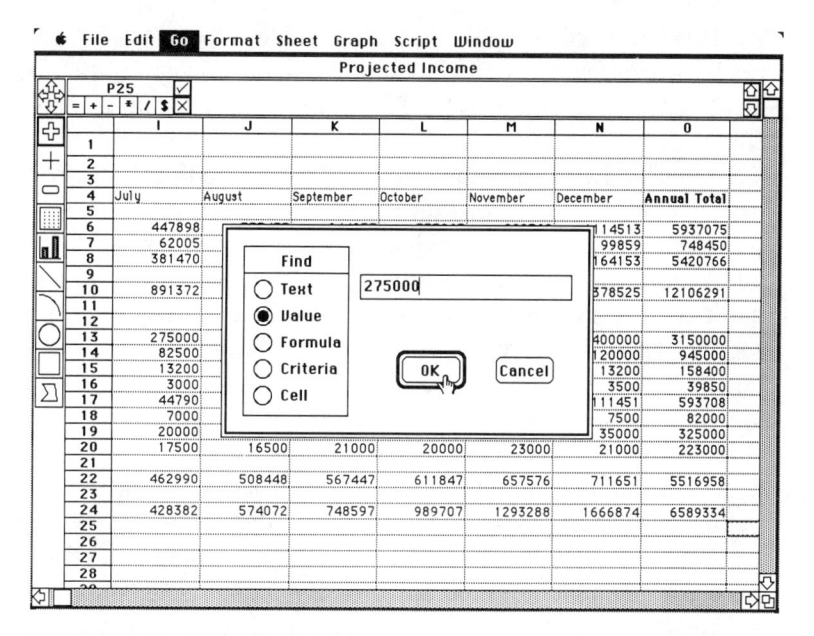

FIGURE 6-34 The Find Dialog Box.

the end of the worksheet. If you start the search at a place other than at the beginning of your worksheet, Wingz may not be able to find what you specify.

While there is no specific Replace command in a Wingz spreadsheet, you can create a Script that uses the Find... command in conjunction with a replacement action. We discuss creating and using scripts in Chapter 11.

PROTECTING YOUR WORK

There are several ways to protect your work from accidental or unauthorized changes, a safeguard that becomes far more important if you're working with sensitive data, or with files that must be shared by several users.

You can protect a file on disk by assigning one or two passwords to it. The first password is a **read/write password**; that is, only those users knowing the password will be able to open the file. The second password can be a read/write password, or a read only password. A **read only password** allows anybody to open and read the file, but no changes can be made to data in the file.

To put password protection on a file, choose the Protection command on the Sheet menu, and select the Password option. Type one or two passwords of 15 characters or less, beginning with a letter. (Write it down separately, and keep that memo in a different, safe place so that you can find it if you can't remember your own password.) Click the Read Only button for the second password, if you use one. Then choose the OK bar. The next time anyone tries to open the file, Wingz will ask for the password or passwords, which must be typed correctly for the file to be opened.

If you want to remove password protection, go through the Protection procedure again, but in the Password box delete the password or passwords.

You can encrypt and decrypt your files the same way as you use a password. Just choose the Encrypt button on the Protection dialog box to save the file in encrypted form. Only those users who know the proper password will be able to open the file in decrypted form.

You can also selectively protect the contents of a document, in essence locking one or more cells so that the specific contents can't be changed until the cell is unprotected. Protecting a cell is accomplished in two steps. First, you select the cell or cells you want protected with the Protection command. Then you choose the Protect option on the submenu. (Once you've chosen Protect for any cell on your worksheet, the Enable Protection command is checked; if you choose Disable Protection, any protected cells become unprotected.)

You can also hide a cell. When you hide a cell, the cell's contents are not displayed on the worksheet when the cell is selected. However, the cell contents appear in the Formula Bar when the cell is selected. To hide one or more cells, select the Attribute command on the Format menu, and check Hidden on the submenu. The selected cells are then hidden on the worksheet. To make the cell contents reappear, again select the Attribute command and turn off the Hidden checkmark.

Protecting a chart works much the same way as protecting a document. You can protect and unprotect cells containing data that are reflected in the chart, and you can assign password protection to a chart. However, you can't hide the chart.

SUMMARY

This chapter has shown you a number of editing commands and techniques, and given you some practice examples so that you could see how these commands and techniques work. Wingz's editing capabilities let you fine-tune your worksheet, moving and changing data, inserting and deleting cells as needed, letting you search for text, values, formulas, and the like, using windows to display several worksheets at once, and using several techniques for protecting data while you work.

CASE STUDY 4:
Wingz In A Law Firm

Robert G. Leeds, P.A.
1956 Whitney Way
Clearwater, Florida 34624

Leeds has been an attorney for 14 years, specializing in business litigation, and has used the Macintosh in a wide variety of applications. He has written manuals, beta tested a lot of Macintosh software, and currently consults for Apple Computer, Inc. He also writes columns for MacWorld and Juris magazines.

He uses spreadsheet programs in matrimonial work a lot, where he needs to present financial information to the court. He has learned to be careful with some of the graphs, however, since some judges are reluctant to accept charts as evidence, there being (in one case) "no showing of the underlying reliability of the factual data." The court would accept, however, the raw data, but not its pictorial representation. (He later learned that the real reason was because the charts were too good—his opponents couldn't cope with something that clear.)

He decided to use Wingz after hearing about it, deciding it would be perfect to help him track stock price fluctuations in a federal securities fraud case. It became apparent that the price of a certain stock would rise after certain people got involved, then decline after they sold out.

Wingz's charts have helped him demonstrate how stock prices have moved as a result of what he is attempting to show is stock manipulation. The charts display these relationships clearly.

Leeds considers Wingz "one of the handful of truly innovative programs on the Mac—it has evolved into something impressive. I'm very impressed with HyperScript," he commented recently.

7

File Management

When you open a Wingz worksheet for the first time, the data you enter are stored in RAM. All your changes and corrections, all the formulas and values resulting from formulas, all the formats and color selections are kept in the computer's memory. If you create a chart from your newly entered data, it gets stored in RAM too. Thus, if you turn off the computer, or if you lose power accidentally, all your work is erased. If you intend to use your work again, you need to save it as a disk file, a simple process using the File menu.

This chapter will show you how to save your work, retrieve it and use it again, open and use files from other spreadsheet packages, and share files with other users.

OPENING A NEW WORKSHEET

When you start Wingz, you start with an empty worksheet on your screen (see Figure 7–1). Anything you enter on the worksheet is saved in RAM. It

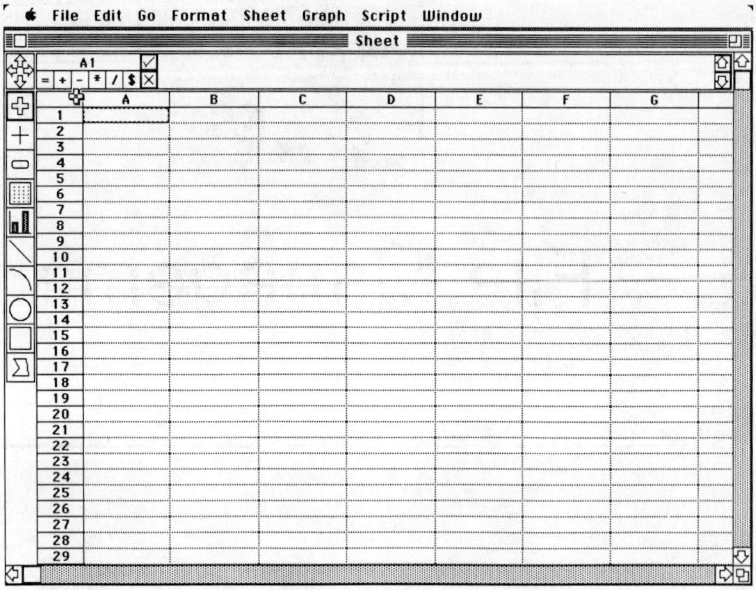

FIGURE 7-1 Empty Worksheet.

stays there until you replace the data with something else, or turn off the computer.

You can open a new worksheet any time you want, with the New command on the File menu. When you do, you'll see the same blank worksheet that overlays your previous work. This previous work, however, is still in RAM. And if you want, you can open still more new worksheets, each of which is considered to be open within its own "window," hence the commands on the Window menu. Each of these sheets contains data that are stored in RAM.

When you save the current worksheet, you aren't necessarily removing it from RAM; you're simply making a copy of it and storing the copy on disk. Only when you use the Close command do you actually remove the worksheet from RAM.

You can move back and forth between the open worksheets with the Window menu. Listed at the bottom of the Window menu are the names of the currently open worksheets; if you haven't saved them, they're listed as Sheet1, Sheet2, and so forth. If any has been saved, its filename is shown. The name associated with the worksheet currently being displayed has a checkmark beside it. To display a different worksheet from the current one, simply choose the name associated with it.

SAVING YOUR WORK

When you get your work to a point where you're willing to save a copy of it (and this can be in unfinished form, or in final form), choose either the Save or Save As command on the File menu. The first time you do this, you'll be prompted for a file name by this Save dialog box. (see Figure 7-2). This box is the same for both the Save and Save As commands the first time you save a file. Type the filename you want to use in the shaded box. The File Type box default shows that the file is saved as a Wingz file.

Filenames already in use in the current folder are listed in the box above shown in Figure 7-2. The name of the current folder is shown next to the folder icon above the list of filenames, and the name of the current disk drive is shown in the upper right corner next to the Drive icon.

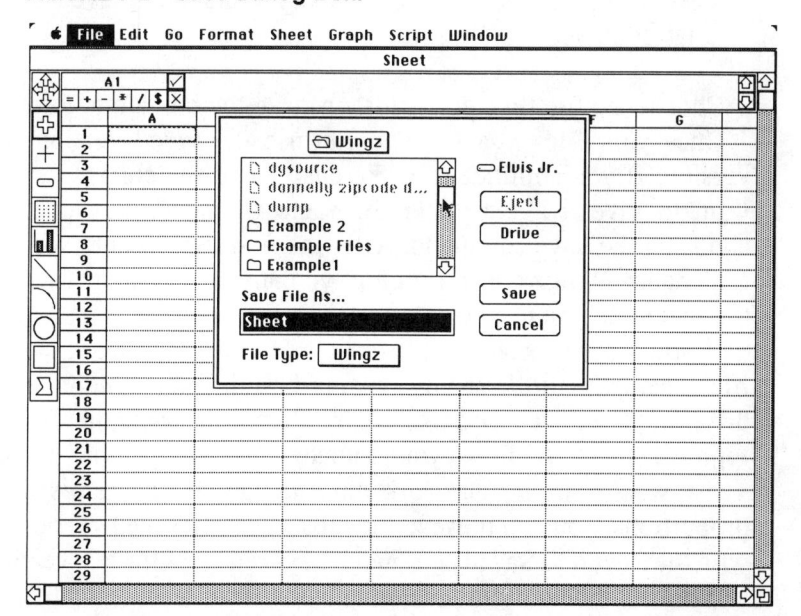

FIGURE 7-2 Save Dialog Box.

You can specify a different drive, folder, or file type than the one shown. To change drives, simply click on the drive box. (Once the file has been saved, each time you come back to this box, you'll be able to click on the Drive button.) If you click the Drive box, you can change drives. If you click the Folder icon, you'll be shown the list of files in the current folder. If you pull down on the folder icon, you'll see the "parent" folder, and a list of folders available within that. Use this to store a Wingz file in some other folder.

If you move the pointer to the File Type box and pull down, you'll see a list of acceptable file types:

Wingz files are those created by Wingz.

DIF files are those used by some older spreadsheet programs, usually based on VisiCalc; numbers, text, and formulas become unformatted text.

123-1a files are those used by Lotus 1-2-3, version 1a; numbers and text are kept intact, as well as all formulas except those Lotus 1-2-3 does not support.

123-2.0 files are those used by Lotus 1-2-3, version 2.0 and higher; numbers and text are kept intact, as well as all formulas except those Lotus 1-2-3 does not support.

Text All numbers, text, and results of formulas are saved as unformatted, tab delimited, ASCII text.

Choose the file type you want, or leave the box alone for a Wingz file.

Once your file is saved, you can use the saved version or the current version. If you continue to make changes to the current version, you may want to save it again under the same filename. You do this simply by choosing the Save command. After the first time, where you had to specify a filename, Wingz doesn't prompt you any more for the filename, and uses the same one you used last time.

If you want to save the current version of your work under a different filename, or with the same filename in a different folder or on a different drive, use the Save As command. You'll see the same dialog box you saw in Figure 7-2, which allows you to change any of those file parameters.

If at some point in your work you find you've made a mistake of awesome proportions, you can retrieve the most recently saved version of your work with the Revert to Saved command. This retrieves the last version you saved, and replaces the current version in RAM. This feature is particularly helpful if you've saved your work periodically, as you don't have to start all over from the beginning, retyping all your data, redoing the formatting, and reconstructing your formulas.

CLOSING A FILE

Choosing the Close command does not have the same effect as using the Save or Save As command. The Close command simply removes the current worksheet from RAM, regardless of what you changed. If you've made any changes at all, you are prompted by the Save Changes dialog box (see Figure 7-3). If you choose the Yes button, Wingz behaves as if you'd chosen the Save As command, prompting you for a filename. If you choose the No button, Wingz removes the file from RAM. You can also choose to cancel the Close operation.

FIGURE 7-3   Save Changes Dialog Box.

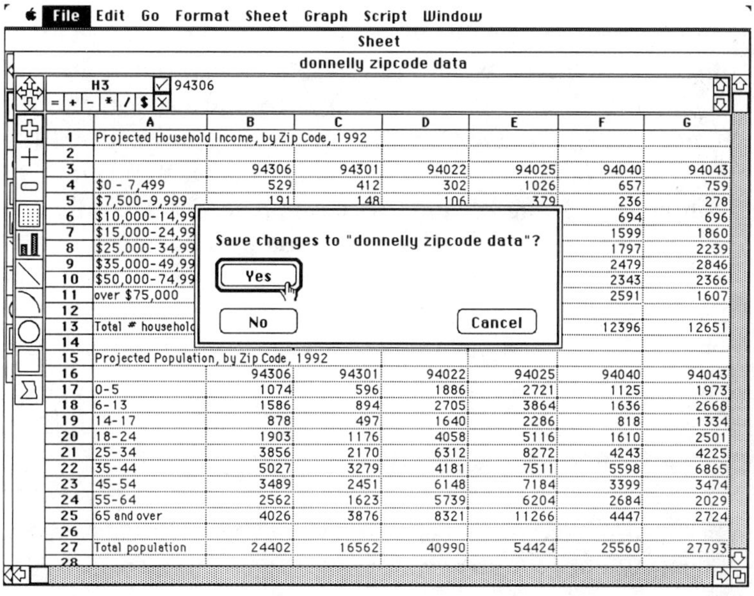

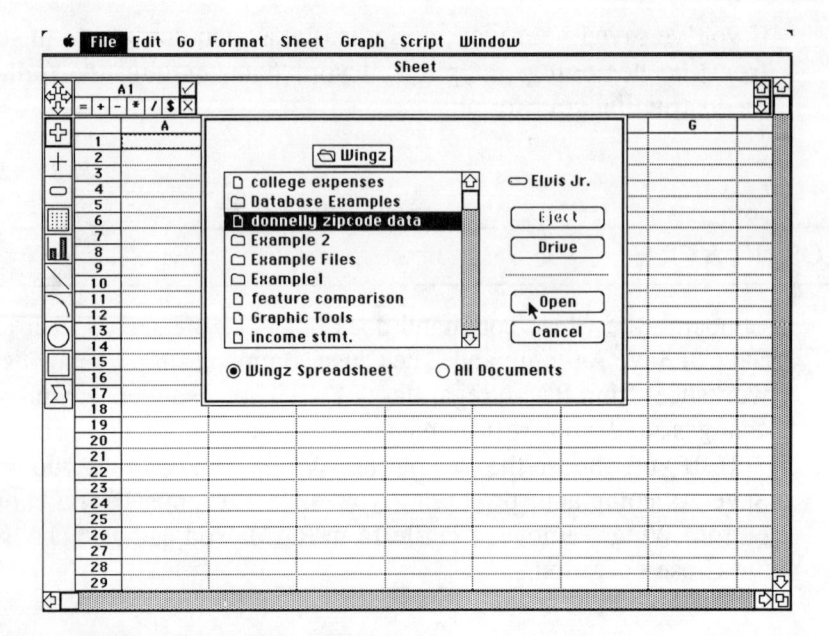

FIGURE 7-4 File Open Dialog Box.

RETRIEVING A SAVED FILE

Choose the Open command to retrieve a file you've previously saved. Wingz displays a dialog box, letting you specify just where this file is located (see figure 7-4). The Folder icon shows the current folder. To change folders, simply click on it and choose from the list shown. The drive box shows the current drive. Change drives by clicking on the icon. The buttons at the bottom specify the file type: Wingz spreadsheets, or all documents. Choose whichever one fits the kind of file you want to open.

Once you've specified the parameters for the file you want, look through the available filenames and highlight the one you want, then click the Open button. This action opens the file, which is displayed on your screen.

CLOSING A FILE WHEN YOU QUIT Wingz

If you still have files open when you choose the Quit command on the File menu, Wingz closes them for you. If you've made changes to any of them,

Wingz displays the dialog box you saw in Figure 7-3, allowing you to save the changed version of the file. Wingz then proceeds to remove the files from RAM, one by one, and exits the program.

SUMMARY

This chapter has given you a brief look at file management within Wingz. In Chapter 10 we'll look at some more facets of file management, including topics related to using files in a network environment, sharing files with other programs, and importing graphics from nonspreadsheet programs.

CASE STUDY 5:
Wingz in Publishing

MacGuide Magazine
Dave Duty, Publisher
550 S. Wadsworth
Lakewood, Colorado 80226

MacGuide Magazine was one of the first to receive pre-beta versions of Wingz. Publisher Dave Duty had several uses for it: not only did he need to use it to produce the snazzy graphs and charts to back up the figures in the prospectus for the magazine, but he wanted a package that could really be useful in the workplace that the offices of MacGuide represent. The package has been used to produce charts and graphs for the magazine itself, as well as tracking the data and resulting staff memos that support the business side of the magazine.

When the package arrived at MacGuide, staffers put it through its paces and wrote the following:

"It is not every day that a new Macintosh product moves jaded Macintosh magazine editors to blurt out gasps of "oohs" and "aahs." But that was what happened at the MacGuide offices in late July when we witnessed a preview of Wingz, the new spreadsheet from Informix.

"Wingz is more than a spreadsheet; it is a presentation aid that could be just what business people have been hoping for. . . .

"Whatever you call it, Wingz has some tremendous specs. Try these for size: 32,768 rows by 32,768 columns; text fields up to 22" x 22" with multiple fonts, styles, and sizes; 20 basic chart types, including scientific charts; 3D rotation of charts; drawing tools, over 80 windows open at once (try that one); HyperScript, a programming language similar to HyperCard's HyperTalk; multi-user capability; all the data import options you could need; more than 180 built-in functions; and a palette of 16 million colors (on a Mac II). . . .

"The simplicity with which these charts were created was startling. Once the data were entered, the bar and pie graphs were produced with a few point-and-click functions. There is more, but we do not want to gush too much over a pre-beta version of a product."

—MacGuide Magazine, Fall/Winter 1988

The MacGuide staff received updated copies as Wingz progressed through the beta test phase, and staffers continued to feel very positive about the software. Duty used it to produce several circulation projections:

Given data about the sales and a projected growth rate of 20% per year for the Macintosh, Duty calculated figures to show the quarterly installed base through 1992. He then calculated circulation and market share for each month of the five years.

With final projected circulation figures, he created a chart to show circulation growth:

	A	B	C	D
1	GROWTH RATE OF MAC PER YEAR	20 %		
2	Domestic Newsstand Sell Thru	40 %		
3	International Newsstand Sell Thru	50 %		
4		TOTAL	DOMESTIC	INT
5	INSTALLED MACS 3RD QUARTER 1988	1,600,000	1,000,000	600,000
6	INSTALLED MACS 4TH QUARTER 1988	2,000,000	1,340,000	660,000
7				
8	INSTALLED MACS 1ST QUARTER 1989	2,095,238	1,403,810	691,429
9	INSTALLED MACS 2ND QUARTER 1989	2,195,011	1,470,658	724,354
10	INSTALLED MACS 3RD QUARTER 1989	2,299,536	1,540,689	758,847
11	INSTALLED MACS 4TH QUARTER 1989	2,409,037	1,614,055	794,982
12				
13	INSTALLED MACS 1ST QUARTER 1990	2,523,753	1,690,915	832,839
14	INSTALLED MACS 2ND QUARTER 1990	2,643,932	1,771,435	872,498
15	INSTALLED MACS 3RD QUARTER 1990	2,769,834	1,855,789	914,045
16	INSTALLED MACS 4TH QUARTER 1990	2,901,731	1,944,159	957,571
17				
18	INSTALLED MACS 1ST QUARTER 1991	3,039,908	2,036,739	1,003,170
19	INSTALLED MACS 2ND QUARTER 1991	3,184,666	2,133,726	1,050,940
20	INSTALLED MACS 3RD QUARTER 1991	3,336,316	2,235,332	1,100,984
21	INSTALLED MACS 4TH QUARTER 1991	3,495,189	2,341,776	1,153,412
22				
23	INSTALLED MACS 1ST QUARTER 1992	3,661,626	2,453,290	1,208,337
24	INSTALLED MACS 2ND QUARTER 1992	3,835,989	2,570,113	1,265,877
25	INSTALLED MACS 3RD QUARTER 1992	4,018,656	2,692,499	1,326,156

226   Mastering Wingz

Window 1 (9:53) — OTHER FILES for Wingz — Cell F318

	A	B	C	D	E
319	International Newsstand	90,713	7.86%	181,426	
320	Controlled	68,966	1.97%	68,966	
321	Total	758,626	21.70%	993,506	
322					
323	GROWTH PATTERN FOR CIRCULATION				
324	Feb-89	100,590			
325	Mar-89	111,100			
326	Apr-89	118,690			
327	May-89	127,127			
328	Jun-89	136,522			
329	Jul-89	147,000			
330	Aug-89	158,705			
331	Sep-89	171,800			
332	Oct-89	186,469			
333	Nov-89	202,922			
334	Dec-89	213,713			
335	Jan-90	225,185			
336	Feb-90	237,386			
337	Mar-90	250,364			
338	Apr-90	264,174			
339	May-90	278,871			
340	Jun-90	294,515			
341	Jul-90	311,173			
342	Aug-90	328,912			
343	Sep-90	347,808			
344	Oct-90	367,939			
345	Nov-90	389,391			

Window 2 (9:50) — OTHER FILES for Wingz — Cell B8 =B6*(B1/4.2)+B6

	A	B	C	D
40	GROWTH RATE - US Newsstand 1991	2.00%		
41	GROWTH RATE - Int. Newsstand 1991	5.00%		
42				
43	Feb-89	Circulation	Market Share	Copies Printed
44	US Subscriptions	25,000	1.78%	25,000
45	International Subscriptions	800	0.11%	800
46	US Newsstand	55,000	3.92%	137,500
47	International Newsstand	15,000	2.17%	30,000
48	Controlled	4,790	0.23%	4,790
49	Total	100,590	4.80%	198,090
50				
51	Mar-89	Circulation	Market Share	Copies Printed
52	US Subscriptions	35,000	2.38%	35,000
53	International Subscriptions	1,000	0.14%	1,000
54	US Newsstand	50,000	3.40%	125,000
55	International Newsstand	15,000	2.07%	30,000
56	Controlled	10,100	0.46%	10,100
57	Total	111,100	5.06%	201,100
58				
59	Apr-89	Circulation	Market Share	Copies Printed
60	US Subscriptions	39,900	2.71%	39,900
61	International Subscriptions	1,100	0.15%	1,100
62	US Newsstand	51,000	3.47%	127,500
63	International Newsstand	15,900	2.20%	31,800
64	Controlled	10,790	0.49%	10,790
65	Total	118,690	5.41%	211,090
66				

Duty has been using Wingz to track the ordinary data that runs a business, but has also used it to develop the graphics for the fledgling company's first offering of stock.

8

Using Wingz as a Database

Databases can be highly useful tools. In a manner similar to that of a card filing system, databases allow you to store information in an easy to use format, and then sort that information into a format that is useful to you.

Figure 8-1 shows a card file database. Unlike a card file, a database allows you to do more with your information than just store it. You can automate a search for particular kinds information, merge and sort several databases, and create a report about your database, each with just a few keystrokes (see Figure 8-2).

A database in Wingz is simply a standard spreadsheet that has been restructured so that it can better handle database information. This is a common method of creating a database, because it has two inherent advantages:

1. Spreadsheets and databases can generally be created one from another because the display format that is most often used for a completed database is in essence identical to that used for a spreadsheet.
2. Any data in the database that you wish to use within a spreadsheet is already in the correct data format for use with the spreadsheet.

Admittedly, there are some problems associated with using a spreadsheet as a database. A big one that persisted until recently was the inability of a database to share information with another database. While this feature has been available on large corporate databases for some time, it wasn't until

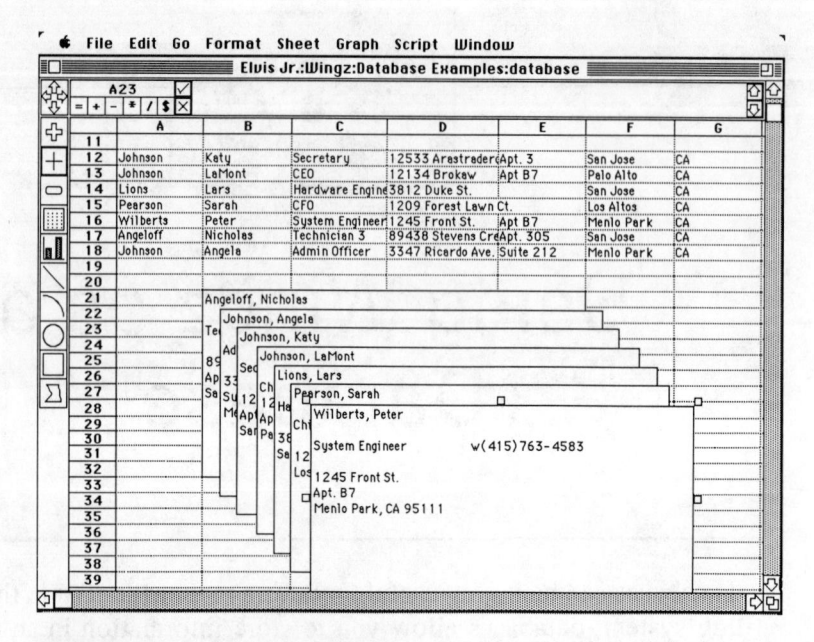

FIGURE 8-1 A Card File Database.

FIGURE 8-2 A Sample Database Form.

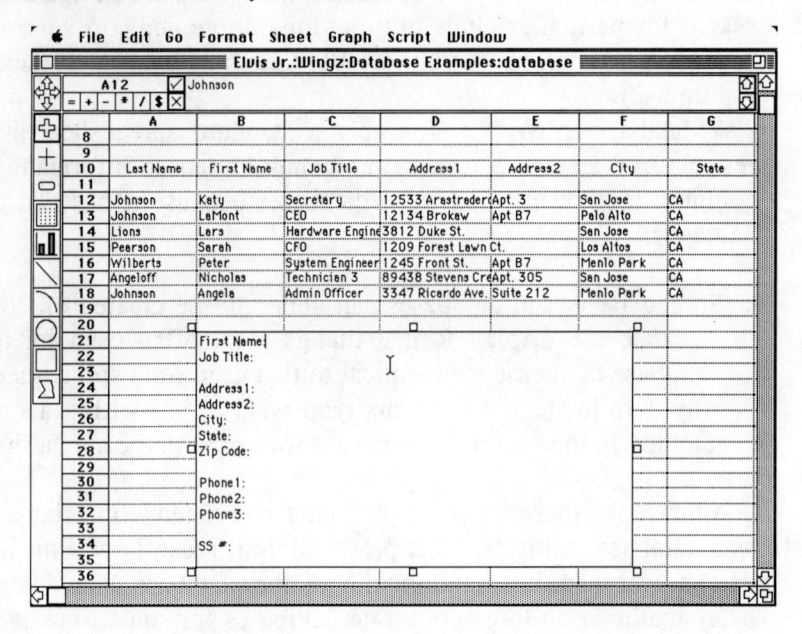

the advent of file-linking spreadsheets that this feature became commonly available to database users on smaller computers (see Figure 8-3).

Another problem with using a spreadsheet as a database is that the database will inherently perform at a lower level than a dedicated database would. Although this isn't usually a problem with small, uncomplicated databases, it can become one with some large databases.

Fortunately, Wingz has dealt at least in part with both of these problems. As a result, Wingz performs much better as a database now than many commercially available databases would have as little as six years ago.

Creating Your Own Database

Before you start to create your own database, you should understand some of the terms that you will be using when you create your database.

A **database** is generally considered to be a file where you store your data. In Wingz, as in many spreadsheet-based databases, a database is a section

FIGURE 8-3 Sharing Information with Another Database.

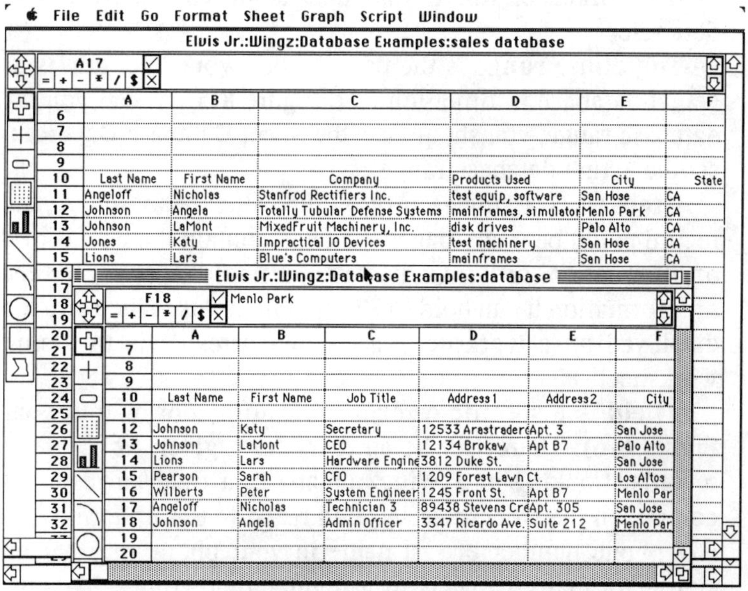

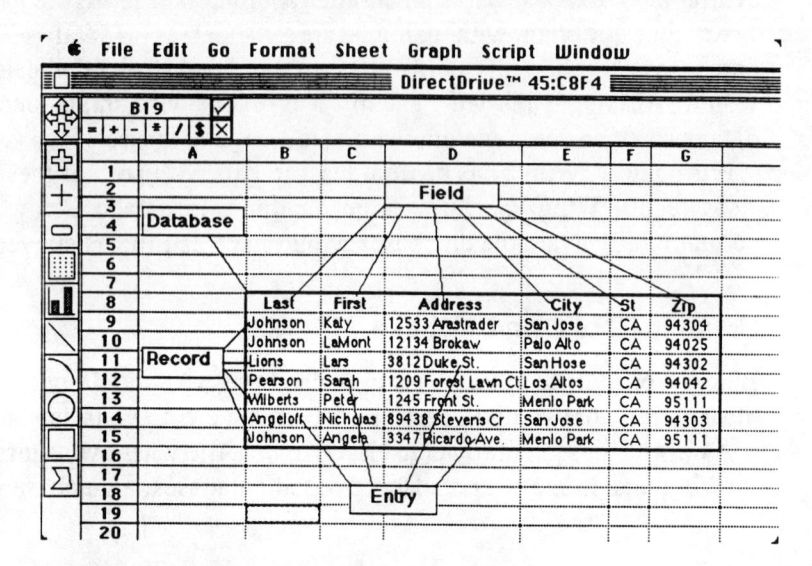

FIGURE 8-4 A Sample Database.

of the worksheet where your data is stored. Figure 8-4 shows a sample database.

A **database range** is the part of your worksheet that is used to store the actual database information (see Figure 8-5). When you want to declare a database range, you should use the Sheet Database Data Range command to set the actual database range.

A **record** is a single-entry within your database. In some databases, a record could be many pages long and contain thousands of different pieces of information. In Wingz, however, a single record is limited in the amount of information it can hold to 32 seperate fields. When you look at a database displayed on a worksheet, a record corresponds to a single line of that worksheet.

A **field** is a specific category of information within your database (see Figure 8-6). There will be an entry for a given field in every one of your records. Looking at a Wingz database, a field corresponds with a single column on the worksheet. A good real-life example of a field in a database is a phone number or last name in your phone list. A **computed field** is similar in many respects to a regular field. But it has one important dif-

Using Wingz as a Database 233

	A	B	C	D	E	F
10	Last Name	First Name	Company	Products Used	City	State
11	Angeloff	Nicholas	Stanfrod Pectifiers Inc.	test equip, software	San Hose	CA
12	Johnson	Angela	Totally Tubular Defense Systems	mainframes, simulator	Menlo Park	CA
13	Johnson	LaMont	Hi-edFruit Machinery, Inc.	disk drives	Palo Alto	CA
14	Jones	Taty	Impractical IO Devices	test machinery	San Hose	CA
15	Lions	Lars	Blue's Computers	mainframes	San Hose	CA
16	Pearson	Sarah	Dewey, Cheatham, & Howe, Attys	PCs, software	Los Altos	CA
18	Wilberts	Peter	Pol'd HilSpec	mainframes, test equip	Menlo Park	CA

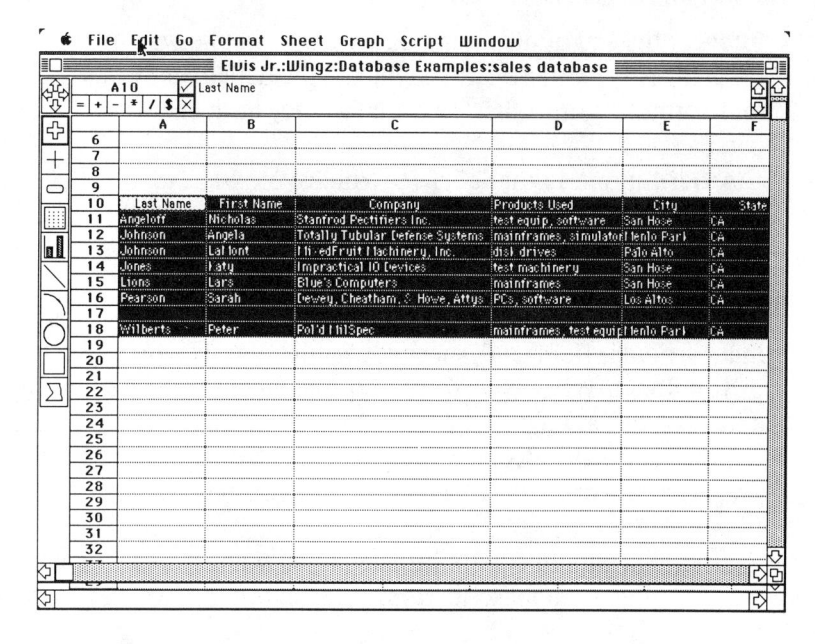

FIGURE 8-5   A Database Range.

FIGURE 8-6   A Computed Field.

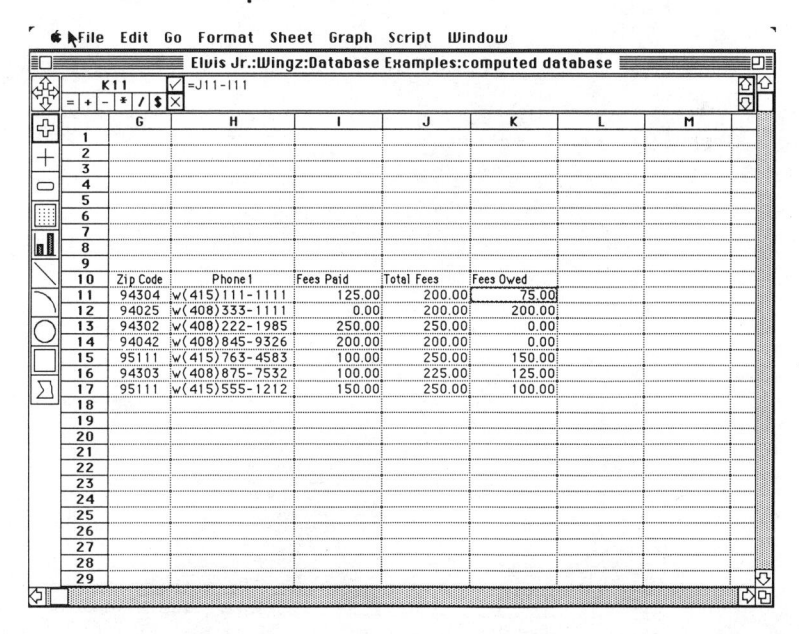

	G	H	I	J	K
10	Zip Code	Phone1	Fees Paid	Total Fees	Fees Owed
11	94304	w(415)111-1111	125.00	200.00	75.00
12	94025	w(408)333-1111	0.00	200.00	200.00
13	94302	w(408)222-1985	250.00	250.00	0.00
14	94042	w(408)845-9326	200.00	200.00	0.00
15	95111	w(415)763-4583	100.00	250.00	150.00
16	94303	w(408)875-7532	100.00	225.00	125.00
17	95111	w(415)555-1212	150.00	250.00	100.00

ference. Instead of dispaying data entered in one way or another by the user, the field only contains a formula, and the data displayed are computed using that formula from other data elsewhere, both inside and external to your database.

A **field name** is the label by which you want to designate each field. It should be a descriptive name for the field, such as "LastName" for a field containing last names, or "PhoneNum" for a field with phone numbers. While there may be cases where you don't want to provide a field name for a particular field, you should anyway—first, because it lets you organize that particular field, and, second, because Wingz won't accept your database if you don't. When you display a database in Wingz, the top row of the database will always contain your field names.

Once you have decided to create a database in Wingz, there is a little preperatory work you should do before you actually start to enter data. (See Figure 8–7.)

First, you should decide just what you want stored in your database. Are you creating a database to store information on your sales contacts, or on

FIGURE 8-7 A Sales Database.

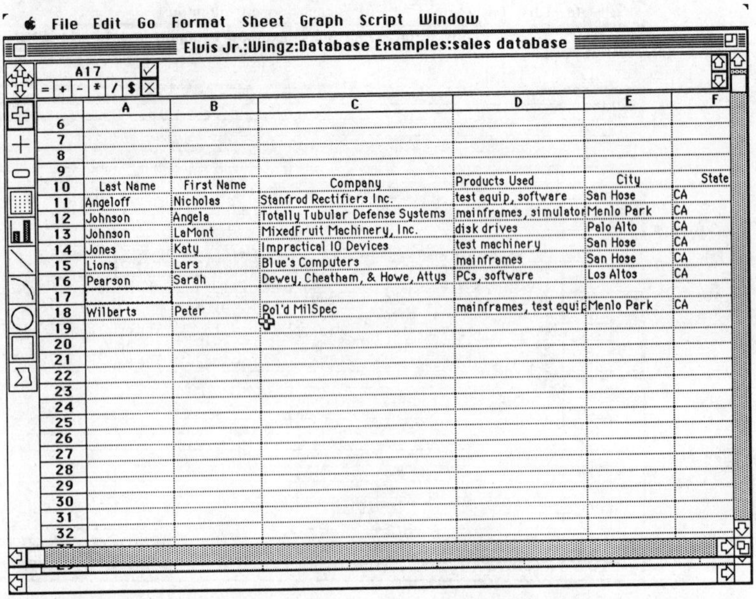

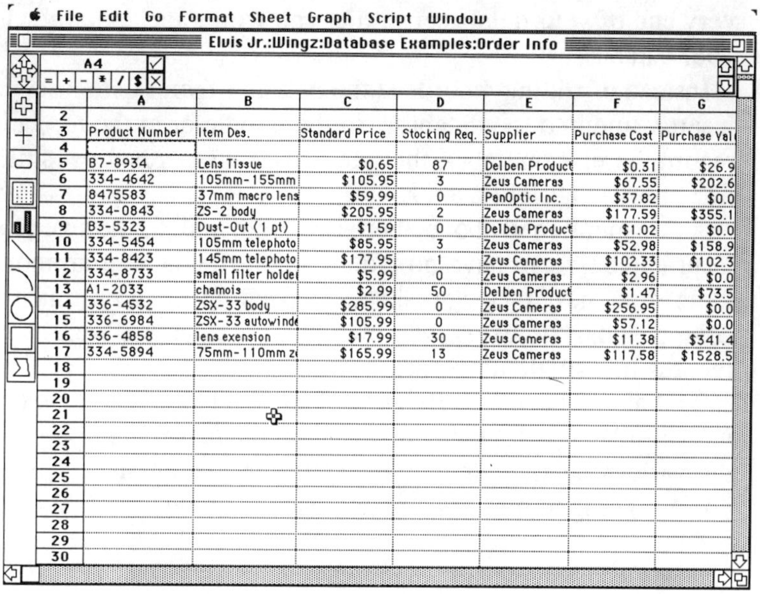

	A	B	C	D	E	F	G
2							
3	Product Number	Item Des.	Standard Price	Stocking Req.	Supplier	Purchase Cost	Purchase Val
4							
5	B7-8934	Lens Tissue	$0.65	87	Delben Product	$0.31	$26.9
6	334-4642	105mm-155mm	$105.95	3	Zeus Cameras	$67.55	$202.6
7	8475583	37mm macro lens	$59.99	0	PanOptic Inc.	$37.82	$0.0
8	334-0843	ZS-2 body	$205.95	2	Zeus Cameras	$177.59	$355.1
9	B3-5323	Dust-Out (1 pt)	$1.59	0	Delben Product	$1.02	$0.0
10	334-5454	105mm telephoto	$85.95	3	Zeus Cameras	$52.98	$158.9
11	334-8423	145mm telephoto	$177.95	1	Zeus Cameras	$102.33	$102.3
12	334-8733	small filter holde	$5.99	0	Zeus Cameras	$2.96	$0.0
13	A1-2033	chamois	$2.99	50	Delben Product	$1.47	$73.5
14	336-4532	ZSX-33 body	$285.99	0	Zeus Cameras	$256.95	$0.0
15	336-6984	ZSX-33 autowinde	$105.99	0	Zeus Cameras	$57.12	$0.0
16	336-4858	lens exension	$17.99	30	Zeus Cameras	$11.38	$341.4
17	334-5894	75mm-110mm z	$165.99	13	Zeus Cameras	$117.58	$1528.5

FIGURE 8–8 A Product Inventory Database.

your sales records? In one case, you will want to store one type of information, while in the other, you will want to store a completely different set of data.(See Figure 8–8.)

Second, you should decide just what fields are appropriate to your particular database, given the general information that you have decided to store. Is your database dedicated to storing information on your product line? Then product codes, descriptions, and recommended prices will all be fields you want in your database. Or are you storing a phone list? Then you'll want fields for first and last names, phone numbers, and possible mailing addresses. As you can see, different databases require different information.

Once you have decided what you want your database to store and how you want it to store that information, it is time to start creating your database. First, select the block of cells that you want to use to start your database. You can have as few as four or five lines in your database, but you will want one column in the database for each field. Now enter your field names across the top row of the space where you want your database. Remember to enter one field name per cell. Below that, you can enter as many records as you want to. But you should remember to keep one or two blank records at the very end of your database, so that you won't accidentally add fields below your database.

Instead of adding records at the bottom of your database, you can instead insert a line into the database, in the middle or at the top, and add the new record there. Remember, though, that new records must still fall below the line containing field names.

As we mentioned above, there is a finite limit to the size of your database. Your database can have no more than 32 fields, and no more records than there are lines in a worksheet. Depending on how much memory your computer has, however, you may be able to create well over ten thousand records in a single database.

So that you have a really good chance to learn how the database structure works in Wingz, let's create a sample database that you can use to try out the various commands in Wingz. In this particular case, the database that you are going to make is a phone list. The fields are designed, however, so

FIGURE 8–9 The Field Names.

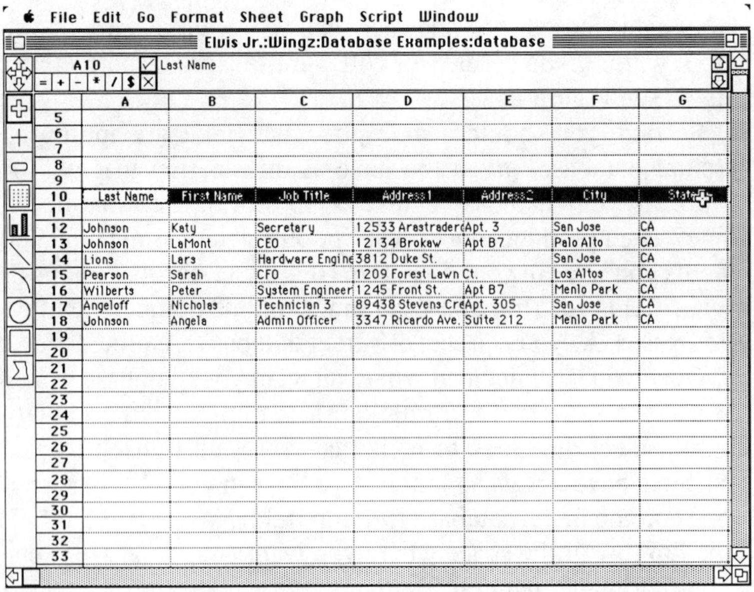

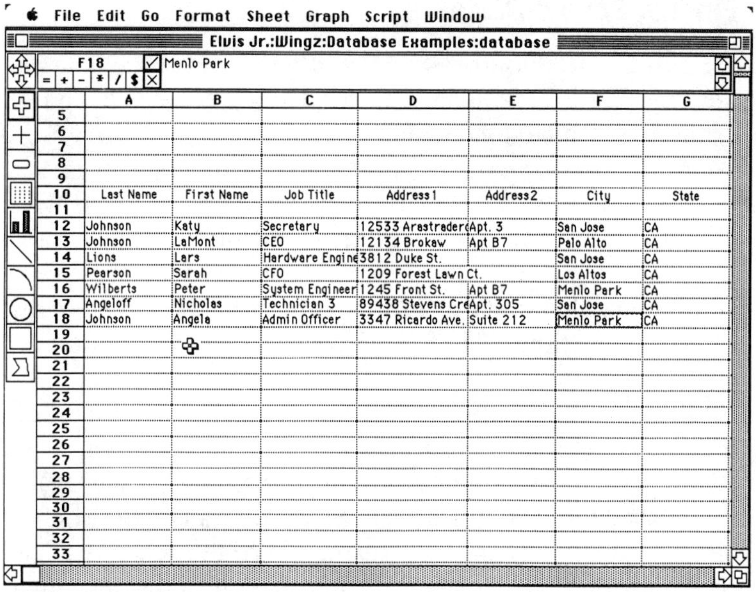

Using Wingz as a Database 237

FIGURE 8-10 A Sample Database.

that they can also be used to create mailing labels with a little work (see Figure 8-9).

The first thing you need to do is to establish the actual fields that will be used for the database. For a phone list, it makes sense to separate out someone's first and last names, so that you can alphabetize your database using the last names. Therefore, these are the fields that you will want to put in for this database. You should adjust the column widths so that the field names will fit at least within their columns.

Last Name, First Name, Job Title, Address1, Address2, City, State, Zip Code, Phone1, Phone2, and Phone 3

Remember to put the field names in one row, so that they will be at the top row of the range you will eventually declare as a database.

Now you should enter several made-up entries in the space below the field names, so that you have something to work with. Remember that you don't need to keep any kind of order in these entries, as you will be learning how to create Sorting keys later in this chapter.

Finding Specific Data

Having a database is all well and good, but if the data just sit there they aren't going to do anyone much good. We need to figure out something useful that can be done with that data.

One of the first operations that was made available on a database was Find. In one form or another, that capability has been available in almost every database ever made. What it generally involves is finding all of the occurances within a given field of a particular set of criteria.

In Wingz, the Find capability has been implemented in the form of a pair of search functions. The first of these is the Find function, while the second is Extract.

Find, as implemented in Wingz, allows you to use a set of search criteria to look through your database, selecting all of the records that match the criteria you have set for your database (see Figure 8-11). Once you have established the search criteria in a Criteria Range, the Find command allows you to actually implement a search. Once the search has been finished, all of the records that meet the criteria you specified will be highlighted, so that

FIGURE 8-11 Using the Find Command.

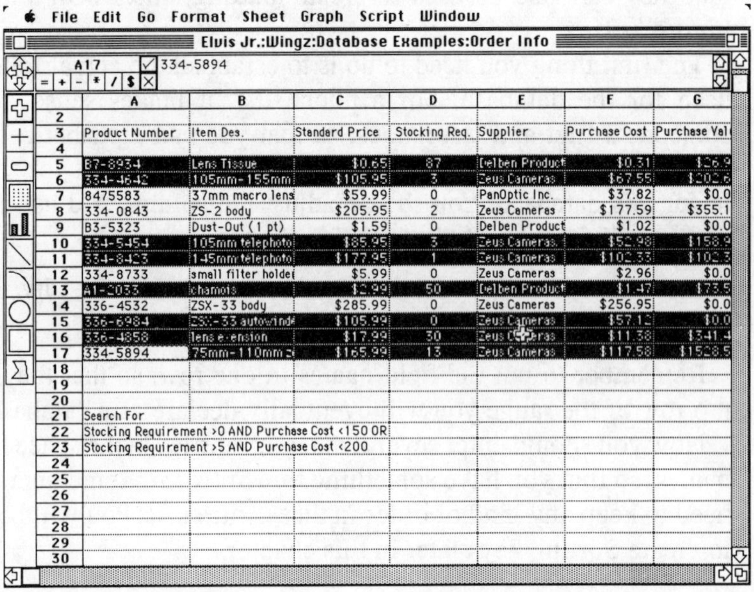

you can do things with them, such as using the Copy or Cut commands from the Edit menu.

When you want to use the Find command, you need to do several things. First, you must create a Criteria Range so that Wingz will know what it needs to search for. After you have created the criteria range, select the Format Database Criteria Range command. This designates the range with your criteria as the Criteria Range that the computer should be looking at.

But what if you are interested in only part of each record? There is a command available to perform that type of search as well: the **Extract command**. The Extract command is similar to the Find command in many ways. But whereas the Find command selects all of the records that match your Search critera, allowing you to do whatever you want to with them, the Extract command instead allows you to look at only part of each database record. And instead of leaving the appropriate records in the middle of your database, highlighted though they may be, the Extract command automatically copies all of the information you have stated an interest in into a separate range, known as the **Extract Range** (see Figure 8-12).

FIGURE 8-12 An Extract Range.

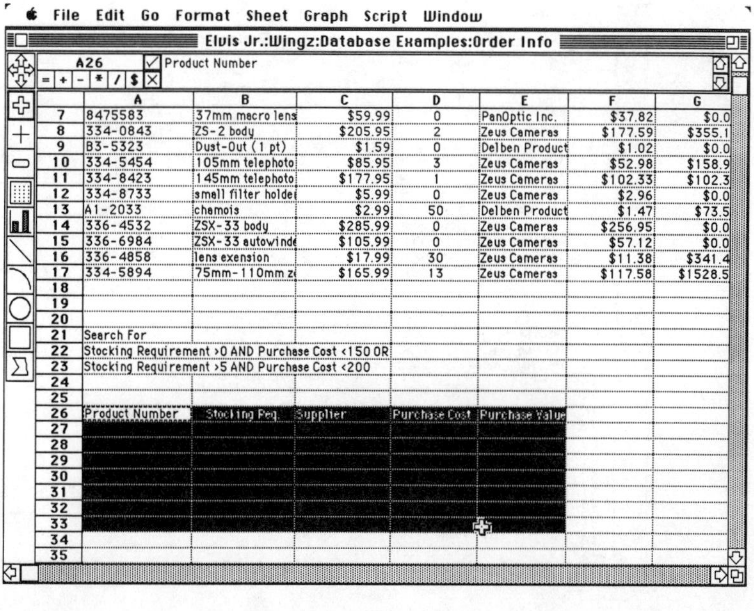

Using the Extract command is quite similar to using the Find command. First, create and designate a Criteria Range, so that Wingz will know what it is looking for. Next, create an Extract Range, which is where your information will be copied during the search.

To create an Extract Range, you simply need to decide what fields you want copied from your database. Enter the field names, exactly as they appear in your database, across the top row of the space where you want the Extract Range to appear. The fields don't need to be in any particular order, but it is very important that all of the information about the field names that you want copied appear in the cell containing the field name for your Extract Range. Included in this are such things as alignment, specificity of numbers in the cell, and almost anything else that could be designated from the Format menu. As you will probably quickly discover, the easiest way to do this is simply to Copy and Paste the field names that you are interested in.

Once you have entered the appropriate field names at the head of the Extract Range, it is time both to create the Extract Range, and to start the Extract command in motion. Select all field names that you want as part of

FIGURE 8-13 Establishing an Extract Range.

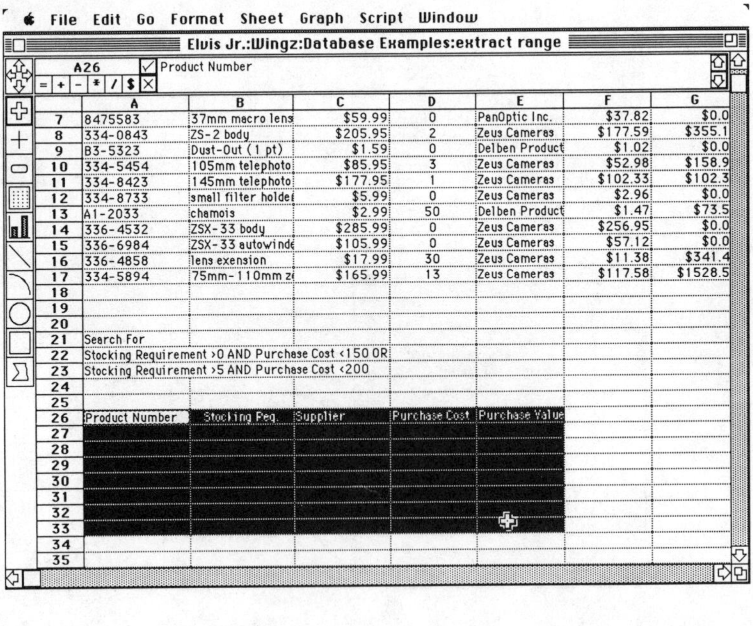

the Extract Range, as well as enough rows below that one that you can deal with all of the records so that fit the Search criteria. Now, select the Sheet Database Extract command. When you do this, you are simultaneously informing Wingz that the range you have selected is the Extract Range, and that it is to go ahead with the Extract command (see Figure 8-13).

Once you start the Extract command, Wingz searches through your database, looking for all of the records that match your search criteria. As they are found, the portions of each record that match the fields listed at the top of the Extract Range are copied into the appropriate locations within the Extract Range.

Criteria Ranges

When you are using the Find or Extract functions, one of the things that you will have had to specify is a Criteria Range. Criteria Ranges are, to put it simply, sections of the worksheet where the criteria for a search are specified (see Figure 8-14). The range itself consists of a block of cells, the top row

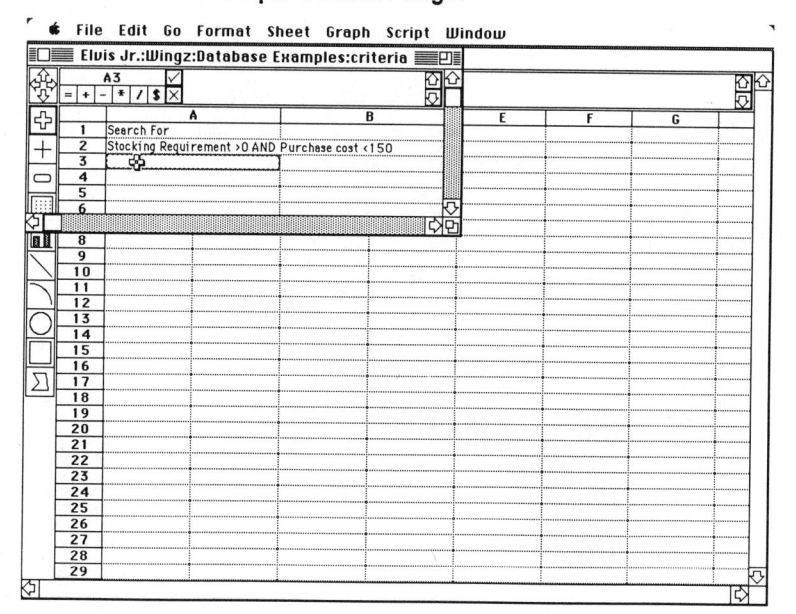

FIGURE 8-14 A Sample Criteria Range.

of which contains the names of the fields that are going to be searched. In the rows below the field names are the various search criteria.

Each search criterion must follow a specific format to allow the search to work. Each individual search criterion, when it is created, is regarded as an individual formula. As a result, the search criterion must be written in a format that Wingz will recognize as a legitimate TRUE/FALSE test. The format that should be used for a search criterion is similar to this:

=A5<1000

Using this format either a 1.00 or a 0.00 is displayed in the cell containing the actual formula. The cell reference within the search formula should refer to the topmost cell within the appropriate record that you want the search criterion to look at. The formula itself should reflect the criterion that you are trying to find (see Figure 8-15).

FIGURE 8-15 Multiple Search Criteria.

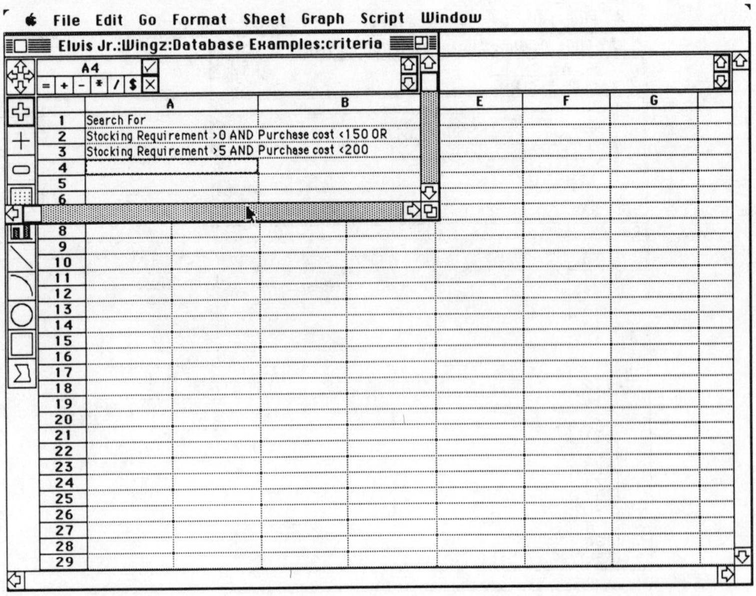

Using Wingz as a Database 243

One of the nice things about Wingz is that the structure of your search criteria allows you to help determine how the search is executed within your database. The reason for this is that depending on how you put a given set of criteria in, you can create one of two different types of multiple criteria.

The most common type of search criteria that you will be creating is an "AND" criteria. To create an AND set of criterion, simply place all of the individual elements of the criteria on the same line. In effect, they create a criteria that says

"if a AND b AND c are true..."

Figure 8-16 shows an AND search criteria.

The other type of criteria that you can create is an OR criteria. In this type of criterion, the separated criteria elements are placed on different lines. As a result, if you had a series of criteria elements in cells below each other, they would create a criteria saying

FIGURE 8-16 An AND Search Criteria.

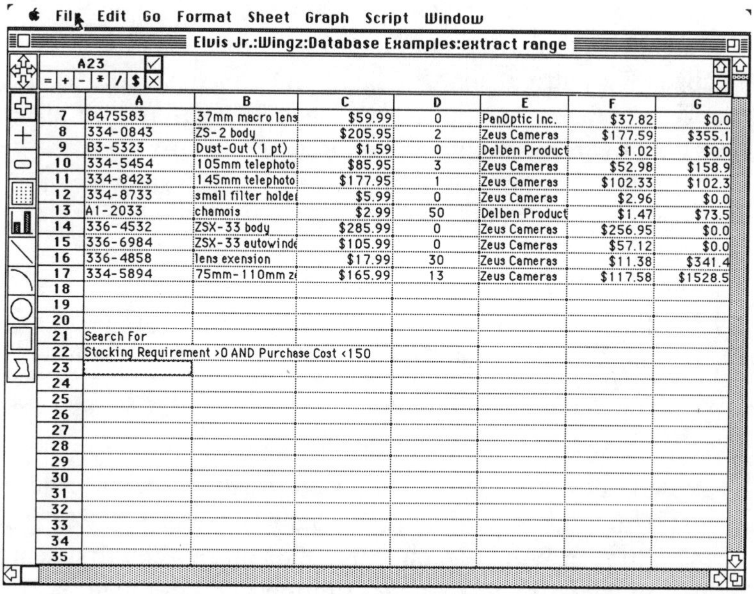

244 Mastering Wingz

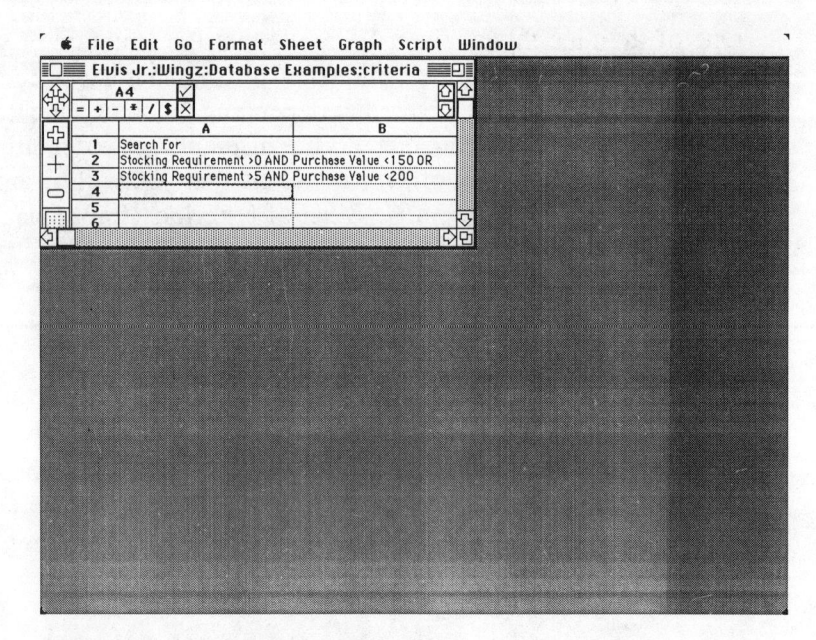

FIGURE 8-17 An OR Search Criteria.

"If a OR b OR c are true. ."

Figure 8-17 shows an OR Search Critera.

It is also possible to combine these types of criteria in a given Criteria Range. By putting all of a given set of AND criteria on one line, and separating the various different sets of OR criteria on different lines, it is possible to create a quite complex search criteria.

To give you an example, the search criteria shown in Figure 8-18 would be interpreted by Wingz as

	A	B	C	D	E	F
1	Find either an entry which has a stocking requirement greater than 0 and a purchase value					
2	of less than $150, or a stocking requirement greater than 5 and a purchase value of less than $					
3	then $200.					

when it was looked at by Wingz during the completion of a search.

Now that you understand how to create a search criteria and use that criteria to find things in your database, let's practice using the search capabilities in Wingz on our sample database. The first search that you are going to try will use a single criterion with an OR in it. You are going to

Using Wingz as a Database 245

```
  File  Edit  Go  Format  Sheet  Graph  Script  Window
                    Elvis Jr.:Wingz:Database Examples:database
   A25
        A            B           C            D           E          F         G
  5
  6
  7
  8
  9
 10  Last Name    First Name  Job Title       Address 1      Address 2    City        State
 11
 12  Johnson      Katy        Secretary       12533 Arastrader Apt. 3    San Jose    CA
 13  Johnson      LeMont      CEO             12134 Brokaw   Apt B7      Palo Alto   CA
 14  Lions        Lars        Hardware Engine 3812 Duke St.              San Jose    CA
 15  Pearson      Sarah       CFO             1209 Forest Lawn Ct.       Los Altos   CA
 16  Wilberts     Peter       System Engineer 1245 Front St. Apt B7      Menlo Park  CA
 17  Angeloff     Nicholas    Technician 3    89438 Stevens Cre Apt. 305 San Jose    CA
 18  Johnson      Angela      Admin Officer   3347 Ricardo Ave. Suite 212 Menlo Park CA
 19
 20
 21
 22  Search For
 23  Stocking Requirement >0 AND Purchase Value <150 OR
 24  Stocking Requirement >5 AND Purchase Value <200
 25
 26
 27
 28
 29
 30
 31
 32
 33
```

FIGURE 8-18 A Sample Search Criteria.

search your database for all of the entries that are in one of two ZIP code areas.

First, you should find a space off to the side of your database that you can use as a Criteria Range. Select the cell containing the Zip Code field name, and choose the Copy command from the Edit menu. Now select the cell at the top of your Criteria Range, and choose the Paste command from the Edit menu. In this way there is no question that the field names of your Criteria Range and of the database match.

Next, enter the ZIP codes that are going to be searched for. In this particular case, the ZIP codes that we chose to search for are 94303 and 95111. As a result, the search criteria would look like the set in Figure 8-19. You should use your search criteria to hunt through your database. Select the criteria table that you have created, and choose the Criteria Range command from the Database submenu on the Sheet menu. Then select the Find command to execute the search. If you have written your criteria correctly, then you should get results like those shown in Figure 8-20.

Now try extracting the Last Name, First Name, and Phone2 fields for some of the entries in your database. In a clear space on your worksheet, copy the

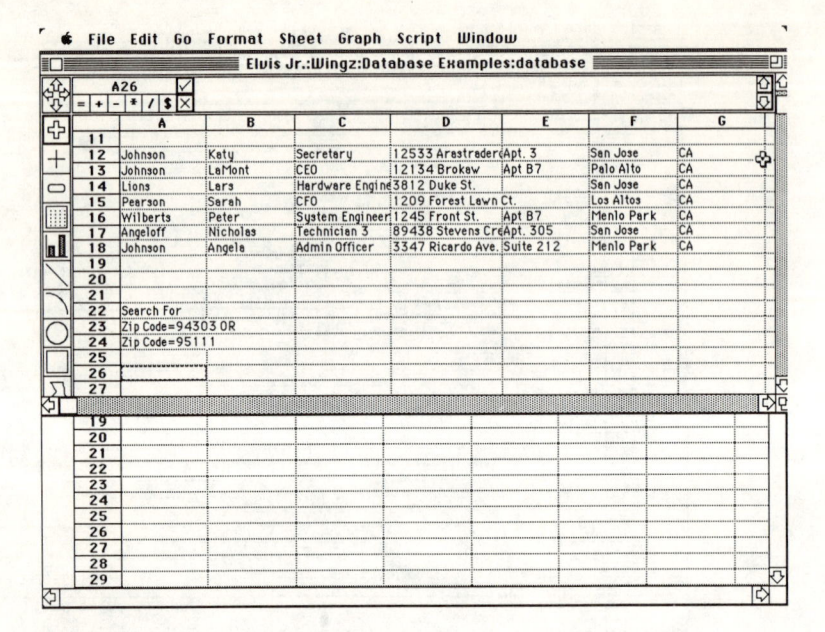

FIGURE 8-19 A Set of Search Criteria.

FIGURE 8-20 Searched-For Entries in the Database.

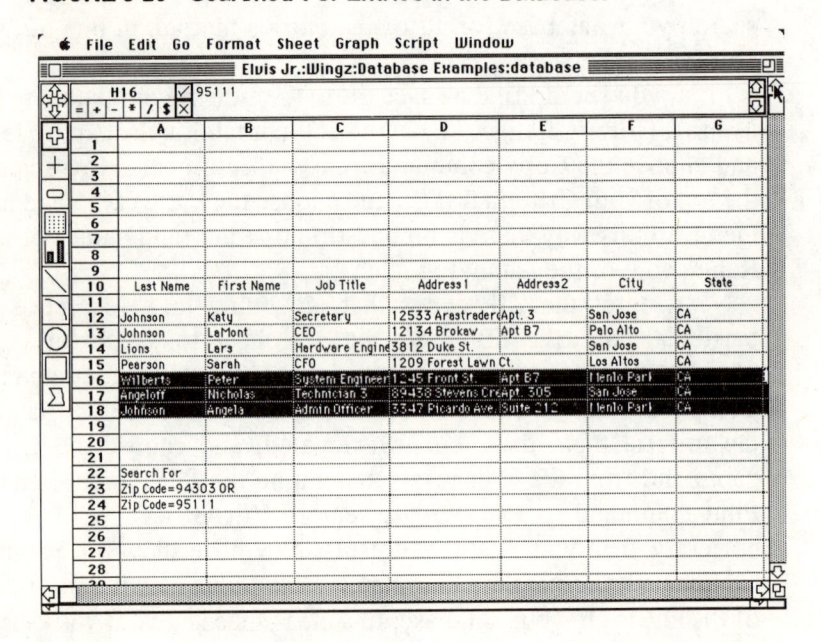

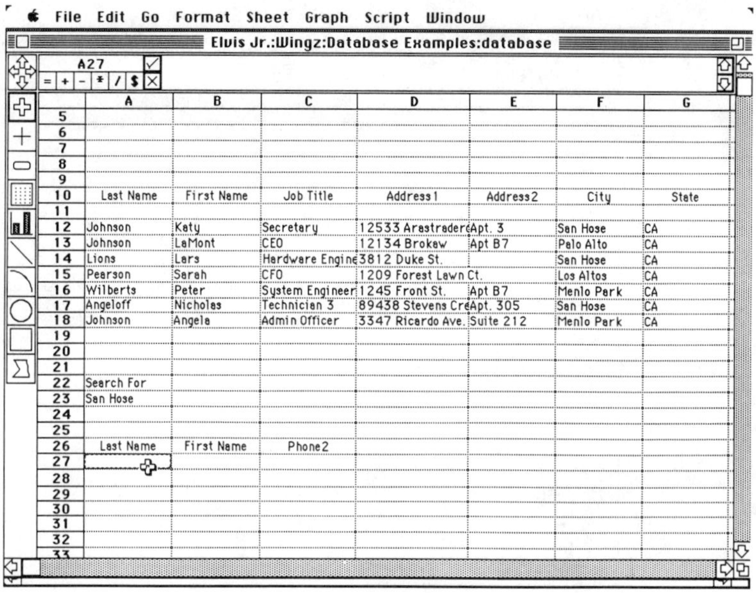

Using Wingz as a Database   247

FIGURE 8-21   A New Criteria Range.

Last Name, First Name, and Phone2 fields so that they are side by side. Move to your Criteria Range, and enter a set of practice criteria. In our case, we chose to search for all of the entries in the City of San Jose. Figure 8-21 shows the new Critieria Range.

You should remember that you must delete the old set of criteria, and redeclare the Criteria Range before you start your search this time. Once you are ready to execute your search, select the three fields in your extract range, as well as enough rows below them that there is no danger of filling the range, and choose the Extract command from the Database submenu. Once your search is completed, you should wind up with data like those shown in Figure 8-22. As you can see, the Extract command doesn't disturbe your database. It merely copies the appropriate data into your extract range, so that you can do what you find appropriate with the data.

Sorting Your Data

Besides digging through your data, you can do other things with it. One of the more common things that you might want to do is sort the data into an

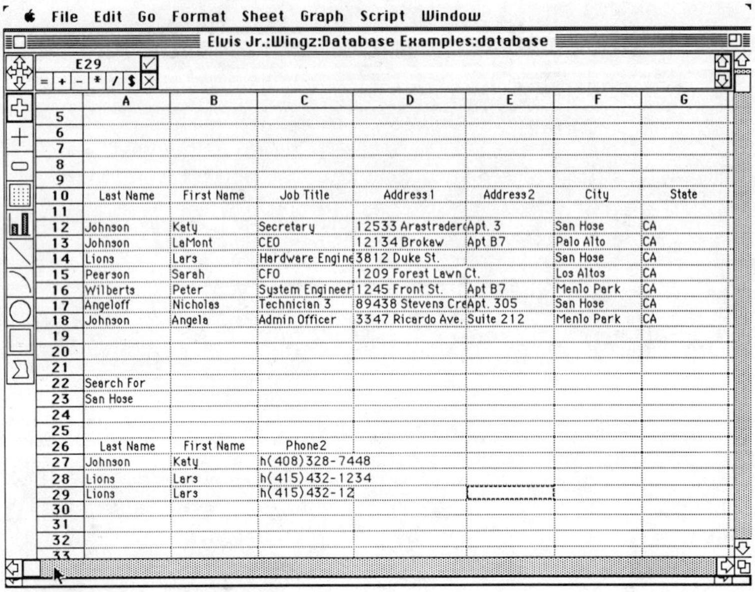

248 Mastering Wingz

FIGURE 8-22 Extracted Data.

ascending or descending order, using one or more of the fields in your database as criterion for the sort.

The Sort function included in Wingz can be used with more than just a database, and it allows you to sort by as many keys as you want to take the time to define. In addition to working in the database, the Sort function also works with any other section of a worksheet that you want to sort.

Depending on how complex you wish to get with your sort, and how you define it, you can do quite a bit. You can specify multiple keys, different directions of sort for different keys (that is, ascending or descending), subkeys within an already defined key or set of keys, and subsets of keys within a given sort. Figure 8-23 shows a Sort menu. Each of these different options is actually controlled through a very simple and abbreviated command structure. The order and manner in which you specify your search keys will in large part decide the order in which your sort keys are approached. In general, when you designate your search keys, you are dictating a queue, with each entry containing the queue and an indication whether the key is ascending or descending.

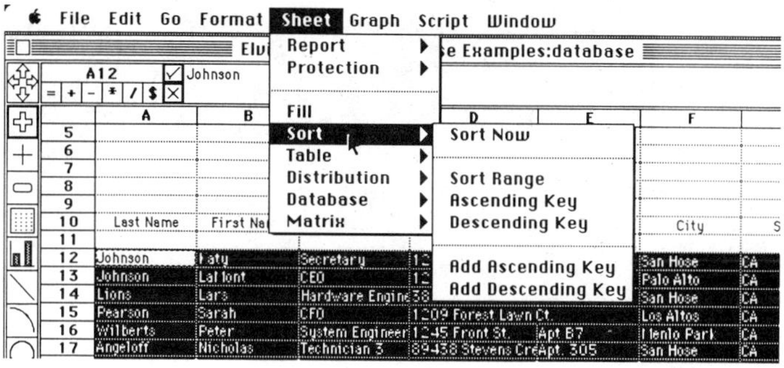

Using Wingz as a Database   249

FIGURE 8-23 The Sort Menu.

One thing that you will definitely want to remember is that you only want to use the Ascending Key or Descending Key command once in any given set of sorting keys. When either of these commands is used, it resets all of the sort keys for your database, eliminating all of your previously declared search keys. If you really do want to reset your search keys, then you should go right ahead and use the Ascending Key or Descending Key command to set a new sort key. But if you just want to add another sort key, then you should be using the Add Ascending Key and Add Descending Key commands.

The order in which you add your search keys is very important, because when you declare each search key, you are adding that key to a stack of search keys that are dealt with strictly in the order that they were declared.

Now you will have a chance to practice doing a sort. Why not alphabetize your database?

First, select the entire database. Now choose the Sort Range command from the Sort submenu on the Sheet menu. Next, select the entire contents of the Last Name field, or click on the column and choose the Ascending Key command from the Sort submenu. But, if you are going to alphabetize

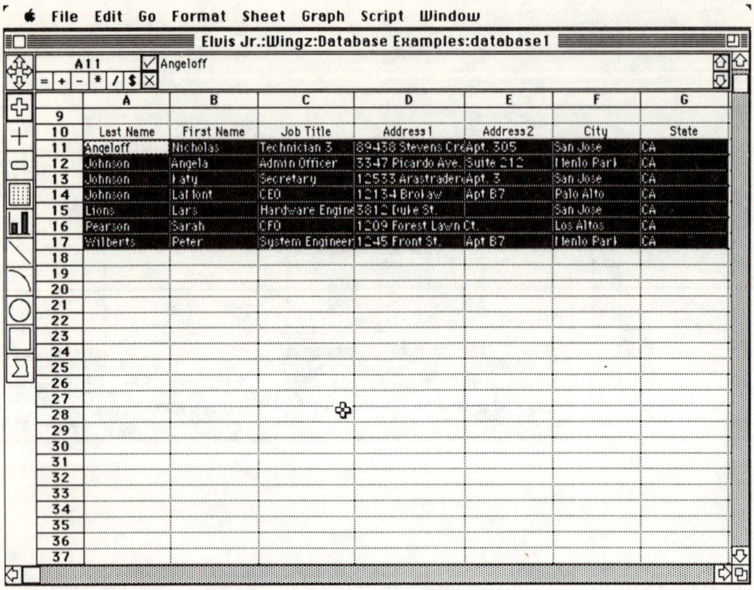

[Figure 8-24: screenshot of a Wingz spreadsheet showing a sorted database with columns Last Name, First Name, Job Title, Address1, Address2, City, State]

FIGURE 8-24 A Sorted Database.

your list, you may have some duplicate last names that will mess things up. Thus you should use the First Name field to perform a subsidiary sort of your database. Select the contents of the First Name field, and choose the Add Ascending Key command from the Sort submenu. Now you are ready to sort out your database. Choose the Sort Now command from the Sort submenu. You should end up with an alphabetized phone list like the one shown in Figure 8-24.

When you create a sort for your database you should always remember to avoid selecting the field names as part of your sort range or sort keys. If you do happen to select the field names as part of your sort, you will have to sort the field names into your database by whatever criteria you declared.

Inserting and Deleting Data

Adding and removing entries from your database probably seems to be an interminable problem. It's easy enough to tack new entries on the end of your database, but since the database won't be extended, you would have to redefine the database range every time you added a new set of entries. But

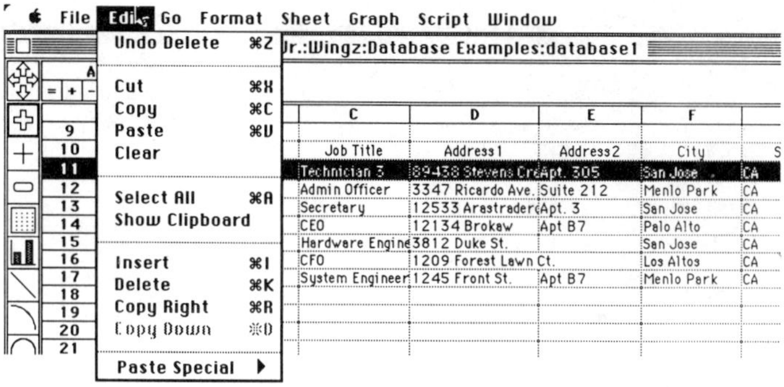

FIGURE 8-25 The Edit Menu

if you look closely at the Edit menu, there are two commands that are just right for dealing with this problem: Insert and Delete (see Figure 8-25).

By using the Insert command, you can insert a new line either all the way across the worksheet, or just in the segment of the worksheet that contains your database (see Figure 8-26). Similarly, the Delete command can remove all or part of a line in a worksheet. In either case, the command operates by having you select where within the worksheet you want the new line inserted or deleted. Once that segment of the worksheet has been selected, then just choose the appropriate command.

So long as it doesn't matter whether you insert a new line all the way across the worksheet or not, it is usually easier to select the entire row and insert a line that way. If it does matter, however, select only the cells above which you want to have a new line. Once you have selected whatever you have decided is appropriate, choose the Insert command from the Edit menu, and a new line will be inserted (see Figure 8-27).

If you want to delete a line, you will want to follow roghly the same procedure. Select the row if you want to delete the entire row, or just the

252 Mastering Wingz

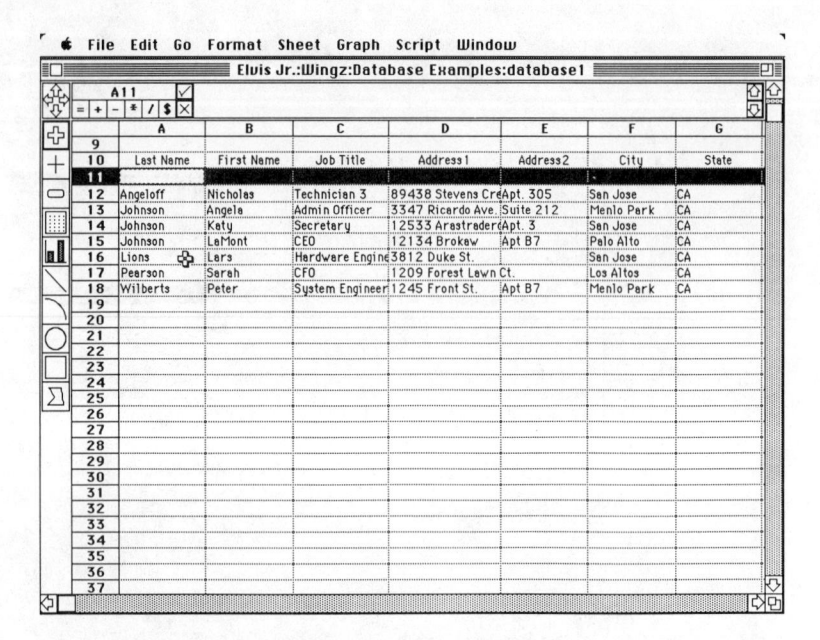

FIGURE 8-26 Adding a New Line to a Worksheet

FIGURE 8-27 Adding Part of a New Line to a Worksheet.

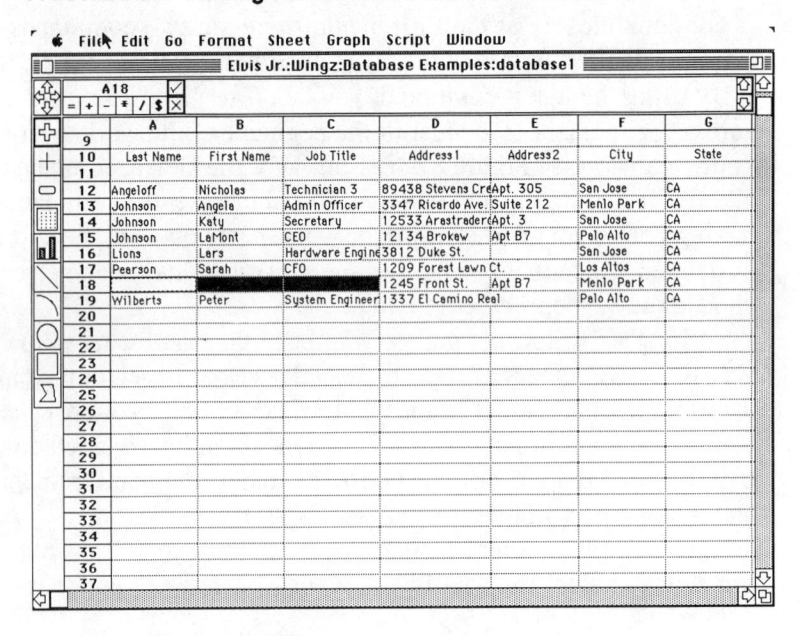

Using Wingz as a Database 253

FIGURE 8-28 A Database Range Before Inserting a New Line.

FIGURE 8-29 A Database Range After Inserting a Line.

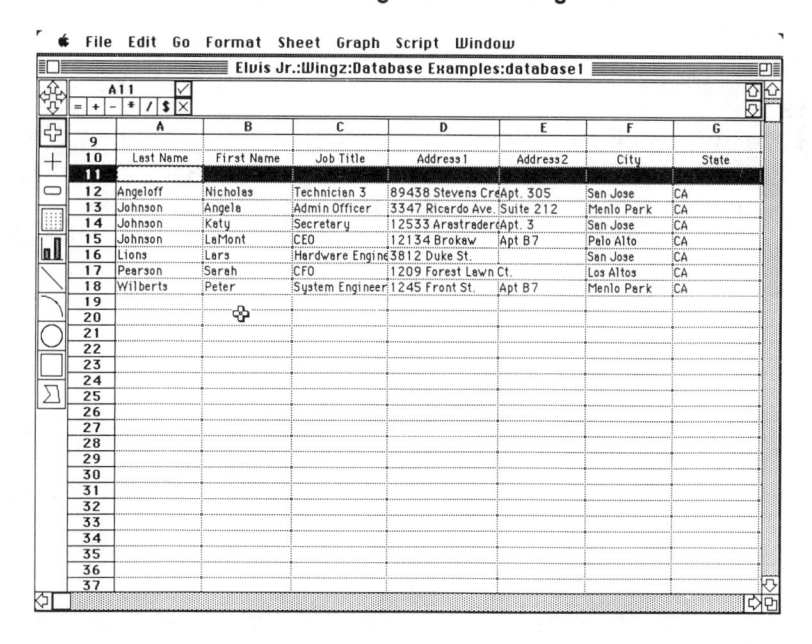

cells you want to delete if you can't delete the entire row, and then choose the Edit Delete command.

One thing you should notice about the Insert and Delete commands is that, provided the range of cells extends the full width of a defined cell range, using the Insert or Delete command will actually alter the range. If you use the Insert command to insert a new line across a range, the range will stretch as many lines as you have added, while if you delete part of a range, the range will shrink appropriately.

If you remember this feature when you are working with your database, you can take advantage of it to avoid having to redefine the database range whenever you have had to enter or remove some data in your database. Merely insert your data inside the database using the Insert command whenever you want to add new records, and the database will always automatically expand to suit your needs.

If you use the Delete command to remove information, you can keep your database range only as large as it needs to be; that is, you can use the space below your database for other purposes. Most important, there isn't any danger that the information below the database will be mixed up with the information inside the database.

SUMMARY

By this point you should have a grasp of the many things that can be done with a database in Wingz. Given the scripting capability in conjunction with a database, it is feasible that a database in Wingz could equal the performance possible in a commercially available, purpose-designed database.

CASE STUDY 6:
Wingz in TV Election Result

Jose (Pepe) Sabat
Computer Marketing Group
Banco de Ponce Building
Avenue Munoz Rivera #268
Hata Rey, Puerto Rico 00918

Sabat's firm contacted Informix about the possibility of using Wingz to display graphs on live television on KSJN as returns came in for the National election of November 8, 1988. They'd need a lot of 3D pie graphs, including a number with exploded pie slices, and they'd need to have the calculations done fast (inside two minutes).

The Nov. 8 election was an important one for Puerto Rico. In addition to electing the governor of Puerto Rico, voters would be electing 61 of the local alcalde's (precinct governors) and 150 other offices. Over 1,750,000 people voted that day—95% of Puerto Rico's eligible voter population.

The station set up four Macintosh II's on a video switching system, allowing instantaneous feed of Wingz screens into the millions of homes watching the election returns. Wingz was used in combination with some other software which stripped out the menus and added text, and operators entered data as it came in. The resulting Wingz graphs, showing results of the most interesting elections, were shown live on KSJN's election coverage that night, an event spanning some 15 hours.

9

Printing

Printing your work from a Wingz file is a very simple process. Simply make sure that your printer is connected, choose the Print command, select the options you want, and click the OK button. However, you have a number of options about what and how you print, and this chapter will look at these.

PREPARING YOUR PRINTER

If you haven't already specified a printer, use Chooser (a Desk Accessory file available under the Apple symbol at the left end of the Menu Bar) to do so.

If you're going to be printing charts, you'll want to use a laser printer, though you can print charts on a dot matrix printer. Because the laser printer allows far greater resolution, not only you will be better able to see shapes and lines, but you'll also be able to differentiate more shades of gray. Depending on your needs and the abilities of your printer, you may want to request one of the auxiliary fonts or use faster bitmap printing when you print. Check the Page Setup menu when you change printers on the Chooser dialog box.

You may find that different printers handle Wingz documents in ways not strictly comparable to their stated features. For instance, with Version 1 of Wingz, it appears that Apple LaserWriter IISC prints slightly sharper bar charts than does either the IINT or IINTX.

You can also print Wingz documents in color, if you have an appropriate color printer. For instance, to produce color charts on one of the Tektronics color laser printers, all you have to do is choose the Color box on the Print dialog box. If yours is a black and white screen, you'll need to choose the colors for various elements on your chart before you print. If yours is a color monitor, however, the colors printed will be related to the colors on your screen, depending on what colors are available with your printer.

Once you've specified a printer, you can proceed with other printing specifications.

PAGE SIZE AND ORIENTATION

You can specify how big your pages are, with options on the dialog box that appear with either the Page Setup or Print commands. This set of options has to do with the actual size of the sheet, not the printing area.

The page size options in the dialog box include:

Option	Page Size
US Letter	8.5 x 11 inches
US Legal	8.5 x 14 inches
Computer paper	14 x 11 inches
A4 Letter	8 x 11.5 inches
International fanfold	8.25 x 12 inches

Wingz adjusts the printable area to fit within the page size specified, allowing a reasonable margin. However, you can reduce the margins to expand the printable area; how much of the page can be printed depends on your printer. An Imagewriter can print on almost the entire page, but the LaserWrite can't. A LaserWriter, for instance, will print only up to an area 8.0 inches by 10.9 inches when a US Letter page has been specified. If you're

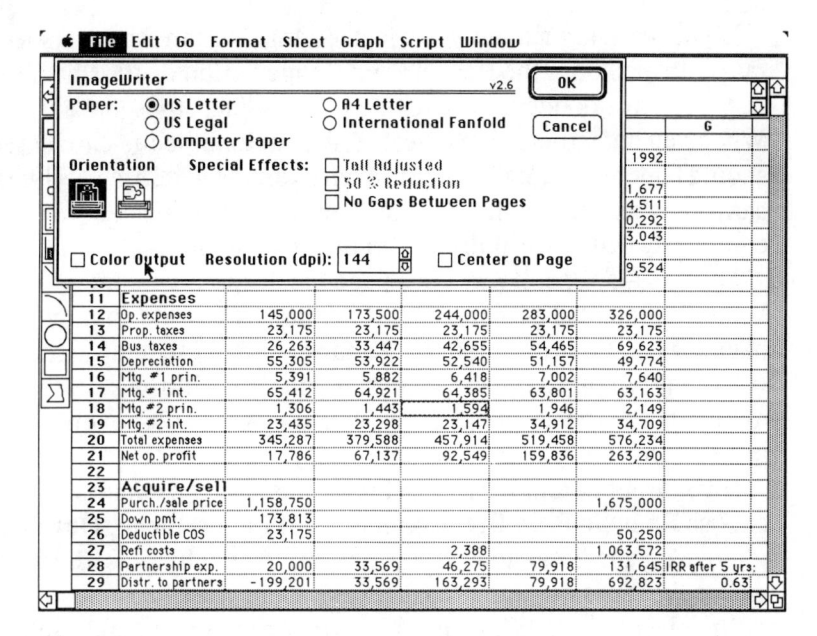

FIGURE 9-1 Print Dialog Box.

printing spreadsheet columns, Wingz will not allow printing of a partial column, and will adjust the number of columns printed so that complete columns are printed.

The page orientation option allows you to print pages either vertically (the normal way pages are printed, also sometimes referred to as **portrait orientation**), or horizontally (sometimes called **landscape orientation**). Click on the appropriate icon to specify which orientation you want to use.

CREATING A REPORT

Normally what you see on your screen as a worksheet gets translated by Wingz into a report when you go to print the information: Wingz breaks up your worksheet into pages and adds page numbers. You can add some fine touches to the printed report, with options available with the Report command on the Sheet menu. These include specifying the range to be printed, and adding your own page breaks, headers, and footers.

If you want to print only a selected range within the worksheet, select the range, then choose the Report Print Range option on the Sheet Report menu.

A **page break** occurs where one page of data stops and a new one begins. When you construct a worksheet, Wingz automatically calculates where this should happen (normally about seven columns wide, and 59 lines long). You can see where this will occur on your data if you select the Page Preview command, which we'll discuss in the next section.

You can also specify where a page break should go, rather than relying on Wingz' calculated placement. Select the last row or column to appear on a page, or position the cursor in the lower right cell, and select the Add Page Break option on the Sheet Report menu. Data in rows below and columns to the right of the new page break will appear on subsequent pages, and their page arrangement will be automatically recalculated.

If you want to remove a page break, position the cursor the same way, and choose Remove Page Break on the Sheet Report menu. However, you can't remove a page break that Wingz has automatically placed. If you don't like where Wingz is breaking a page, select a row above or a column to the left of the place where Wingz has placed its page break, and use the Add Page Break option.

Headers and **footers** appear on every page of your printed report. Since they are text, they can be edited, formatted, and colored the same way you'd modify any other Wingz text. You enter the text in one or more cells (all in one row or one column), then select the cells involved, and choose the Report Header Range or Report Footer Range option, as appropriate, on the Sheet Report menu.

Text in each cell should not exceed 255 characters. If you're using text in more than one cell, the text in each cell will appear on a separate line.

You can produce headers and footers for a printed report in a format that differs from the way the text appears in your worksheet. Be sure the cells containing the header or footer information have been selected and declared as headers or footers under the Sheet Report menu. (The appropriate option should appear with a checkmark beside it.) Use the Report Header or Report Footer option under the Select command on the Go menu. Once so selected, you can apply any of the applicable options on the Format menu to the print versions of the header or footer.

PREVIEWING YOUR PAGE

The Page Preview command on the File menu lets you see a small version of your pages, as Wingz has them currently arranged. (This includes all page breaks, either specified by you or calculated by Wingz.) This command is particularly useful because it lets you tinker with the page breaks, or any other page arrangement details, before you actually print.

When you select the Page Preview command, you see the first page of your printed report, along with some buttons at the bottom (see Figure 9-2). Note that while it's difficult to see all of your data, the preview-size pages let you see how the page will appear in general. You can move forward and backward through the pages in your report, using the Next and Prev buttons at the bottom.

Note also that Wingz orders the pages first from left to right, then top to bottom. At this time, the only way to change pagination order is to move the data around on your worksheet.

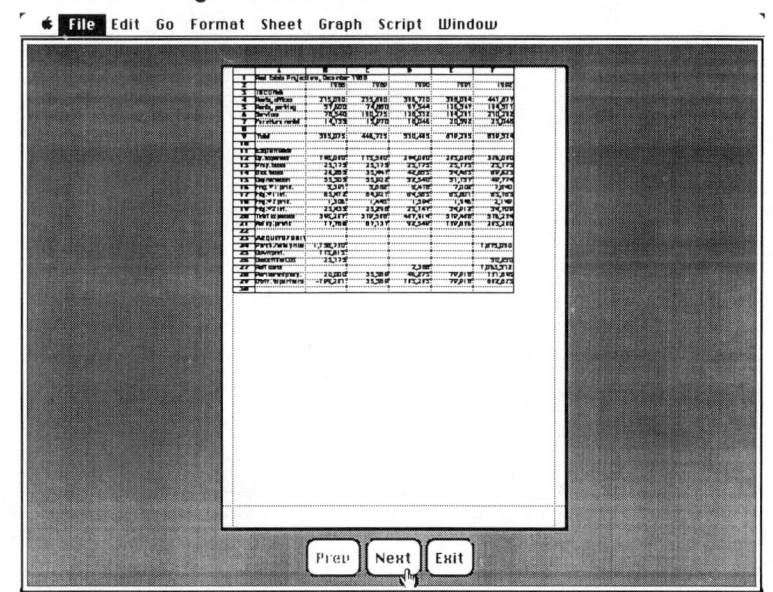

FIGURE 9-2 Page Preview Box.

PRINTING YOUR WORK

Normally, you'll want to print your entire worksheet. To do so, select the Print command on the File menu, then choose the applicable options on the dialog box (see Figure 9-3). You can specify which pages are to be printed if you don't want them all, how many copies are to be printed, and whether the paper feed is automatic or by hand.

You don't have to print everything on the entire worksheet when you select the Print command. However, you must have selected what you want to print before you choose Print. We mentioned earlier how to print a selected range. Be sure you select the range, then choose the Report Print Range option on the Sheet Report menu before you choose the Print command.

If you want only selected information printed, use the Show command on the Window menu to select what you want printed. Because anything that is checked will be printed, to print only selected kinds of items choose the checked items, one at a time, that you want to hide for that particular report.

FIGURE 9-3   Print Command Dialog Box.

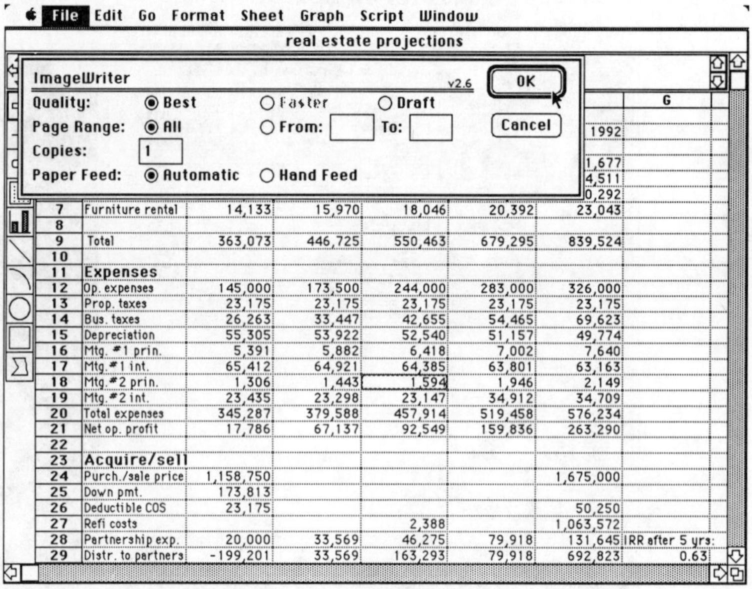

Then choose the Print command. If you want to hide headers or footers, choose the Hide Report Header or Hide Report Footer options on the Sheet Report menu.

SUMMARY

This chapter has shown you how to print your worksheet, tailoring it to specific printers or reporting situations.

10

Talking tothe Outside World

Many Wingz users will find that they're using Wingz in a network environment, or that they need to be able to share their worksheet files with others in a company. This chapter addresses the concerns of those who need to be able share their data with others.

LINKING TO OTHER Wingz SPREADSHEETS

One of the most common applications of the use of multiple spreadsheets is the construction of monthly and annual budgets, and the comparison of budgeted amounts with actual income and expenses. It is not uncommon for a department to construct an annual budget for the fiscal year, then break that down into budgets for each month. Those monthly budgets are then used to compare against departmental performance, and the results are reported elsewhere. Figure 10-1 shows an example of one such use of a spreadsheet. Notice that there is data here from at least three different sources:

1. The annual figures are drawn from the annual budget, as are the monthly budget figures. The budgeted year-to-date figures could come from the annual budget, or from the previous month's budgeted-vs.-actual figures if they are added to the budgeted figures for the current month.

266   Mastering Wingz

	A	B	C	D	E	F
1	August Budget vs. Actual	Aug-88	Aug-88	Year-to-date	Year-to-date	Annual
2		Act. expenses	Budg. expenses	Act. expenses	Budg. expenses	Budget
3	Salaries, professional	42065	41000	279719	275750	455750
4	Salaries, clerical	27945	28250	215487	209400	338400
5	SSI, employer	2302	2181	15944	15282	25016
6	SDI	807	810	5819	5676	9292
7	Contract work	22465	24500	217130	220500	332500
8	Rent	1750	1750	14000	14000	21000
9	Utilities	634	700	6097	5900	8875
10	Telephone	744	675	5316	5075	7875
11	Equipment	784	800	6128	6400	9600
12	Supplies	412	400	3197	3200	4800
13	Postage	214	200	1601	1600	2400
14	Transportation	387	350	2774	2800	4200
15	Subscriptions	34	50	418	400	600
16						
17	Total expenses	100543	101667	773630	765983	1220307

FIGURE 10-1 Budgeted vs. Actual Expenses.

2. The actual year-to-date figures come from the previous month's worksheet, and are added to the current month's figures.
3. The actual figures for the current month are entered each month.

With the exception of the current month's figures, you could automate the worksheet such that each time it is used, it would open the appropriate external files, copy the appropriate information to the current worksheet, and perform the necessary calculations to reflect the current status.

How Would We Do That?

If when you first started using Wingz, you ran Test Flight, the program on disk that comes with the Wingz program diskette and demonstrates some of Wingz' capabilities, one of the files you probably saw was the Worldwide financial reports. This file includes data drawn from summary reports from the United States, Europe, and the Orient. Each of these reports, in turn, draws on other regional files for its own summary data. The Orient file, for instance, draws its data from individual files for Taiwan, China, and Japan. If you change one of the sales figures on the China chart, you'll also change the figures on the Orient file because of the link between the two. Note that the summary figure for each quarter on the China chart winds up on the row for China for each quarter. If you were to change, the leasing figure for Q2 on the China chart, the total for Q2 would change both on the China chart and on the Orient chart.

Because of this linking, then, you can use data from another chart without having to copy it (although copying and moving are other ways of getting data from one place to another). Instead of the normal cell references, Wingz uses an external reference format so that it knows where to look for the data you want.

When you use a cell reference locally in a worksheet to duplicate data that are in another cell, you type something like

=C15

in the current cell. This tells Wingz to retrieve whatever is in C15 and to store it in the current cell. Whenever the data in C15 change, so will the current cell.

An **external reference** works the same way, except that it refers to a cell outside the current worksheet. An external reference is stated as the name

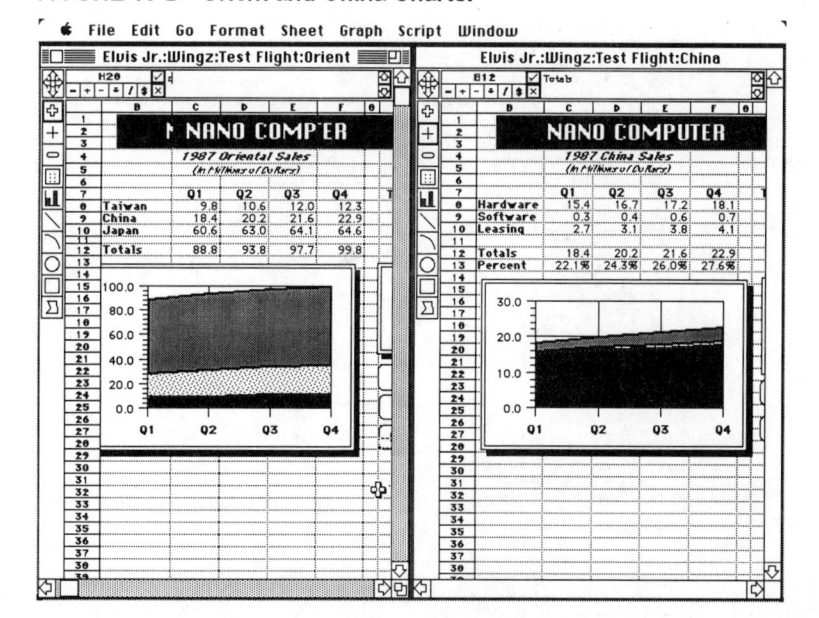

FIGURE 10-2   Orient and China Charts.

of the worksheet file containing the data you want, followed by a colon, followed by the cell address within that worksheet. For instance, suppose we are working on the budget vs. actual expenses for the month of August, and we want to use the monthly and annual budget figures from the file BUDGET1988. The annual budget might look something like this: Figure 10-3 depicts an annual budget, and Figure 10-4 shows the monthly budget statements for it.

To compute the August figures, we need to activate two other worksheets: the annual budget, and the monthly budget for the prior month. Starting at the right edge of the August budget statement, we can retrieve the annual budget figures by an external reference to the annual budget file. For instance, to retrieve the "Salaries, professional" figure from the annual budget, type the external reference

=Annualbudget:N3

FIGURE 10-3 Annual Budget.

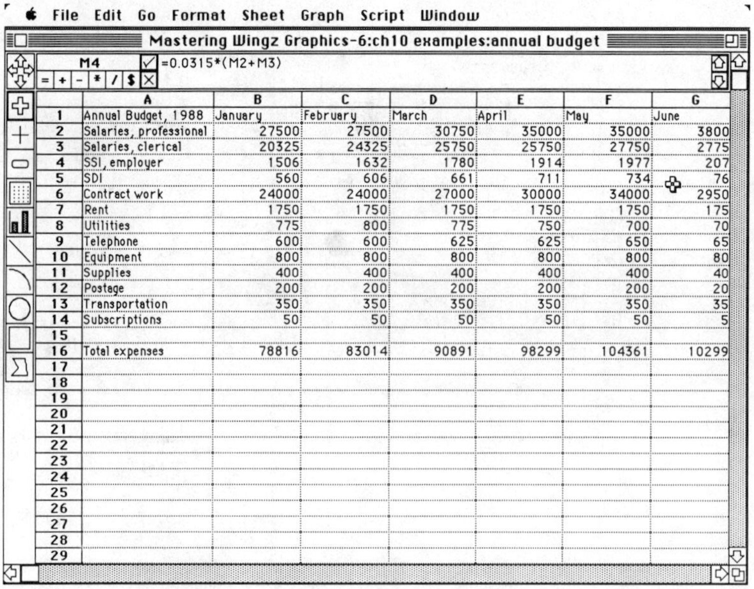

	A	B	C	D	E	F	G
1	Annual Budget, 1988	January	February	March	April	May	June
2	Salaries, professional	27500	27500	30750	35000	35000	3800
3	Salaries, clerical	20325	24325	25750	25750	27750	2775
4	SSI, employer	1506	1632	1780	1914	1977	207
5	SDI	560	606	661	711	734	76
6	Contract work	24000	24000	27000	30000	34000	2950
7	Rent	1750	1750	1750	1750	1750	175
8	Utilities	775	800	775	750	700	70
9	Telephone	600	600	625	625	650	65
10	Equipment	800	800	800	800	800	80
11	Supplies	400	400	400	400	400	40
12	Postage	200	200	200	200	200	20
13	Transportation	350	350	350	350	350	35
14	Subscriptions	50	50	50	50	50	5
15							
16	Total expenses	78816	83014	90891	98299	104361	10299
17							
18							
19							
20							
21							
22							
23							
24							
25							
26							
27							
28							
29							

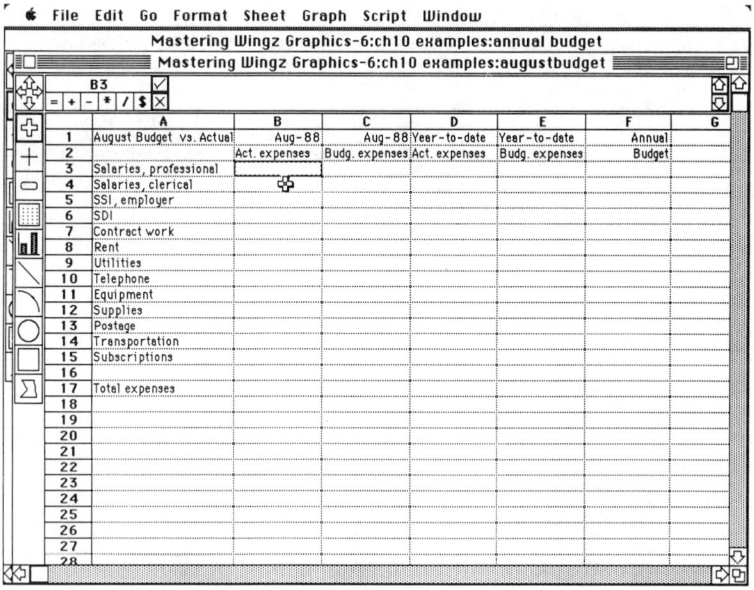

FIGURE 10-4 Monthly Budget.

This tells Wingz to retrieve whatever is in cell N3 in the file named Annualbudget. (Note that the filename in an external reference must not contain a space, even though Macintosh filenames may have spaces between words.)

Since we're after everything in column N from row 3 down on the annual budget, we can simply copy the external reference formula on the August worksheet down the column; Wingz will adjust the cell references for each row. The formulas in column F on the August worksheet will look like this:

=Annualbudget:N4

=Annualbudget:N5

=Annualbudget:N6

etc.

The figures from the annual budget now appear on the August worksheet (see Figure 10-5).

Mastering Wingz

	A	B	C	D	E	F
1	August Budget vs. Actual	Aug-88	Aug-88	Year-to-date	Year-to-date	Annual
2		Act. expenses	Budg. expenses	Act. expenses	Budg. expenses	Budget
3	Salaries, professional					455750
4	Salaries, clerical					338400
5	SSI, employer					25016
6	SDI					9292
7	Contract work					332500
8	Rent					21000
9	Utilities					8875
10	Telephone					7875
11	Equipment					9600
12	Supplies					4800
13	Postage					2400
14	Transportation					4200
15	Subscriptions					600
16						
17	Total expenses					1220307

FIGURE 10-5 August Worksheet with Annual Figures.

We could have copied the figures from the annual budget to the August worksheet, by using the Edit Paste Special command and choosing the Values option. However, this would have copied the figures only as stated at the time of copying. To make sure that the figures being transferred reflect the current state of the external file, including any changes, use an external reference. Each time the files are opened, whatever is currently in the cells in the external references is used as values.

We can also get the August budget figures from the Annual budget file: they're in column I. An external reference to retrieve the "Salaries, professional" figure is:

=Annualbudget:I3

Again, once the formula has been typed in C3 on the August worksheet, we can copy the formula down the rest of column C (see Figure 10-6).

We now need two more sets of figures from elsewhere. Both the Year-to-Date sets of figures for August need to use the Year-to-Date figures from

Talking to the Outside World 271

```
                     File  Edit  Go  Format  Sheet  Graph  Script  Window
                  Mastering Wingz Graphics-6:ch10 examples:annualbudget
                    Mastering Wingz Graphics-6:ch10 examples:augustbudget
            C17            =annualbudget:I17
         =  +  -  *  /  $  X
                      A                 B              C              D              E              F            G
         1   August Budget vs. Actual   Aug-88         Aug-88        Year-to-date   Year-to-date   Annual
         2                              Act. expenses  Budg. expenses Act. expenses Budg. expenses Budget
         3   Salaries, professional                    41000                                       455750
         4   Salaries, clerical                        28250                                       338400
         5   SSI, employer                             2181                                         25016
         6   SDI                                       810                                           9292
         7   Contract work                             24500                                       332500
         8   Rent                                      1750                                         21000
         9   Utilities                                 700                                           8875
        10   Telephone                                 675                                           7875
        11   Equipment                                 800                                           9600
        12   Supplies                                  400                                           4800
        13   Postage                                   200                                           2400
        14   Transportation                            350                                           4200
        15   Subscriptions                             50                                             600
        16
        17   Total expenses                            101667                                      1220307
        18
        19
        ...
```

FIGURE 10-6 **August Budget with August Figures.**

July, added to the August Actual and August Budget figures, respectively. Again, we can reteive these with an external reference formula.

In the case of the Year-to-Date Budgeted Expenses, the formula for "Salaries, professional" is:

=Sum(Annualbudget:B3..I3)

This tells Wingz to sum the figures in B3 through I3 in the file Annualbudget.

And the comparable figure for Year-to-Date Actual Expenses uses this formula:

=Julybudget:D3+B3

This formula tells Wingz to use the figure in D3 on the file Julybudget and to add to it the figure in B3 on the current worksheet, which happens to be the actual expenses for August for "Salaries, professional." As before, you can copy the formulas down columns D and E to fill in the areas.

Figure 10-7 shows how the August budget worksheet looks at this moment. Now the only thing left for you to do is to enter the August actual expenses. As soon as you enter a figure in column B, the comparable figure in column D changes to reflect the new data.

Figure 10-8 shows how the finished August budget vs. actual worksheet looks like:

One reminder about using external references: the files involved must be currently open. You can easily move from file to file while you're constructing a worksheet with external references if you use the Window menu to select the worksheet you need.

EXCHANGING FILES WITH OTHER PROGRAMS

Wingz lets you use files created under other spreadsheet programs, as well as ASCII text files created elsewhere. You open one of these files with the

FIGURE 10-7 August Budget without August Actual

	A	B	C	D	E	F
1	August Budget vs. Actual	Aug-88	Aug-88	Year-to-date	Year-to-date	Annual
2		Act. expenses	Budg. expenses	Act. expenses	Budg. expenses	Budget
3	Salaries, professional		41000	237654	275750	455750
4	Salaries, clerical		28250	187542	209400	338400
5	SSI, employer		2181	13642	15282	25016
6	SDI		810	5012	5676	9292
7	Contract work		24500	194665	220500	332500
8	Rent		1750	12250	14000	21000
9	Utilities		700	5463	5900	8875
10	Telephone		675	4572	5075	7875
11	Equipment		800	5344	6400	9600
12	Supplies		400	2785	3200	4800
13	Postage		200	1387	1600	2400
14	Transportation		350	2387	2800	4200
15	Subscriptions		50	384	400	600
16						
17	Total expenses		101667	673087	765983	1220307

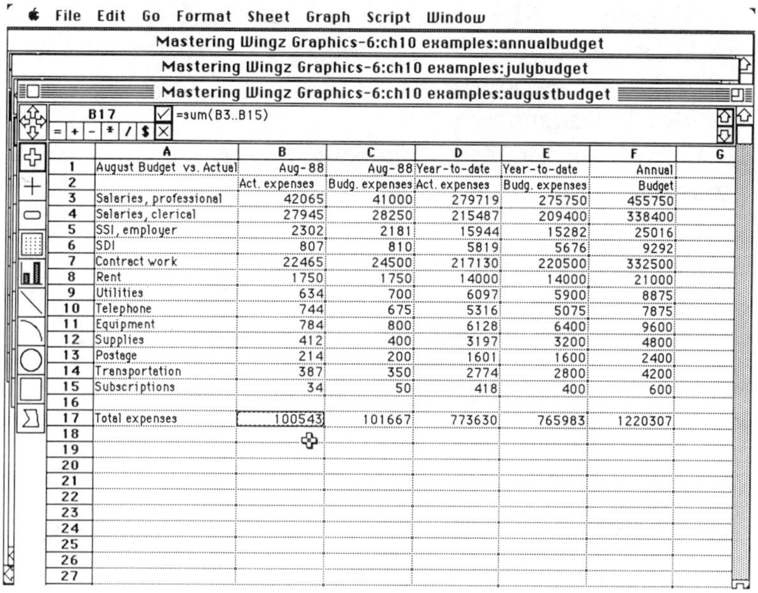

FIGURE 10-8 Completed August Worksheet.

File Open command. How Wingz adapts them for its own use depends on the file format.

Wingz also lets you save worksheets in formats that can be used by other programs. Use the File Save As command, and at the bottom of the dialog box, pull down the File Type box, then choose the format in which you want the current worksheet saved.

Lotus 1-2-3

Files created under Lotus 1-2-3, either version 1A or version 2, can be used by Wingz, and Wingz can produce files in either .WKS (version 1A) or .WK1 (version 2) formats. All number and text formats are used the same way. Wingz evaluates all formulas the same way except for those Wingz does not support. Any text used in formulas, or formulas that produce text as a result will be translated intact to a version 2 file format, but because Lotus 1-2-3 version 1A does not support text formulas, they will not be translated to a version 1A file format.

Wingz uses a different method of reporting errors than does either version of Lotus 1–2–3. Lotus 1–2–3 supports the error values NA and ERR, and while Wingz supports those values, it also reports error messages as ERR followed by a number.

Wingz allows references to single cells, to cell ranges, and to multiple selections. Neither version of Lotus 1–2–3 supports references to multiple areas.

The maximum size of a Lotus 1–2–3 version 1A worksheet is 2048 rows by 256 columns; with version 2A the maximum is 8192 rows by 256 columns. While Wingz can handle a worksheet of up to 32,768 rows by 32,768 columns, and therefore will be able to handle any size Lotus 1–2–3 worksheet, the reverse is not true. When saving a Wingz worksheet in a Lotus 1–2–3 format, any data to the right of column IV, or below row 2048 for version 1A, or below row 8192 for version 2 will be ignored.

Neither version of Lotus 1–2–3 handles external references. Any external references in a Wingz worksheet will not be converted when the file is saved under either Lotus 1–2–3 format.

SYLK

The SYLK format is used by Microsoft Excel for the Macintosh and Microsoft Multiplan. You can import a SYLK file into Wingz, but Wingz cannot save a worksheet in SYLK format, nor can Microsoft Excel for the Macintosh recognize Wingz files. Files created under the SYLK format are translated with number and text formats transferred intact. All formulas except those Wingz does not support are kept intact.

Date formulas may pose a problem, however. Microsoft Excel for the Macintosh uses a different starting point for the date/time serial number than does Wingz. Under Excel for the Macintosh, serial number 1 is equivalent to January 2, 1904; under Wingz, serial number 1 is equivalent to January 1, 1900. For example, the serial number under Wingz for December 14, 1988, is 32491, but the serial number under Microsoft Excel for the Macintosh for the same date is 31029. (Under Microsoft Excel for the PC, serial number 1 is also equivalent to January 1, 1900.)

DIF

Files created under a program that uses the DIF file format (usually VisiCalc and derivative programs) can also be used by Wingz. Numbers and text are transferred intact, but formulas are ignored.

ASCII

Files created under a program using an ASCII text format (usually a text file) are used by Wingz with numbers and text intact. Formulas are ignored. Columns are separated by tabs, and rows by carriage returns, but all other formatting is lost.

Wingz can also save the current worksheet as ASCII text, with the same conditions as above. This option makes it easy to transfer the contents of a worksheet, which may include text and numbers, into a word processor document.

If Wingz is asked to open a file and can't detect an allowable format, it will open the file as an ASCII text file.

IMPORTING GRAPHICS AND TEXT

Anything that can be put on the Clipboard can be imported into a Wingz worksheet. Thus, any Macintosh application using the Clipboard can contribute information to your Wingz worksheet.

To send text to a Wingz spreadsheet, open the other file containing the text you want, and cut or copy the part you want to to the Clipboard. Then open the Wingz worksheet, click the worksheet tool, click in the text field, and choose the Edit Paste command.

Importing graphics is a little more involved. Any graphic image you want to use must be in .PIC (picture) format. However, you then have two choices:

1. You can copy the graphic file to the Clipboard, and paste it into place much as we described above for imported text.
2. You can use the HyperScript command READ PIC with the appropriate arguments, and copy the picture file into a particular range on your worksheet. (We discuss HyperScript in more detail in Chapter 11.)

USING Wingz IN A NETWORK

Just as you can trade data from Wingz files with other applications on a single machine, you can also use Wingz in a network environment. Wingz simply looks at the network as yet another place to get and send files.

You open a file that's not on your machine the same way you open a file that's not in the Wingz folder. Simply choose the File Open command, and when the dialog box appears, click on the name of the network you need, then click on the folder names until you find the file you want.

One caveat, however: when you're openly sharing files on a network, it pays to add an extra level of protection to your own work, so that the data can't be altered without your permission. The lowest level of this protection, which uses the Cell Protection or Enable Protection commands on the Sheet menu, "freezes" the cell contents as displayed for the cells on which protection is applied. You'll use this form of protection when it's okay for others to see your file, and even make changes to the data, so long as they're careful enough to remove cell protection. You may want to use this form of protection when you have formulas and labels in certain cells that really shouldn't be changed, but data in others that may be changed by any user. Templates are a good example for this form of protection.

The second form of protection is available with the Password option with the Sheet Protection command. You can apply two levels of passwords to your file. (When a file is password-protected, anyone attempting to open it must correctly type the password, or is denied access.)

You can also mandate that anyone opening it is given read-only permission; that is, they may read it but not write it. (Note, that someone could save your file on their own system. If they find the correct password, they could then remove the read-only restriction, and modify the data. For most uses, however, this won't be a problem.)

Finally, you can encrypt the file. Thus, even if someone can get at your file, unless they have the encryption key or the password that tells Wingz to decrypt the file, they can't use the data.

There is a very practical problem with using passwords to protect a file: people forget them. Even the standard warning about writing down the password and keeping it in a safe place doesn't always work—if you can find the password, so can someone else, even if accidentally. Password protection, however, is extremely useful in normal business situations where moderate amounts of security are beneficial.

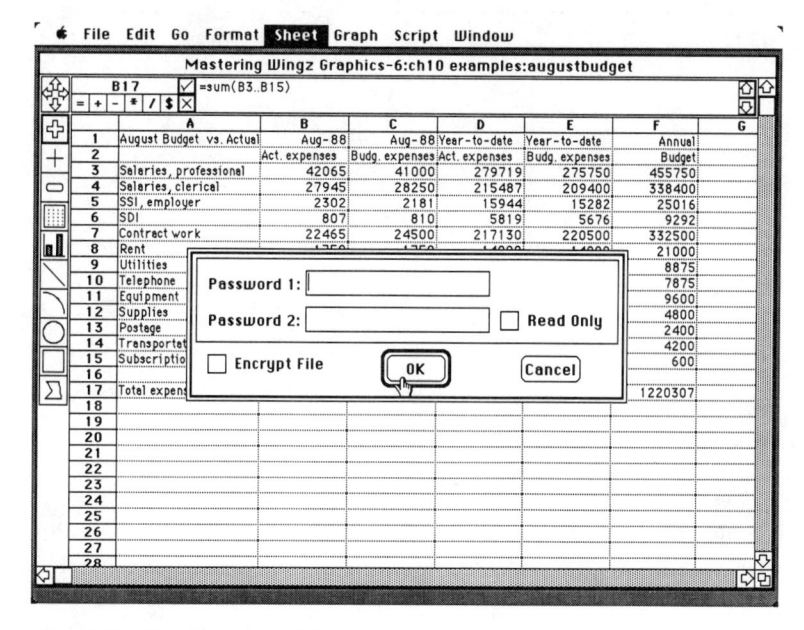

FIGURE 10-9 Password Dialog Box.

SUMMARY

This chapter has looked at some aspects of using Wingz in an environment where more than one file is used, or in network situations. There are also some HyperScript commands that let you access external files from within one of your own script files. We'll look at HyperScript in Chapter 11.

11

Programming in HyperScript

By this point in the book it should be fairly clear to you that Wingz is a very powerful tool. We will now examine an even more powerful aspect of Wingz that will give you more control and flexibility than is available in any comparable software: the HyperScript programming language. This chapter will provide examples of what can be done with HyperScript in a number of different applications. The basic structures will be explained with scripts that will demonstrate these structures.

The best part about writing HyperScript routines is that Wingz has a **learn mode** that even someone with no programming background at all can master in a single session. The learn mode writes scripts for the user simply by following the actions of the user and providing HyperScript code in the script based on the action. For example, if you select the range of cells from **a1** to **c15** by dragging the mouse over them while in the learn mode, the script

select range a1..c15

will be written in the selected Script window. So, there is no need to avoid scripts if you are not a programmer. You can do them inthe Learn mode, and by adding a few "hand-typed" lines of your own, you can quickly enhance your applications.

WHAT IS HYPERSCRIPT?

HyperScript is the control language of Wingz. It has some characteristics similar to HyperCard (the programming environment provided by Apple Computer, Inc., with all new Macintosh computers). However, HyperScript is also different from HyperCard. HyperScript is not centered around cards, but instead uses the sheet environment of Wingz, a much broader field. Nevertheless, if you are familiar with writing scripts in HyperCard, learning HyperScript will be a bit easier. HyperScript also has features similar to those for programming languages C, Pascal, Forth, and even BASIC.

Direct Commands

One of the best ways to start off with any programming language is to use the immediate or direct mode. That is, write a command line and watch it execute immediately. Let's start off with a few direct commands to provide a feel for HyperScript, and then begin creating scripts with the Learn mode.

To get going, load up a new sheet. Write the following line in the Entry bar:

put "Monday" into a1;select range a1..f1; fill

Figure 11-1 shows how it should look in the Entry bar.

Now press the **command key** and **<Return key>** at the same time. As soon as you do this, your screen should look like the one shown in Figure 11-2.

Let's see what happened in that line of script. Since the semicolons separate each command, by removing the semicolons we can break it down into three parts.

Programming in Hyperscript 281

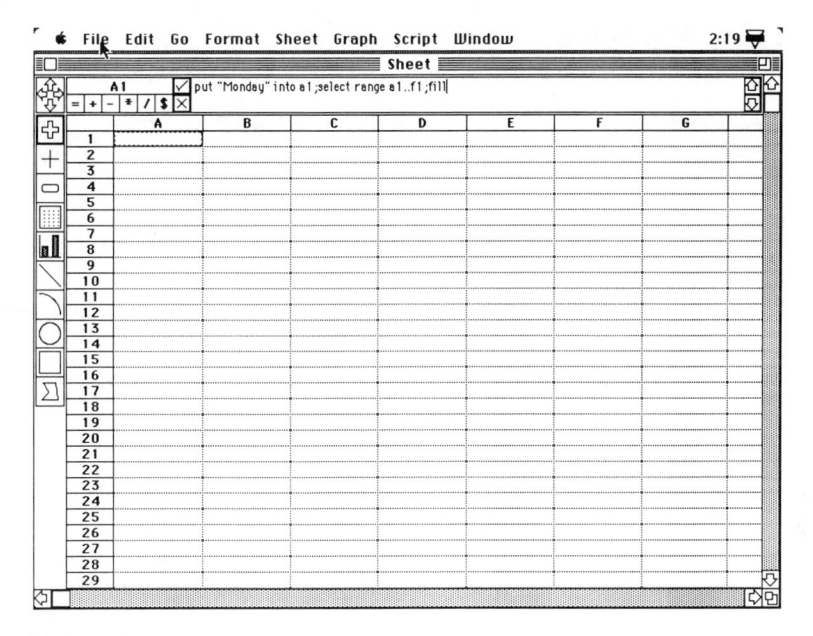

FIGURE 11-1.

FIGURE 11-2.

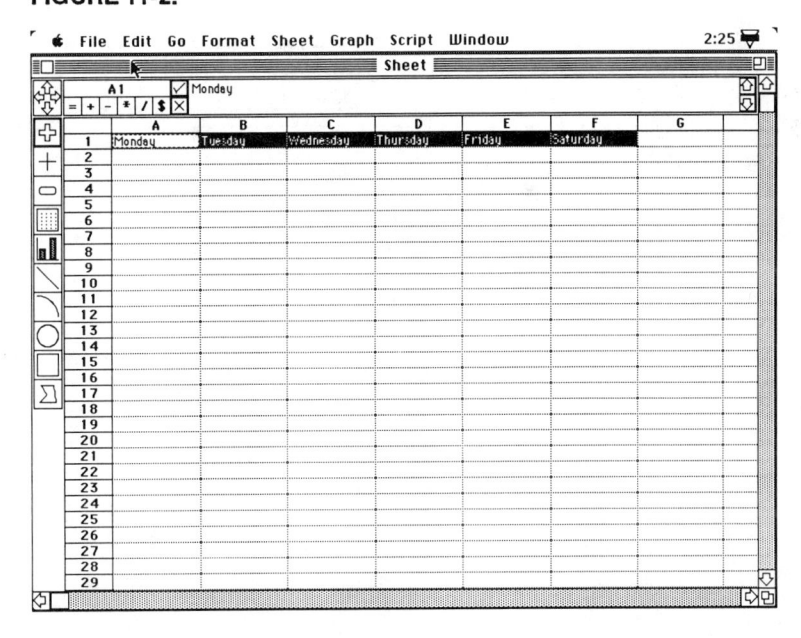

Command Line	Action
put "Monday" into a1	Writes the word Monday into the cell a1.
select range a1..f1	Selects the cells a1 through f1.
fill	Fills in the days Tuesday through Saturday

For practice and to get an inkling of what is happening, put in the line shown in Figure 11-3.

Once the line has been written as shown in the window, see if you can determine the results before looking at Figure 11-4. Now press <Return> and see if you have guessed correctly what will happen.

Breaking down the command again, we find,

Command Line	Action
put "Your Name" into a1	Writes your name into a1.
put a1 into d10	Writes the contents of a1 to d10.

FIGURE 11-3.

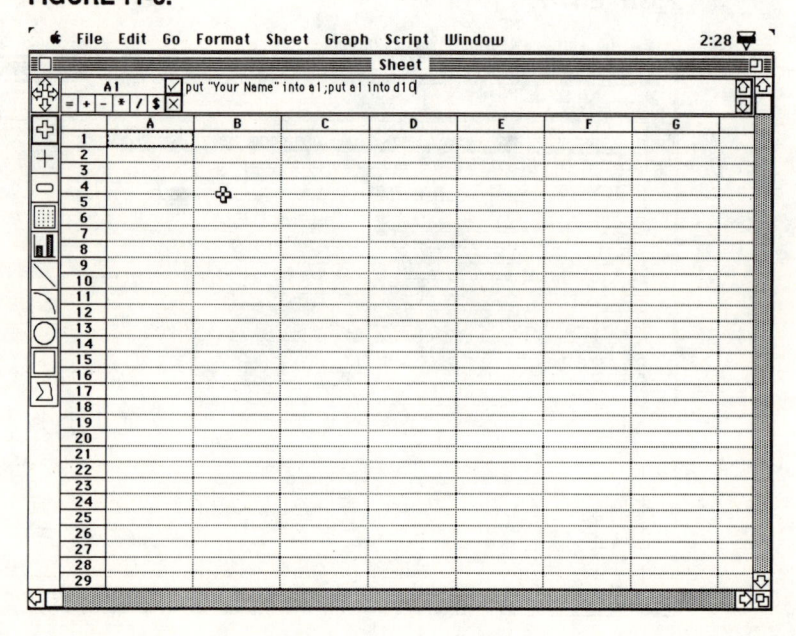

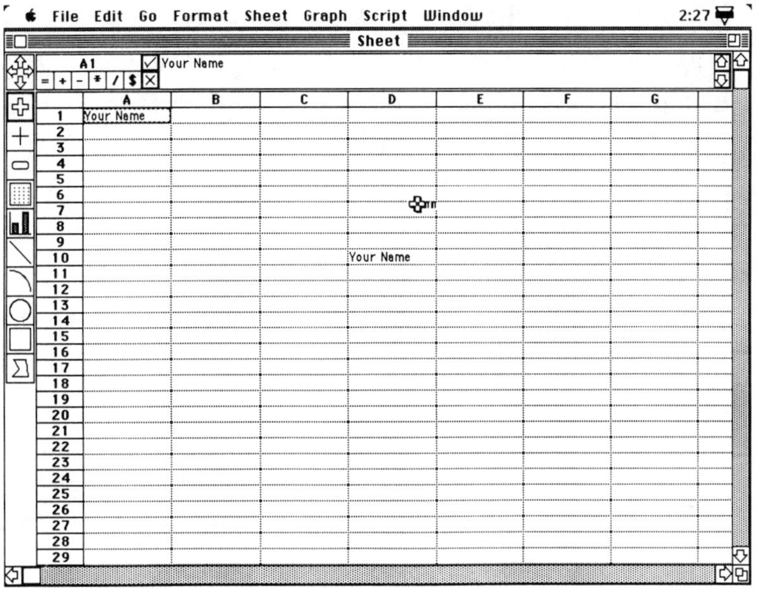

FIGURE 11-4.

From these samples, you can see that it is pretty simple to put data into cells, and take data from one cell and put it into another. To get some practice and a feel for some more commands, enter the following HyperScript direct command and execute them from the Entry box:

    put 10 into a1; put 20 into b1; put a1 + b1 into c1

    put 15 into a1; put 80 into d10; select range a1..d10;fill

    text font "Monaco"; text size "9"; put "Message" into a1

    put "Wingz" into a1;select range a1..e16;copy down;copy right

The above four little lines of script should give an idea of what the screen looks like when script is executed. In turn, this will provide a visual explanation of what the scripts do so that when you start writing your own scripts you can see the relationship between the commands and the actions.

Learn Mode: Button Scripts

Probably the best way for you to get started with HyperScript is to create button scripts with the learn mode. The Learn mode can be turned on and off from the script menu. Before the learn mode can be turned on, first a script must be selected. In the examples in this section, we will select the button script. To get started, let's use the following procedure:

1. Select the button tool from the toolbox.
2. Create a button by dragging the mouse from a9 to a13. (Figure 11-5 shows how the button should appear.)
3. Select Button Info... from the Format window.
4. When the dialog box appears use the name Test Table for the button and click on "OK." (Figure 11-6 shows how it should look.)
5. Choose Button Script from the Script menu.
6. When the button script appears, click the Window menu and return to the sheet view.

FIGURE 11-5.

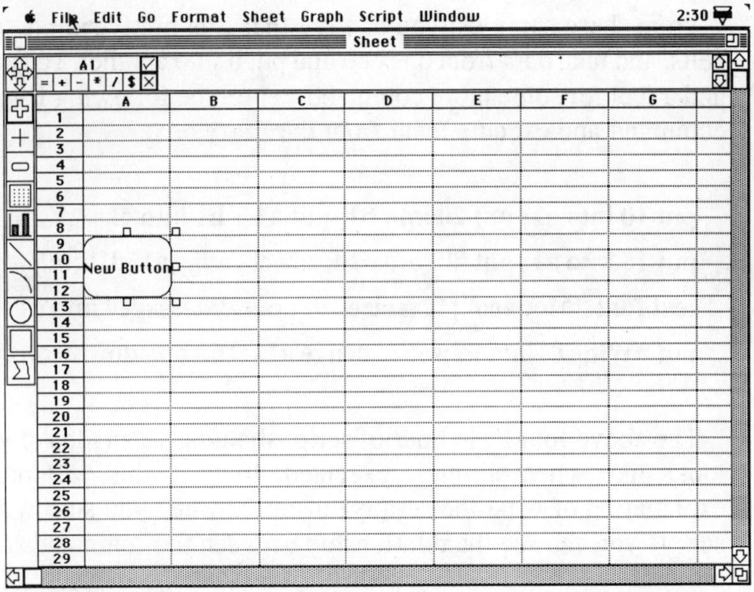

Programming in Hyperscript 285

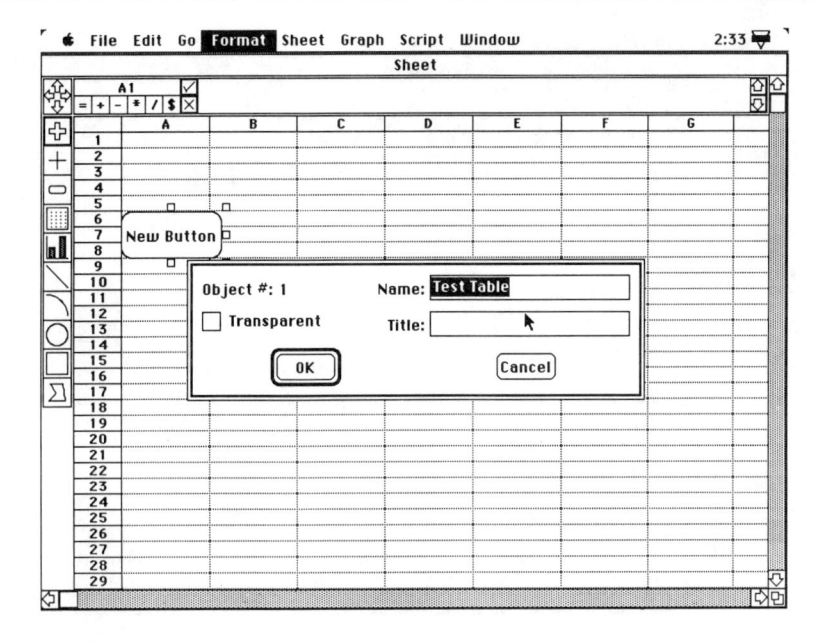

FIGURE 11-6

7. From the Script menu, select Learn. (*Note:* From this point on until Learn is turned off, every action you take will be recorded in the button script; so be careful to follow the next steps precisely.)
8. Place the cursor in cell a1 and write,

    =rand()*1000

    in the Entry bar and press <Return>.
9. Select cells a1 through d7 by dragging the mouse from a1 to d7.
10. From the Edit menu, select Copy Down and then Copy Right.
11. With the cells still selected, from the Format menu choose, Precision. . . and set precision to 0.
12. Click Learn from the Script menu to turn off the learn function.
13. Deselect the a1. . .d7 range by clicking cell a1. Your screen should look like the one in Figure 11-7.

Close the button script, clear all the cells with numbers in them, and click the Test Table button. You'll see that all the cells fill up with random integer

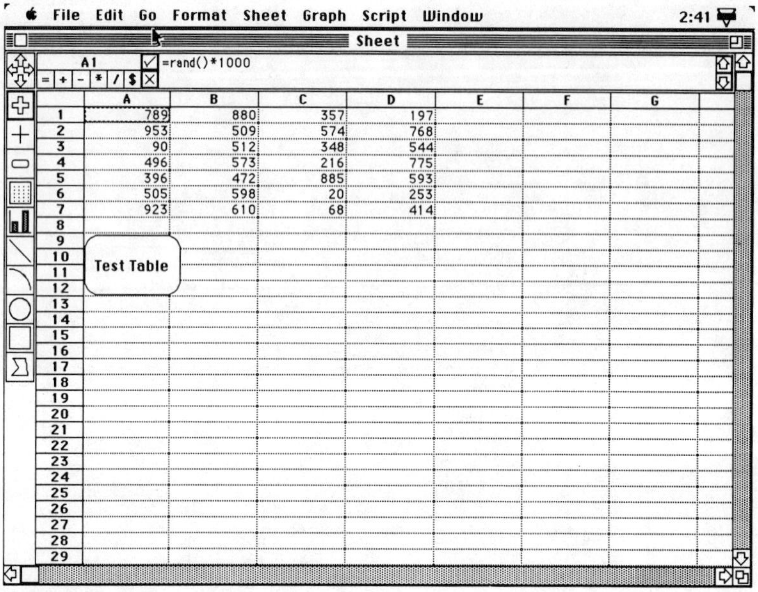

FIGURE 11-7.

numbers. This particular example illustrates several different things that the Learn mode can do with HyperScript. To see what has happened select the button, and choose the button script view from the Window menu. The following script (without line numbers) should be in the button script.

```
select range A1
Put "=rand()*1000" Into A1
select range A1..D7
Copy Down
Copy Right
precision 0
```

Think of the script as a set of instructions you would give a friend whom you are teaching to use Wingz. In fact, it is even easier since the menu items are chosen by themselves and not as a subset of a menu. That is, it is unnecessary to specify the menu before specifying the menu item (for example, you don't have select the Edit menu before selecting Copy Down.)

About the only thing in the whole script with which you may not be familiar is the random function, expressed as

rand()

The function returns a random fraction between 0 and 1. It was multiplied by 1000 in the example and then rounded to the nearest integer. Thus, the line

rand()*1000

generated numbers between 10 and 999.

Learn Mode: Sheet Scripts

Now that we have an idea of what can be done with the Wingz Learn procedure, let's see if we can put together something practical, but instead of a button script, we will use a sheet script. It's a good idea to have a script that hides all extraneous materials not wanted on a printout. The following script does all those things and takes the user to the Print Dialog box. Use the following procedure to create a script that will accomplish those tasks:

1. Choose Sheet Script from the Script menu.
2. From the Window menu, return to Sheet.
3. Turn on the Learn mode from the Script menu.
4. Deselect the following from the Show item in the Window menu: (remove the checkmark)

   Toolbox
   Cell Grid
   Title Grid
   Entry Bar
   Heading Grid
   Headings

5. Select Print from the File menu.
6. Turn Learn off from the Script menu.

The sheet script now has a little program that instructs Wingz to hide the Toolbox, grids, and headings and start the print procedure. Change the view from the sheet to the script from the Window menu, and you'll see that the following script has been generated:

```
Hide Toolbox
Hide Cell Grid
Hide Title Grid
Hide Entry Bar
Hide Heading Grid
Hide Headings
Print Dialog
```

To see the effects of running the script, first choose Compile from the Script menu, and then Run from the Script menu. Everything from the screen will disappear, and the Print dialog box appears. (Just click Cancel when it does.) Use this with some of your completed spreadsheets to see how easy it is to use.

Learn Mode: Independent Scripts

Independent scripts are similar to sheet scripts except they are not attached to any particular script. They can be initiated with New Script from the Script menu, and later recalled with Open Script.. from the Script menu. They are saved in the same way as are sheets using the Save option from the File menu. A useful application for an independent script is one that restores all of the grids, Toolbox, and other items hidden when the sheet was set up for printing. The following procedure does this:

1. Select New Script from the Script menu.
2. Return to the sheet view using the Window menu.
3. Choose Learn from the Script menu.
4. From the Show item in the Window menu, select the following:

Toolbox
Cell Grid
Title Grid
Entry Bar
Heading Grid
Headings

5. Turn Learn off from the Script menu.

Once you complete these steps, select Save from the File menu, and save the file as Show. Now, whenever it is necessary to restore all of the material to the sheet, all you need to do is to open and compile Show and then select Run from the Script menu. All of the restoration will be done automatically. Your Show script will look like this:

```
Show Toolbox
Show Cell Grid
Show Title Grid
Show Entry Bar
Show Heading Grid
Show Headings
```

As you can see, all the script does is what would have been done by the mouse. But, unlike the mouse, once a script has learned the routine, it will do it automatically.

Note: To remove the rectangle around the printed output, it is necessary to remove the borders. To do this, first choose Select from the Go menu, and then at the very bottom of the menu choose Report Border. Next from the Format menu, select Border... and change the border line to None.

WRITING SCRIPTS

From experimenting with the Learn mode, you can see how much the HyperScript programming language resembles a fairly natural language.

However, we can do a number of things beyond the Learn mode in writing scripts. Now, we'll cover these and provide examples with applications that can be used to make any task with Wingz even simpler.

As a quick and simple example, let's create a couple of button scripts that select different types of graphs from the sheet. Such buttons are very useful in situations where we want to switch from one type of graph to another. By clicking the buttons, we can change the graph type. First let's create four buttons, as shown in Figure 11-8.

Be sure to place the buttons where they are shown. The four buttons represent types of graphs that cannot immediately be seen on the Graph menus of Macintosh Plus and Macintosh SE computers. Since these Macs have smaller screens than the Mac II's, the menu items have to be on the extended part of the menu. (The extended menu is indicated by a downward pointing triangle on the menu.) By having the buttons on the screen, it makes it much easier for you to select these different types of graphs, not only for the smaller Macs, but for the big ones too.

FIGURE 11-8.

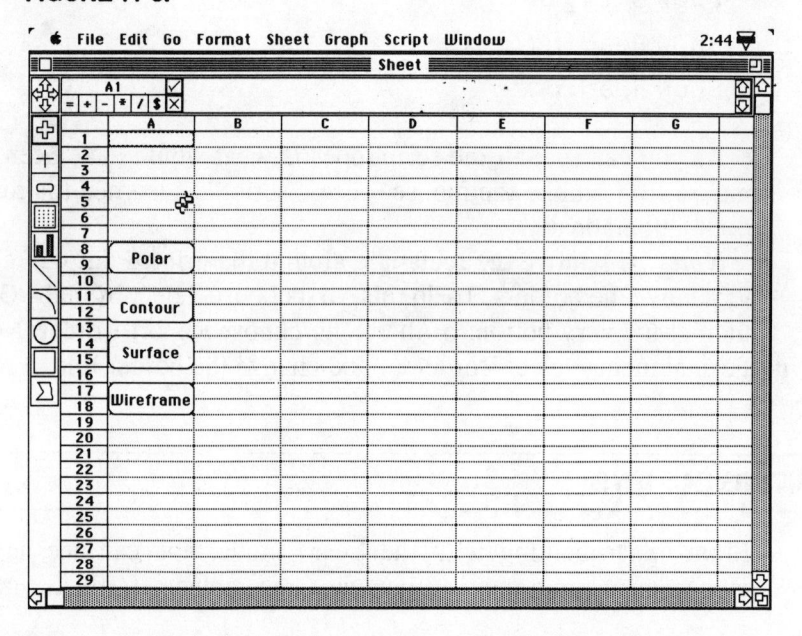

Next, let's generate a graph and some data. We have seen how to use the **rand** function to generate random numbers, and we can write a script to create the data. Select New Script from the Script menu, and type in the following script. (Save the script as Instant Data.

```
{Make an automatic generating field of data}
select range A1
put "=rand()*1000" into A1
precision 0
select range A1..E7
copy down
copy right
{Add the chart covering some of the data}
add chart range B1..F18 using A1..E7
hide legend
```

All of the text inside the curly brackets constitutes remarks and is not compiled into the running program. They are added to help understand what the different components of the script are doing. About the only new commands are the ones adding the chart and hiding the legend.

The "hide legend" line is fairly self-explanatory, but the line to add a chart to the sheet needs some explanation. Let's break it down to see how it works.

Script	Action
add chart	adds a chart to the sheet
range B1..F18	covers the cells in the range indicated.
using A1..E7	uses the data in the indicated cells

Compile and run the script. Remember that the last script compiled runs when the Run option from the Script menu is selected. Also, the sheet onto which the data will be written must be selected. Figure 11-9 shows how the screen will appear after the script has been executed.

Our next task is to create scripts for the four buttons. The chart is Object 5 since the buttons took up Object numbers 1 through 4. All the button scripts

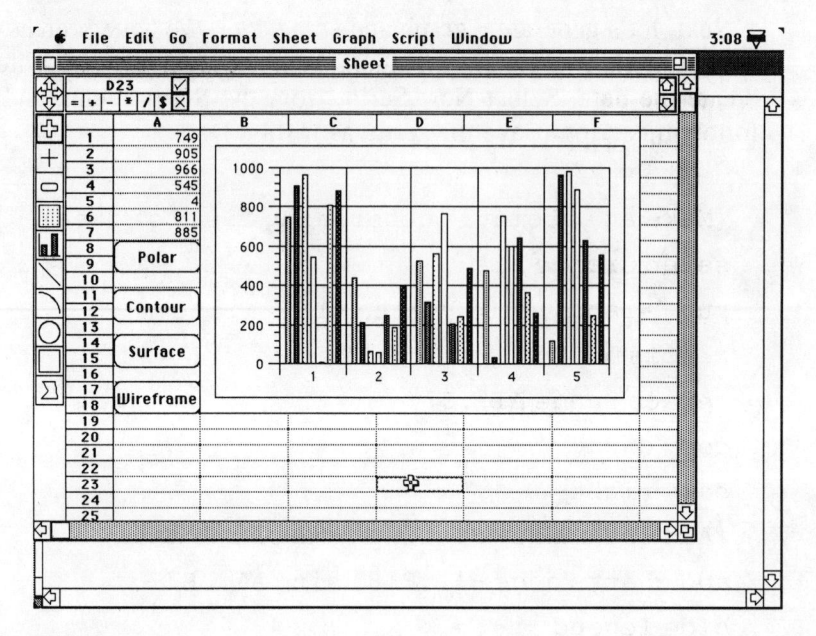

FIGURE 11-9.

have to do is to select the chart (Object 5) and select the type of chart to be drawn.

Polar

    select Object 5
    polar

Contour

    select Object 5
    contour

Surface

    select Object 5
    surface

Wireframe

    select Object 5
    wireframe

Programming in Hyperscript 293

To see if everything is working correctly, test one of the buttons. Try the Surface button. If it works correctly, your screen should look like the one in Figure 11-10.

The script has given the use of a maximum amount of screen, but in an application, it may prove to be inconvenient to have a graph cover the active cells. To make the application more useful, let's add two more buttons, Hide and Show, that will make the graphic appear and disappear. In that way, if the numbers need to be changed, the graph can be hidden while the changes are made. Once the changes are complete, the chart can be shown. It is important not to cut and paste the chart or to create a new one each time the graphics are removed. If we do that, a new object is created, and the reference to Object 5 in the button script no longer applies to the chart object. To make the graphic appear and disappear, we need two buttons. One button, called Hide has the script

```
hide graphics
```

FIGURE 11-10.

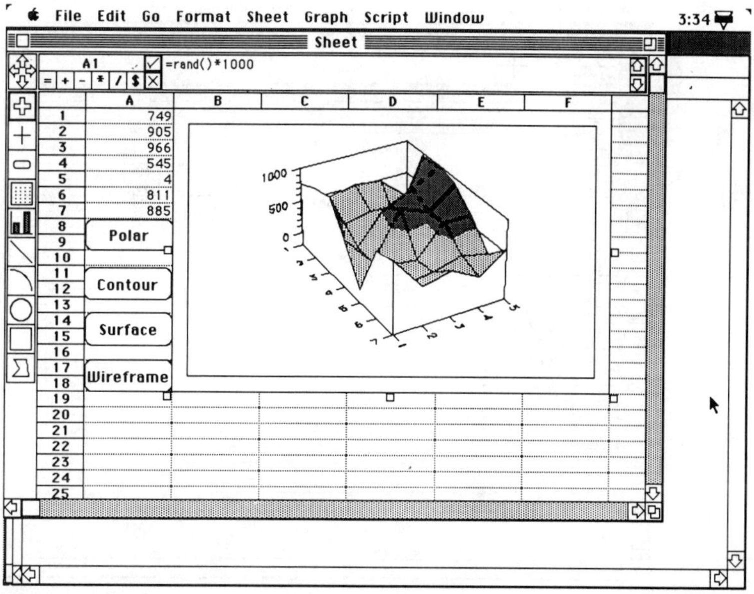

and the other button, Show, has the script

```
show graphics
```

to retrieve the chart. To add the two new buttons, move the original four buttons using the object tool from the toolbox. Figure 11-11 shows how the screen will look when the buttons are all placed and the Hide button has been clicked.

MAKING MENUS

Besides the menus that are available when you start up Wingz, you can write scripts that will create additional menus or even whole new Menu Bars. This section shows how to make your own menus and menuitems.

FIGURE 11-11.

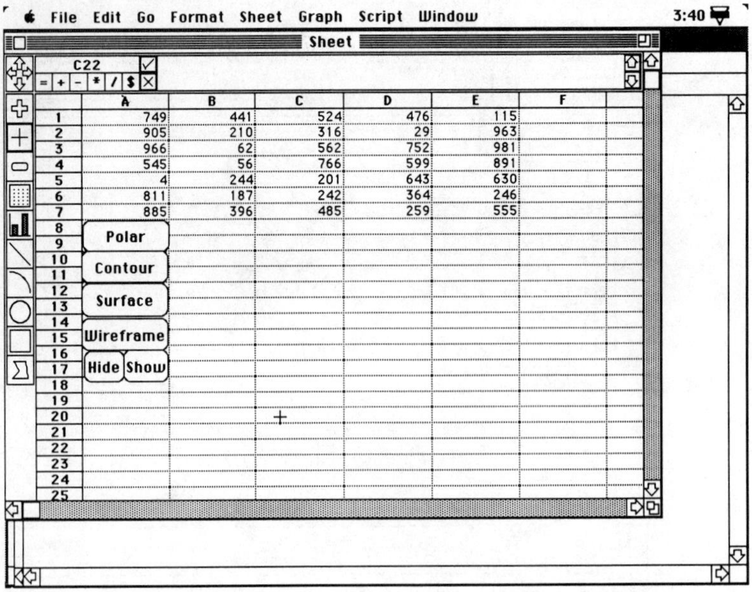

The command for adding a menu is

add menu "Title"

Each item in the menu is referenced as **menuitem**, and all menuitems that follow an **add menu** command will be placed in that menu. For example, the script

add menu "New"
add menuitem "PrintClear"

would add an additional menu called "New" to the existing menu bar with the single menu item called "PrintClear."

Menuitem Commands

The real power of HyperScript comes into play when we add the Menuitem commands. These commands are just like the other HyperScript commands we have discussed. They execute when a given menuitem is selected. The format is

add menuitem "Title" command "com1;com2;com3..."

The commands in the list are separated by semicolons, and all of the commands are enclosed by quotation marks. If a command in the list references something that requires quotation marks, you must use two sets of quotes. For example, a command line that selects the Window menu will have to use the syntax

.."select menu ""Window""". . .

so that the command line would not misinterpret the quotation marks as indicating the end of the command list. To see a practical application, let's take the little hide-and-print routine and create a menu that will do everything we want done. This is far easier than loading the script and running it. Everything will be done from the menu. Create a new script and type in the following routine:

```
add menu "Special"
add menuitem "Hide & Print" command "Hide Tool
  Box;Hide Cell Grid;Hide Title Grid;Hide Entry
  Bar;Hide Heading Grid; Hide Headings;Print
  Dialog"
add menuitem "Show" command "Show Tool Box;Show
  Cell Grid;Show Title Grid;Show Entry Bar;Show
  Heading Grid;Show Headings"
add menuitem "Remove Me" command "Select Menu
  ""Special"";remove menu"
```

The HyperScript lines were indented so that you can better use what goes with what. The last line removes the menu from the Menu Bar. Notice the use of the double quotation marks around "Special."

Note: Even though we are no longer showing examples of writing scripts using the Learn mode, it is possible to combine script writing with and without the Learn mode. If there is a certain part of your script that is easier to write using the Learn mode, simply turn on Learn, use it, and then turn it off for the part of the script where direct entry is used. Also, to aid in your learning of HyperScript, try turning on the Learn mode to help learn the syntax of the language.

USING EVENT HANDLERS

We have seen how simple it is to create a button script and use the buttons in Wingz. All buttons have a built-in event handler. Whenever a button is clicked, its script is executed. The event handlers

on mouseup

.

.

end mouseup

bracket the script even though we cannot see them. For buttons (controls), seven different events are handled:

mousedown

mousedoubleclick

mousemove

error

mouseup

repaint

mousestilldown

Each event handler begins with **On** and terminates with **End**.

Between the beginning and end of the handler is the script that takes an action initiated by the event. To see how this might works, let's take a simple script using the "mousedoubleclick" event. This will require a double instead of a single click of the button to activate the script. Figure 11-12 shows an example of how a double click button works. The script is a button script shown simultaneously with the sheet. Use the immediate mode command

arrange windows

followed by the <Return> command to place both the sheet and the script window side by side on the screen.

To test it, single click the button. Nothing should happen. Next, double click the button, and the cells from a1 through a5 should be selected. A double click button is useful in applications where you want the user to think twice about an action, such as clearing a range of data.

SHEET EVENTS

Sheets may also handle events, but there are a set of events different from those handled by buttons (controls). The five events for sheets are

activate

deactivate

recalc

idle

error

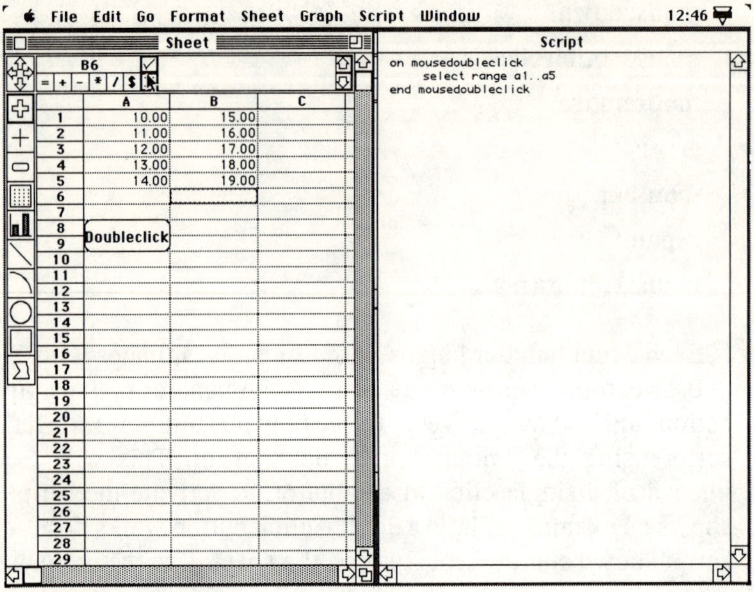

FIGURE 11-12.

The most likely events to be handled are Activate and Deactivate. When the sheet is activated, there are a number of things that might have to be automatically done such as change the Menu Bar, load functions into memory, put a Slide bar on the screen, and get the current date.

A useful example is a script that places the current date on the screen as soon as the sheet is activated. We'll use the **message** statement

```
on activate
   message "Todays date: "&adate(now(),"month
   dd,yyyy")
end activate
```

When the sheet is activated, it automatically shows the date in a dialog box that the user must click to continue. Figure 11-13 shows how the screen appears as soon as the sheet is activated.

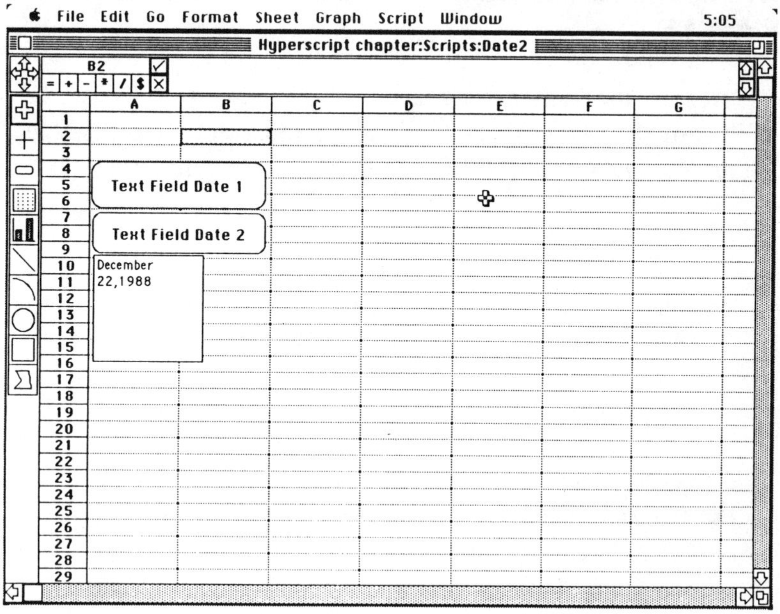

Programming in Hyperscript

FIGURE 11-13.

Another interesting use of time and event handlers in sheet scripts is using the Idle handler. Basically, this handler commands actions while nothing else is going on. As a result, it is simple to make a clock in a cell. Use the following sheet script to make a "clock" in cell a1.

```
{Set the text to bold face}
text style "B"
{When nothing else is happening (idle), have cell
 a1}
{serve as a clock}
on idle
    put atime(now(),"hr: mn sc") into a1
end idle
```

VARIABLES

Before continuing, let's stop for a second and discuss how variables are handled in HyperScript. First, we must define a variable. The definition process reserves space in memory. For example, the line

define x

reserves space for a variable called "X." When more than a single variable is defined at once, commas are used to separate the variables in the format,

define var1,var2

Variable names must begin with a letter, but they can be combinations of letters and numbers. If two-word variables are used, underscores must connect them. For example,

past_performance

is an acceptable variable name.

There is no difference between the way string and numeric variables are defined or formatted. The following sheet script gives a quick example of defining and using variables.

```
define x,y
x=55
y="This is text"
put x into a1
put y into a2
```

As can be seen in the example, quotation marks surround the string variable (line 3), while the numeric variable is simply equated without any bracketing marks at all (line 2). By "string variables," we simply mean that the variable contains text instead of numbers. When numbers and text are combined in a variable, they are string variables. For example, "Catch22" is a string variable.

In naming variables be careful not to use cell names—names such as "v2" or any combination of up to four letters followed by one or more numbers. For example, try the following script in a sheet script and run it.

```
define way1
way1 = "2222"
put way1 into way1
```

When you attempt to run the program, you get an "Expected Range" error message in the dialog box because Wingz uses combinations of letters in the range from "A" to "AYLH" with numbers from 1 to 32768 as cell references. However, removing the numbers from the end of the variable name will fix this error. For example, the following script works well.

```
define way
way = "2222"
put way into way1
```

A final precaution in naming variables: it is best not to use reserved words. Although in some cases you can actually use reserved words as variables, it is a bad habit to acquire, for it can be very confusing whether the words are being used as commands or as variables. For example, the script

```
define put
put= "Put"
put put into put1
```

may work, but no script could be more confusing! In naming variables, use these rules of thumb:

1. Avoid using command names as variables.
2. If numbers are used in variable names, either put them in the middle of the name or use the underscore to separate them from the main name of the variable (for example, use Map_1 **and not** Map1 as a variable name).
3. Use descriptive names so that you know what your variable is doing unless it is too close to a command name.

302 Mastering Wingz

OTHER CONTROLS

The standard control buttons (push buttons) are relatively easy to set up, but it is also possible to set up other types of controls. In this section we'll examine sheets that use the different types of control. At the same time, we'll progress with the HyperScript programming language.

Slide Bar

You can use the slide bar to move quickly through a range of values to see what effect they have on a constellation of data. At the same time slide bars cover a wide range of values specified by the user. To add a control unit such as a slide bar, first, add it to the sheet using the statement
    add control unit range cell-1..cell-n

The same format is used for all control units, from number wheels to list boxes.

Create Script

```
{Make the slide bar}
Add Slide bar range a1..c17
Show control title "Tax finder"
Show Control Name "Amount of Sale."
Slide Bar Major divisions 10
slide bar minor divisions 5
slide bar range 0 to 50
slide bar precision .01
slide bar position 0
{This sets up the screen for the control script.}
put "Amount" into d1
put "Tax" into d2
put "Total" into d3
select range d1..d3
```

```
text style "B"
put 0 into e1
  put 0 into e2
  put 0 into e3
  select range e1..e3
  format currency
```

CTVALUE()

Once the control unit has been created, it is now necessary to write a control script to make the control do what you want. The ctvalue(c#,i#) function returns the value of

control number (the object number of the control unit)

item number (the number of the item in the control unit.)

FIGURE 11-14.

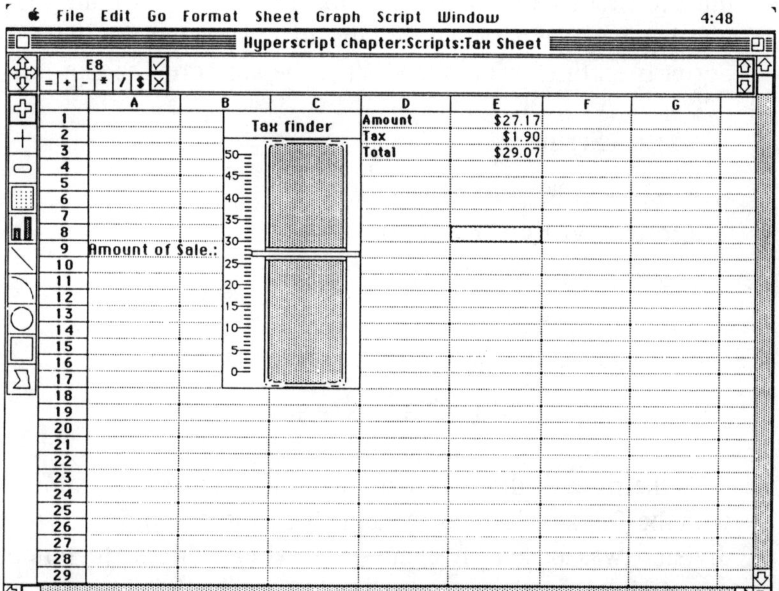

To return the current position of the slide bar we use the item number 0. With other control units, 0 is used to indicate the currently selected item. For example, in Object number 3, if there are four radio buttons, and ctvalue to be returned is the Current button, the ctvalue is

ctvalue(3,0)

To get item information on a specific item only, the script calls for that item number to be specified in the second position. For instance, if you want a result only when the third box is checked in a Check Box control unit, and the object number of the unit is 2, the ctvalue would read,

ctvalue(2,3)

Applications with single correct answers would be an example of using only single items.

The control script for the slide bar uses 0 for the item identifier since it returns the current location of the bar based on the smallest unit division of the bar. In fact, most of the other control units we'll examine will also use 0 for the item identifier.

Note: In order to write a control script for a specified control unit, you must to first use the object tool to select the control unit. Once the control unit has been selected (little tabs appear around the unit), choose Control Script from the Script menu. Write the script on the Control Script:

Control Script
```
define amount,tax
amount =ctvalue(1,0)
tax= amount*.07
put amount into e1
put tax into e2
put amount + tax into e3
```

To the right of the slide bar, you will see that the Amount changes along with the Tax and Total as the slide bar is used. Note that because the pricing division was based on cents—it is very difficult to pinpoint an amount exactly by using the control bar. Had we used a larger unit, such as dollars, or even tenths or quarters of dollars, the slide bar could have more easily placed the exact amount we desired. A longer slide bar is always more precise than a short one.

Amount	$27.17
Tax	$1.90
Total	$29.07

Check Box

The Check box is created very much like the slide bar. But instead of having to name all of the parameters of the slide, you now must name the various boxes. The following example of a script shows how to use the ctvalue function to return only a positive value when a particular cell is checked. Notice what happens to the score when the wrong answer is checked or the correct answer is unchecked.

Create Script
```
hide cell grid
Add check box "Football","Baseball","Horse Racing",
   "Basketball" range a1..d12
Show control title "Sports Quiz"
Show Control Name "Largest attendance?"
put "Score" into e4
select range e4
text style "B"
```

Control Script
```
    put ctvalue(1,3) & " Points" into e5
```

Figure 11-15 shows how the screen looks when the correct answer is chosen. Try checking the different combinations to see what value is generated by ctvalue with the different combinations.

Notice how "1 Points" changes to "O Points" when Horse Racing has the X removed from the Check box. Because ctvalue returns only a one or zero

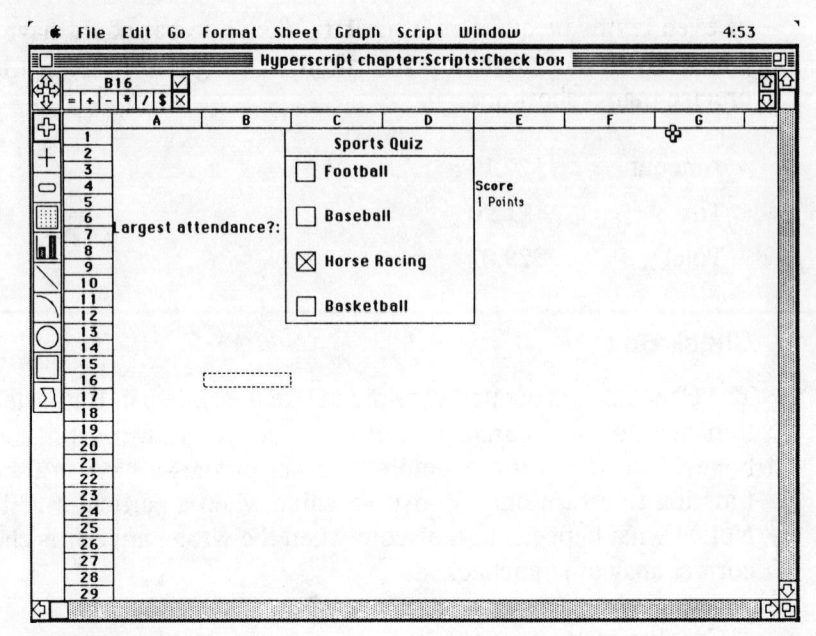

FIGURE 11-15.

when a specific item is indicated in the second parameter of the ctvalue function, all of the other choices also return "0 Points" when checked. That's In this case it works like a true or false function in that it returns a 1 only if the correct choice is made. Otherwise, it returns a 0.

Popup Menu

CTSTRING(). The Popup menu provides a good control unit to illustrate how the ctstring function works. Instead of returning a number as ctvalue does, ctstring returns the string with the name of the item. It uses exactly the same parameters as does ctvalue, but generates text instead of numbers. In the case of the Popup menu, each menu item is the string returned by ctstring when that item is selected.

The following Create script clears most of the screen and makes the Popup menu. It is a demonstration script that shows the difference between how ctvalue and ctstring work. However, it can be a very practical application if you use it actually to open different spreadsheets created on Wingz.

Create Script

```
{Conceal everything but the tool box}
Hide Cell Grid
Hide Title Grid
Hide Entry Bar
Hide Heading Grid
Hide Headings

{Script to create the popup menu}
Add popup menu "Marketing", "Promotions",
"Development", "Public Relations" range a1..d7
show control title "Department Data"
Show control name "Department->"
put "CTVALUE=" into c10
put "CTSTRING=" into c11
select range c10..c11
text style "B"
```

The reason the toolbox was not hidden in the sheet script that created the Popup menu was that we need the Object tool to select the control unit to access the control script. The control script contains the command to hide the toolbox.

In the last line we used the ampersand to concatenate (tie together) the text Open with the string returned by ctstring. That is to show how the ctstring function might be used with the command open to open a spreadsheet for one of the departments listed in the Popup menu. (Notice there is a space between the last letter of Open and the second parenthesis in line 3 of the control script.)

Control Script

```
Hide tool box
Put CTValue(1,0) into D10
Put "Open " &CTString(1,0) into D11
```

Figure 11-16 shows how screen appears when you use the Popup menu.

List Box

IF Statement   Let's use List box to illustrate how to use Wingz's conditional statement IF. The general syntax for IF is

IF condition
   action 1
ELSE
   action 2
END IF

For example, a script might call for a flag if a certain client's name comes up. An important client may warrant special attention, and if his or her name

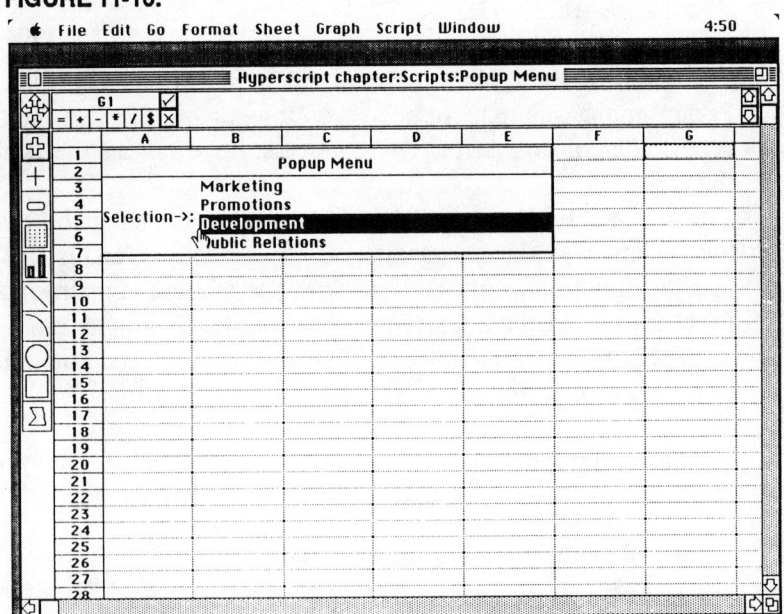

FIGURE 11-16.

is accessed, the message "VIP is special!" could remind the user that the client is important to the business. Thus, the script

    Define VIP

    VIP=ctstring(1,0)

        if VIP = "Warbucks"

            message VIP &" is special!"

        end if

    generates the message,

    Warbucks is special!

whenever the name is picked from a control unit with an item named "Warbucks."

In some applications, there is a special condition for a lot of different events. Instead of having a single name, number, or other condition, the script looks for several different conditions and each condition requires a different action. A different IF format is used in these cases:

IF condition 1
   action 1
ELSE IF condition 2
   action 2
ELSE IF condition 3
   action 3
  •
  •
END IF

The List box is something like the Popup menu except that it does not pop up. All of the text is listed in the box on the screen. The following Create and Control scripts use the IF structure to create a simple "Phonebook."

Create Script

```
Add list box
"Jack","Betty","Pete","Sue","John","Jose","Dave",
"Joann"
range a1..c17
   Show control title "List Control"
   Show Control Name "Phone Book"
```

Control Script

```
{Get phone number}
   put ctstring(1,0) into E3
if ctstring(1,0) = "Jack"
   put "555-1234" into e4
elseif ctstring(1,0) = "Betty"
   put "555-4321" into e4
elseif ctstring(1,0) = "Pete"
   put "555-8888" into e4
elseif ctstring(1,0) = "Sue"
   put "555-0128" into e4
elseif ctstring(1,0) = "John"
   put "555-0099" into e4
elseif ctstring(1,0) = "Jose"
   put "555-5691" into e4
elseif ctstring(1,0) = "Dave"
   put "555-9183" into e4
elseif ctstring(1,0) = "Joann"
   put "555-1100" into e4
end if
```

FIGURE 11-17 shows how the screen appears once the phone book is in place and working correctly.

Radio Button

Case Conditional. We'll use the Radio button control unit to illustrate how the CASE statement will be used. It is similar to the IF..ELSE IF conditional. The basic syntax for CASE is

Case
   When condition 1
      action 1
   When condition 2
      action 2
   When condition 3
      action 3

FIGURE 11-17.

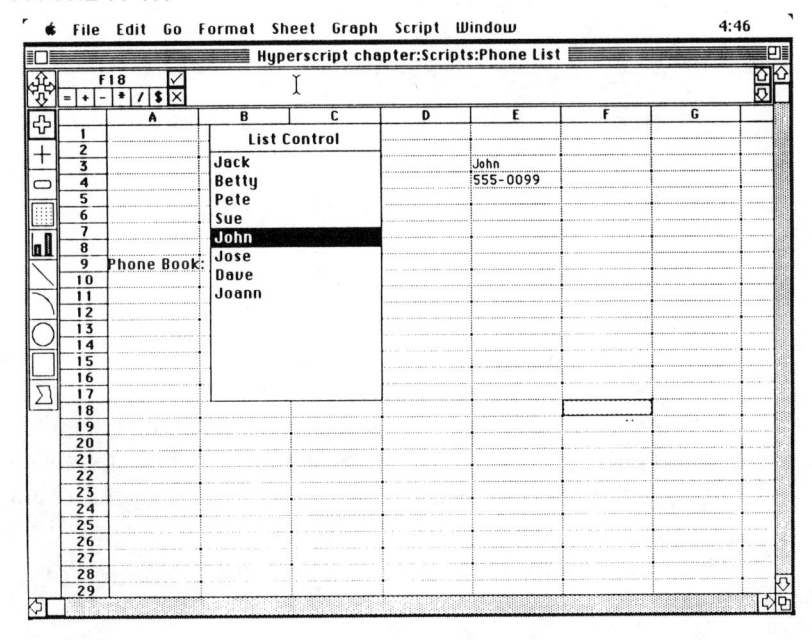

Otherwise
>   action x
End Case

This format would be a good one to apply to the phonebook example used with the List box. In this example, let's create a simple tool for reading the results of Radio buttons with the ctvalue function.

Create Script
```
Hide cell grid
add radio button "Poor","Fair","Good","Excellent"
range a1..b10
```

Control Script
```
define hozbusiness
hozbusiness = ctvalue(1,0)
Case
  when hozbusiness=2
    Message "We're surviving."
  when hozbusiness=3
    Message "Pretty good this year."
  when hozbusiness=4
    Message "Business is booming!"
  otherwise
    Message "We're in trouble"
  end case
```

Notice that the action following the Otherwise statement applies to any other condition. If there were twenty Radio buttons and only buttons 2 through 4 were in When lines, as is the case in the example, the other seventeen buttons would come up with the message "We're in trouble." Figure 11-18 shows the screen when a button has been clicked.

Programming in Hyperscript   313

There are other control units, but they are scripted in a very manner similar to the control units discussed above. Try out the other control units to see how they act with the set of commands discussed in this section.

LOOP STRUCTURES

There are two loop structures, the **FOR** loop and the **WHILE** loop. Like all loop structures, these loops repeat certain sets of commands and statements until the termination condition has been met. The syntax for the FOR loop is

FOR beginval TO endval STEP increment
    statements/commands
END FOR

FIGURE 11-18.

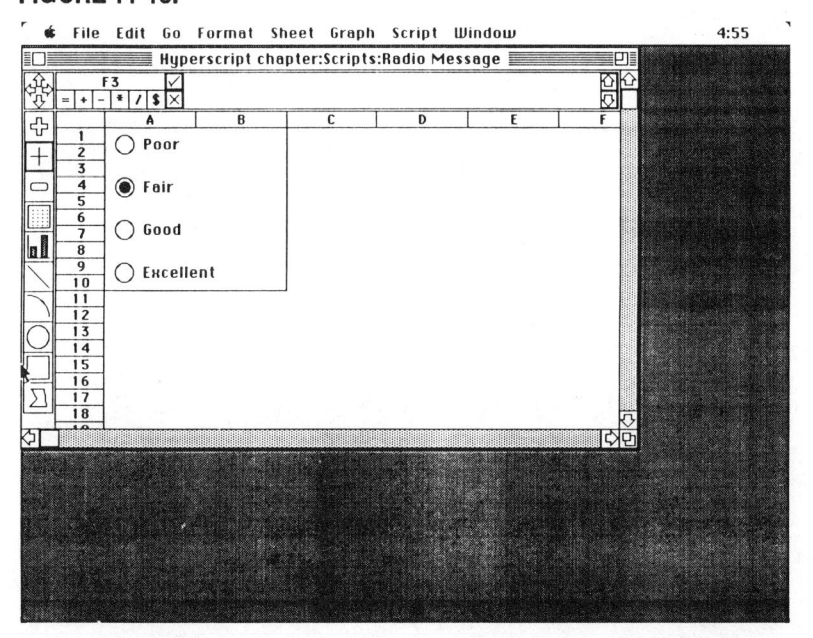

For example, the following script generates values from 35 to 85 with increments of 5.

define x
for x=35 to 85 step 5
    put x into a1
end for

The script would not do anything too interesting since it would simply put all of the values into a single cell. However, there are occasions when it is necessary to read data from individual cells or put them into individual cells. Our next example shows how to use a FOR loop to put data into sequential cells and columns. The following button script generates sequential data, but, more important, it shows how to use variables to access various cells. (Use a button script for this one. See Figure 11-19.)

define count,cell,column

```
{Column A}
column="a"
for cell=1 to 10
  put cell into column & cell
end for

Column B}
count=0
column="b"
for cell=11 to 20
  *count=count+1
  put cell into column & count
end for
```

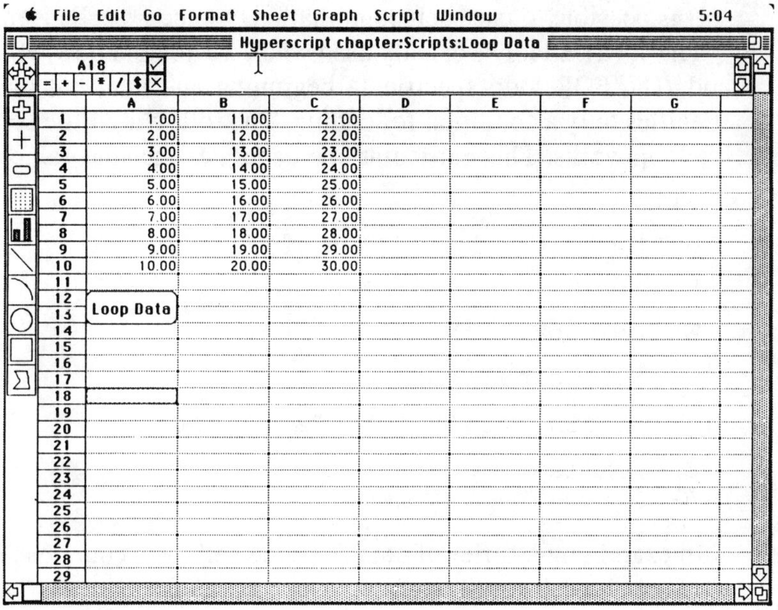

FIGURE 11-19.

```
Column C}
count=0
column="c"
    for cell=21 to 30
  count=count+1
put cell into column & count
end for
```

The variable name "cell" was used in the loop to generate values from 1 to 10, from 11 to 20, and from 21 to 30. In the first loop, the variable "column" was defined to be "a." The first time through the loop, the value of "cell" was "1." By concatenating "column" and "cell" using the ampersand (&), the name generated was "a1."

column	"a"
cell	1
column & cell=	"a" & 1 or "a1."

It is possible to use such combinations to access cells from scripts.

The WHILE loop is usually used when we do not know when the loop will end. The FOR loop specifies a beginning and end, but the WHILE loop specifies only a condition for ending. The following little script shows how the loop works. This particular one generates the sine values from 1 to 15.

```
define total
total =0
While total <15
   total=total + 1
   put sin(total) into "a" & total
End While
```

In examining a series of data from the cells, we could use a WHILE loop to check the cells until we found a certain value.

FUNCTIONS

The last major element we'll discuss in HyperScript is functions. There are several functions built into Wingz, but it is possible to create your own functions. Creating and using functions is a two-step process. The first step is to write a script that defines the function. Next, the function must be called into memory with the GET statement. Then, once the function is in memory, it is referenced by the file name of the function and the function name. This procedure may seem a bit awkward to you, but if you think of functions as macros and you should see that it is possible to create a whole library of functions and then call them from any script you write.

To see how the procedure works, let's use a very simple example that has all of the elements required for a function. We'll make a cube function that returns the cubic measurement based on a single value. (The sides of the cubes in this example must all be equal.) Write the first script and save it as "MyCube."

Function

```
Function cube(side)
   return side ^3
End function
```

Once the function is saved under an easily remembered name, it can then be called by that name and used. The following script shows how:

Function Used

```
define a
{First call the function script into memory}
   get script "MyCube"


{Optionally, place function return value into variable}

   a=MyCube:Cube(5)
   put a into a1
```

From this simple example, we can expand the contents of a function to be complex scripts.

Local Variables in Functions   Once last item before concluding this brief glimpse of HyperScript. Whenever a variable is defined, it takes up room in memory. To save memory and speed up applications, we can use local variables in defining functions. For example, changing the "MyCube" script, we can see how a local variable will work. (Save the following script as "VarCube.")

Function cube(side)

```
define s
   s=side ^3
return s
End function
```

The variable "s" is local only to the function defined as "cube" in the script in which it is saved. With the following script, you can use the revised function. However, see what happens if you attempt to use the local variable "s" in the new script. It will not work.

```
define a
get script "VarCube"
a=VarCube:Cube(5)
put a into b1
put s into b2}
```

Remove the brackets from the last line after "VarCube" is loaded into memory and attempt to compile the script. It will return an error message.

SUMMARY

This short chapter has barely touched the capabilities of HyperScript. It is a full-blown computer language and one that will assist in quickly developing very powerful programs on Wingz. By means of the examples in this chapter, you will be able to vastly increase your use of Wingz, and not be afraid to experiment and see what you can create. Begin slowly, and then develop more and more scripts to help your work go more smoothly and easily.

For those of you who have never programmed before, think of HyperScript as a vastly improved macro language. The little scripts (or even big ones) can be treated as macros. While getting used to the idea of having a lot of macro power, use the Learn mode to create button and sheet scripts. In a very short time, you will be able to develop both for you and for others, an astoundingly wide range of applications of Wingz.

APPENDIX

Macintosh Spreadsheet Feature Comparison

	Wingz	Excel	Full Impact
Spreadsheet Basics			
Maximum Spreadsheet Size	32,768 x 32,768	16,384 x 256	2,084 x 256
Memory Constraints	RAM	1 Megabyte	Virtual
Sparse Matrix Memory	yes	yes	no
On-Line Help	yes	yes	yes
Keyboard Equivalents	yes	yes	yes
Icon Equivalents	yes	no	yes
Password Protection	2 levels	yes	2 levels
Auditing Tools	yes	no	no
"AppleShare" ® Aware"	yes	yes	yes

	Wingz	Excel	Full Impact
Spreadsheet Analysis			
Built-In Functions	303	131	100
Minimal Recalculation	yes	yes	yes
Background Recalculation	yes	no	no
English Names in Formula	yes	yes	yes
Multiple WKS Open	unlimited	unlimitied	8.00
Linked Worksheets	unlimited	unlimited	8.00
Linked Data, Graph, Text	yes	Data/Gr	Data/Gr
What If? Tables	yes	yes	yes
Matrix Arithmetic	yes	yes	no
Cell Annotation	yes	no	no
Auto Data Series Entry	yes	yes	yes
Spreadsheet Graphics			
# of Chart Types	21	7	7
# of Predefined Charts	unlimited	42	unlimited
Overlay Charts	yes	yes	yes
Arrows on Chart	yes	yes	yes
Free Text on Chart	yes	yes	yes
Independent Axis Scaling	yes	yes	yes
Linear/Log Scaling	yes	yes	yes
Presentation Capabilities			
# Colors Displayed	256	8	8
# Fonts on Worksheet	256	1	8
Bold, Italic	yes	yes	yes
# Built-In Formats	32	19	9
Customized Formats	yes	yes	yes
Variable Column Widths	yes	yes	yes
Variable Row Heights	yes	no	yes
Text Fields (Basic WP)	yes	no	yes
Graphics/Drawing Tool	yes	no	yes
Scanned Images	yes	no	yes

	Wingz	**Excel**	**Full Impact**
Customized/Macros			
Macros	yes	yes	yes
Macro Recorder	yes	yes	yes
Autoexec Macros	yes	yes	yes
Custom Menus, Dialog Boxes	yes	yes	no
Definable Functions	yes	yes	no
Macro Error Messages	yes	yes	yes
Database Management			
Integrated Database	yes	yes	no
Sort Levels	256	3	N/A
Link Database to Worksheet	yes	yes	N/A
Data Entry Validation	no	no	N/A
Wild Card Searches	yes	yes	N/A
File Compatibility			
WKS	yes	yes	yes
WK1	yes	yes	yes
WK1 Macros	no	no	yes
SYLK	yes	yes	yes
DIF	yes	no	yes
ASCII	yes	yes	yes
Binary File Format	no	yes	no
dBASE II/III	no	no	yes
Special Features			
MultiFinder ™ Support:			
Background Recalc	yes	yes	yes
Background Macros	yes	yes	no
Freeze Frames	no	yes	no
WP-SS Warm Links	no	yes	no
Mixed Text, Data, Charts	yes	no	yes
3-D Surface Charts	yes	no	no

	Wingz	**Excel**	**Full Impact**
Chart Rotation	yes	no	no
Chart Elevation/Scaling	yes	no	no
Style Sheets	yes	no	no
HyperScript Language	yes	no	no
Customizable Icon Bar	no	no	yes
Zoom/Enlarge Feature	scale	no	yes
Reduce Mode	scale	no	yes

ABOUT THE AUTHORS

Elna R. Tymes has been involved in the computer field, in various capacities, for almost twenty years. She has worked on mainframe and minicomputers, as well as on personal computers. As a business person herself and consultant to various businesses, she has always been a strong advocate of the use of computers in business. She also believes that computer literacy should be a part of a sound educational curriculum. An author of many successful computer books, her works have helped many personal computer users learn popular business productivity software. Her books include: *Mastering AppleWorks, 1-2-3 from A to Z, SuperCalc: Home and Office Companion, Multiplan: Home and Office Companion, WriteNow Right Now,* and *The PC Works Primer* (Bantam, 1988).

Frederic E. Davis was Editor-in-Chief of *MacUser* magazine. Prior to this he was Editor-in-Chief of *A+* magazine. He is the author of several books on the personal computer, including *Adobe Illustrator 88: The Official Handbook for Designers* (Bantam, 1988).

Index

A

ABS function, 120
Absolute reference, 46-47
ACOS function, 120
ACOSH function, 121
ADATE function, 87
ADDDAYS function, 88
ADDHOURS function, 88
ADDMINUTES function, 88
ADDMONTHS function, 89
ADDSECONDS function, 89
ADDYEARS function, 89
Alignment, of data and text, 59-61
AND search criteria, database, 243
Arc tool, 43-44
Arguments, and functions, 73-74
ASCII, use by Wingz, 275
ASIN function, 121
ASINH function, 121
ATAN function, 121
ATAN2 function, 122
ATANH function, 122
ATIME function, 89
AVG function, 99
Axes, charts, 146-147

B

Bar charts, 14-15, 150
BONDPRICE function, 76
BONDYTM function, 76-77
Borders
    adding, 200, 203-205
    border command, 164
Budgets
    annual budget, 268-271
    cell reference, use of, 267
    data sources in, 265-266
    external referencing, 267-268, 272
    monthly budget, 271-272
Business functions, 64, 76-86
    BONDPRICE, 76
    BONDYTM, 76-77
    CTERM, 77
    DDB, 77
    FV, 78
    FVL, 78
    INTEREST, 79
    IRR, 79-80
    LOANTERM, 80-81
    NPV, 81-83
    PMT, 83
    PRINCIPAL, 83-84
    PV, 84
    PVL, 84
    RATE, 85
    SLN, 85
    SYD, 85-86
    TERM, 86
Button scripts, creating, 284-287, 290-293
Button tool, 43

C

CASE
    control script, 312-313
    syntax for, 312
CELL function, 112
Cell note, 209-210
Cells, 41, 45-49
    absolute reference, 46-47
    current or active cell, 47-48
    data entry, 49-55
    editing contents, 180
    hiding cell, 214
    maximum number of characters, 56
    mixed reference, 47
    moving cells, 187-188, 190
    protection, 214
    ranges, 48
    relative difference, 46
    selection criteria, 48-49
    width, 56-57, 61
CELLTEXT function, 113
CHAR function, 106
Charts, 13-30
    adding/deleting new elements, 154, 156-157
    axes, 146-147
    bar charts, 14-15, 150
    colors and patterns, 158-166
    combination charts, 22, 24
    contour charts, 29-30
    data points, marking, 146
    divisions, 132
    elements to change, 141
    enlarging, 138-139
    footnotes, 142-143
    hiding data series, 157
    HiLo charts, 24
    horizontal bar charts, 16
    layer charts, 21-22
    legends, 142

326 Index

line charts, 19
moving elements in, 148
pie charts, 16, 19, 150
polar charts, 26-27
scatter charts, 24-25
series, 132
   labels, 144-146
stacked charts, 148
step charts, 15-16
steps in making chart, 132-142
surface charts, 27, 29
three-D charts, 14, 15, 19, 21, 22, 135, 38
titles, 142, 144
wireframe charts, 27
X-Y charts, 26
Chart tool, 43
Check box, creating, 305-306
CHOOSE function, 113-114
Circles and ovals, drawing, 168
Circle tool, 44
Clear command, 176, 181
Clipboard, 188
Closing file, 221, 222-223
CMONTH function, 89
CODE function, 106
COL function, 114
COLLATE function, 106
Color, 59
   adding, 200-203
   charts, 158-166
Color printing, 258
COLS function, 114
Columns
   address style, 46
   width, 46, 61
Combination charts, 22, 24
CONTAINS function, 107
Contour charts, 29-30
Control units
   check box, 305-306
   control script, 303-305
   List box, 308-311
   popup menu, 306-308
   radio button, 311-313
   slide bar, 302-305
Copy command, 176, 196
Copy Down command, 177, 192

Copying data, 190-200
   Copy Right and Copy Down, 192
   into formula bar, 195
   versus moving data, 190
   names or functions into formula, 195-196
   specific cell/data attributes, 193
   windows, 210
Copying objects, 157, 196-200
Copy Right command, 177, 192
COS function, 122
COSH function, 122-123
COUNT function, 99
Create Names command, 179
Criteria Ranges, database, 241-247
CTERM function, 77
CTVALVE function, 303-304
CURRENCY function, 107
Cut command, 175-176, 188, 198
CWEEKDAY function, 90

D

Database, 12
   AND search criteria, 243
   creating database, 235-237
   Criteria Ranges, 241-247
   database range, 232, 241-242
   definition of, 231
   deleting data, 251, 254
   Extract command, 239-241, 247
   field, 232, 234
   field name, 234
   Find command, 238-239, 245
   inserting data, 250-251
   OR search criteria, 243-244
   phone list, example of, 236-237

   range, and adding/removing data, 254
   record, 232
   size limitation, 236
   sorting, 247-250
   spreadsheets as databases, 229-231
Database functions, 64, 103-105
DAVG, 104
DCOUNT, 104
DMAX, 104
DMIN, 104
DSTD, 105
DSTDEV, 105
DSUM, 105
DSUMSQ, 105
DVAR, 105
DVARIANCE, 105
Data entry, 49-55
   data series, 53-55
   date and time, 51-52
   Fill command, 53-54
   logical values, 52
   numeric data, 50-51
   text, 50
   too wide contents, 50, 57
Data modification
   borders/color/patterns, adding, 200-205
   cell selection and, 180
   clearing data, 181
   commands used, 175-180
   copying data, 190-200
   deleting data, 180-183
   inserting data, 183-187
   moving data, 187-190
   text, adding to worksheet, 205-210
Data series, 53-55
Date and time
   entering, 51-52
   formats, 58
   formulas, 64
   operators, 71
Date and time functions, 64, 87-95
ADATE, 87
ADDDAYS, 88
ADDHOURS, 88
ADDMINUTES, 88

Index

ADDMONTHS, 89
ADDSECONDS, 89
ADDYEARS, 89
ATIME, 89
CMONTH, 89
CWEEKDAY, 90
DATE, 90
DATEVALUE, 90-91
DAY, 91
DAYNAME, 91
HOUR, 91-92
MINUTE, 92
MONTH, 92
MONTHNAME, 93
NOW, 93
SECOND, 93-94
TIME, 94
TIMEVALUE, 94
YEAR, 94-95
DATEVALUE function, 90-91
DAVG function, 104
DAY function, 91
DAYNAME function, 91
DCOUNT function, 104
DDB function, 77
Define Name command, 179
DEGREES function, 123
Deleting data, 180-183
  database, 251, 254
  delete command, 177, 183
DIF, use by Wingz, 275
Divisions, charts, 132
DMAX function, 104
DMIN function, 104
Drop, 164-165
DSTD function, 105
DSTDEV function, 105
DSUM function, 105
DSUMSQ function, 105
DVAR function, 105
DVARIANCE function, 105

E

E function, 123
Encrypting and decrypting
  files, 214, 276
ERR function, 95
Event handlers, 296-297
EXACT function, 95-96

EXP function, 123
Expected Range error, 301
EXPONENTIAL function, 123
Expressions, 71-72
  item lists, 72
  logical expressions, 71
  numeric expressions, 71
  ranges, 72
  text expressions, 71
External referencing, 212, 267-268, 272
Extract command, database, 239-241, 247

F

FACTORIAL function, 124
FALSE function, 96
Field, database, 232, 234
Field name, database, 234
Fill command, 53-54, 61, 159-160, 163
FIND function, 107-108
Find command, 178, 212-213
  database, 238-239, 245
Flags, in scripts, 308-309
Footnotes, charts, 142-143
FOR loop, 314-316
Formatting, 56-62
  alignment of data and text, 59-61
  date and time formats, 58
  number formats, 58-59
  row height, changing, 61, 62
  text formats, 59
  width of column, changing, 61
Formula bar, copying data into, 195
Formulas, 62, 64
  copying names or functions into, 195-196
  date and time formulas, 64
  entering formulas, 69-72
  expressions, 71-72
  numeric formulas, 64
  operators, 70-71
  parentheses in, 72
  text formulas, 64

  values, 70
Functions
  arguments and, 73-74
  business functions, 64, 76-86
  creating new functions, 316-318
  database functions, 64, 103-105
  date and time functions, 64, 87-95
  local variables, 317-318
  logical functions, 64, 95-99
  numeric functions, 64, 120-128
  parenthesis in, 73
  pasting functions, 75
  spreadsheet functions, 64, 112-120
  statistical functions, 64, 99-103
  syntax of, 73
  text functions, 64, 106-112
  See also specific types of functions.
FV function, 78
FVL function, 78

G

GOAL function, 124
Graphics
  circles and ovals, 168
  importing, 275
  importing graphics from applications, 171
  importing scanned graphics, 167
  lines, 167-168
  polygons, 170-171
  See also Charts.
GUESS function, 124

H

Handlers
  event handlers, 296-297
  Idle handler, 299

328 Index

sheet events, 297-299
Headers and footers, printing, 260
Help, 38, 40
HiLo charts, 24
HLOOKUP function, 114-115
Horizontal bar charts, 16
HOUR function, 91-92
HyperScript, 10, 30-31
   commands, 31, 280-283
   control units, 302-311
   events, 31
   handlers
      event handlers, 296-297
      Idle handler, 299
      sheet events, 297-299
   Learn mode, 30, 279-280, 296
   loop structures
      FOR loop, 314-316
      WHILE loop, 316
   menus, creating, 294-296
   scripts
      button scripts, 284-287, 290-293
      graphics in, 290-294
      independent scripts, 288-289
      sheet scripts, 287-288
      writing scripts, example of, 290-294
   user-defined functions, 31
   variables, 300-301
      Expected Range error, 301
      naming variables, 300, 301
      numeric variables, 300
      string variables, 300

I

Idle handler, 299
IF function, 96
IF statement, 308-311
   control script, 310-311
   formats for, 308, 309
Importing files
   graphics, 275
   other file formats
      ASCII, 275
      DIF, 275
      Lotus 1-2-3, 273-274
      SYLK, 274
      text, 275
Independent scripts, creating, 288-289
INDEX function, 115-116
INDIRECT function, 116
INFORMAT function, 117-118
Insert command, 176-177, 183
Inserting data, 183-187
   database, 250-251
INT function, 125
INTEREST function, 79
Interior Brush/Interior Pen, 166
IRR function, 79-80
ISBLANK function, 97
ISERR function, 97
ISNA function, 97
ISNUMBER function, 97-98
ISRANGE function, 98
ISSTRING function, 98
Item lists, 72

L

Landscape orientation, 259
Layer charts, 21-22
Learn mode, 279-280, 296
   script writing
      button scripts, 284-287, 290-293
      independent scripts, 288-289
      sheet scripts, 287-288
LEFT function, 108
Left-aligned, 59, 61
Legends, charts, 142
LENGTH function, 108
Line charts, 19
Line command, 163
Lines
   drawing, 167-168
   shadow, 164-165
Line tool, 43
List box, creating, 308-311
LN function, 125
Loading Wingz, 37-38
LOANTERM function, 80-81
Local variables, functions, 317-318
LOG function, 125
Logical expressions, 71
Logical functions, 64, 95-99
   ERR, 95
   EXACT, 95-96
   FALSE, 96
   IF, 96
   ISBLANK, 97
   ISERR, 97
   ISNA, 97
   ISNUMBER, 97-98
   ISRANGE, 98
   ISSTRING, 98
   SIGN, 98
   TRUE, 99
Logical operators, 71
Logical values, entering, 52
LOGN function, 125
Loop structures
   FOR loop, 314-316
   WHILE loop, 316
Lotus 1-2-3, use by Wingz, 273-274
LOWER function, 108-109

M

MAKECELL function, 116-117
MAKERANGE function, 117
MATCH function, 109
MAX function, 100
Menu Bar, 41
Menus creating, 294-296
   Menuitem commands, 295-296
   Popup menu, 306-308
MID function, 109
MIN function, 100
MINUTE function, 92
Mixed reference, 47
MOD function, 126

Index   329

MONTH function, 92
MONTHNAME function, 93
Moving cells, 187-188, 190
Moving data, 187-190, 190
   versus copying data, 190
   text boxes, 200

N

N function, 117
NA function, 117
Name command, 179, 195
Navigation box, 42
Networking, 276
NORMAL function, 126
NOW function, 93
NPV function, 81-83, 196
Number formats, 58-59
Numeric data, entering, 50-51
Numeric expressions, 71
Numeric formulas, 64
Numeric functions, 64, 120-128
   ABS, 120
   ACOS, 120
   ACOSH, 121
   ASIN, 121
   ASINH, 121
   ATAN, 121
   ATAN2, 122
   ATANH, 122
   COS, 122
   COSH, 122-123
   DEGREES, 123
   E, 123
   EXP, 123
   EXPONENTIAL, 123
   FACTORIAL, 124
   GOAL, 124
   GUESS, 124
   INT, 125
   LN, 125
   LOG, 125
   LOGN, 125
   MOD, 126
   NORMAL, 126
   PI, 126
   RADIANS, 126

RAND, 127
ROUND, 127
SIN, 127
SINH, 127
SQRT, 127-128
TAN, 128
TANH, 128
UNIFORM, 128
Numeric operators, 70
Numeric variables, 300

O

Objects
   copying, 157
   creating, 153-154
   and handles, 153
   moving, 158
   removing, 158
Object tool, 42-43, 154
Offset dials, 165
Operators, 70-71
   date and time operators, 71
   listing of, 129
   logical operators, 71
   numeric operators, 70
   parentheses in, 128
   prioritization order, 72
   relational operators, 71
   text operators, 70
OR search criteria, database, 243, 244

P

Page breaks, printing, 260
Page orientation, printing, 259
Page size, printing, 258-259
Passwords
   types of, 213-214
   using, 214
Paste command, 176, 188, 198
Paste Formula command, 178, 195

Paste Special command, 177-178, 193-194
Patterns
   adding, 200-203
   charts, 158-166
PI function, 126
Pie charts, 16, 19
   exploded segments, 150
PMT function, 83
Polar charts, 26-27
Polygons, drawing, 170-171
Polygon tool, 44
Popup menu, creating, 306-308
Portrait orientation, 259
Presentation software,
      categories of, 4
PRINCIPAL function, 83-84
Printing
   color printing, 258
   headers and footers, 260
   page breaks, 260
   page orientation, 259
   Page Setup menu, 258
   page size, 258-259
   previewing page, 261
   selected information only, 262-263
PROPER function, 110
Protection
   levels of for networking, 276
   methods of, 213-214
PV function, 84
PVL function, 84

R

RADIANS function, 126
Radio button, creating, 311-313
RAND function, 127
RANGE function, 118
Ranges, 48, 72
   contiguous and noncontiguous, 48
   database, and adding/removing data, 254
RATE function, 85
Recalc command, 178

Index

Recalc Info command, 178
Record, database, 232
Rectangle tool, 44
Referencing
 absolute reference, 46-47
 mixed reference, 47
 relative difference, 46
Relational operators, 71
Relative difference, 46
Remove Names command, 179
REPEAT function, 110
REPLACE function, 110
RIGHT function, 110-111
Right-aligned, 59-60
ROUND function, 127
Rounding errors, 57
Row height, changing, 61, 62
ROW function, 118
ROWS function, 118

S

S function, 118
Saving, 219-221
 file types for, 220
 options, 220
 retrieving saved versions, 220-221, 222
Scatter charts, 24-25
Scripts, HyperScript
 button scripts, 284-287, 290-293
 graphics in, 290-294
 independent scripts, 288-289
 sheet scripts, 287-288
 writing scripts, 290-294
Scroll box, 42
SECOND function, 93-94
Select All command, 176
Select command, 178-179
Series
 charts, 132
 labels, 144-146
Shadow, lines, 164-165
Sheet events, 297-299
Sheet scripts, creating, 287-288

Show Clipboard command, 176, 188
SIGN function, 98
SIN function, 127
SINH function, 127
Slide bar
 control script, 303-305
 creating, 302-305
SLN function, 85
Sorting, database, 247-250
 alphabetization, 249-250
 ascending or descending order, 248-249
 search keys, 248-249
Spreadsheet, 10, 12
 as database, 229-231
 worksheet, main body, 41
Spreadsheet functions, 64, 112-120
 CELL, 112
 CELLTEXT, 113
 CHOOSE, 113-114
 COL, 114
 COLS, 114
 HLOOKUP, 114-115
 INDEX, 115-116
 INDIRECT, 116
 INFORMAT, 117-118
 MAKECELL, 116-117
 MAKERANGE, 117
 N, 117
 NA, 117
 RANGE, 118
 ROW, 118
 ROWS, 118
 S, 118
 VLOOKUP, 119
SQRT function, 127-128
Stacked charts, 148
Statistical functions, 64, 99-103
 AVG, 99
 COUNT, 99
 MAX, 100
 MIN, 100
 STD, 100-101
 STDEV, 101
 SUM, 101
 SUMSQ, 102
 VAR, 102
 VARIANCE, 102

STD function, 100-101
STDEV function, 101
Step charts, 15-16
STR function, 111
STRING function, 111
String variables, 300
SUM function, 101
SUMSQ function, 102
Surface charts, 27, 29
SYD function, 85-86
SYLK, use by Wingz, 274

T

TAN function, 128
TANH function, 128
TERM function, 86
Text
 adding to worksheet, 205-210
 entering, 50
Text boxes
 cell note, 209-210
 creating, 206
 moving, 200
Text expressions, 71
Text field, word processing functions, 208-209
Text formats, 59
Text formulas, 64
Text functions, 64, 106-112
 CHAR, 106
 CODE, 106
 COLLATE, 106
 CONTAINS, 107
 CURRENCY, 107
 FIND, 107-108
 LEFT, 108
 LENGTH, 108
 LOWER, 108-109
 MATCH, 109
 MID, 109
 PROPER, 110
 REPEAT, 110
 REPLACE, 110
 RIGHT, 110-111
 STR, 111

Index

STRING, 111
TRIM, 111
UPPER, 111-112
VALUE, 112
Text operators, 70
Text tool, 43
TIME function, 94
TIMEVALUE function, 94
Titles, charts, 142, 144
Toolbox, components of, 42-44
Topics, choosing, 38, 40
TRIM function, 111
TRUE function, 99
Typeface, default, 62

U

Undo command, 175, 180
UNIFORM function, 128
UPPER function, 111-112

V

VALUE function, 112
Values, 70
VAR function, 102
Variables
  functions, local variables, 317-318
  HyperScript, 300-301
    Expected Range error, 301
    naming variables, 300, 301
    numeric variables, 300
    string variables, 300
VARIANCE function, 102
VLOOKUP function, 119

W

WHILE loop, 316
Windows
  copying data, 210
  new window, creating, 210
  rearranging windows, 210
Wingz
  capabilities of, 4-13
  charts, 13-30
  examples of use
    hydrological study, 33-35
    investment banking, 173-174
    law firm, 216
    market analysis example, 5-13
    political election, 255
    publishing company, 224-227
    quasi-crystal study, 66-68
  HyperScript, 10, 30-31
Wireframe charts, 27
Worksheet, 40-42
  adding text to, 205-210
  cells, 45-49
  moving between, 218
  new, opening of, 217-218
Worksheet tool, 42
Worldwide financial reports, 266-267

X

X-Y charts, 26

Y

YEAR function, 94-95